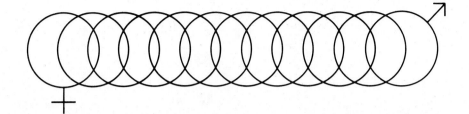

Gender and Communication

Judy Cornelia Pearson
Ohio University, Athens

wcb

Wm. C. Brown Publishers
Dubuque, Iowa

Printed in the United States of America
10 9 8 7 6 5 4 3 2

Contents

3   Images of women and men   66

Contents

10   Public contexts   314

Preface

Interest in the complex relationships among women, men and communication has progressed at a geometric rate in the past decade. Although Jespersen (1922), Stopes (1908) and Parsons (1913) are credited with the origins of interest in gender and communication (Thorne, Kramarae, & Henley, 1983), the work of countless researchers in the past 10 years has encouraged the examination of differences in the communicative patterns of women and men.

A variety of models have guided the research on gender and communication. The initial lack of investigations on women promoted stereotypical images and a model of effective communicative patterns that were derived from the interactions of men. Implicitly, communicative success was equated with male practice. Today, the communicative behaviors of both women and men are examined and behavioral research is replacing "folk linguistics."

The purpose of *Gender and Communication* is to synthesize the research findings into a single, manageable source. Although the text includes hundreds of citations, at least as many were deleted from inclusion. An attempt was made to include the various findings on each issue, to include at least one or two citations from the major researchers, and to suggest the breadth of research in this area. At the same time, manageability of the text, considerations such as length of the book, and concern about the teaching value of the text suggested some restraint.

Organization of the text

Gender and Communication includes both theory and practice. It is divided into four major parts: Considerations which includes an introduction to gender and communication, the self-perceptions of women and men, and the images of women and men. Components, Section II, includes self-disclosure, self-assertion, listening, and empathy. Section III, Codes, includes a consideration of the language usage of women and men, interpersonal attraction and physical attractiveness, and nonverbal codes. The fourth section of the text is entitled Contexts and includes both intimate and public contexts. Each chapter contains an opening outline of it's content and summary, at its close. A variety of exercises are included throughout the text.

Teaching gender and communication

Gender and Communication will provide interesting reading to the lay reader, but it was written primarily for the classroom. A certain amount of controversy surrounds the question of teaching courses in the area of gender and communication. First, critics have suggested that the area of gender and communication is without a model or a theoretical base. Second, they argue that courses on gender and communication emphasize gender to the minimization of communication. A third argument in this series of sorities is that gender and communication pedagogy encourages an outdated notion of communication. Recent evidence suggests that the "trait" approach to communication with its attendant cross-situational consistency may be out of vogue. A fourth consideration is the divisiveness that is said to accompany courses on gender and communication. The social scientific research methods focus on differences between women and men. Gender research may encourage bipolarity and mutual exclusivity between the sexes.

What response can be offered to such criticism? A Chinese curse reads, "May you live in changing times." Brenton (1966) writes that we live "in a world of unprecedented changes and choice. Change itself is nothing new. Cultures are always shifting; people are always discarding old ways, trying new ones. But the pace and intensity of change in today's society are unprecedented, making tremendous demands on the individual's ability to adjust (p. 33)." It is essential in these times of change that we encourage courses on gender and communication.

Theories change in a variety of ways. Knowledge may increase in an incremental way in which we add small bits of new knowledge to that which is already known. Or, we may gain knowledge as we clarify more precisely that which is already known. Finally, Kuhn (1970) suggests that theories may change through revolution in which new information which runs counter to the prevailing knowledge precipitates a crisis and leads to the development of a new paradigm.

The pluralism that exists in epistemology is further complicated by the myth of value-free social science. Researchers may disagree on the means by which knowledge is generated or they may recognize the role of axiology in research and agree with Gouldner (1962) who explained that physicists before Hiroshima talked of a value-free science, but were less sure in the 1960's. Our knowledge about gender is similarly subject to the values of the culture. Kramarae (1981) writes, "Scientific statements about gender are made to fit the changing 'needs' and myths about society. . . . Social scientific research is not impersonal, apolitical, and factual, but interpretative (p. vi)." Gender and communication research has not followed the same pattern as have other areas of investigation, it is not based on the same value structure that underlies other research, and it is more applied than theoretical, yet it has a theoretical-base.

Courses on gender and communication treat both gender *and* communication; they cannot be expected to teach communication to the exclusion of gender. The study of communication has substance as well as form. We cannot study human communication unless we are allowed to include some humans to study. Heisenberg's Principle of Uncertainty reminded social scientists that they could study both position and momemtum, but the more accurately they were able to measure one, the less accurately they could assess the other. As we focus more critically on women and men, we are less able to draw generalizations about communication. This is not a criticism, however, it is a tautology.

Social environments, or contexts, precede individuals who exist within those environs. Symbolic interaction is predicated on a notion of social process. The human biological organism is modified and channeled through interactions with others (Cooley, 1972). We are social in character (Homans, 1950), we are role-taking animals (Morris, 1962), and we are influenced by the actual, imagined, or implied presence of others (Allport, 1969). We cannot study human communication without an understanding of biology, sociology, and psychology. As James A. Doyle (1983) reminds us in his new text, *The Male Experience,* "Too often experts from one academic discipline become so enmeshed in their own discipline's viewpoint that they exclude the findings of any other discipline (p. xiii)."

Gender is sometimes treated simplistically in our research; however, gender is a complex notion which is far more than biology. Examination of gender variables in the communicative process does not necessitate a trait approach to communication. Gender need not be treated as a dispositional variable. Endler and Magnusson (1976) suggest that gender is acquired from a complex interaction among the contextual features of the situation and the dispositional features of the communicators. Pearson (1981), in a modest attempt to illustrate that context does affect the communicative behavior of women and men, demonstrated that setting and gender interact in predicting self-disclosure.

Researchers on gender variables in the communicative process have relied upon a trait perspective in their work. At the same time the communication field has been enamored with this point of view. The only conclusion that is warranted is that gender communication researchers, like their colleagues, have been consistent with an overriding paradigm. Furthermore, we are beginning to observe researchers viewing gender as more complex than a univariate trait, just as research in other areas of communication are relying increasingly on multivariate designs and are becoming more interested in the importance of the communication context. We might predict that research on gender variables will be similarly complex and will be concerned with the same issues that are expressed in other areas of communication theory.

Courses on gender and communication sometimes focus on differences rather than similarities which reflect our social scientific methodology and our research in this area; however most researchers and instructors encourage the enlargement of behavioral repertoires, not the prescription of continued difference. John Money and Patricia Tucker (1975) are probably accurate when they write, "When it comes down to the biological imperatives that are laid down for all men and women, there are only four: Only a man can impregnate; only a woman can menstruate, gestate, and lactate (p. 38)." The long history of psychological research on sex differences, however, has demonstrated a variety of personality, attitudinal, and behavioral differences between women and men. Most recently psychologists have questioned their position on examining differences between people on the basis of anatomical, physiological, or intrapsychic bases and have begun to assess gender differences within a social context. Perhaps the strongest appeal came from Naomi Weisstein (1971) who authored the monograph, *Psychology Constructs the Female, or the Fantasy Life of the Male Psychologist*. In her article, Weisstein effectively argues that many psychological correlates for biological differences could be explained by invoking such concepts as conformity to social pressure, expectancy effects, differential socialization practices for females and males, and experimenter bias. We have noted, since the Weisstein article, a sharp upswing of research interest in the social variables that underly sex differences.

The emphasis on differences between women and men is probably disheartening for most people who write or teach in the area of gender and communication. We find ourselves constantly emphasizing that which we wish, symbolically and pragmatically, to de-emphasize: the differences between females and males. Ambert and Ambert (1976) wrote,

> For, in spite of current research trends and ideologies, the sexes are more alike than dissimilar. We are in the presence of a range of human potentialities and qualities and the more important observation resides in the overlap of human traits between the sexes in spite of a socialization process that encourages cleavage (p. 7).

While we write and talk of differences, our emphasis remains to remind ourselves and others of the great overlap of human traits and the large range of human potential. Notions of psychological androgyny, behavioral flexibility, and communication competence mark most of the recommendations on gender and communication.

Instructor's resource manual

Gender and communication is a fairly new addition to the curriculum. As a consequence, instructors may be more or less prepared to teach the course. For those instructors with limited experience, a thorough instructor's manual is available. For those instructors who have extensive experience, the manual may provide some new ideas and should be useful in providing examination questions that have been classroom tested. The Instructor's Resource Manual includes approximately 25 true-false and 25 multiple-choice questions for each chapter in the text and about 6 activities or exercises for each chapter.

The author

Judy C. Pearson is committed to the research and teaching of courses on gender and communication. She has developed and taught such courses at four universities. She earned her doctorate at Indiana University and has been on the faculty at Bradley University, Indiana University-Purdue University at Fort Wayne, Iowa State University, and Michigan State University. She currently serves as an Associate Professor of Interpersonal Communication at Ohio University.

Acknowledgments

Gender and Communication is a cumulative effort by publishers, editors, critic-evaluators, students, fellow teachers, and the author. Encouraged by Louise Waller who originally signed the contract for this book and the birth of Rebekah Kristina Pearson Nelson who provided me six weeks of maternity leave on which to write a large part of the manuscript, the book was begun. The text was completed through long and loving hours of research and writing.

Many other people deserve my special thanks. The people at Wm. C. Brown Company Publishers have earned my appreciation and also the reviewers they have selected: Dencil K. Backus, Purdue University at Calumet; Mary Anne Fitzpatrick, University of Wisconsin at Madison; H. Lloyd Goodall Jr., University of Alabama; Patricia Riley, University of Southern California at Los Angeles; Don W. Stacks, University of South Alabama; Constance M. Staley, University of Colorado at Colorado Springs; William R. Todd-Mancillas, University of Nebraska at Lincoln. I am also grateful for the helpful suggestions from faculty members who evaluated the manuscript at several stages of development. Five people at Ohio University were instrumental in the completion of the book: Debbie Nissley typed the manuscript in her usual flawless manner; Lisa Charney and Shirley A. Williams provided library research as they double-checked bibliographic citations; and David Bennett and Colleen Romick provided invaluable assistance in proofreading the final manuscript. I was granted research release time by the School of Interpersonal Communication at Ohio University to complete this book and to all of my colleagues, I am grateful.

Ambert, A. and Ambert M. *Sex Structure*. Don Mills: Longman Canada, 1976.
Cooley, C. H. "Primary Groups and Human Nature." In J. G. Manis and B. N. Meltzer (Eds.). *Symbolic Interaction, a Reader in Social Psychology*. Boston: Allyn and Bacon, 1972, 158–160.
Doyle, James A. *The Male Experience*. Dubuque, Iowa: William C. Brown Publishers, 1983.

Endler, N. S. and Magnusson, D. "Toward an Interactional Psychology of Personality." *Psychological Bulletin,* 1976, 83, 956–974.

Gouldner, Alvin W. "Anti-Minotaur: The Myth of a Value-Free Sociology." *Social Problems,* Winter 1962, 9, 199–213.

Homans, G. C. *The Human Group.* New York: Harcourt, Brace & World, 1950.

Jesperson, Otto. *Language: Its Nature, Development and Origin.* London: Allen & Unwin, 1922.

Kramarae, Cheris. *Women and Men Speaking.* Rowley, Massachusetts: Newbury House Publishers, Inc., 1981.

Kuhn, Thomas S. *The Structure of Scientific Revolutions.* Chicago: University of Chicago Press, 1970.

Money, John and Tucker, Patricia. *Sexual Signatures.* Boston: Little, Brown, 1975.

Morris, C. W. "Introduction: George H. Mead and Social Psychologist and Social Philosopher." In C. W. Morris (Ed.), *Mind, Self and Society.* Chicago, Illinois: University of Chicago Press, 1961.

Parsons, Elsie Clews. *The Old-Fashioned Woman: Primitive Fancies about the Sex.* New York: G. P. Putnam's Sons, 1913.

Pearson, Judy C. "The Effects of Setting and Gender on Self-Disclosure." *Group and Organizational Studies: The International Journal for Group Facilitators,* 1981, 6, 334–340.

Stopes, Charlotte Carmichael. *The Sphere of "Man": In Relation to That of "Woman" in the Constitution.* London: T. Fisher Unwin, 1908.

Thorne, Barrie; Kramarae, Cheris; and Henley, Nancy (Ed.) *Language, Gender and Society.* Rowley, Massachusetts: Newbury House Publishers, 1983.

Weisstein, Naomi. *Psychology Constructs the Female, or the Fantasy Life of the Male Psychologist.* Boston: New England Free Press, 1971.

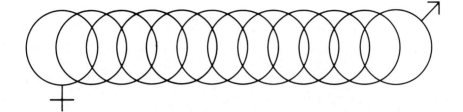

Gender and Communication

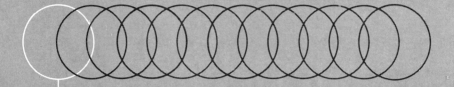

Section 1

You are about to begin the exploration of one of the most salient topics in contemporary life: an examination of the communicative behavior of women and men. In order to accomplish this task, certain basic considerations must be discussed. This first section of the text lays the groundwork for the material which is to follow.

In this section you will be introduced to some new terms and you will learn to define some familiar terms in specific ways.

This section includes three chapters. Chapter 1 provides an introduction to gender and communication, defines relevant terms, and presents a model by which we may view the communication between women and men.

Considerations

Chapter 2 considers the self-perceptions of women and men, explaining how people acquire images of themselves as women or men, how women and men are characterized, and how they differ in their self-concepts. Chapter 3 discusses the images of women and men that people hold. This chapter analyzes the language that is used to describe women and men, determines the portrayal of women and men in humor and delineates the portrayal of women and men in mediated sources such as magazines, newspapers, advertisements, popular music, television, and television commercials.

1 An introduction to gender and communication

4

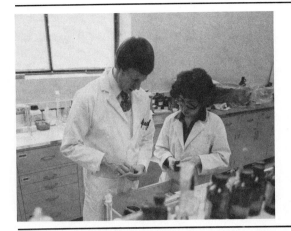

Introduction

A judge in Wisconsin claims that a 5-year-old girl involved in a sexual assault case was "promiscuous," and the case receives national attention as local citizens demand the recall of the judge. In 1977 a Massachusetts father is the first male to win child custody in that state, and the movie *Kramer vs. Kramer* shows a father in the role of single parent for his son. Betty Friedan authors a new book in 1981, *The Second Stage,* in which she implies that her first book, published in 1963, *The Feminine Mystique,* is out of date. In *The Second Stage* she puts forth a new challenge for women, overcoming the "feminist mystique."

The changing roles of women and men are inescapable. The contemporary women's movement, which had its auspices in Betty Friedan's *The Feminine Mystique,* has obscured the clear perceptions of women and men which once prevailed in our culture. New definitions of "male" and "female" in the psychological literature call into question traditional masculine and feminine sex roles. Consistent with this new approach, the changing sociological nature of the family requires flexibility and demonstrates that the "nuclear family" is obsolete.

The topic of "gender and communication" is relevant today because of the vast sociological and psychological changes which are part of our culture in the 1980's. Whether we choose to entertain ourselves with the movies, television, or the radio, we encounter this topic. In the best-selling books we select, the magazines or newspapers we read, we are confronted with the importance of "gender and communication." And, whether we focus on legal decision-making, governmental action, or religious tracts, we see the central, but often hidden, role of this newly emerging topic of consideration.

Why are we concerned with the issue of gender and communication *today?* Why are research studies that focus on the communication of women and men, nonexistent twenty years ago, now filling traditional journals and necessitating the creation of new journals which are devoted solely to this topic? Why are courses on sex differences in communication, female/male communication, and sex and communication being introduced on campuses throughout the country?

Thomas Kuhn, in *The Structure of Scientific Revolutions,* offers some theoretical explanation for the prevalence of the topic of gender and communication. Describing the stages through which people perceive knowledge, Kuhn suggests that when we believe a set of "facts," we have what is known as a *paradigm.* A paradigm may be thought of as a set of beliefs which are internally consistent and which are derived from an over-riding belief or "fact." For instance, at one time people thought that the world was flat and developed theories based on that central belief. Later, people believed that the world was round and replaced their outdated theories with contemporary views that were in line with their new paradigm. The time span between the two paradigms, when some people hold to one point of view and others maintain the other perspective, is known as a *paradigm shift.*

In the same way that scientific knowledge moves through differing paradigms, our belief systems also change. At one time, we believed that women and men had specific roles to play and that deviation from these roles was suspect. For instance, women have been viewed to be nurturers of children, while men have been perceived to be hunters, or providers of food. Today, these perceptions appear to a number of people to be unusual and impractical.

We are now undergoing a paradigm shift concerning women and men in our culture. In the United States the sharp divisiveness over the Equal Rights Amendment demonstrates the positions of the two bodies of belief. On the one hand, there are persons who support the traditional perspective in which men and women are viewed as more different than alike; on the other, there are those who propose a more contemporary view in which men and women are viewed as more alike than different. The traditionalists do not maintain that men and women are completely different, and persons with the contemporary perspective do not hold that men and women are completely alike. Nonetheless, a considerable gap exists between the perceived proportions of similarity and dissimilarity which are ascribed to persons who are labeled "female," and "male."

Why is the topic of gender and communication important to *you?* Every day of your life you communicate with members of the same sex and members of the opposite sex. At school, you attend classes with women and men, and your instructors may be female or male. At work, you find that women and men fill jobs as subordinates, superiors, and co-workers. At home, you interact with members of both sexes. It is unlikely that you do not communicate with members of both sexes in every communication context in which you find yourself. The combination of communication and gender is important, then, because of its pervasiveness.

The association of communication and gender is also important because of its difficulty. Each of us is involved, directly or indirectly, in understanding our environments, in making predictions about outcomes, and in controlling situations to our own satisfaction. For example, you may wish to receive a high grade in a public speaking class. You observe that people who receive high grades generally attend class, read the required textbook, and plan their speeches carefully. You "predict" that you will receive a high grade if you engage in these behaviors. You engage in the behaviors and find that your prediction is accurate resulting in the desired outcome and personal satisfaction.

Similarly, when we communicate with members of our own sex or the other sex, we attempt to understand, predict, and control. You may observe that when you touch the shoulder of a member of the opposite sex, he or she cuddles to your touch. You may conclude that the other person enjoys being

touched by you and is positively affected by your behavior. The other person's positive response appears to be the outcome you desire, and consequently you feel personal satisfaction with the interaction.

The difficulty of communicating with same-sex and opposite sex people is that the responses of others are no longer as predictable as they once were. This cartoon illustrates the complexity of the changes with which we are dealing. Women are no longer limited to secretarial roles and men are not excluded from them. At the same time, women and men have skills that allow them to perform traditional jobs in their new professions. For instance, the female manager may be able to do her own shorthand or transcription, and the male nurse may be able to handle jobs that require great strength. The result is confusion for all of us. Let us consider another situation. As we shall see in chapter 7, the example of touching another person, described above, may have been fairly accurate in the past and may, indeed, be an accurate description of what still occurs in some places today. Now, however, a male touching a female may be as likely to elicit a negative response as a positive one; similarly, a female touching a male may result in confusion.

The association of gender and communication is an important topic for you because of the frequency with which you communicate with members of the opposite and same sex and the difficulty of explaining and predicting successful communication interactions. Without a knowledge of the contrasting and similar communication styles of women and men, you are likely to encounter defeat in your interactions with others. It is less probable that you will have satisfying personal relationships, and your chances for success in your career are reduced. To the extent that you are able to understand the information in this text and to apply it to your interactions with others, you will be more likely to understand, predict, and have successful interactions with others.

What is "gender and communication"?

As you have been reading this introductory section in the first chapter, you may have felt you understood, in a general sense, the meaning of the phrase "gender and communication." On the other hand, you may have thought that you were not completely certain about what would be, and what would not be included in such a discussion. In order to clarify the content of this book and to set up the parameters within which we will be working, we will explain our terms, beginning with definitions of the two words separately.

Gender

Recently the word "gender" has been used in place of the word "sex." Why? A special program on Home Box Office was entitled, "Sex Is a Three Letter Word." Although the word "sex" is not imposing in length, it carries a great deal of emotional weight and has a number of different meanings. If you were asked to write a "sex joke," what would you write? Students, in a recent study, were asked just that. What were their responses? Some students wrote jokes based on confusion about whether the principals were male or female; others wrote jokes about the women's movement; still others wrote jokes in which sexism was a dominant theme; but most of the students wrote jokes about sexual intercourse (Pearson, Miller & Senter, 1982). If you are asked your "sex" on a drivers' license application, you are likely to focus on the word as a request to distinguish between male and female, even though the person filling in "once or twice a week," "not enough," and "please" are common humorous responses to the question.

Sex
The word "sex" is used in a variety of different ways, and the context or situation in which we are involved provides some cues as to which definition applies. "Sex" may refer to a classification schema based on reproductive functions: male and female. "Sex" may mean the sexual urge or instinct as it manifests itself in behavior, for example, the behavior of sexual intercourse. Finally, "sex" may refer to physiological, functional, or psychological descriptions of persons who are characterized as male or female.

The meaning of "sex" becomes cloudy when we add the last definition, which includes not only physiology but also functional or psychological descriptors of sex. We will examine this notion in more detail in a later section of this chapter, but we need to recognize the difficulties that are entailed when persons use the terms in this way.

When someone comments on a man who is a gossip and states, "He's such an old woman!" Or, when another person mentions a highly assertive businesswoman and asks, "Who does she think she is, a man?" we gain some idea of the confusion about the terms "woman," "man," and "sex." Through these remarks we also acquire some notion of the negative feelings toward women in our culture, since males who behave negatively are perceived to be women, while women who behave in positive ways are regarded as men. With this brief description of the confusion among the definitions of "sex," in mind, let us consider some other "sex-related" terms.

Sex-related terms

Two other terms that have become widely used in the past decade that relate to sex are "sex role orientation" and "sexism." "Sex role orientation" is a central concept in our understanding of "gender and communication." It refers to the extent to which a person has internalized society's sex-typed standards of desirable behavior for men and for women. Persons are classified as "feminine" if they have internalized traits which are desirable for women and have rejected the traits of men; they are considered "masculine" if they have internalized the desirable traits for men and rejected the traits of women. Later in this chapter we will explore some problems with this concept and suggest some alternatives to being "feminine" and "masculine."

"Sexism" refers to discrimination by members of one sex against the other, especially by males against females, based on the assumption that one sex is superior (Morris, 1975), or the extent to which a person believes that typical behaviors and specific dispositions exist which are appropriate for each of the sexes (Pearson, 1975). You have probably noted that both "sex role orientation" and "sexism" rely on stereotyping of men and women.

You may be interested in how these concepts relate to each other. In other words, you may wish to understand if persons who are biologically classified as women tend to be more or less sexist than are persons who are biologically men. Or, you may wish to know the relationship between biological sex and sex role orientation. A high correlation has been found to exist between biological sex and sex role orientation; that is, women tend to be feminine and men tend to be masculine (Pearson, 1980). In addition, a relationship exists between sex and sexism, which suggests that women tend to be less sexist than are men (Pearson, 1980; Whitehead & Tawes, 1976). Additional relationships between sexism and other variables clarify these relationships.

Sexism may be related to a number of personality characteristics. Both men and women who hold negative attitudes toward women tend to rate high in defensiveness (Albright & Chang, 1976) and high in dogmatism, the quality of being close-minded, narrow, and believing in the absolute correctness of one's own set of beliefs (Whitehead & Tawes, 1976). Age and educational level have no effect on the sexism of men; but older and less educated women tend to be less supportive of women, in general (Unger, 1979). Sexist men tend to have lower self-esteem than do men who view the sexes as equals (Miller, 1974). While these studies suggest that sexism may be related to a number of other characteristics, at least one researcher has concluded that sexism seems to exist almost independently of other characteristics and that negative attitudes toward women may represent a social judgment rather than an individual attitude (Goldberg, 1974).

You may be interested in an apparent relationship between attitudes about women, attitudes about homosexual relationships, and attitudes about sexuality. At least one study has demonstrated that these attitudes appear to cluster together. Persons who are sexist or nonfeminist tend to hold conservative sexual attitudes and to hold anti-homosexual attitudes (Minnigerode, 1976). In general, it appears that persons who hold negative attitudes toward women, homosexuals, and a nonconservative sexuality have more stereotyped attitudes about persons and define acceptable sexual behaviors more narrowly. At the same time, sex role orientation appears to show little relationship to this set of beliefs (Unger, 1979).

In this text, the term "gender" is used in place of the word "sex." Birdwhistell (1970) wrote,

> There has been . . . an increasing realization that intragender and
> intergender behavior throughout the animal kingdom is not simply a response
> to instinctual mechanisms but is shaped, structured, and released both by the
> ontogenetic experiences of the participating organisms and by the patterned
> circumstances of the relevant environment (p. 40).

Birdwhistell distinguished between primary, secondary, and tertiary sexual characteristics. He defined primary sexual characteristics as those that were physiological and primarily reproductive in nature including hormonal differences. Secondary characteristics were those that were anatomical and included such differences as body hair, bone structure, and physical size. Tertiary characteristics are learned and situationally produced differences. "Sex" differences are far more complex than we might originally have surmised.

The term "gender" tends to be less confusing than does "sex." For instance, we rarely confuse a question about our gender with one about our sexuality or with one which concerns coital behavior. At the same time, the word "gender" is broad enough to include psychological as well as biological differences between persons. "Gender" is traditionally defined as a set of two or more categories such as feminine, masculine, or neuter, categories into which words are divided on the basis of psychological associations, vivacity, or other characteristics. This perspective serves our purposes well.

In order to have the opportunity of experiencing different sex role behaviors, other than those you typically enact, this exericse is useful. As you engage in the exercise, observe how people respond to you in your selected or assigned role and how you feel about portraying the particular role. You can participate in this exercise with members of your class or friends in an informal setting.

Each person should select, or be assigned to, one of the following roles.

Female Roles

1. **Good Old Mom**   You are an older woman who enjoys nurturing and helping others. You enjoy listening to other peoples' problems and offering advice.

2. **Mrs. Anybody**   You are dedicated to the traditional idea. You are a wife and mother who puts the needs of your children and husband before yourself. You do all of this unselfishly.

3. **Ms. Somebody**   You have internalized all of the new teachings on feminism. You do not wear make-up or clothing that is designed to attract male attention. You are concerned about women being treated as sex objects.

4. **Sensuous Woman**   You have a terrific figure and you like to show it off. You dress in a manner to attract attention—no neckline is too low and no skirt is slit too high. You flirt overtly with all of the men and have little time for the women.

5. **Little Girl**   You have found that the best strategy in gaining what you desire is through never growing up. You dress in a juvenile manner and generally act helpless.

6. **Professional Person**   You perceive your role as a professional and behave accordingly. You dress in business suits, even for social occasions. You want to be taken seriously and in order to accomplish this, you always appear goal-oriented and business-like.

Male Roles

1. **Playboy of this world**   You view yourself as highly sophisticated and very subtle in the seduction of women. You enjoy capturing the attention of the women you meet. Your relationships with women are primarily sexual; every woman is a conquest, regardless of her marital status.

2. **Mr. C. Pig**   You believe that women have a limited role in our society and that they should maintain it. Men should be men and women should be women and no confusion between sex roles should occur.

3. **Helpless Harry**   You have found that women like to "mother" you and you enjoy it. You continually forget important items, but you know that someone will take care of you.

4. **Feminist Male**   You are highly sympathetic with the struggle of women. You demonstrate genuine interest and concern. You perceive biological gender to be less important than other factors about a person.

5. **"Jock" Ewing**   You have been an athlete all of your life. You have a very strong and well developed body and you are proud of it. You believe that men should work out every day and should be physically fit; you are less convinced of the importance of exercise for women.

6. **Dandy Dad**   You see yourself as someone who can offer years of experience to younger people that you meet. You are eager to provide advice on any topic. You tend to be patronizing sometimes; paternalistic always.

Male or Female Roles

1. **Pat Prude**   You believe that discussions of sexuality are best left in the bedroom between intimates, if at all. You think that sex is reserved for married people of the opposite sex and you do not mind sharing your moral views with others.

2. **Intensive Intellectual**   Sexual topics are discussed in biological and impersonal terms. You discuss current research in the fields of sociology and psychology in order to explain sexual matters, but you never disclose your own feelings.

3. **Me, First**   You have a view of the world in which you are the center. Every topic of discussion must center on you. Regardless of the topic that others introduce, you manage to bring the conversation back to yourself.

4. **Happy Together** You have been involved in a committed relationship for a number of years. While you and your partner have had the same difficulties which others have had, you have worked together to be supportive of each other and to build a relationship satisfying to both.

5. **Complete Self** You have had a variety of life experiences and have grown and learned from them. You are a person who truly appreciates the complexity of yourself and of others. You allow yourself and others the freedom to be who they are.

After you have selected one of these roles or been assigned a role to play, consider how you will dress, walk, talk, and behave. After you have had some opportunity to experiment with the new behavior, interact with the others in a social situation, or a role-playing social setting, in which you play your new role. Interact with others at the "party" for at least one hour. After you have mingled with the other "people," discuss your feelings. What did you learn about the role you were playing, what did you learn about other sex roles, and how do people respond to the variety of roles presented? Do you think these sex roles actually occur? Which of the roles are preferable? Which ones do you normally play? Which roles would you like to avoid?

Communication

The term "communication" comes from the Latin *communicare* which literally means "to make common." Communication occurs when persons negotiate the "meaning" of any phenomenon. Earlier definitions of communication have identified messages or thoughts as the objects of communication. Neither of these terms is as accurate as "meaning." The term "message" does not imply any level of understanding. We may listen to a radio station which transmits its signal from Mexico City and be able to repeat words and phrases that we hear (the message), but have no notion of the meaning since we do not speak Spanish. The term "thought" is bothersome since thoughts are difficult to define and analyze. How do we know another person's thoughts? The term "meaning" is more accurately the object of communication.

Communication as a process
Communication is not an end product, but a *process* which is characterized by change and movement. Alterations occur within people as they are communicating; the context of communication may be different; differing messages are selected; and the nonverbal elements of the exchange are altered.

Communication is marked by shifts and turns, variation and modification. None of us can stop the process of communication nor does communication have a beginning or an end. David Berlo, a communication scholar explains,

> If we accept the concept of process, we view events and relationships as dynamic, ongoing, ever-changing, continuous. When we label something as a process, we also mean that it does not have a beginning, an end, a fixed sequence of events. It is not static, at rest. It is moving. The ingredients within a process interact; each affects all of the others (Berlo, 1960 p. 24).

The process nature of communication is especially important in a text on gender and communication. The variety of changes in our society—growth in scope and size, changes in relationships, the influence of media on reality, altering family structures, increasing numbers of older people, greater mobility and physical movement, and changes in the economic condition of the country—all call to mind the relevance of a process notion.

The negotiation of meaning

Communication involves *negotiation.* When we negotiate a matter, we attempt to reach a common agreement about the phenomenon. A sound argument can be made for the assertion that over 3 billion languages exist in our world; in other words, each of us has a different notion of what particular words mean. While we may hold similar conceptions of words, we also have unique experiences with them which alter our perceptions. For instance, I may share with others the idea that a mouse is a small, brown rodent; but I may have a particular fondness for mice, based on my experience with them as pets. The word *mouse,* then, elicits a different response from me than it might from another person.

Although each one of us has a unique language, we must rely upon this mode of behavior to communicate with others. How do we use disparate symbol systems to interact effectively with others? We negotiate the meaning of the words which we use and the order in which we arrange them. When we are using more descriptive language, or concrete words, like *desk, chair, Santa Claus, walk, drink* or *type,* we have less trouble in establishing a common meaning for the terms than when we use abstract or ambiguous words like *beautiful, honest, kind, ugly, loving, warm,* or *phony.* You may find that most of the disagreements you have with others come from a lack of negotiating the meaning of such terms.

Similarly, we negotiate the meaning of phrases and sentences by the order in which we put them together. For instance, we commonly place adjectives before the words they modify. If someone asserts that, "It's a beautiful day, but I have a terrible cold," we assume that *beautiful* modifies the kind of day it is and that *terrible* modifies the condition of the cold. Sometimes we put words together in unusual ways, however. Suppose the person interacting with you states, "It's a beautiful day today, isn't it?" Would you assume they are asking a question or making an assertion? The other person's anger or apparent frustration when you do not answer may tell you that your conclusion that the person had made an assertion was incorrect. Your sensitivity to the feedback will help you in the negotiation process.

Communication begins with self and others

Communication begins simultaneously with ourselves and with others. Communication begins with ourselves in one sense. Carl Rogers wrote, "Every individual exists in a continually changing world of experience of which he is the center" (Rogers, 1951, p. 483). All of our communicative behavior is viewed from the perspective of ourselves. Chapter 2 discusses the central role of self in communication and stresses the importance of self-awareness and self-concept in communication.

How does our self-centered perspective affect our communication with others? Dean Barnlund, a communication scholar, suggested that "six people" are actually involved in every "two person" communicative situation. The six people include (1) how you see yourself; (2) how the other person sees himself or herself; (3) how you see the other person; (4) how the other person sees you; (5) how you believe the other person views you; and (6) how the other person believes you view him or her. Barnlund's model implies that we "create" views of ourselves and of others in our transactions with them (Barnlund, 1970).

An example may clarify Barnlund's model. Suppose you are a woman dating a man. You view yourself as a slightly overweight, bright, assertive, complex person. The man you are dating views you as physically attractive, funny, and opinionated. He views himself as a muscular, fairly intelligent, happy-go-lucky, partier. You view him as a humorous person who keeps in shape, but is not terribly bright. You believe that he is attracted to you because of your intelligence and the help that you have given him in some of his classes. You believe that he perceives you as very bright and complicated. He believes that you are attracted to him because of his muscular physique and his social nature. He believes that you see him as a popular athlete.

As we negotiate meaning with others, we need to keep in mind that our skills in establishing common meanings are limited by our unique perspectives. As we describe, explain, and evaluate the communication transactions in which we take part, we reflect a great deal of ourselves. As communicators, we are limited by our own view of the situation. After a heated argument between the two people in the example above, the woman might respond, "I wonder why he keeps talking about my body—we both know I have ten pounds to lose," and the man might inject, "I don't know why she wants to talk about philosophy all the time—she knows that physical education is my major!"

In another sense, communication begins with others. Although we view communication from our own perspective and with our unique perceptual processes, the self we know is learned from others. George Herbert Mead explains that self originates in communication. The child, through verbal and nonverbal symbols, learns to accept roles in response to the expectations of others (Mead, 1977). We establish our self-image, the sort of person that we believe we are, by the ways that other people categorize us. The positive, negative, and neutral messages that others offer us, enable us to determine who we are. Our self-definition, then, arises through our interactions with others.

Communication also begins with others in the sense that the effective communicator considers the other person's needs and expectations as he or she selects appropriate messages to share. The effective communicator understands that a large number of messages can be shared at any time, but sensitivity and responsiveness to the other communicator is essential. Thus we observe that communication begins simultaneously with the self, defined by others, and with others, defined by self.

Communication in context

Communication occurs in a context. We do not communicate in a vacuum. Sometimes we communicate with one other person in an intimate setting; other times, we communicate with a small number of people in a task-oriented small group; and finally, we occasionally give public speeches to large groups of people. The changes in these contexts affect our communication. We sit, stand, and move differently, depending upon the context. When we are talking to someone we love, we use different words than when we are speaking to a crowd. The levels of formality, the amount of preparation, the places that communication can occur, the topics which are appropriate, and the purposes it serves, all vary as a result of differences in context.

Communication involves codes

Communication involves codes and consists of encoding and decoding. *Codes* are systematic arrangements or comprehensive collections of symbols, letters, or words that have arbitrary meanings and are used in communication. The codes which are used in our interactions with others may be classified into verbal or nonverbal. *Verbal codes* are the words we use and their grammatical arrangement. *Nonverbal codes* are all the symbols which are used that are not words; they include bodily movements, space, time, clothing and other adornments, and sounds that are not words.

The process of communication can be viewed as the process of encoding and decoding. *Encoding* is the act of putting a message or a thought into a code; *decoding* is the assignment of meaning to a message. If you are feeling morose and you want to explain your feelings to a small child, you might encode your message by stating, "I feel sad today," or "I feel like a day when the skies are cloudy and the rain drizzles all day long." The child would then decode your message by considering the word "sad," or the meaning of a gray day. Your ability to encode your message and the child's ability to decode it are essential in establishing common meanings.

As you considered the example above, you might have felt that the process of communication did not sound like a process at all, or that it sounded somewhat slow-moving and artificial. The relationship between encoding and decoding has been viewed in three ways by researchers. Some scholars believe that encoding and decoding are separate processes and that one person encodes and then the other decodes in the manner suggested in the example above. A second perspective is that encoding and decoding are successive phases of a single ongoing process. Finally, some persons conclude that encoding and decoding are the same operation viewed from opposite ends of the system. You may wish to consider your own experiences with communication to determine which of these perspectives appears to be accurate.

Communication is transactional. Our interpretation of the relationship between encoding and decoding may affect the way we view communication. Historically, people viewed communication as *action*. An action perspective meant that one person sent a message (encoded) and the other person received it (decoded). This perspective is comparable to a juggler tossing a ball to a second person.

The second view of communication that emerged more recently is that communication is an interaction in which one person sends a message to a second person (encodes), the second person receives it (decodes) and then sends a message back (encodes). When we view communication as an interaction, we perceive communicators taking turns encoding and decoding messages. This point of view is comparable to two jugglers throwing a ball to each other. However, one juggler cannot throw a ball until he or she has caught it from the other person.

A final perspective on communication which emerged most recently is that communication is *transactional*. This point of view suggests that communicators are simultaneously receiving (decoding) and sending (encoding) messages. The jugglers each have multiple balls which are tossed to each other continually. In addition, they might be receiving balls from other sources (the environment, other persons) and they may be sending balls to other sources (to others in the environment, to no one in particular). Finally, some of the balls may be intended for the other communicator, but may never reach their destination.

When we consider communication to be a transaction, we do not perceive one person to be a sender of messages and another person to be a receiver of messages. Both people are simultaneously senders and receivers, and neither has the status of the initiator of the message. Two communication scholars coined the term "transceivers" (Zelko & Dance, 1965) to describe the communicators in a transactional perspective. According to this point of view, people are continually sending and receiving messages; they cannot avoid communicating with others. This perspective is adopted in this text and is consistent with the notion of communication as the "negotiation of meaning."

Communication consists of bargaining

Communication consists of bargaining. A *bargain* is an agreement between two parties determining what each should give and receive in a transaction between them. Bargains may be explicit and formal such as the kinds of agreements we reach with others to share tasks, attend a social event, or behave in particular ways. Bargains may also be implicit and informal as an agreement you make to avoid profane language around your parents. You may not be aware of some of the implicit, tacit agreements you have with others with whom you communicate.

Two researchers, in a study on interpersonal bargaining, find that three essential features of a bargaining situation exist. They include:

1. both parties perceive that there is the possibility of reaching an agreement in which each party would be better off, or no worse off, than if no agreement is reached;

2. both parties perceive that there is more than one such agreement which could be reached; and

3. both parties perceive each other to have conflicting preferences or opposed interests with regard to the different agreements which might be reached. (Deutsch & Kraus, 1962, p. 52).

Some common bargaining situations are when you and the person you are dating wish to attend different events on the same night; when two roommates have different styles and one wishes to stay up late in the room studying while the other wants to go to bed early and study in the morning; or when two people use a word in two different ways.

Bargaining is obvious in those communication settings in which people are arguing over a particular phenomenon, behavior, or person. It is less obvious when we consider that bargaining occurs, to some extent, in nearly every interaction. Consider the following conversation that occurred between a ten year old girl and her four year old brother.

B   I'm really smart.
G   What is 2 times 3?
B   I know what a giraffe is.
G   What is 2 times 3?
B   I know all about giraffes—where they live, what they eat, and what they do all day.
G   What is 2 times 3?
B   What is 2 times 4?

In this conversation, the two children were attempting to negotiate some meaning for the concept of "really smart." For the ten year old girl, the concept meant that a person could do multiplication problems; for the four year old boy, it meant that a person had some understanding of animals. The boy correctly perceived that his sister was going to maintain her position regardless of his knowledge about giraffes and cleverly attempted to change the focus of the application of the definition of "really smart" from him to her.

Bargaining may be nearly invisible in interactions. For instance, in this conversation, the two people have a different conception of the word "several," but they never appear to disagree.

Husband   Don't hurry—we have several minutes before we need to go.
Wife   Do I have time to use my hot rollers?
Husband   No, unless you can do it quickly.
Wife   It usually takes about ten or fifteen minutes.
Husband   We need to go sooner than that.
Wife   Okay, I'll be right down.

The husband in this instance perceives "several minutes" to mean about "five minutes;" while the wife perceives it to be about "fifteen minutes." The two bargain, but in this instance, they never appear to become angry or sharply disagree.

Two researchers considered the importance of bargaining in interpersonal interactions. They concluded that all relationships are bargaining ones.

The point should be made . . . that whatever the gratifications achieved in dyads, however lofty or fine the motives satisfied may be, the relationship may be viewed as a trading or bargaining one. The basic assumption running throughout our analysis is that every individual voluntarily enters and stays in any relationship only as long as it is adequately satisfactory in terms of his rewards and costs (Thibaut & Kelley, 1959).

These writers stress the central role of bargaining in interpersonal relationships and they also underline a notion of cost-benefit analysis that appears to occur.

Communication includes costs and benefits. When we choose to interact with another person, we are free to select from a variety of behaviors those that will have the most positive outcomes for us. In other words, we attempt to maximize the benefits or rewards and minimize the costs. The rewards may be personal gratification, satisfaction of ego needs, or demonstration of status. The costs include anxiety, mental and physical effort, and possible embarrassment.

To illustrate the cost-reward consideration in communication, suppose that you have an acquaintance who is going through dissolution of her marriage. After she has confided in you and has asked for your understanding, you decide to disclose to her that you, too, had a marriage that ended. You may never have considered talking about your own dissolution with her because the relationship had not been very close, and you may have determined that she would have judged you negatively if she knew about this incident.

In this exercise you will experience the negotiation inherent to communication. Write down something which another person could do for you that you would enjoy. For example, you might write down that you would like someone to give you a backrub, that you would like someone to type a paper for you, that you would enjoy someone preparing a meal for you, or that you would like someone to babysit for your children. Select a partner from your class with whom to interact. During your conversation, you each need to negotiate your wishes. The other person may want you to go to a movie with him or her and you may want the other person to go on a run with you. Engage in bargaining in order to gain agreement for both of your goals. In order for this exercise to work effectively, you must honestly engage in the interaction. In other words, do not simply respond that you will do something unless you actually will engage in the behavior. You may find that you reach agreement fairly quickly, if you want something that is relatively easy for the other person to do, but rather slowly, if you want something that is relatively difficult for the other person to do, or not at all, if you want something which the other person would not, or could not, perform. After your interaction with the other person, discuss what occurred. What strategies appear to facilitate agreement? What communication attempts appear to result in failure to negotiate? What have you learned about two-person interactions from this exercise?

The cost, prior to this interaction was higher than any potential reward that you could determine. After she has disclosed to you, you reassess the situation and determine that it is appropriate to tell her about your own unsatisfying marriage. In this instance, you perceive the cost (her negative judgment of you) to be minimal, while the reward (her perception of you as someone who is understanding and experienced in dealing with difficult relationship termination) would be maximized. Homans, a social psychologist, offers a recommendation about successful interactions,

> The open secret of human exchange is to give the other man [or woman]
> behavior that is more valuable to him [or her] than it is costly to you and to
> get from him [or her] behavior that is more valuable to you than it is costly to
> him [or her] (Homans, 1961, p. 62).

Complementary and symmetrical interactions

Communication interactions are either symmetrial or complementary. Watzlawick, Beavin, and Jackson (1967), in their classic treatise on communication, offer the communication principle that, "All communicational interchanges are either symmetrical or complementary, depending on whether they are based on equality or difference" (p. 70). They discuss the two kinds

of interaction and explain that symmetrical interchanges are those in which the two people tend to mirror each other's behavior. Complementary interactions occur when one partner's behavior complements the other. Symmetrical interactions minimize differences and complementary interactions maximize differences. Complementary interactions include communicators who are of different status, within the confines of the interaction. One person is perceived to be superior, primary, or the initiator; the other person is perceived to be inferior, secondary, or the responder. Some complementary interactions occur because of social or cultural norms about various roles. For instance, a doctor may be perceived to be superior to her or his patient, who is considered to be inferior. A parent may be viewed as superior in an interaction with his or her child. Complementary relationships may also exist in interpersonal exchanges as a result of implicit agreement between the communicators. One essential feature to note is that one person cannot be superior unless the other agrees to be inferior, and vice-versa. The complementary relationship is dependent upon both people engaging in what becomes an interlocking pattern.

Watzlawick, Beavin, and Jackson (1967) emphasize that the symmetrical or complementary definitions of interaction are descriptive and that persons should not associate them with "naturally" good or bad relationships. Either can be satisfying to the participants and either can be used for good or ill. They conclude, ". . . the symmetry-complementarity paradigm comes perhaps closest to the mathematical concept of *function,* the individuals' positions merely being variables with an infinity of possible values whose meaning is not absolute but rather emerges only in relation to each other" (p. 71).

To recapitulate the essential features of a definition of communication discussed in this section of the chapter, we note that communication is the process of negotiating meaning which begins with ourselves, occurs in a context, involves codes and consists of encoding and decoding, is transactional, consists of bargaining, has costs and benefits, and occurs in interactions which are either symmetrical or complementary. This definition with its unique features will guide our understanding of the communication that occurs within and between women and men.

Women and men both hold a number of stereotyped beliefs about the opposite sex, and they are both frequently curious about how it might feel to be of the opposite sex. In this exercise you will gain an opportunity to talk to members of the same and opposite sex about questions you have always wanted to ask, but never felt comfortable asking. First, make a list of questions that you would like to ask members of the opposite sex. Then, share these questions with members of the same sex, creating one master list. After you have completed this, join with all of the others and take turns asking each other questions. For example, one of the men and one of the women might serve as spokespersons and take turns asking the questions generated by the individual lists and by the groups. Some examples of questions might be, "How does it feel to be pregnant?" "How do you cope with feelings of emotional inadequacy?" "Do men want to be fathers?" "Do you like to initiate conversations?" "What communication skills are most important for a member of your sex?" Although this exercise may begin in a fairly structured and uncomfortable manner, you will probably find that it loosens up as the discussion ensues. All of the men and all of the women should feel free to add comments about their own feelings; however, individuals should be discouraged from judging the feelings of others. For instance, if a man discloses that he tries to be understanding and sensitive in his relationships with women, none of the women should disagree or argue with him. As you engage in this exercise, observe how talking to the opposite sex appears to be essential in understanding and relating to them.

Gender and communication

When we put the terms "gender" and "communication" together and join them with the conjunction "and," we are allowed a great deal of latitude in our area of consideration. When we study gender and communication, we may be examining communication that occurs before, during, and after sexual intercourse, communication about sexual intercourse, communication between women and men, communication about women and men, communication between persons who are "feminine" and "masculine," communication about persons who are "feminine" and "masculine," communication between persons who are functionally male and female, or communication about persons who are functionally male and female. You may be surprised to know that we will at least touch upon all of these topics in this text.

Our primary focus will be the communication which occurs between women and men, but the other topics will be considered. We will discuss communication in intimate settings in chapter 9, where we will explore other contexts of communication as well. We will consider communication about men and women, about persons who are "feminine" and "masculine," and about persons who are functionally male and female in chapter 6, where we discuss the role of language and semantics. We will attempt to include information about communication between people who are "feminine" and "masculine" or functionally male and female throughout those chapters which consider topics on which research has been conducted. For example, we will consider the influence of sex role orientation in chapter 10, when we discuss public speaking, since research has examined both sex and sex role orientation in this area. Nonetheless, the primary emphasis in the text will be on male/female communication.

Viewing communication between women and men

One of the continuing threads through this chapter has been the changing nature of our society; this has resulted in confusion and a certain amount of chaos in the relationships between women and men. In the same way, persons who have been interested in understanding, explaining, and predicting communication behaviors between women and men have tried alternative approaches, differing methods, and distinctive philosophies. Let us briefly review the research on sex-related variables and communication.

Early research

The origin of research on sex-related variables in communication probably can be traced to the earliest studies in which many people included biological sex as a category to determine whether it affected the particular area of communication under consideration. However, most of these studies treated biological sex as an almost accidental feature, rather than as the primary area of interest in the study (cf. Ball, 1958; Bryan & Wilke, 1942). About twenty years ago researchers began to examine sex differences in communication as a central concern. During this first wave of research a number of differences in communication were determined (cf. Bostrom & Kemp, 1968; Brooks, 1974). This kind of work proceeded until Bem reintroduced the importance of **androgyny**, the internalization of both masculine and feminine characteristics in 1974, a term which was used by the ancient Greeks with essentially the same meaning, but had little currency in modern history. Research in communication, after 1974, replaced biological sex with psychological sex role orientation (cf. Talley & Richmond, 1980; Greenblatt, Hasenauer, & Freimuth, 1980; Montgomery & Burgoon, 1980). The Bem Sex Role Inventory (BSRI; Bem, 1974) was used by most researchers to "operationalize"—specify the components of—the concept. Criticism of the instrument (cf. Strahan, 1975; Spence, Helmreich, & Stapp, 1975; Pedhazur & Tetenbaum, 1979; Locksley

& Colton, 1979) resulted in the development of new methods of tapping the androgyny component (cf. Spence, Helmreich, & Stapp, 1975; Heilbrun, 1976; Wheeless & Wheeless, 1981; Wheeless & Dierks-Stewart, 1981) and communication researchers accordingly shifted their understanding of sex role orientation.

The early studies that used sex role, rather than biological sex, appeared to hold some promise. While the use of biological sex had resulted in mixed findings, the utilization of the new sex role instruments appeared to clarify the findings and sharpen the issues. However, the research using sex role began to break down, too, and people became unclear about the meaningfulness of their findings. In addition, re-examining all of the previous research on communication by replacing biological sex with psychological sex type became tedious and tiresome.

Researchers began to ask themselves about the purpose and goal of their work. They began to perceive that the research on gender variables and communication had little conceptual base. In other words, when they had completed a study they were no closer to an explanation for the communication behaviors of people than before, and could not offer predictions that were useful or clear. In short, the research did not answer the basic questions about why research was being completed or what purpose was to be served once the answers were to be found.

The theorists and practitioners

Communication theorists were simultaneously working on constructs that would provide theoretical undergirding for effective communication. Hart and his associates developed the Rhetorical Sensitivity construct (cf. Hart & Burke, 1972; Hart, Carlson, & Eadie, 1980) and defined the rhetorically sensitive person as one who characterizes herself or himself as a changing, fluctuating person who appropriately adapts to situational or environmental variations. Norton (1978) created the Communicator Style construct which offered an integrated schema for organizing communication behavior into specific style categories. Among the styles he identified are the dominant, contentious, precise, attentive, friendly, open, relaxed, animated, and dramatic. Of importance in communicator style is the general assessment of the effectiveness of an individual's style of communication. Other researchers considered the importance of communication competence (Bochner & Kelly, 1974; Brunner & Phelps, 1980; Cegala, 1981; Duran & Wheeless, 1982) which included an element of adaptability or flexibility. These instruments and others were created to tap effective and appropriate communication. In general, they acknowledged the importance of sensitivity to oneself, to the other communicator(s), the context, and the message variables inherent in communication. Overriding these concerns was the importance of flexibility, adaptability, and situational appropriateness.

At the same time that behavioral researchers were considering effectiveness in communication and the relationships among communication and a variety of gender-related variables, theorists and practioners were offering prescriptive advice to people about how they should behave. Some of them simply stated that women and men communicate differently and *vive la difference.* Marabel Morgan's best-seller, *Total Woman,* for instance, promised fulfillment to women who were willing to limit themselves to stereotypically feminine behaviors. (An excellent rhetorical analysis of *Total Woman* is available by Solomon, 1981).

Others pointed up the difficulties in achieving success which women have had in our culture and suggested that women adopt some of the behaviors of men. For instance, John Molloy's *Dress for Success Book* and its companion, *The Women's Dress for Success Book,* recommended that men, and then women, dress in prescribed ways which would lead to success in the business world. Women were also encouraged to become more assertive; to say *no;* to be outspoken, aggressive, and shrewd (cf. Phelps & Austin, 1975; Bloom, Coburn, & Pearlman, 1975). Women were pictured in the popular literature in roles that were previously reserved for men in our culture, as illustrated above.

Other people observed the highly technological culture and suggested that all of us should adopt the behaviors of women. By becoming more co-operative, more emotional, more supportive, and more nurturing, our culture would become qualitatively better. The writings of these theorists were consistent with communication prescriptions for empathic understanding and active listening skills. The suggestions of these theorists were popularized in cartoons like the one above.

The largest group of people, however, suggest that we become more behaviorally flexible (cf. Pearson, 1983). Behavioral flexibility, the ability to change and to alter behavior in order to adapt to new situations and to relate in new ways as necessary, became the keystone. Persons who were behaviorally flexible listened actively with empathic understanding when it was appropriate and were similarly able to self-disclose and be assertive in their communication when these communication behaviors were called for. The competent communicator was sensitive to the other person or people with whom she or he was communicating, the situation in which they were communicating, the level of intimacy in the relationship, and other variables that were involved.

Behavioral flexibility was difficult for the most committed person who attended to all of the stimuli in the environment, sorted it out, considered alternative behaviors, and then responded appropriately.

Finally, women found that when they communicated in ways that traditionally were associated with men—they talked loudly, interrupted, used large gestures, and smiled less frequently—they were negatively evaluated (cf. Bradley, 1981). Similarly, men found that when they cuddled to the touch of another person, used expressive facial gestures, demonstrated nonverbal sensitivity, and relied upon adjectives such as "lovely," "adorable," or "quaint," which had been stereotypically associated with women, they were provided with negative feedback. The culture did not appear to be prepared for behavioral flexibility.

The basis of this text

Gender and Communication rests on these historical developments in the communication of women and men. This book has a perspective on the communication within and between the sexes. The most useful research in communication dealing with gender variables appears to be that which is well grounded in a philosophy or theory and which offers a framework from which to understand, explain, and predict communication between women and men. This book rejects the notions that men and women should be encouraged to communicate differently. It supports the belief that a continuation of distinctive patterns of communication will encourage the superordinate/subordinate status existing between men and women. It rejects the idea that women should simply become men. When women adopt the communication behaviors of men and reject the communication behaviors of their own sex, they limit their behavioral options. Similarly, men who simply adopt the behaviors of women are limited by an incomplete set of communication skills.

Gender and Communication proposes that behavioral flexibility holds the most promise of success in communication between women and men; however, it recognizes the complexity of the notion of behavioral flexibility. Behavioral flexibility is not simply a matter of selecting "three behaviors from Column A and three behaviors from Column B." It is not merely a matter of adding a few behaviors from those that are stereotypically associated with members of the opposite sex. It does not offer simple prescriptions for a complex communicative problem.

Behavioral flexibility has intuitive logic and is consistent with the research being conducted in communication. It is compatible with Hart's *Rhetorical Sensitivity,* Norton's *Communicator Style,* and Duran and Wheeless' *Social Management Scales.* It also has logical coherence with the notion of androgyny. Researchers have demonstrated the relationship among these constructs (cf. Wheeless & Duran, 1982; Talley & Richmond, 1980; Montgomery & Norton, 1981; Wheeless & Wheeless, 1981; Pearson, 1981).

Behavioral flexibility requires that each of us develop large repertoires of communication skills which will provide us with the tools we need for the complex and varied situations in which we communicate with others. The development of these skills will allow us to become more effective communicators only if we recognize the basic principles of communication that are presented in this chapter. We must recognize that communication is the process of negotiating meaning. No *one* of us is permitted to determine the meaning in an interaction alone. We must enter into an exchange with another person to determine a meaning which we can share. Similarly, the process notion of communication requires that we continue to redefine and renegotiate shared meanings.

We need to appreciate and understand that communication interactions begin simultaneously with ourselves and with others. We must be sensitive to the sociological characteristics we possess, the stereotypical representations we offer, and the unique personal characteristics that affect our communication with others. Our awareness and appreciation of the various "selves" offered by the other person must be taken into consideration in our interactions with them. The roles we play are largely determined by others and the roles that others play are largely defined by us.

We recognize that communication occurs in a context and that changes in context result in changes in the kinds and types of communication which occur. For instance, a married couple who work in the same organization must recognize the differences in appropriate behavior in each context. The influence of other people and environmental changes as well as alterations which occur because of the passage of time or changes in the culture affect appropriate communication.

We know that communication consists of codes and involves encoding and decoding behavior. We will see in later chapters that women and men are socialized to learn different sets of codes, and they may actually decode differently. The essential nature of encoding and decoding in communication, as well as the historical and sociological differences between women and men, must be considered as we observe the communication behavior across these sub-cultures.

We understand that communication is transactional. We cannot assume that because we have offered a message to another person they have received it. The other person may not have been able to "catch" our message, may have been preoccupied with "throwing" one of her or his own, or may have been distracted by other bombarding stimuli. Similarly, we do not allow one person to be perceived as the exclusive initiator of ideas and the other person to be viewed as the respondent, or receiver of ideas. Both parties can initiate and can respond.

We recognize that communication consists of bargaining. We accept that women and men will be better off, or at least no worse off, if they can communicate with each other. We believe that there is more than one way that agreement can be reached between women and men, recognizing that women and men frequently have conflicting preferences or opposed interests with regard to the different agreements which might be reached.

We accept the idea that communication involves costs and rewards, that we risk exposing ourselves, experiencing personal hurt, being frustrated, becoming angry, or feeling embarrassment when we communicate with others. At the same time, we stand to gain a better understanding of ourselves, a better understanding of others, closer personal relationships, and more satisfying occupational careers through our communication.

Finally, we know that communication interactions are either symmetrical or complementary. We recognize that men may be in "one-up" positions in relation to women's "one-down" situations in conversations, just as men and women may be viewed as symmetrical equals. Women may be the superiors in interactions, with men as the subordinates. Neither sex should be "naturally" complementary or symmetrical to the opposite sex. At the same time, we understand the historical traditions which have appeared to place men and women in complementary relationships and that continue to affect the relationships that can occur between women and men.

The perspective taken by this text is consistent with other textbooks in the communication field. An analysis of 22 interpersonal communication texts was completed which examined the symbolic and actual inclusion of the gender identity construct. The survey determined that most interpersonal texts favor or encourage androgyny. Preference is given to masculine traits in the areas of power, problem-solving, and self-esteem. Preference is given to femininity, mediated by masculinity, in the areas of emotions and relationships (Dorris, 1981).

To the extent that this text helps people develop extensive repertoires of communication behaviors which are not limited by their particular gender, it will have achieved its purpose. Insofar as women and men are better able to communicate with members of their own sex and with members of the opposite sex, the book will have succeeded. To the extent that it allows all of us to describe, explain, and predict effective communication strategies for the complex, changing world in which we live, it will have met its goal.

Conclusions

In this chapter you have been introduced to the subject matter of the book. You are probably more aware now of the relevance of this topic for you as a communicator. You examined a variety of ways to use the term "gender," learned about "communication," and placed the two concepts together to determine the variety of topics considered in this text.

Research in the last decade has altered our conceptions of masculinity and femininity, while emphasizing the notion of *androgyny*. While some changes have occurred in the characterizations of women and men, stereotypical notions still predominate. Communication research and theory in the area of gender-related variables is new and somewhat fragmented. In this text we maintain that *behavioral flexibility* is the most useful framework in which to consider the communication between women and men; but we recognize that this does not provide simple, straightforward prescriptions for the communicator as the most useful at the current time.

You are living in a highly exciting time in the history of our culture. Alterations in knowledge are occurring all around you. The curricula in academic institutions are rapidly changing in order to attempt to meet the needs for skills in innovative and unusual career paths which are developing. In mass communication, electronic "newspapers" are replacing those printed on paper, and movies of every type are available in people's homes at times when they choose to see them. In interpersonal communication, the changes are no less dramatic. Women and men who were once offered prescriptions on how to communicate effectively with each other now find that these modes of communication are outdated and result in disintegrating personal relationships. In order to communicate effectively with the same sex and with the opposite sex, new skills are required. Your ability to understand the material in this text and to put into practice the skills that are suggested may be critical to your personal relationships and to the successful accomplishment of your goals.

2 The self-perceptions of women and men

Introduction

In the last chapter the assertion was made that communication begins simultaneously with self and with others. Each of us views communicative exchanges from his or her own perspective, and the way we view ourselves affects our interactions with others. At the same time, our self-perception is based on our verbal and nonverbal exchanges with others. In this chapter we will explore the centrality of self and others in communication by considering the role of self-image and how we gain images of ourselves as women or men, the ways that women and men are characterized in our culture, and how women and men differ in their self-concepts.

Although we are beginning our examination of gender and communication with the self-perceptions of women and men, we do not hold a self-centered theory of communication. In the last two decades, a variety of books such as *Looking Out for #1, How to Be Your Own Best Friend,* and *Pulling Your Own Strings* suggested such an approach. These books were written with the assumption that one's own needs, attitudes, and experiences were primary, and that the needs, attitudes and experiences of others were far less important. The perspective of this text is much closer to the position taken by Daniel Yankelovich in *New Rules: Searching for Self-Fulfillment in a World Turned Upside Down.* Yankelovich (1981) offers the concept of an ethic of commitment which, he explains, shifts the axis away from self to connectedness with the world. This foundation will be useful as we attempt to understand how women and men negotiate meaning as they strive to communicate with each other in a variety of different contexts.

Gaining self-image

Self-awareness is our cognizance of ourselves as unique beings. We become aware of ourselves as we interact with others. As small children, we learn to recognize the boundaries of where we stop and someone else begins. When we are three or four years of age we develop an awareness of our own autonomy and recognize the distinctness of ourselves from our parents, our siblings, and other significant persons in our world.

Biological explanation

When we consider how people gain images of themselves as women or men, or how we gain a "female" or "male" self-awareness, the question appears to be fairly straightforward. Biological answers to such questions appear to be simple and to place people in one of two categories. You have already discovered in chapter one, however, that the question of "femaleness" and "maleness" is more complex than it appears. Even if we are to limit our answer to

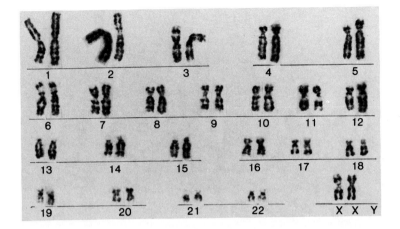

biology, the question still remains fairly complex. Each of us has 44 chromosomes that are not related to our sex and two of them that are. In figure 2.1, you are provided with a visual depiction of the 46 chromosomes of a female before birth. This person had normal chromosomes and is determined to be a female because chromosome 45 and 46 are both X's. Typically, women have two X chromosomes (one from the mother and one from the father); a typical male has an X and a Y chromosome (an X from the mother and a Y from the father). However, everyone does not have two X chromosomes or an X and a Y chromosome.

People may have an unusual combination of sex chromosomes, with or without associated physical or mental defects. Four of the most common are the Triple-X syndrome, Klinefelter's syndrome, Turner's syndrome, and the XYY syndrome. The *Triple-X syndrome* refers to a condition in which one has three X sex chromosomes rather than two. Persons with this condition are known as "superfemales," but they are generally not unusually feminine. They may, however, be mentally retarded.

Klinefelter's syndrome refers to the condition of having two X chromosomes and one Y chromosome. These men are generally very tall and thin, have small primary sexual organs, and sometimes develop breasts at puberty. They are sterile and may have some mental impairment. They are usually relatively inactive sexually.

Turner's syndrome is the condition of having only one sex chromosome which is an X. Women with Turner's syndrome appear to be physically immature, to be in a prepubescent state. They may have no ovaries or have ovaries present in only a rudimentary form. They are often physically short and their intelligence may be impaired.

Another abnormality, the *XYY syndrome,* has received a certain amount of publicity in the past five years. A high percentage of men with the XYY configuration have been found imprisoned for crimes involving violence or sex. XYY persons are thoroughly masculine in appearance, tend to be more than six feet tall, and show a normal range of intelligence. Any causal connection between their abnormal sex-chromosome pattern and their behavior patterns remains to be established, although such speculation has been offered by a number of researchers. Thus, we conclude that biological explanations alone, are not as straightforward as we might have assumed in determining one's sexuality.

Socialization

Becoming men and women, however, is a question that goes beyond biology. Socialization begins at birth, shaping persons to behave in appropriate, prescriptive ways. Examinations of other cultures demonstrate that men and women are guided by different sex stereotypes in other nations (cf. Williams & Best, 1982). In our own culture, we dress male and female babies in different colored clothing and parents respond differently to male and female infants (cf. Moss, 1970; Bell & Carver, 1980). Similarly, male and female babies are described with different adjectives; boys are described as strong, solid, and independent, while girls are described as loving, cute, and sweet. People describe identical behavior on the part of infants differently if they are told the infant is a "boy" or a "girl." (Condry & Condry, 1976). Preschool children observe commercials and cartoons on television, are read books, and play with toys in which "appropriate" sex roles are depicted.

Since the messages about sex roles are ubiquitous, it may be surprising that children do not develop specific sex role conceptions earlier than they currently do. It appears that before 3 years of age, children have litle conception of sex roles; but between the ages of 3 and 5, sex roles appear to be developing (cf. Seegmiller, 1980). Children between 3 and 5 years of age similarly sex type others (Haugh, Hoffman, & Cowan, 1980). Between the ages of 5 and 7, *gender constancy* or the tendency to see oneself consistently as a male or female, appears to develop in most people (cf. Tibbits, 1975). Communicative differences can be traced at a fairly early age as well. Graves and Price (1980) studied the communicative behavior of middle school children. They found that differences in usage occurred, but no differences in language abilities were present. They concluded that the expectations of others, rather than innate ability, affected the perceived differences in communicative behavior. Other investigators who have determined differences in the communicative behavior of women and men have suggested that differences in the expectations of others, rather than alternative explanations, is most parsi-monious (cf. Martin & Craig, 1983; Fishman, 1978). Communicative behav-ior reflects an understanding of distinctive sex role socialization. One of the factors that affects the perception of self as "male" or "female" are the role models that are available to children.

Role models
People communicate appropriate behavior through role models. Males appear to be more rigid than females in their sex roles and in determining appropriate behavior. For example, when children were told, before they performed an activity, that "girls do better at this task," "boys do better at this task," or "both boys and girls do well at this task," boys performed poorly when it was specified as appropriate for the opposite sex. Girls did not perform differently if the experimenter suggested that opposite sex persons generally performed better (Gold & Berger, 1978; Lane, 1983). The authors of this study suggest that it may be more difficult for boys to achieve masculine sex identity than it is for girls to achieve feminine sex identity because young boys initially iden-tify with their mothers and then must switch their identification to the male role. Girls, on the other hand, can retain their female identification since they identify with their mothers and remain with that identification. The process of rejecting feminine roles is salient to young boys. The researchers conclude that if the boys' need to reject feminine activities arises because of the tra-ditional mother's role as caretaker of the children, this tendency could be de-creased by introducing more males into early child-rearing. Boys might then be provided with greater opportunities to learn their sex role by having more contact with male models.

Role models affect children's notions of sex roles. When children of non-working mothers were compared to children of working mothers, the children in the first group gave far more sex-role stereotyped answers when asked about the appropriateness of certain adult and child activities than did the children of working mothers. These second grade students who had working mothers labeled eleven of twelve activities sex-neutral while the students who had non-working mothers labeled most of them appropriate for women or men (Jones, 1980). Maternal employment, one kind of role model, affects attitudes about appropriate sex roles.

Educational institutions
Educational institutions provide clear messages about sex roles. Children who are enrolled in nursery schools and day care centers appear to develop ster-eotypical beliefs earlier than other children. Two- and three-year-old children enrolled in a nursery school demonstrated substantial knowledge of prevalent

sex role stereotypes (Kuhn, Nash, & Brucken, 1978). While traditional educational environments can encourage the stereotyping of persons, based on sex, non-sexist schools may have the opposite effect.

A comparison of traditional schools which emphasize sex role socialization and open schools which stress the individual development of each child has been made. Pre-school age children were divided between the two schools and the type of school in which the child was enrolled affected her or his sex-typing. Children enrolled in the traditional school tended to have more stereotyped notions of sex roles than did children enrolled in the open school (Bianchi & Bakeman, 1978).

Games and toys

Just as role models and educational institutions affect sex role socialization, the games and toys which children select encourage notions of sex differences. Young children do not show any preferences for toys based on sex-appropriateness; but as they move through the lower elementary grades, they begin increasingly to avoid non-traditional sex role play objects (Viera & Miller, 1978). Differences in the playing behavior of children include that boys play outdoors more than girls and engage in more team sports and fantasy games. Girls tend to play indoors with dolls and board games. Girls often play alone while boys tend to play with others. Boys tend to play in more groups of children of different ages with the youngest child playing on the same level as the oldest child in the group. Girls rarely play in groups of varying ages; but when they do, the oldest girls play on the level of the youngest in the group.

As a result of these differences in play behavior, girls are more restricted in their bodily movements and vocal expressions, while boys are provided with more training for independence. Boys experience more controlled and socially approved competitive situations in which they learn the role of a person on a team. This situation may improve their ability to deal with interpersonal competition. Girls' games provide training for the development of more delicate socio-emotional skills (Lever, 1976).

Traditional game-playing encourages sex role divisions in our society, while nontraditional game-playing may encourage alternative behaviors. Fourth- through sixth-grade children were first given the freedom to select any toy they wished from a group of stereotyped feminine toys (dolls and doll furniture) and masculine toys (vehicles). Only the girls demonstrated stereotyped responses; that is, they consistently chose dolls and doll furniture. Nonetheless, the stories and games that were created by children playing with feminine toys were feminine and the play constructions for the masculine toys were masculine. In a second situation, the children were provided with either feminine or masculine toys, rather than being free to select their own choices.

"If that's what you want, Honey, then Mommy and Daddy want you to be the very, very, very best female impersonator you possibly can."

GUINDON 2-6   © 1980 L A Times Synd

In this situation, the play construction was consistent with the toy rather than the gender of the child. In other words, a boy playing with a doll would create a feminine story while a girl playing with a vehicle would construct a masculine story (Karpoe & Olney, 1983).

Children's literature

In addition to the games children play, other influences encourage traditional sex roles. Perhaps one of the most pervasive influences is the literature, or written communication, that children read and that others read to them. Many surveys of children's literature and textbooks have been conducted. They tend to confirm that many of these materials provide limited roles for females, a predominance of males, limited occupational goals for women, and stereotyping which results in less than the full range of human interests, traits, and capabilities for either sex (cf. Schulwitz, 1976; Stewig & Knipfel, 1975).

Girls and boys are frequently depicted differently. Girls are pictured as kind, attentive and serving, while boys are pictured as adventuresome and strong (Oliver, 1974). The basic difference between the sexes was summed up as "boys do," and "girls are" in one investigation (Rachlin & Vogt, 1974).

This idea means that boys are shown as active participants while girls are shown as passive observers. Boys are referred to by the functions they perform or the activities in which they engage while girls are known in terms of their appearance or the way they look to others.

What other differences between males and females appear in children's literature? Broverman, Broverman, Clarkson, and Vogel (1970) listed male-value items in children's literature as "aggressive, independent and adventurous;" and female-value traits as "very gentle, very interested in own appearance, and very strong need for security." In a random sampling of children's picture books, 21 out of 58 women pictured wore aprons (Nilsen, 1971). Most books for elementary children have a stereotypical family which consists of a mother who doesn't work, a father who does, two children (an older boy and a younger girl), and two pets (a dog and perhaps a cat); and the sexes of the animals mirror those of the children (Howe, 1971).

Finally, in an examination of the pictures in selected children's books, boys were shown in three primary male activities including fishing, building, and camping. Fewer of the girls were shown in activities of any kind; but those that did engage in activities were shown swinging, jumping rope, and playing in the sand. Women's leisure activities were shown as sedate, structured, and confining, while men's were characterized by physical action, aggression, and adventure. Girls were encouraged to be domestic and boys were encouraged not to engage in domestic activities (Liebert, McCall & Hanratty, 1971). Given these findings, it may not be surprising that boys prefer to read about boys; while girls have no preference for stories about boys or girls (Connor & Serbin, 1978). The boys may prefer stories about boys since they are more exciting and about their own sex. Girls, on the other hand, may have a difficult time choosing between a more exciting story or a story which is about people of the same sex.

Some efforts have been made to alter the way that girls and boys are depicted in children's literature. A comparison of stories from the decade of the 1930's with stories written between 1964 and 1974 was revealing. Males were prevalent more often than females, and the range of occupations for males was much broader than for females in both eras. Three changes were evident from one period to the other: (1) a broadening of sex role standards was evident in the later period, (2) many of the changes in sex role stereotyping occurred because women were becoming increasingly "masculine," not because of a similar change in both genders, and (3) differences between men and women were most apparent in the area of occupational choice as very little change occurred between the two decades studied (Hillman, 1974).

Does sexism still exist in children's literature? Yes, it is still apparent in many of the books that children read (cf. Kingston & Lovelace, 1977–1978; Britton & Lumpkin, 1977; Kyle, 1978; Tibbits, 1979). These results in recent studies are particularly surprising since a number of major publishers have called for the elimination of sexism in their materials (Macmillan Publishing Company, 1975; Scott, Foresman, and Company, 1972).

The manner in which males and females are presented in stories affects the way that the child reader views himself or herself. Girls who read about women in limited, stereotyped roles may limit their own self-perceptions and aspirations. Girls who read non-traditional stories were shown to rate traditionally male jobs as more appropriate for females than did girls who read traditional stories (Ashby & Wittmaier, 1978).

Similarly, when women were placed in nontraditional roles in stories, children's perceptions of the appropriateness of various activities for girls increased significantly. However, the children did not perceive any nontraditional roles other than those presented in the story (Scott & Summers, 1979). In other words, the children did not originate any nontraditional activities, but they were willing to accept those that were presented to them in the story.

Summary

Let us summarize how women and men gain images of themselves. We have observed in this section of the chapter that a number of factors account for our views of "maleness" and "femaleness." Biological differences are more complicated than we realize, but these differences are used from birth to determine how we will be treated. Socialization processes, which occur through interaction with others, including role models, educational institutions, children's games, and children's literature, all affect the way individuals perceive themselves. We shift our attention now from the way we learn how to perceive ourselves as women or men to the way women and men are characterized in our culture.

Characterizing women and men

Sex roles

In our consideration of how persons become women and men in our culture, we have alluded to personality characteristics and other traits that tend to distinguish women from men. You will recall that in the last chapter we discussed sex role orientation, explaining that people have a feminine sex role orientation if they internalize the desirable behaviors for women in our culture and reject the behaviors of men, and that persons are said to have a masculine sex role orientation if they internalize the desirable behaviors for men and reject the behaviors of women. Our sex role is based on the kinds of behaviors and attitudes which are expected of us because of our physiological sex.

The characteristics that comprise each of the sex roles are determined by people in a society. As individuals we sort stimuli, select some data, and reject others. We attend to, categorize, and store certain pieces of data; and we neglect, fail to categorize, and reject other data. Through our selective perception we determine the reality around us. Categorizing information allows us to have some predictability in our lives. If we decide that women are generally more compliant or yielding than men, we can make certain predictions about their behavior after we know their sex. Categorization is necessary if we are to have order and predictability in our lives. Furthermore, our language systems are based on categories, so categorization is essential to communication.

Stereotyping

Stereotyping refers to the process of assigning people, groups, events, or issues to a particular, conventional category. When we stereotype, we do not take into consideration the individualistic, unconventional, or unique characteristics of a particular person, group, event, or issue. We base our judgment, or characterization, on an oversimplified conception, opinion, or belief. Nonetheless, a certain amount of generalization is necessary in our interactions with others.

We cannot begin communicating with each new person with no assumptions about his or her behavior. For instance, we generally assume that people in our culture speak English and we thus stereotype them as English-speaking persons. If we could not assume this, we would be forced to begin each conversation with attempts to communicate in a variety of different languages until we found one in which we could all speak. Relevant to the subject matter of this text, Richmond and Robertson (1977) found that the stereotypes that people held about the supporters and opponents of the women's movement affected the interpersonal communication between women and men.

44   Considerations

What stereotypes do people in our culture hold? Listed below are a group of adjectives which can be used to describe people. Place an "M" for male and an "F" for female next to each item to designate it as part of the male stereotype or part of the female stereotype in our culture.

_____	1. Appreciative	_____	11. Excitable
_____	2. Aggressive	_____	12. Cynical
_____	3. Considerate	_____	13. Fearful
_____	4. Arrogant	_____	14. Deliberate
_____	5. Contented	_____	15. Fickle
_____	6. Assertive	_____	16. Frank
_____	7. Cooperative	_____	17. Friendly
_____	8. Autocratic	_____	18. Industrious
_____	9. Dependent	_____	19. Sentimental
_____	10. Conceited	_____	20. Outspoken

After you have completed these ten items, compare your response with the reactions of your classmates. Do you agree on most items? On which items do you disagree? How do you account for the disagreement?

Negative aspects

While stereotypes serve some useful functions, stereotyping has a negative connotation, especially in the area of sex differences among people. Stereotyping men and women is harmful for at least three reasons. First, stereotyping limits people from becoming complete beings. In table 2.1, two lists of characteristics which are traditionally associated with women and men are provided. You will observe that these are the lists from which the exercise above was derived. You may wish to examine your response to the exercise to determine whether your answers are consistent with the findings of the research which determined the two lists. (You will notice that the odd-numbered items are "feminine" and the even-numbered items are "masculine.")

As you examine Heilbrun's masculine and feminine scale items in Table 2.1, the problem with stereotyping women and men becomes apparent. Persons who are "feminine" are allowed one set of behaviors and persons who are "masculine" are allowed another set. However, our common sense tells us that each list contains characteristics which are useful in certain circumstances. For example, it is appropriate to be confident and assertive when you are giving a public speech. It is appropriate to be considerate and sensitive in interacting with family and friends. By stereotyping, we limit ourselves to something

Table 2.1   Masculine and feminine scale items (Heilbrun, 1976).

Masculine Items		Feminine Items	
Aggressive	Hard-headed	Appreciative	Jolly
Arrogant	Industrious	Considerate	Modest
Assertive	Ingenious	Contented	Praising
Autocratic	Inventive	Cooperative	Sensitive
Conceited	Masculine	Dependent	Sentimental
Confident	Opportunistic	Emotional	Sincere
Cynical	Outspoken	Excitable	Submissive
Deliberate	Self-confident	Fearful	Sympathetic
Dominant	Sharp-witted	Feminine	Talkative
Enterprising	Shrewd	Fickle	Timid
Forceful	Stern	Forgiving	Warm
Foresighted	Strong	Friendly	Worrying
Frank	Tough	Frivolous	
Handsome	Vindictive	Helpful	

less than the full range of human experience. This cartoon suggests that the traditional male experience with large impersonal corporations limits their opportunities to be interesting, unique people.

Moreover, stereotyping is limiting as we apply these concepts to others. You will recall that we stated in chapter 1 that the roles we play are largely determined by others and the roles that others play are largely defined by us. When we interact with someone who is physically a female, but behaves in a way we expect men to behave, aggressive, strong, and shrewd, for instance, we tend to negatively evaluate the person. Men are especially likely to be judged negatively for behaving in feminine ways in our culture. A recent study showed that college instructors are particularly vulnerable to negative judgments when they behave in a manner that is outside of their assigned stereotype. Students in this study were not able to learn well when they had women professors who did not behave in accordance with the stereotype for women in our culture. In addition, students were asked to evaluate four different categories of professors: men who used negative nonverbal cues including leaning sideways, avoiding eye contact, and not smiling; men who used positive nonverbal cues including a great deal of smiling, nodding their heads indicating agreement, and maintaining eye contact; women who used the same negative nonverbal cues; and women who used the same positive nonverbal cues. The students evaluated the women who demonstrated positive nonverbal cues the highest of the four groups, evaluated the men who used the positive or negative cues equally well, and evaluated the woman who demonstrated the negative nonverbal cues the lowest of the four groups (Esp, 1978). It appears, in this study, that women are "punished" when they do not live up to their stereotype.

"You don't realize how eighteen years with that large, impersonal corporation has changed you, Fred."

COCHRAN!

Basis in myth

Second, stereotyping creates problems because many of the differences between women and men are based on myth. Behaving as the "ideal" woman or the "ideal" man is difficult because the behaviors or attitudes of the stereotype are not accurate. One report dispelled seven myths about children. It showed that there is no basis for the beliefs that girls are more social than boys, that girls are more suggestible than boys, that girls have lower self-esteem than boys, that girls lack motivation to achieve, that girls are better at rote learning and simple repetitive tasks, that girls are less analytic than boys, and that girls are more affected by heredity while boys are more affected by environment (Jacklin & Maccoby, 1974). While the differences between persons are not "natural" or even accurate, we persist in believing them and in forcing people into categories. In the same way that Cinderella's shoe would not fit her stepsisters, persons cannot be forced into stereotypes that do not fit.

"This is fun, Mommy. I'm glad you wrecked the car."

Superior-inferior positions

Finally, stereotypes about men and women are harmful because one sex is placed in a position superior to the other sex. We live in a competitive, industrial-technological society in which instrumentality, shown in such characteristics as assertiveness, strength, confidence, dominance, forcefulness, industriousness, and shrewdness, is highly useful in achieving goals. At the same time, expressive characteristics, including being considerate, contented, cooperative, dependent, friendly, helpful, modest, sincere, submissive, and warm are less useful, given our cultural orientation. The masculine stereotype with its roots in instrumentality and the feminine stereotype with its roots in expressiveness not only differentiate between persons, but they provide a built-in prejudice against women. In other words, when women and men behave consistently with their stereotypical behavior, men have an advantage in this culture.

This third point should be distinguished from the first negative aspect of sex role stereotyping that was offered earlier. The first point was that women and men are both limited in their behavioral options when stereotyping occurs. This point suggests that, in addition, an evaluative dimension occurs between the two sets of characteristics which commends the male characteristics over the female characteristics, in general. Consistent with the first point would be a conclusion that both men and women are negatively judged when they behave "out of role." That is, that women who behave in an aggressive, outspoken, dominating manner are viewed negatively, just as are men who express sensitivity and vulnerability. Both sexes suffer from the limitations placed upon them by stereotyping. Consistent with the third point is that women are negatively judged when they behave within their stereotypical role. This cartoon is typical of the negative judgments made about stereotypical female behavior. Women are incorrectly perceived to be poorer drivers than are men, while men have far more automobile accidents than do women.

A variety of studies have demonstrated that women are judged more negatively than men. For instance, studies on the competence of men and women have shown that women are generally judged to be less competent than are men. When persons are asked to judge the quality of two essays, one supposedly written by a male author and one by a female author, they judge the quality of the essay supposedly written by a male as higher than that written by the female (cf. Goldberg, 1968). When individuals are provided with essays that are written by a male author, a female author, and an author whose sex is unknown (initials rather than a first name is provided), they select the male's essay as best, followed by the essay authored by the person of unknown sex, followed by the female's essay (Paludi & Bauer, 1983). Similarly, when persons are told that the source of a speech is a female, the speaker receives lower competence ratings than when the source for the same speech is identified as a male (Miller & McReynolds, 1973).

Further, in a study in which men and women were asked to judge the essays of attractive and unattractive persons, differences were found. Essays "written" by attractive women were judged to be better than were essays supposedly written by unattractive women when men made the judgments. Women judges were not affected by the attractiveness of the supposed female author. Neither men nor women were affected by the attractiveness or unattractiveness of male authors in judging the quality of essays (Kaplan, 1978). It appears that men are perceived to be more competent than women and that attractive women are assessed as more competent than unattractive women. Even small children are aware of the more positive evaluations of men. One researcher found that a substantial number of pre-school girls wished they were boys or daddies, but very few pre-school boys showed any desire to be girls or mommies (Clifton & Lee, 1976).

It is intriguing that stereotyped women are not selected for jobs, even when their stereotype would suggest that they, rather than stereotyped men, would be better suited for it. When people evaluate candidates for agentic (masculine) roles, they prefer masculine individuals for those roles. However, when they evaluate candidates for communal (feminine) roles, they prefer persons who are masculine or androgynous. Feminine individuals are almost never chosen for either the agentic or the communal roles (Hansson, O'Connor, Jones, & Mihelich, 1980).

The term *misogynist* means the hatred of women. A number of theorists have stated flatly that our culture appears to devalue, and even hate, women. Examine the following jobs and professions. Place an "M" by those jobs you would prefer to be performed by a man if you were the consumer and a "W" by those jobs you would prefer to be handled by a woman if you were the consumer. If you have no preference, place an "N" in the blank provided.

_____ 1. Bartender
_____ 2. Hair stylist
_____ 3. Physician
_____ 4. Professor
_____ 5. Lawyer
_____ 6. Accountant
_____ 7. Elementary school
     teacher
_____ 8. Airline pilot
_____ 9. Nurse
_____ 10. Housekeeper/cleaning
     person
_____ 11. Babysitter
_____ 12. Restaurant serving
     person
_____ 13. Cook
_____ 14. Automobile mechanic

Examine your responses. How many of the positions could be filled by either sex for you? Do your prefer women in traditional roles like nursing, elementary school teaching, and babysitting and men in such roles as airline piloting, automobile mechanics, and bartending? What conclusions can you draw about your own responses? Compare your feelings with those of your classmates.

Which of the positions that are listed above generally earn a great deal of money and which generally result in small incomes? Place a "+" after each job that generally results in a salary that is above average and a "−" behind each that is generally below average. Now examine those jobs which are predominately held by women and those that are predominately held by men. Are men or women associated with occupations that are lower paying? How do you account for this difference?

Finally, the assistance that we provide to others suggests that we perceive women to be in more need of help than are men. We regularly help women with doors, coats, carrying packages, and other routine matters. Bostrom, Humphreys, and Roloff (1981) showed that men help females more willingly than they help males, while females help others regardless of gender. The inherent message in the discriminatory helping behavior is that women are not as competent or capable as men. We translate our perceptions about women and men into specific communicative behavior.

Changing conceptualizations

In the introduction to the first chapter, changes in our culture concerning the sex roles of women and men were forecasted. In this chapter we have been examining traditional attitudes and stereotypes about women and men. The research on masculine and feminine sex roles has undergone drastic changes in the last decade. Until the mid-1970's, the sex role conceptions were quite clear and generally unquestioned. Similarly, communication behaviors were more predictable and aligned with traditional roles. The personality characteristics that were assigned to men and women were similar to those provided in table 2.1, earlier in this chapter. The traits that are identified in that chart were determined on the basis of the behaviors that were more characteristic of males, who identified with masculine fathers (masculine), and behaviors more characteristic of females, who identified with feminine mothers (feminine).

Other researchers determined lists of masculine and feminine items based on societal conceptions of the "ideal man" or the "ideal woman" (cf. Bem, 1974). Regardless of the manner in which the lists of characteristics were generated, all of the available research suggested that masculinity and femininity represented the opposite ends of the same quality. In other words, the more masculine a person was found to be, the less feminine she or he was said to be. Masculinity and femininity were thus characterized as opposites.

Beginning in the mid-1970's, the view that masculinity and femininity simply represented the opposite ends of a single dimension was questioned. Bem (1974) is generally credited with the development of the first instrument in which masculinity and femininity were treated as independent attributes. Essentially, Bem (1974), Spence, Helmreich, and Stapp (1974, 1975), and Heilbrun (1976), among others, argued that we could measure the extent to which a person was feminine or non-feminine separately from our measurement of a person's masculinity. Using the simplest analysis, people could be characterized as high in masculinity and high in femininity; high in masculinity and low in femininity; low in masculinity and low in femininity; or low in masculinity and high in femininity. These four potential outcomes are depicted in the figure below. By shifting masculinity and femininity to separate dimensions, researchers saw a need for a term to refer to those persons who were high in masculinity and high in femininity. The noun that was used is "androgyny" and the adjective was "androgynous." These terms refer to those persons who combine masculine and feminine characteristics.

Subsequent to the development of the instruments which measured androgyny, a great deal of research had been conducted to demonstrate that persons who are androgynous are behaviorally more effective than masculine or feminine persons (cf. Bem, 1975; Heilbrun, 1968; Spence, Helmreich, & Strapp, 1975). While conflicting evidence is available concerning the superiority of androgyny, the new conceptions of masculinity and femininity are

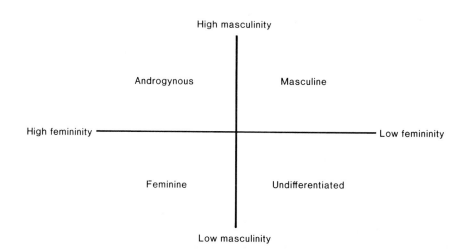

helpful. Persons may feel that they are freer to behave in alternative ways in different situations. That is, a man might feel that it is "normal" to nurture a baby and a woman might feel that it is acceptable to be aggressive in a business setting. In general, the new conceptions of masculinity and femininity had the potential of freeing people from one set of stereotypical characteristics.

Current characterizations of women and men

The current research provides an optimistic perspective from which to consider the changing roles of women and men, though we must be careful not to be too easily persuaded by the recommendations in the literature. The effects of research findings are limited and mixed, at best. On the one hand, we have suggestions that women and men are changing. For example, two representative national surveys were compared, one of which was conducted in 1957 and one of which was conducted in 1976, and differences were determined. Among men, the achievement motive remained stable, the affiliative motive decreased, and power motives increased. For women, the motives for achievement and power increased (Veroff, Depner, Kulka, & Douvan, 1980).

Other studies similarly point to change. Women may have more liberated attitudes and a greater sense of self if the amount of graffiti written in women's restrooms serves as an indicator. An examination of such graffiti demonstrated an increase in the past few years (Tahir, 1979). In addition, women and men appear to be judged on a more individual basis than on the basis of their stereotypes currently (Locksley, Borgida, Breicke, & Hepburn, 1980).

For each study which suggests that new, broader conceptions of women and men exist, we are able to find a contradictory study which demonstrates that "the more things change, the more they stay the same." Although the study was completed over 10 years ago, the persistence of traditional sex roles was demonstrated as pervasive and unchanging (Broverman, Broverman, Clarkson, Rosenkrantz, & Vogel, 1972). This cartoon illustrates the negative evaluation that sometimes occurs when women behave outside their traditional roles.

Recent studies provide similar trends. For example, high school counselors' attitudes were assessed, and male counselors were found to perceive female students to be less interested in math and science, less skilled in business, less adventurous, and less self-confident. Female high school counselors maintained that women were more submissive, illogical, sneaky, uncomfortable with their own aggression, and more dependent than men. They also felt that men were not more knowing about the ways of the world and better able to separate feelings from ideas than were women. In this study, the male counselors held fewer traditional beliefs than did the female counselors (Petro & Putnam, 1979). In other words, female counselors are more limited, and may be more limiting in their recommendations than are their male counterparts. We can speculate that the female counselors' experience with reality may have suggested that people are more limited in their options than the male counselors' experience has led them to believe.

Another study was conducted with college students who were asked to rank, in order, fifteen descriptions that they thought best characterized the average female and the average male, the ideal female and the ideal male, and themselves. The results of this study demonstrated considerable agreement between the female and male students concerning the average and the ideal female and male. Both groups continue to believe that sex role stereotypic differences exist between the average female and the average male (Freeman, 1979). The question which opened this section of the chapter remains a question.

Summary

To summarize, women and men are characterized on the basis of their sex roles and by stereotyping. Others influence our communicative behavior as they make assessments of who we are and communicate their expectations to us. We influence the behaviors of others to the extent that we use data such as biological gender and psychological stereotypes in making judgments about them and in communicating our expectations to them. To a certain extent we must rely on stereotypes in order to communicate with others. At the same time, stereotypes are harmful, inasmuch as they limit the behavioral options of women and men, as they are based on myths, and as they place one sex in a superior position to the other. Women tend to be judged more negatively than are men in our culture. Conceptualizations of sex roles are in a state of flux.

Differing self-concepts

We have examined how people gain images of themselves as men and women and how men and women are characterized. We are now prepared to consider how women and men differ in their self-concepts. Our *self-concept* is our consciousness of our total, essential, and particular being; it includes all of the "selves" that are products of the responses we gain from others to our communication (Mead, 1977). It may be analytically divided into two components: *self-image* and *self-esteem*. Our self-image is the sort of person that we

To what extent do you believe that our attitudes about women and men have changed? Arrange to interview at least two men and two women who are at least 60 years of age. Prepare a set of interview questions in which you inquire about the roles of women and men 40 years ago, 20 years ago, and today, from their perspective. Consider asking similar questions about each 20-year-interval. For instance, you may want to ask what percentage of women worked outside the home at each point in time, how women who worked outside the home were viewed, how many children were raised in each family, how much day-care and other child-care was available, how frequently a family would hire an evening babysitter, how a woman would spend a typical day, how a man made a living, how many hours a day a man worked, what kind of work was typical for a man, how much time men spent with their children, and how men were viewed who spent a lot of time with their families and less time engaged in their job or occupation. Be sure to include questions about the attitudes of the person you interview toward any changes she or he perceives. Does this person believe people were happier? Were people able to achieve their goals? Why? Write a short report on your findings and draw some conclusions from your investigation.

believe we are, as we come to know ourselves through our interactions with others. It is the "I" of self-concept. If we explain to someone that we are an electrical engineer, a father of three children, and a part-time student, we are verbalizing our self-image. Those elements that are relevant to us are learned from others. For instance, a well-known author on a television interview, might mention that he or she has written four other books, graduated from a midwestern university, and has received a coveted award. He or she might not mention that he or she is married, has two young children, and dislikes cats. It is fairly obvious that our self-definition, or self-image, is directly affected by the subtle and unmistakable messages of others.

Self-esteem is how we feel about who we are; it is the "me" of self-concept. If we add to our self-description that we feel badly about the lack of humanness in electrical engineering, about our inability to spend quality time with our children, or about the pressures of attempting to handle a number of different roles at the same time, we are referring to our self-esteem. Just as our self-image is determined by our interactions with others, so is our self-esteem. Many highly accomplished individuals feel that they have not done enough. A scientist with many discoveries feels badly about his work because he has never won the Nobel Prize; an author with a number of successful books feels like a failure because she has never had a best-seller; and a parent feels

like he or she has not succeeded because one of his or her children has committed suicide. In each case, another person or group of people have provided a response which is interpreted negatively.

Self-image

Our self-image is not innate, but rather is based on categorization by other people who place us in particular roles: mother, woman, part-time student, homemaker, househusband, child, man, daughter, grandfather. It is also based on personality traits that others attribute to us: angry, moody, spirited, immature, enthusiastic, shy. Self-image is dependent, too, on our physical characteristics: short, stoop-shouldered, square, thin, tiny, huge, rotund.

One part of our self-image is how we perceive ourselves to be as a communicator. Montgomery and Norton (1981), for instance, found that women tend to view themselves as animated communicators. Women similarly report slightly more communication apprehension than do men (McCroskey, Simpson, & Richmond, 1982). Throughout this text we will explore relationships between our self-image and our communicative behavior.

Self-esteem

Our self-esteem is based on the positive or negative reactions that people offer us; our self-esteem is not "natural." An illustration is provided in this cartoon. If we develop favorable attitudes about ourselves based on the evaluations of others, we are said to have "high self-esteem;" if we develop unfavorable attitudes about ourselves, we have "low self-esteem." Our self-esteem affects the way we communicate, how frequently we engage in communication, and how we view opportunities to communicate with others. At the same time it is our communication with others that provides us with our self-esteem.

One of the misconceptions about self-image and self-esteem is that they are highly correlated. In other words, people who make a great deal of money, have international fame, or have particular possessions are happy and that people who are poor, unknown, and without many worldly goods are unhappy. The relationship does not withstand the scrutiny of empirical testing. Two people may have similar self-images—view themselves as "career women," for instance, and have dramatically different levels of self-esteem. One recent study showed that no correlation exists between self-esteem and educational goals, career goals, and career commitment (Zuckerman, 1980).

Gender differences in self-esteem

Self-esteem has been thoroughly examined in the literature. Apparently members of minority groups frequently suffer from negative self-evaluations which occur as they internalize the evaluations of the dominant culture (Rovner, 1981). For instance middle class individuals have higher self-esteem than do lower class individuals and Euro-Americans have higher self-esteem than do Mexican Americans (Fu, Koslund, & Hinkle, 1980). Similarly, older children have higher self-esteem than younger children (Burge, 1980). The studies that have focused on men and women have provided mixed findings. Some have found no difference in the levels of self-esteem between men and women (Seidner, 1978; Drummond, McIntire & Ryand, 1977; Zuckerman, 1980) and others have determined that men are higher in self-esteem than are women (Stoner & Kaiser, 1978; Smith & Self, 1978; Gold, Brush, & Sprotzer, 1980; Loeb & Horst, 1978; Judd & Smith, 1974; Berger, 1968; Bohan, 1973).

Similarly, the self-concepts of women and men may change in different ways. A number of studies have suggested that the stability, or enduring nature, of the self-concept may be different for women and men (cf. Myamoto, Crowell, & Katcher, 1956; Shamo & Hill, 1975; Judd & Smith, 1974, 1977). In other words, women and men may have self-concepts that are relatively different from each other and these self-concepts may alter differently as a result of similar experiences. We might not be surprised, then, that Judd and Smith (1977) found that a beginning communication course resulted in different changes in self-concept for men and women.

More specific findings are available in the literature. In particular, men tend to score higher on personal self, or how they view themselves as a person without regard for others; social self, or how they view themselves as a person interacting with others; and self-criticism, or their ability to identify problems in their behavior. At the same time, no significant differences are found in the areas of physical self, how they view their bodies; moral-ethical self, or how they view their own value systems; family self, or how they view themselves as a member of a family unit; identity, or who they believe themselves to be; and self-satisfaction, or how comfortable they are with their achievements (Stoner & Kaiser, 1978).

The perceptions of children's self-esteem appear to be affected by the children's gender and the gender of their teachers. Fourth and fifth grade children rated themselves on self-esteem and their teachers rated them on self-esteem. The boys rated themselves higher than the girls; female teachers rated the girls higher than the boys; and male teachers rated the boys higher than the girls (Loeb & Horst, 1978).

From the time of adolescence, men have a higher expected success rate on non-social skills than do women. When actual performance lags behind expected success, men are still perceived as more successful (Gold, Brush, & Sprotzer, 1980). In other words, we perceive men to be more successful; the reality of their being less successful in some instances does not intrude upon our perceptions. We persist in believing that men are more successful in non-social skills than are women.

Men appear to be more dominant and assertive than females during the process of decision-making. In addition, people perceive men to be more influential in decision-making, an observation which is consistent with traditional sex-role stereotyping. Two authors found that the differences in male-female decision-making appears to be the result of differences other than variations in self-esteem. Females tend to be more open-minded, open to persuasion, lower in performance-specific self-esteem than males, but not lower in general self-esteem. Males' self-esteem is evaluated on the basis of instrumental capabilities, such as achieving a goal, completing a task, or finishing a project; whereas, females are evaluated on criteria such as emotional warmth and sociability. Thus we see that differences in male-female behavior may be due to differing views of self, rather than differences in self-esteem (Stare & Stare, 1979).

Other variables affecting self-esteem

Do other factors affect the different self-esteem expressed by males and females? A number of variables have been identified. A child's caretaker affects his or her self-esteem. Children whose fathers were their major caretakers had the lowest self-concept scores; children whose parents both served as major caretakers ranked next in self-concept; children whose mothers were caretakers ranked next; and the highest self-concept scores were reported by children whose parents cite others as their major caretakers (Burge, 1980). This study may serve to alleviate the guilt which working women feel when they place pre-school-age children in the care of others when they work.

Depression also appears to intervene with self-esteem. Low self-esteem is related to depression (Wilson & Krane, 1980). Women report depression at a ratio of about 2 to 1 to men (Hammen & Padesky, 1977). The following influences may contribute to this figure: the strains of multiple roles; the limitations of some roles; the socialization of women, including *learned helplessness*, (e.g., the condition in which women are taught that they cannot perform specific behaviors such as changing a tire, fixing the plumbing, or disciplining children); reinforcement of *passivity,* or the tendency to accept others' behavior without objection or resistance; the reinforcement of *futility,* or the belief that change is not possible and that women must accept their situation; and *guilt,* or taking responsibility for wrongdoing.

It may also be that women and men experience the same *degree* of depression, but they *express* it differently. Depressed men generally report an inability to cry, a loss of social interest, a sense of failure, and somatic complaints, (complaints about the body), while depressed women generally report indecisiveness and self-dislike (Hamman & Padesky, 1977). Men tend to withdraw socially and use more adaptive responses such as becoming involved in activities. Women engage in a wider variety of behaviors when they are depressed than do men. They deal with their depression on a cognitive level by telling themselves they should not be depressed; they state that they would probably go to a close friend to discuss their problems; and they may engage in affective disorders such as over-eating, hostility, self-deprecating statements, and writing about their feelings (Funabiki, Bologna, Pepping, & Fitzgerald, 1980).

Traditional and liberated women also appear to differ on measurements of self-esteem. Traditional women tend to base their self-esteem more on friendships and social involvements and less on interests and abilities, while liberated women tend to base their self-esteem on interests and abilities rather than on friendships and social involvement. In addition, traditional and liberated women tend to choose tasks based on their expected performance satisfaction, despite the fact that satisfaction from success actually differs little with the task (Pomerantz & House, 1977). In other words, a liberated woman might select an analytical or managerial problem to solve, based on her expected success with the task, rather than choosing to deal with a domestic problem, based on her expected lack of success with the task. Nonetheless, she would probably be as capable of handling the domestic problem as the analytical or managerial problem. Similarly, traditional women might select problems related to interpersonal relationships rather than job-related problems, but in reality could handle either task equally well.

Single women appear to have different levels of self-esteem than do married women. We might hypothesize that the roles of wife and mother are so important in our society that a person who fulfilled neither of these roles would suffer from a lowered self-esteem. However, this does not appear to be the case. Instead, single women value personal growth and achievement, stating that they are self-determined, while married women value personal relationships and describe themselves with the associated characteristics, kinship roles, and household activities. A relationship seems to exist among education, occupation, and single status. Single women have a different level of self-esteem than married women, but it is in a positive, rather than a negative, direction (Gigy, 1980).

Dating and married couples have also been studied to determine their levels of self-esteem. Dating couples tend to select others with similar levels of self-esteem. An examination of the self-esteem scores reported by married couples yielded a moderate correlation between the persons, but the relationship did not increase over a period of time. Similarity in self-esteem, then, is probably due to initial selection of someone who is similar in self-esteem, rather than as a result of marital interaction (Schumm, Figley, & Fuhs, 1980).

To summarize, persons with low self-esteem do not achieve as much as people who are high in self-esteem, but the former may be higher in affiliation or association with others as they seek and offer help to others. Given these findings, you may be curious about whether self-esteem levels can be changed.

Altering self-esteem

Our feelings about ourselves are always in process. We do not view ourselves in the same way all of the time with all the people and all the situations that we encounter. Similarly, we know that our self-esteem changes in the course of time. You may have felt more negative or more positive about yourself when you were in elementary school than you did when you were in high school. You may feel better about yourself now than you ever have before.

Table 2.2 Differences in self-esteem

Summary

* Men rate higher on personal self, social self, and self-criticism; no differences occur on physical self, moral-ethical self, family self, identity, or self-satisfaction.

* Fourth and fifth grade boys rate themselves higher on self-esteem than fourth and fifth grade girls; female teachers rate their female students higher, while male teachers rate their male students higher.

* Men have a higher expected success rate on non-social skills than do women; even when men do not perform better, people perceive that they do.

* Individuals from the middle class score higher on self-esteem than do individuals from the lower class.

* Individuals from Euro-American backgrounds score higher on self-esteem than do individuals from Mexican-American backgrounds.

* Older children score higher on self-esteem than do younger children.

* Children whose caretakers were someone other than their parents score higher on self-esteem than do children who were cared for by their own parents.

* Low self-esteem is related to depression.

* Traditional and liberated women base their self-esteem on different factors.

* Single women have higher self-esteem than do married women.

* Similarity in self-esteem appears to be a factor in selecting someone with whom to date or have a relationship.

The differential in self-esteem between women and men is generally explained in terms of socialization which favors men. Nevertheless, women may overcome these differences through skill development. Women who possess instrumental skills (commonly associated with masculinity) are as likely as men to display high self-esteem (Smith & Self, 1978). In other words, women who are able to develop task-orientation, or be goal-directed, may be viewed to be as high in self-esteem as are their male counterparts.

Locus of control similarly allows women to perceive themselves as favorably as men. Sixth grade girls who had high internal locus of control (they perceived themselves rather than outside forces to be responsible for the events in their lives) viewed themselves as favorably as did sixth grade boys. Sixth grade females with a strong external locus of control (they perceived people and events outside of themselves controlling their lives) viewed themselves significantly lower on measures of self-esteem (Seidner, 1978). Girls who have an external locus of control may be more susceptible to the debilitating effects of the sex-biased culture than are girls who look within for control of the events

Table 2.3 Changes in self-esteem

Summary

* Women who possess instrumental skills tend to display high self-esteem.

* Females who have internal locus of control have higher self-esteem than do females who have external locus of control.

* Individuals who score high in masculinity score high in self-esteem.

* Consciousness raising groups, discussion groups, and classes can assist individuals to alter their self-esteem.

of their lives. This explanation is reinforced by a study which shows that women overcome negative evaluations by women, in general, by focusing on the unfairness of the society (Rovner, 1981).

The relationship between psychological sex roles and self-esteem has been determined. The highest levels of self-esteem are found among people who are high in masculinity and low in femininity which is categorized as "masculine" (Gauthier & Kjervik, 1982; Stericker & Johnson, 1977) or in persons who are high in masculinity, regardless of whether they are low in femininity (categorized as masculine) or high in femininity (categorized as androgynous) (Orlofsky, 1977). Since stereotypical masculine sex-role identification is associated with high self-esteem, optimal self-esteem and optimal sex-role behavior may be inverse in women. Or, as a study cited earlier in this section indicated, women may need to adopt instrumental skills in order to score as highly as men on measures of self-esteem.

Women may have some special problems in establishing positive self-esteem. One author suggests that the female sex role encourages low self-esteem and depression insofar as it teaches women that they are weak and not in control of their own fate. This investigator determined, however, that women can alter their self-esteem by participating in consciousness raising groups. Women who participated in such groups tended to overcome low self-esteem, reduce depression in their lives, decrease their tendency to blame others, and felt that they were more in control of their own lives (Weitz, 1982).

Self-esteem can be altered; and methods such as consciousness raising groups, discussion groups, and other forms of communicative interaction may assist people in affecting change. Self-esteem appears to be lower in women than in men, and low self-esteem appears to result in lower achievement and higher affiliation. People who wish to alter their self-esteem should be able to determine methods of doing so; at the same time, they need to recognize the

All of us have a view of our "ideal" self: the self we aspire to be. Consider your favorite childhood storybook character, a sports figure, a politician, a musical star, a television celebrity, a dancer, a musician, a movie star, a political activist, or another well-known person with whom you identify. Write a short essay on the qualities of this character that are important to you, explain the influence he or she has had on your life (if any), and tell how this person is different from you. In your essay, consider some of the stereotypical characteristics of women, including expressive, reactive, emotional, warm, caring, and dependent, as well as the stereotypical characteristics of men, including task-oriented, aggressive, egocentric, strong, silent, responsible, and competitive. To what extent does the person you select exhibit either set of characteristics? To what extent do you endorse or reject the stereotypical characteristics of your gender? Consider the material in this chapter describing how we gain images of ourselves as women or men through biology and socialization, how women and men are characterized, and how women and men differ in their self-concepts. What conclusions can you draw?

consequences of their behavior. Higher levels of self-esteem appear to be related to "masculine" instrumentality, achievement, and goal-orientation, but lower levels of self-esteem appear to be related to seeking and offering assistance to others, behaviors traditionally associated with the "feminine" stereotype.

Conclusions

In this chapter we considered the self-perceptions of women and men. We determined that people acquire or develop images of themselves, partly because of biological differences, and largely through their interactions with others. The role models each of us holds, the educational institutions we attend, the children's games we play, and the children's literature we have read, all contribute to our notions of being women or men. Women and men are stereotyped to have certain characteristics. While stereotyping is necessary in order to communicate, it has certain harmful elements when it is applied to people: it places limitations on both women and men, it is largely based on mythology, and it assigns one sex to a position superior to the other sex. We are observing changing conceptualizations of women and men at this time in our history, but we also have elements of resistance to change in our culture. Women and men differ in their self-concepts. Men appear to have higher self-esteem than women, but women can increase their self-esteem. Changes in self-esteem may result in changes in other behaviors, including our communicative behavior. Persons who wish to alter their self-esteem should recognize that this is probably part of a cluster of behaviors which includes instrumentality and goal-orientation and may exclude an emphasis on relating to others.

Communication begins with self and with others. The images we have of ourselves as women or as men affect the way we communicate with others; the way other people perceive us because of our "maleness" or "femaleness" affects the way that they will communicate with us; and our self-concept, a product of how others see us, affects how we perceive ourselves as communicators. The material presented in this chapter will be useful to you as foundation material upon which you begin to analyze how women and men negotiate meaning as they strive to communicate with each other in a variety of contexts. In the next chapter we will consider self-disclosure and self-assertion, two communication behaviors which are closely related to an individual's perception of himself or herself.

3 Images of women and men

Introduction

In this chapter we will investigate the relationship of language and media to women and men. We will consider the language which is used to discuss women and men, and then examine the portrayal of women and men in the media. We will observe that both our language and our media reflect the sexist nature of our society and serve to continue the current social order. Suggestions will be made about alterations in both of these modes of communication which could affect changes in our contemporary culture.

Language about women and men

During the past two decades educators, feminists, and other groups of people have expressed concern about language which discriminates between women and men, excludes women, and encourages the domination of women by men. Some of the concern has been minimized by people who have not understood the issues that are involved. Others have disparaged the problems in language because they have felt that social changes in other spheres were more worthy of their time.

Language which refers to women and/or men deserves our consideration. Our perception of the world is closely linked to our language, and language serves to shape the way we perceive reality. Edward Sapir, a linguist, and Benjamin Lee Whorf, a fire-insurance expert, developed the notion that our perception of reality is determined by our thoughts and our thoughts are limited by our language. Therefore, our perception of reality is dependent upon language. This perspective, known as the Sapir-Whorf Hypothesis, has been widely quoted. The hypothesis contends that if you have a large vocabulary for colors, for instance, you will be able to perceive a wide range of colors. Similarly, if you reside in Southern California, you may have a variety of terms for differing kinds of surf and be able to perceive the surf differently than would someone from the Midwest. As we shall determine, this idea has direct implications for "man-linked" words and "generic" pronouns, two areas we will consider next.

Man-linked words

One area of concern about the language which describes men and women includes words which are known as man-linked. *Man-linked words* are those which include the suffix, "man." Examples include postman, serviceman, fireman, milkman, salesman, telephone lineman, and craftsman. One position is that such words refer to men, exclusively, rather than to women. Another position is that such words are "generic," and refer to women and men equally.

Sometimes people argue that the names we are called are irrelevant to the way we perceive ourselves. For instance, being called a "girl," a "lady," or a "woman" are synonymous, they argue, and women who object are being picayune. As we demonstrated in this section of the text, words have appreciable impact on peoples' perceptions of themselves and of others. Complete the following sentences to determine your own meanings for these words.

1. A bitch is _____

2. A witch is _____

3. A lady is _____

4. A gentleman is _____

5. A man is _____

6. A girl is _____

7. A bastard is _____

8. A wizard is _____

9. A woman is _____

10. A boy is _____

You may be interested to know that #2 and #8 are female and male equivalents just as are the pairs #3 and #4, #5 and #9, #6 and #10. Consider the relationship between #1 and #7. What conclusions can you draw based on this exercise? Attempt to identify other pairs that are female/male equivalents. Do these words have negative or positive meanings for most people? Can any of the pairs be interpreted so that the male term is positive and the female term is negative or vice-versa? Why do you think this occurs?

A number of research studies have systematically investigated the meaning people ascribe to man-linked words. Many of these studies were summarized by Todd-Mancillas (1981) whose work in this area is both extensive and respected. These investigations allow us to respond more scientifically to the meaning which man-linked words have for persons in our culture. The first study considered job advertisements. High-school seniors read 12 job advertisements for positions such as appliance sales, photographer, telephone frameman, taxicab driver, assistant buyer, telephone lineman, and others. Some of the jobs were man-linked (*e.g.,* telephone lineman, telephone frameman) and some of them were neutral (*e.g.,* photographer, taxicab driver). Three conditions were used in the experiment. In one condition, the jobs were sex-biased. Jobs traditionally associated with men—the man-linked jobs—were described as "men" working with other "men." Similarly, jobs that were stereotypically held by women, e.g., telephone operator, dental assistant and some of the other jobs that were not man-linked, were described as an opportunity for a "woman" to work with other "women" or "girls." In a second condition, the jobs were described without a sex-referent or with both sex referents. Traditionally male and female jobs were described for "people" or for "men and women." Third, the jobs were sex-reversed. Jobs that were traditionally male were described as opportunities for women, and positions that were stereotypically female were described as possibilities for men. The study found that in the sex-biased condition, only 5% of the women and 30% of the men were interested in applying for "opposite-sex" jobs. In the sex-unbiased condition, 25% of the women and 75% of the men were interested in applying for "opposite-sex" jobs; and in the sex-reversed conditions, 45% of the women and 65% of the men were willing to consider the "opposite-sex" jobs. The authors of this study suggest that sex-bias in the wording of job advertisements appears to alter the appropriateness of applying for positions by women and men (Bem & Bem, 1973). Man-linked words and workers described as "men" or "women" appear to alter people's perceptions of the appropriate gender in the job description.

A second study by the same authors achieved similar results. Female college students rated the advertisements in *The Pittsburg Press.* Two conditions were present in this study: In one condition the students read job advertisements that were listed under the "Jobs-Male Interest" or "Jobs-Female Interest" columns. In the second instance, the jobs were not segregated into gender-related interest groups. In the first case, when the jobs were divided on the basis of sex, only 46% of the subjects were as likely to apply for the male-interest jobs as were willing to apply for the female-interest jobs. In the non-segregated condition, 86% of the subjects preferred the male-interest jobs (Bem & Bem, 1973). The placement of the jobs under a gender-interest label influenced the selection of the female students.

Another researcher asked college students to rate the perceived masculinity or femininity of certain titles. She used man-linked words like "chairman" and non-man-linked words like "chairperson" and "individual." Males, in this study were more likely than females to identify male referents when the word "chairperson" was used; and there were only slight differences in the degree of masculinity or femininity associated with man-linked rather than non-man-linked words (Shimanoff, 1975).

The impact of man-linked words on paper-and-pencil vocational interest tests were examined. High-school-age women completed one of four parallel forms of Holland's Vocational Preference Inventory and of the Self-Directed Search. These instruments included one of the following four forms of man-linked and non-man-linked items: draftsman/draftswoman; life insurance salesman/life insurance salesperson; policeman/police officer; real estate salesman/real estate salesperson. This study, like the previous one, demonstrated no systematic tendency for persons to rate the non-man-linked terms more frequently than they rated the man-linked terms (Gottfredson, 1976).

Declarative sentences and paper-and-pencil completions were used in a fifth study. A total of 18 sentences were used which included the word "man" or a man-linked word such as, "The potentialities of man are infinitely varied and exciting." In nine cases, students were asked open-ended questions in which they would describe, in their own words, the gender of the persons discussed in the sentences. The remaining nine sentences were followed by forced-choice options in which students were required to identify the gender of the person as male or female. In the open-choice condition, the person was described as a male 66% of the time, as a female 5% of the time, and as neither male nor female, 29% of the time. In the forced-choice condition the person was identified as a man 86% of the time and as a female 9% of the time (Kidd, 1971). Both the forced-choice and the open-choice options resulted in persons perceiving a "man" more frequently as a masculine person rather than as a neutral term which referred with equal likelihood to men and women.

Photographs, rather than language, were used to determine people's perceptions. College students were asked to submit photographs from newspapers and magazines that would be appropriate for illustrating chapters in a college introductory sociology book. Half of the subjects received the table of contents with man-linked chapter titles, such as "Social Man," "Urban Man," "Political Man," "Industrial Man," and "Economic Man." The other subjects received a similar table of contents, but the chapter titles were non-man-linked, including, "Culture," "Population," "Race and Minority Groups," "Families," "Crime and Delinquency," and "Ecology." Those students who received man-linked titles supplied photographs of men at the rate of 64%. In the non-man-linked condition, only 50% of the photographs were of men only (Schneider & Hacker, 1973).

Most recently, Pincus and Pincus (1980) surveyed children in grades 3, 7, and 10, as well as adults, to determine their interpretations of sentences containing the word "man" or "man-linked" words. They determined that gender-marking can be covert or overt, and that even adults found the use of the word "man" to be ambiguous. "Man" and "man-linked" terminology remains a problem.

Although the studies reviewed here are not conclusive, they tend to support the idea that man-linked words are not viewed as referring, with equal likelihood, to women as much as to men. People who use man and man-linked words generically may only be fooling themselves: Their listeners are more likely to perceive their referents as male. Additionally, the use of man-linked words appears to be troublesome, since it narrows the perception of appropriateness of particular occupations and activities for women. Finally, the usage of such terms tends to imply that women are a substandard, or a deviant form. Women are viewed, at best, as after-thoughts or as second-class citizens. The authors of one article state that using man-linked terms is reminiscent of a time in which women were viewed as the possessions of their husbands and fathers (Burr, Dunn & Farquhar, 1972).

Man-linked words are referred to as "exclusionary," since they exclude women in the same way that woman-linked words (*e.g.,* chairwoman, saleswoman) exclude men. Inclusive words, such as chairperson, people, mail carrier, and salesperson, include both men and women. One article suggests that the usage of exclusionary language rather than inclusionary forms is similar to prescribing drugs which guarantee harmful side effects rather than using medication which does its job without harmful side effects (Johnson & Kelly, 1975). The potential danger of misinterpretation, altering behavioral options for one group of people, and continuing to view women as subordinate to men, renders this to be advice worth accepting.

Generic pronouns

A second area of concern about the language that describes men and women are those words which are referred to as generic pronouns. *Generic pronouns* are those pronouns such as "he," "him," "his," and "himself" which are said to refer, with equal likelihood, to women and to men. As early as 1970, the generic nature of such terminology was questioned. One author charged that this language was androcentric, or male-centered, sexist, and used to limit the behavioral options of women (Densmore, 1970). Another author sarcastically stated that it appeared that all persons were male, until proven otherwise (Murray, 1973). In addition, traditional generics were criticized on the grounds that they were confusing (Murray, 1973), ambiguous, exclusive, and unequal (Martyna, 1978); and defined women as secondary or deviant (Farwell, 1973).

Strainchamps (1971) maintained that the use of generic pronouns is evidence that our language retains more of an out-dated sexism than any other civilized language.

Recently, investigations have considered whether traditional generics actually refer to women and men equally. Many of these studies have compared traditional generic terms such as "he," "him," and "his" with alternative pronoun forms. Some of the alternative forms are based on commonly used words such as "he or she," "him or her," and "his or her," or less familiar words like "he/she," "she/he," and "s/he." Finally, some of the alternatives are *neologisms,* or new words, such as "herm" for "her or him," "heris," for "her or his," and "tay" for "he or she."

Just as earlier researchers examined man-linked words in job descriptions, Stericker (1981) investigated the impact of pronouns on job attitudes. She used job descriptions that were perceived as feminine, such as interior decorator and clerk-typist, as masculine, such as lawyer and taxi-driver, and as neutral, such as child psychologist and high school teacher. Stericker used three conditions: one which used "he," one which used "he or she," and one which used "they." Although the males' interest did not alter under the different conditions, she found that the use of "he or she" encouraged female interest in the jobs.

In another study, subjects read essays in which one of five kinds of pronouns were used. In the first condition the essay included the traditional generic forms (he, him, his). In the second condition the alternative generic forms were the feminine form (she, her). In the third condition the alternative generics "he/she" "she/he," "him/her," "her/his," etc., were used. Another alternative generic form was used in the fourth condition, which included "tay" for "he or she," "ter" for "her or his," and "tem" for him or her. In the last condition the alternative generics were "se" for "she or he," "hes" for "his or her," and "hir" for "her or him." Subjects were asked about the gender of the referent, the perceived quality of the essay, and the comprehensibility of the essay. This investigation demonstrated that people are more likely to perceive the word "he" as referring to men than to women, and that none of the alternatives were perceived as significantly affecting the quality or comprehensibility of the essay (Soto, Forslund & Cole, 1975).

In another early study, pronoun citations in children's books were analyzed. Nine-hundred-forty references of the word "he" were found and, of these, 744 referred to male humans, 128 to male animals, 36 to people in male-linked occupations, and only 32 to the unspecified singular subject (Graham, 1973). Similarly, Ernst (1977) determined that seventh-grade students interpreted masculine-oriented (traditional generics) language as masculine rather than as feminine.

Martyna (1978) examined the extent to which people used alternative, rather than traditional, generics in their writing. She asked students to complete six male-related statements, six neutral statements, and six female-related statements. An example of a male-related statement includes, "Before a judge can offer a final ruling. . . ." An example of a neutral statement would be, "When a person loses money, . . ." Finally, a female-related statement would include, "After a nurse has completed training. . . ." This research showed that men were more likely than women to use "he" in the completion of male-related and neutral sentence fragments; that women were more likely than men to use alternative generic forms such as "she," "he or she," and "they" for the neutral sentences; and that both men and women demonstrated a preference for gender-specific pronouns when they completed the male-related and female-related sentences.

In a similar study, subjects read a one-sentence statement and then wrote brief narratives about the person in the statement. Three conditions were used. In the first the subjects read, "In a large coeducational institution, the average student will feel isolated in his introductory courses." Or "Most people are concerned with appearance; each person knows when his appearance is unattractive." In the second condition subjects read the same sentences, but the generic "his" was deleted and the pronouns "his or her" were inserted. In the third condition the word, "their," was inserted for "his." This study indicated a significantly greater tendency for people to write essays describing males in the traditional generic situation than in either of the alternative conditions (Moulton, Robinson & Elias, 1978). Similarly, McKay (1979) found that when college students interpreted the generic "he," they assumed in 87% of the cases that the word referred exclusively to men. In another study one year later McKay similarly found that students who read textbook paragraphs that contained the traditional generic pronouns, but were used to refer to neutral antecedents, assumed the terms referred to men 40% of the time (McKay, 1980).

A recent study confirms those conducted in the 1970s. When college students were asked to complete sentence fragments that referred to traditional male roles, traditional female roles, and gender-neutral roles, their responses were similar to earlier research. The overwhelming response to the completion of sentences that included male roles was to use "he"; the overwhelming response to the completion of sentences that included female roles was to use "she"; and they used "he" or "they" in the neutral condition (Wheeless, Berryman-Fink, Serafini, 1981). At the present time we can determine gender-specific roles, and we can still maintain that the traditional "he" does not communicate both males and females with equal frequency.

Nontraditional generics are neither more difficult to understand nor perceived as less pleasant than traditional generics. A large number of students read different forms of an essay in which one form used the traditional generics; one form used the alternative form "s/he"; and the third form used the neologism, "tey" for "she or he." Subjects read one of the three forms and then completed a comprehension test and also rated the aesthetic quality of the essay. Neither the comprehension scores nor the aesthetic ratings of the essays were significantly different from each other in the three forms (Meyers, 1979). Todd-Mancillas (1982) determined that contrived pronoun forms such as "tey," "ter," and "tem" may result in actual and perceived reductions in comprehension, but that less contrived forms such as "s/he," "him/her," and "his/her" do not cause any difficulties. The use of less contrived forms may be more desirable than using neologisms.

Teachers may be able to alter the pronoun usage of their students. One instructor taught two sections of a child psychology course and substituted the feminine forms, "she," and "her," for the traditional generic pronouns. At the end of the course student papers were examined for the students' usage of pronouns. The results showed that students tended to use "she" in their papers significantly more than did a control group (Adamsky, 1980).

Flanagan and Todd-Mancillas (1982) examined the effects of two approaches in teaching inclusive generics. In one approach, the students decision about using inclusive generics was forced upon them by an instructor telling them that they would be required to use them in all future assignments. In the second approach, material on inclusive pronouns was presented for the students' information only. Flanagan and Todd-Mancillas found that both approaches encouraged the use of inclusive generics, but that the authority model produced more change in pronoun use.

These studies allow us to draw a number of conclusions concerning traditional and alternative pronoun choices. First, just as man-linked words are not perceived to refer with equal likelihood to men and women, traditional generic pronouns are not perceived to refer equally to men and women. Second, alternative generics do not affect the comprehensibility or pleasantness of written work. Last, students will alter their use of pronouns when alternatives are modeled by instructors. The potential change that can occur is encouraging in the light of the possible damage that occurs to women when traditional forms are used.

Alternatives to traditional man-linked words and generic pronouns

What kinds of alternatives exist for man-linked words and pronoun usage? A recent study suggests that we may categorize alternative forms into three possibilities (Todd-Mancillas, 1980). First we can use currently existing words and phrases to avoid sexism. For instance, we can pluralize sentence subjects rather than relying on singular forms. An example of this usage would be, "Writers should consider their audiences," instead of, "A writer should consider. . . ." Another method of change would be to substitute words like "people" for "man," "citizens" for "mankind," and "manufactured" for "manmade." We can also use the indefinite "one;" as in the sentence, "One

can always find tutorial service available at this university." We can substitute the third person plural form, such as "they" or "their," rather than the third person, singular, such as "he," "she," etc. In addition, man-linked words can be eliminated in favor of neutral words: "firefighter" for "fireman," "mail carrier" for "mailman," and "chair" for "chairman."

A second category of alterations includes those changes that require some relatively new forms or words. Forms such as "s/he," "wo/men," "chairperson," and "personkind" are relatively new forms that can be used. Parallel constructions might be considered: Whenever "he" is used, it is followed by (or preceded by) "she." We then use "women and men," "her or his," "him and her." Alternating the usage of the masculine and feminine third person, singular form may also alleviate the sexism which appears inherent in the constant use of traditional pronouns. It may be particularly useful to employ these forms in opposite-sex situations so that a person would use "he" in referring to a nurse, an elementary school teacher, or a homemaker; and would use "she" in referring to a medical doctor, a bank president, or a U.S. Senator. It may be useful to alter pronouns from paragraph to paragraph rather than from sentence to sentence in order to maintain continuity. In either case the use of the word "she" in these instances refers, just as does the use of the word "he," to men and women equally.

Table 3.1 Neologisms for traditional third person, singular pronouns

Miller and Swift	Densmore	Cole	Traditional
tay	she	se	she/he
ter	heris	hes	her/his
tem	herm	hir	her/him

A third category of alteration includes *neologisms,* or new words, which are more difficult to interpret. Three sets of neologisms have been suggested. Miller and Swift (1972) suggest "tay" for "he and she," "ter" for "her and him," and "tem" for "his or her." Densmore recommends "she" for "she or he," "herm" for "him or her," and "heris" for "her or his." Last, Cole offers "se" for "he or she," "hes" for "her or his," and "hir" for "him or her" (Soto, Forslund & Cole, 1975). All of these proposals are for alterations in third person, singular pronouns and are summarized in Table 3.1.

The 1970s were an exciting time of change in the elimination of "sexist" expressions and in "neutralizing" our language. Publishers such as Scott Foresman & Company, McGraw-Hill Book Company, and Macmillan Publishing Company issued statements that assisted authors in eliminating sexist expressions in their writing. Publishers of research journals, including the American Psychological Association, the Speech Communication Association, and the International Communication Association, issued statements concerning the use of nonsexist language in journals and other publications. English teachers, at one time demanding the use of the traditional generics, began to accept and encourage alternatives.

One specific example of change was the new edition of *Roget's Thesaurus,* the book of synonyms and antonyms which is more than 130 years old. The new edition eliminated categories which were sexist. For example "mankind" was replaced with "humankind," a countryman" became a "country dweller," and a "rich man" was replaced with "rich person." Susan Lloyd, editor of the 1980's edition, stated that the source book

> makes much more explicit the existence of women. Before they were just assumed.

Lloyd explained that she did not consider herself a feminist, but that she was "keen on women's rights and men's rights." She added,

> I'm not making a statement. I'm just reflecting the changes in the languages ("Non-sexist Thesaurus Makes Debut," p. 1).

Popular usage has not kept pace, however. Some of the changes in usage which occurred during the 1970s are present today, but others have been eroded. In Bodine's (1975) examination of 33 senior and junior high grammar books, she found that 28 of these condemned the use of "he or she" and the singular use of "they." Instead, the texts encourage students to use the pronoun "he" in their writing. We noted above that college students in 1981 tended to use the plural "they" when referring to neutral referents. Unfortunately, they frequently use the plural "they" with a singular subject (Wheeless, Berryman-Fink, Serafini, 1981).

Purnell (1978) examined political speeches to determine the extent to which women were included. She examined generic terms used for groups of both sexes or individuals of either sex, the gender typically ascribed to working people, the specific references to women and men to determine in what capacity women were used as examples, and the lists of groups of persons, jobs, places, or organizations to determine whether women's concerns and groups were treated in a manner similar to men's. She found that women were not regularly included, and that when women were included, they were sometimes referred to as "housewives." Interestingly, when the speakers listed "Americans," they excluded the category of housewives, perhaps because of their lack of economic contribution. Purnell found a few nonsexist references and a decrease in obvious sexist forms as "fellow" Americans; nonetheless, women appear infrequently in the language of politics.

Changing sexist forms may be particularly important for educators. We observed that teachers can model nonsexist forms and that students alter their language based on these models. A number of communication educators have called for sensitivity to sexism and modifications in usage (cf. Richmond & Dyba, 1982; Todd-Mancillas, 1981; Pincus & Pincus, 1980; Trenholm & Todd de Mancillas, 1978; Karre, 1976; Sprague, 1975). Among the changes called for are attention to the selection of textbooks and other materials to insure that they are nonsexist, modeling nonsexist behavior, encouraging individuality, assisting students in constructively surmounting the constraints of sex roles, including discussions on sexism in communication, the avoidance of sexist forms, and the use of inclusive language forms.

Why have changes in language been so slow and sometimes appeared to be moving back to older, more sexist forms? Part of the reason for this phenomenon may lie in the disparaging of language changes that we have seen occur. For instance, we may hear people ask if they should use forms such as "Portuguese person-of-war," for "Portuguese man-of-war," "personhole cover" for "manhole cover;" and change names like "Forman" to "Forperson," and "Pearson" to "Pearperson." In addition, feminists have been divided over the issue of the relative importance of language changes, given the nature of other forms of inequality (Lakoff, 1973; Nilsen, 1973). In addition, it has been suggested that pronouns may occur too frequently in sentences, making it difficult to monitor them for the average speaker or writer (Lakoff, 1975).

It is frequently easier to eliminate sexist language than we realize. A childrens' book, *Mother Goose and Father Gander: Equal Rhymes for Girls and Boys* (Larche, 1979), includes popular nursery rhymes which have been rewritten without a sexist bias. Some examples follow:

Jill and Jack Be Nimble
Jack be nimble, Jack be Quick,
Jack, jump over the candlestick.
Jill be nimble, jump it too,
If Jack can do it, so can you!

Bo Peep and Joe Peep
Little Bo Peep has lost her sheep
And doesn't know where to find them.
Leave them alone, and they'll come home,
Wagging their tails behind them.

Little Joe Peep has lost his sheep
And doesn't know where to find them.
Let them be, and let them run free,
They're sowing wild oats behind them.

Rub-A-Dub-Dub
Rub-a-dub-dub, three folks in a tub,
And who do you think they be?
The butcher, the baker, the candlestick maker,
They've all gone off on a spree.

These childrens' nursery rhymes demonstrate how simply we can change sexist terminology and forms to nonsexist alternatives. Copy a poem, a piece of prose, or another literary form that includes sexist language or man-linked words. Rewrite the piece to eliminate possible sexist references.

Bate (1978) contends that in writing, people hesitate to adopt terms that they have difficulty expressing, such as "s/he," "Ms.," and "chairperson." She also reminds the reader that language changes occur slowly, that people begin with changes that are most repulsive, then continue with less repulsive forms. For instance, you might alter "men" and "man" quite early, but not change "freshman" to "first year college student" until later. Bate also concludes that both information and significant females with sufficient credibility must be present in order for people to alter sexist forms. All these explanations suggest why changes in our language are slow and sometimes reactionary.

It is disappointing to find a language that is heavily steeped in sexism, and it is discouraging to observe that change is slow to occur. We may feel totally desolate when we determine that some of the changes which have occurred to do not necessarily result in desexing the language. Broverman, Vogel, Broverman, Clarkson and Rosenkrantz (1970) found that the characteristics of an ideally healthy adult were associated with males. Wise and Rafferty (1982) in a replication of the earlier study determined that men and women were defined differently in terms of ideal health. Specifically, there was a difference between the females and the adults on the dimension of health, while no difference existed between the males and the adults. Wise and Rafferty conclude that by simply replacing terms such as "man" with "adult" or "person," we might not be eliminating sex-specific meaning. In other words, the terms "adult" and "person" may elicit the notion of a biological man just as the term "man" has for centuries.

Sexist practices

When we examine the language about women and men on the basis of man-linked words and generic pronouns, we find that women tend to be excluded in a great deal of the language we hear, and allocated to a secondary, subordinate role. In addition to these two systematic methods of excluding women, or of subordinating them, other practices exist which tend to differentiate between women and men. We will consider some of those differences here.

The choice of married names

For centuries, people in our culture have changed their names when they married. Most typically, the female member of the couple assumed her husband's surname. In this, and in a variety of other ways, the woman became a member of her husband's family. Both linguistically and in reality the woman changed her identity. At various points in history women have rejected this alteration in their names. Most recently, with the current women's movement, a number of women have elected to maintain their original names, to use their former last names as a middle name which is written out in full, or to hyphenate the former last names with the new last names.

A current study shows that people with hyphenated names tend to give their children the hyphenated name or the father's last name. When children are given the hyphenated name, the parents report that they understand that the child might maintain this longer name, might select one of the parent's names, or might select an entirely different last name when she or he becomes an adult. In cases where the husband and wife have each maintained their original names, the children are generally given the father's last name (Cherlin, 1978). Although hyphenating surnames or maintaining original surnames is a move toward nonsexism, rarely do the children of such couples receive the surname of the mother exclusively; they frequently receive their father's name.

In our own family we decided to retain our names when we married. The children of this marriage received both last names without a hyphen. However, we soon discovered that people were only using the final last name, which was the name of their father. In order to reinforce their mother's contribution to the child, we felt obligated to hyphenate the children's last names. Thus our children have hyphenated last names which combine their mother's last name and their father's last name, even though neither parent has a hyphenated last name. We would be neither surprised nor alarmed if the children decided to use one of their two last names, or to combine them in some more creative way.

Cheris Kramarae, who is quoted frequently in this text and has made a significant contribution to the understanding of gender and communication, creatively solved the problem of a married name. Kramarae was married in the state of Ohio at a time when the state did not allow women to retain their own names. Her name, upon marriage, became Cheris Rae Kramer. When the state laws were liberalized, she restructured the name and became Cheris Kramarae. William R. Todd-Mancillas, aka William R. Todd de Mancillas, a researcher whose contributions are particularly evident in this chapter, was born William R. Todd. His last name was expectedly that of his father. As an adult, with increased sensitivity to the influence of naming, he changed his name to reflect his mother's family name as well. Others, like artist Judy Chicago, assumed the name of their home cities. Interesting alternatives are available.

Occasionally, people become concerned about the next generation and the possibility of people having four hyphenated last names. They maintain that they have made name changes in order to avoid this problem. Our own point of view is that such problems are not without solution. Furthermore, we need to determine which is the more serious problem: women routinely losing their identity through name changes or persons creatively naming themselves. If persons in our culture changed their last names on some basis other than sex, we will have made another giant step for "genkind!"

The language of the deaf

A somewhat obscure but highly significant example of sexism occurs in the language of the deaf. Ameslan, which is more commonly known as American Sign Language, continues the sexism that we view in the language of the non-deaf. The head, in signing, is divided into two areas; above the center of the ear is used to indicate "he," "him," "his," "man," "father," and "son;" while below the ear are the signs for "she," "her," "woman," "mother," and "daughter." The area closest to the brain is used to designate masculine referents, while the area closest to the mouth is used to designate feminine referents. In order to compliment a woman, a sign is used that begins above the ear and then comes down to the traditional feminine area on the head which suggests that a woman is like a man ("she thinks like a man," "she acts like a man").

Masculine features, then, are used to compliment women. Professions are sex-typed in Ameslan, as the word for "secretary" is a combination of "girl" and "writes" or "a girl who writes." The term "president" is formed by signing the word "man" with a rising flare or a salute from the forehead which suggests "a respected man." Intellectual terms, in Ameslan, are either masculine or neutral. Emotional terms, words for appearance, and words for talking are feminine. This distinction is consistent with the stereotypical beliefs that men are rational and that women are expressive, as we discussed in chapter 1.

A very interesting example is the word for "love" which is expressed differently for women and for men. For women, the term is signed by open palms which are gently crossed over a woman's breasts. For men, the sign is made by crossing his arms at the wrist, with closed fists over his heart. Love appears to be a positive state for women, but one of entrapment for men (Jolly & O'Kelly, 1980).

Religious languages
Another pocket of sexism in language occurs in religious language. All Western religions originated in patriarchal societies, and the language and metaphors used to express their insights are overwhelmingly male-oriented. Nearly always, masculine pronouns are used in reference to God and to humanity. Typically, in Western religions, women are perceived to be less Godlike and less perfect than their male counterparts. In addition, the masculine language is frequently used to maintain the position of males as the heads of the church. It is instructive that the Aztec Indians, who believed that the origin of human beings was one single principle with a dual nature, used one pronoun in their religious writings which referred to a neutral he/she/it being (Miller & Swift, 1976). Religion reflects the society's attitude of sexism or nonsexism.

Sexism in other languages
Do other languages reflect sexism? Languages, other than English, are composed on the basis of sexist forms, but they are frequently quite different than the English paradigms. For instance, French provides neutral possessive forms such as *"son livre"* which means "his or her book," and *"sa chaise"* which means "his or her chair," but the objects themselves, the book and the chair, have a gender and this determines the gender of the pronoun which refers to the antecedent. In these instances, and not surprisingly, the book is masculine and the chair is feminine. Some of the objects which have been designated to be masculine and feminine in French appear to conform to stereotypes of men and women. For instance, *"le toit"* (roof), *"le train"* (train), *"l'arbre"* (tree), *"le sabre"* (sword), and *"le soleil"* (sun) are masculine, while *"la fleur"* (flower), *"l'etoile"* (star), *"la maison"* (house), *"la mer"* (sea), and *"la lune*" (moon) are feminine. Other objects do not follow this pattern, as *"la tour"*

Table 3.2 Terms for women and men

Women		Men	
Chick	Lady	Gent	Boy
Girl	Broad	Man	Stud
Old lady	Woman	Guy	Hunk
Piece	Honey	Male	Bastard
Female	Madam	Husband	
Prostitute	Whore		
Wife	Dog		
Old maid	Cow		
Bitch	Old biddy		

(tower) and *"la guerre"* (war) are feminine; and *"le lait"* (milk) and *"le hasard"* (chance) are masculine. Sometimes the gender of the object has no connection to masculinity and femininity, and sometimes ominous overtones occur, e.g., the word *"la victim"* (victim) is feminine.

The professions in French belie a sexist overtone. Some of the professions, such as that of an actor, lawyer, or nurse, have both male and female forms in the same way the English language offers actor/actress, poet/poetess, author/authoress. Other professions are always masculine, and include *"le medicin"* (doctor) and *"le professeur"* (professor). It is no coincidence, therefore, that French instructors find when students are writing about doctors or professors, they tend to use masculine pronouns, even when the person about whom they are writing is female (Seaman, 1981). French, like other Western languages, is sexist; but the sexism occurs in different forms. We would find this same pattern if we were to study other Western languages.

Definitions of women and men

If you were asked to list all the terms for women and for men that you could name, what conclusions do you believe you would find? In one study, which included elementary-school children, high-school students, and junior college students, the author found that a much longer list was provided for women than for men and that the words for women were generally much less favorable than were the words for men (Kleinke, 1974). In a similar manner, at three different universities I achieved the same results. We appear to have far more names for women than we do for men, and the abundance of the names for women have a negative connotation compared to the more positive connotation of the terms for men. In Table 3.2 some of the terms that are regularly offered by college students are listed. The differences between the two lists in length and positive/negative connotation reflect classroom responses or attitudes.

"Dear Abby" included this letter in her syndicated column on February 11, 1982:

> DEAR ABBY: I found this in the "AORN Journal"—a publication put out by the Association of Operating Nurses:
>
> "The Chickenization of Women"
>
> "Women are frequently referred to as poultry. We cluck at hen parties. When we aren't henpecking men, we are egging them on. In youth we are chicks. Mothers watch over their broods. Later we are old biddies with an empty-nest syndrome. Is it just a coincidence that so many women's wages are chicken feed?"
>
> ANN D'ARCY, OKLAHOMA NURSE
>
> DEAR ANN: No. And ain't it fowl?

Men and women are referred to by a number of slang terms. Women are referred to as "chicks," and men are referred to as "cocks." List some other terms which you and others use to refer to men and women in addition to those that are provided in Table 3.2. After you have listed these terms independently, discuss the terms with your classmates. What similarities and differences occurred among the lists? Which of the terms are negative and which are positive? Determine if your classmates agree about the positive or negative nature of each word. If you disagree on the evaluation of a term, discuss your rationale.

One author examined the differences in definition of the terms "woman" and "man" in the *Oxford English Dictionary* and found discriminatory treatment. The definition offered for "woman" was (1) an adult female being, (2) a female servant, (3) a lady-love or mistress, (4) a wife. For men, these definitions were offered: (1) a human being, (2) the human creature regarded abstractly, (3) an adult male endowed with manly qualities, and (4) a person of importance or position (O'Donnell, 1973). The definitions appear to place men in a more positive light, and women in a subordinate position. It is not surprising that students judge the names for women to be more negative than the names for men. The connotation and the denotation, for "men" and "women" are decidedly different.

The longer list of names for women and their more negative nature is no accident. A variety of reasons account for the differences between women's names and men's names. First, the group in power typically does the naming

Terms for Men	Positive or Negative?	Terms for Women	Positive or Negative?
_____	_____	_____	_____
_____	_____	_____	_____
_____	_____	_____	_____
_____	_____	_____	_____
_____	_____	_____	_____
_____	_____	_____	_____
_____	_____	_____	_____
_____	_____	_____	_____
_____	_____	_____	_____
_____	_____	_____	_____

or labeling. In our culture men tend to name people, places, and things. (How many dictionaries have been written by women, as compared to the number which have been written by men?) Second, women are observed and men are the observers. As we will note in the later chapter on nonverbal communication, women tend to be the objects of observation as they dress in more unusual, provocative, and colorful ways. More names are needed for the objects of observation than for the observer. Third, women are viewed as subordinate to men and consequently have more negative terms applied to them. Last, women have a wider range of behaviors than do men, so that a larger vocabulary might be necessary in order to encompass a variety of roles.

Let us examine some of the specific generalizations we can make about the differences in labeling women and men. First, names for women are sometimes created by adding another word or a feminine marker to a name for men. We are all familiar with terms of address in which a woman is known

> "When a lady never marries, she's an *old maid.*"
> "Then when a man never marries, is he an old butler?"

by her husband's name (Mrs. John Jones) rather than by her own name (Barbara Jones or Barbara Smith). The name is simply that of her husband with the addition of a "Mrs." to indicate that she is his (possessive) wife. Similarly, women's professions are sometimes indicated by adding the suffixes -*ess* or -*ette,* as in changing waiter to waitress, drum major to drum majorette or sculptor to sculptress. Also, women serving in traditional male professions are sometimes referred to by adding the word "female" before the profession, as in, "She is a female doctor"; "She's a female attorney"; or "She is a female senator." In each of these cases women appear to be subordinate to a specific male or to men. They appear to be less important and their work appears to be more trivial.

Second, names for women are frequently sexual. In one study on sexual names, about 10 times more sexual terms were cited which were associated with women than were associated with men (Stanley, 1972). Our *phallocentric,* or penis-centered, culture causes women to take on meaning as a sex object, or object of conquest. Some of the less vulgar sexual terms for women include "broad," "slut," "cherry," "slit," and "whore." Few similar terms for men exist, and most suggest sexual prowess: "hunk," "stud," and "sex machine."

Table 3.3 "Parallel" terms for women and men

Women	Men
Whore	Don Juan
Old maid	Bachelor
Madam	Sir
Mistress	Master
Lady	Gentleman
Governess	Governor
Landlady	Landlord
Queen	King

Third, different metaphors are used for women and men. Women are frequently referred to as some form of food, e.g., honey, sugar, cookie, piece of cake, pudding, tomato, cupcake, which suggests, as one author wrote, that women appear to be "laid out on a buffet" (Nilsen, 1972). Men are sometimes referred to as a "hunk" or a "big cheese," but these terms are far less common than are the many terms for women. Many names of flowers are applied to women, e.g., rose, clinging vine, sweet pea, petunia, while the names of flowers, when applied to men, suggest that they are women, for example, pansy. Women are referred to by animal names which are undesirable—cow, pig, sow, heifer, and dog; by animal baby names—bunny, kitty, chick, or lamb. But men are named aggressive animal names: stud, buck, wolf, and tomcat.

Fourth, polar opposites are used for women and men, thus the term for women is considered negative, but the term for men is positive. Consider the lists of words that are offered in Table 3.3. Although these terms are "opposites," they clearly do not have the same connotations. For example, a governor is viewed as someone who is the head of a state or in charge of land; while a governess is in charge of children. A landlord is typically a person who is respected as the owner of land or property, while a landlady is the rent collector and rule enforcer. Most people would rather be a bachelor than an old maid, a Don Juan than a whore; and one of the most insulting names to call a man is a "woman." As you examine the list of female terms, you might observe that a number of the words have become associated with a sexual woman, e.g., whore, madam, mistress, and lady, or are used for men to suggest that they are "gay": queen.

A current study examined the different connotations that people have for the terms "bitch" and "bastard," two terms which are considered to be similar, but the first is applied to women while the second is applied to men. They found that people had different connotations. Men associated "cold," "untrustworthy," and "deceitful" with bastard, and "insincere," "tactless," and "dominant" with bitch. Women described bastard as "loud," "narrow-minded," and "untrustworthy," and described bitch as "cold," "tactless," and "phony." The authors conclude that when a woman is called a bitch this suggests that she is being moved from a stereotypically feminine role to a masculine role, whereas men who are called "bastard" are only viewed as an exaggeration of their masculine identity (Coyne, Sherman & O'Brien, 1978).

Fifth, more familiar terms are used for women than for men. Women are frequently addressed by their first names, even when they have professional status, while men are more often addressed by their formal titles or as "Mr." In addition, few people would call a man "honey," "baby," "sweetie," "hon," or "sugar", but most females have been addressed by these terms, even by people whom they have not previously met.

Sixth, women are identified by their associations with others far more frequently than are men. We stated above that the identity of many women is given as their hsuband's name with a "Mrs." attached to it. How frequently are men known as Mr. Barbara Jones? Similarly, countless obituary columns, marriage announcements, and other similar personal news stories have been gathered to demonstrate how frequently a woman will be identified as someone's wife, mother, daughter, or sister and how rarely men are identified as someone's husband, father, son, or brother. When women are identified through their associations with others, they are viewed as property, or at least, as possessions. Consider your own experiences: Are women more likely to be introduced as "my wife" by their husbands or are men more likely to be introduced as "my husband" by their wives?

Seventh, women are more likely to be referred to by euphemisms than are men. *Euphemisms* are seemingly inoffensive words which are substituted for more offensive terms. For instance, rather than ask her husband if he would care to "engage in sexual intercourse," a wife might ask if he would like to "make love." A person is more likely to be asked to be excused to go to the "ladies' room," "the little girls' room," or the "powder room" than to clearly and bluntly state his or her intentions. (Notice how inappropriate the "his" seems to be in the sentence: Men never go to the rooms that are euphemistically mentioned!) In the same way that we choose euphemisms to discuss bodily functions (urination, defecation, sexual intercourse), unpleasant matters (death, poverty, psychological impairment) and other topics (becoming drunk, becoming high on drugs), we use euphemisms to talk about women.

The two most common euphemisms for women are "lady" and "girl." In an earlier book (Pearson & Nelson, 1982) we used the example of the word "lady" to illustrate a "dirty four-letter word." Subsequently, many of my students have inquired about the negative connotation of the word. The word "lady" has been popularized and used positively in songs by Kenny Rogers, Barry Manilow, Bob Dylan and others. The word may come to hold even more positive connotations in the future, but many women can still recall the images of a white-gloved, soft-spoken, pretty, polite, and always proper woman that the term tended to create. In the military, the term "lady" is reserved for the wives of officers, while the word "wife" is used for the wives of the enlisted men. To many people, the term "lady" suggests a class struggle in which only some women can hope to become "ladies," while others must be satisfied to be women.

"Girl" is problematic too. The term "girl" refers to a young woman, typically one who has not yet pubesced. When adult women refer to each other as "girls," they may be disparaging their roles as women. They are implying that they are younger, more immature, or less than they actually are. Sometimes older women will use the term in an effort to feel younger; nevertheless, it is inconsistent with reality. The complimentary potential of the word is offset by the connotation that the person is not responsible or serious.

Men are not called by similar euphemistic terms. We rarely call men "gentlemen" or "boys." We more typically refer to men as "men." Euphemisms are neither positive nor negative, they are merely more "polite." When the term "lady" is used in connection with the word "gentleman," it is consistent. Or, when people refer to themselves as "girls and boys," we do not observe blatant sexism. Unfortunately, too frequently women are referred to as "ladies" or as "girls," and men are referred to as "men." These differences are significant.

What occurs when men and women are described in sexist as opposed to nonsexist ways? Dayhoff (1983) determined whether sexist descriptions bias an individual's perception in a realistic setting. After reading simulated newspaper articles describing a candidate running for political office, people were asked to evaluate the candidate. When women were running for masculine-related or neutral-related offices, they were evaluated more negatively if they were described in sexist terms. Only when they were running for a traditionally feminine office were they not devalued. Sexist language tended to make more evident the gender appropriateness of the offices when candidates running for the "masculine" offices were perceived as more "masculine," and candidates running for the "feminine" offices were viewed as more "feminine." Sexist usage encourages sexism.

The essay reprinted below recently appeared in *The Chronicle of Higher Education*. The author offers a unique perspective on sexist language. After you have had an opportunity to read the essay, write a response as though you were writing a letter to the editor of the *Chronicle*. Share your letter with your classmates and listen to their letters. Discuss differences in your perceptions of this complicated issue.

If the 'Miss' Fits, Use it—Sexist Language Is Appropriate to Describe Sexist People
By Robin Barratt

EVER SINCE HIGH SCHOOL, I have been ready at only a few moments' notice to address my creditors as "Dear Friends," or, in a more formal or possibly more impecunious mood, as "Dear Sales Representatives." I recently found myself balking, however, at the prospect of using a nonsexist salutation in a letter to a "feminist" anti-abortion group.

I finally decided on "Dear Sirs"—an opening that did not credit the organization with any political concerns I did not feel it represented. My reluctance to use nonsexist language in this case made me reconsider much of the rhetoric I have routinely used.

Obviously, form is important—without nonsexist language, for example, a child is presented with a world of sex-segregated occupations (fire*men*, sales-*women*). It is no wonder that it was considered an insult when, following the publication of *Burger's Daughter*, the South African government referred to Nadine Gordimer as an "authoress." It is also considered insulting to call my fellow

Portrayal of women and men in humor

Humor is culture-specific, and a great deal of joking is based on ingroup/outgroup relationships. Status affects the object of a joke. Typically, people tell jokes about others who have the same, or lower, status than themselves. They do not direct witticisms at persons who are present who have higher status. Few Americans find it appropriate to tell humorous stories which paint a negative picture of a subordinate group to members of that group. *Sexist humor,* humor that disparages women or men, is an established communicative behavior in our culture. Interestingly, people do not show reluctance to share sexist jokes about women to women (Wrather & Sanches, 1978).

The content of the joke clearly affects the reactions of women and men. For instance, the person who is denigrated in the joke affects its rating. If the joke is about a woman, men perceive it to be more humorous than do women (Chapman & Gadfield, 1976) although both men and women perceive jokes which ridicule women as more humorous than jokes which ridicule men (Losco & Epstein, 1975; Cantor, 1976). In addition, male targets are rated as less humorous than neutral caricatures. (Losco & Epstein, 1975).

Barnard College students "girls"; we are women, thank you.

Still, there are contexts in which the use of feminist-sounding language would be a separation of form from content. Particularly given the current conservative climate, there are meetings women are not likely to be chairing in the immediate future; it would be more misleading than nonsexist to refer to the men who do as "chairpersons."

The *American Heritage Dictionary* defines feminism as "militant advocacy of equal rights and status for women." If a female chairperson is dedicated, rather, to the eradication of women's social/political rights, surely her intent is not reflected by her politically correct title. *Ms.* Schlafly?

Nonsexist language is as much a question of application as of gender. In the interest of accuracy, possibly movements and people who ignore women's rights should be discussed in terms echoing this lack of concern. Simply changing the pronouns in a textbook isn't enough if women are not thought of as part of the audience—and, in history and other courses, as part of the subject as well.

I once took a summer course on the religious experience of *man*kind, which was an accurate description of its content. Granted, female prophets were few and far between, but the role of women within a religion is at least half the religious experience of *human*kind.

Of course, everything's relative, and it is a matter of choice whether one finds the campus eating establishment's advertisement for "waitpersons" to be offensive, humorous, asinine, or a real breakthrough.

Linguistic change is important when it reflects or causes social change; however, acceptance of feminist rhetoric does not guarantee acceptance of women's rights. It only helps when you mean what you say.

Robin Barratt began her senior year at Barnard College in January.

Three plausible explanations for this anti-female bias in humor are offered by one researcher. Cantor (1976) maintains that 1) the socialization process in our society promotes the idea of female inferiority, 2) the cultural expectations about the appropriate behavior of males and females differ, and 3) our expectations affect the perceptions of communication sources who behave in particular ways (for instance, sarcasm may be viewed as clever and witty when used by men but as cruel and critical when used by women). The anti-female bias was demonstrated in a study which varied the gender of the victim and the gender of the dominating person. Again, the gender of the victim rather than the gender of the dominant person appeared to determine whether the joke was viewed as humorous (Cantor, 1976).

Studies of self-disparagement and the disparagement of others show that people with presumably high status and *ethos,* such as male college professors, can disparage their professional fields in their speeches and raise their ratings on wittiness, funniness, and sense of humor without damaging other factors of credibility (Chang & Gruner, 1981).

Images of Women and Men   91

The gender of the person telling the joke appears to interact with his or her disparagement of people of the same or opposite sex. In general, women engage in more self-deprecation than men. In addition, the negative comments that men offer about their own appearance are far less injurious to themselves than are the negative comments made by women (LeVine, 1976). Comediennes such as Phyllis Diller and Joan Rivers are well known for their self-disparaging remarks about their bodies. Women humorists appear to be aware of women's traditionally oppressed role and respond in a manner that is consistent with it. The values of the current social order are evident in their humor.

Another study indicates not only that the humor of women is not anti-male in the same way that a great deal of male comedy is anti-female, but also that most female humor ignores the male. For instance, female comics rarely dress in male attire for their routines, but the female impersonator has been a stock in trade for male comics for some time. The writer states that while men will listen to other men deprecate them, they will not laugh at vulnerabilities or weaknesses when they are pointed out by women. This study concludes that it appears that women humorists may believe that what women will laugh at in mixed company and what they laugh at in all female audiences is very different (Stoehr, 1981).

In a second study on self-disparagement, male storytellers told tales in which they disparaged themselves, in which they disparaged a friend, and in which they disparaged an enemy. Men who engaged in self-disparagement were viewed as less witty, less intelligent, and less confident than when they engaged in disparagement of either friends or enemies (Zillman & Stocking, 1976). The results of this study are consistent with the findings of the first study on self-disparagement. Men appear to be viewed negatively when they fail to present men as successful.

Additional findings in this study are also of interest. Women perceived a male disparaging himself as significantly funnier than a male disparaging an enemy. Men found it significantly funnier to see a male disparage an enemy than himself. Perhaps the socialization of men in order to be dominant encourages them to take more enjoyment from viewing another male in a dominant role, whereas women's socialization to be submissive encourages them to identify with self-disparagement. This research report included the findings that women enjoy female self-deprecation more than men, and that self-disparaging humor is generally viewed as funnier by women than by men (Zillman & Stocking, 1976). This research contends that women, more than men, may be responsible for the continuation of women as objects of deprecation in humor.

One investigation attempted to determine whether women are disparaged more frequently than are men during prime-time television hours. This study demonstrated that men were disparaged far more often than are women, regardless of the sex of the disparager. Women were victimized by men about as often as men were victimized by women. Men, however, were more frequently in the position of making the deprecating remark and thus were the source of the message in a significantly greater number of incidents than were women, regardless of the sex of the victim. Men disparaged other males more than they disparaged women, except in the case of hostile sexual humor, where males disparaged women more than males disparaged men. Females did not disparage other females nearly as much as males disparaged other males (Stocking, Sapolsky, & Zillman, 1977). Men appear to be more aggressive than women in their disparagement of persons. The war between the sexes appears to be especially salient in the area of sexuality.

What are the effects that men and women receive when they attempt to tell humorous stories? An investigation which relied upon male and female professors found gender differences. Any sort of humorous presentation is positively related to appeal, delivery, and teaching effectiveness for male professors. Only humorous hostile humor had the same positive effects for female professors. Female professors who used nonhostile humor lost appeal, receiving lower evaluations on competence, delivery factors, and on a measure of overall teaching effectiveness. The authors conclude that students may expect humor from men while they do not from women. Hostile humor may be viewed positively for women, since it exhibits a degree of aggressiveness which grants women the authority to be humorous (Jennings, Crane, Comisky, & Zillman, 1980). Apparently, women who demonstrate masculine characteristics are allowed the opportunity to behave in other stereotypical masculine ways without incurring negative judgment.

These findings are consistent with folk beliefs that surround gender differences in humor. Two widely held ideas are that women have no sense of humor (Kramarae, 1981) and that women cannot tell jokes (Eakins & Eakins, 1978). Freud suggested that humor serves as an acceptable outlet for aggression, and that women may use less humor in male-female interactions because any show of aggression may be threatening to men. As one writer notes, "The woman has as much natural tendency to enjoy wit as her male counterpart. But if she is clever, she will not show it" (Grotjahn, 1957).

Women probably *choose* not to respond to, or participate in, aggressive humor. Two studies support this notion. Women do not respond positively to aggressive humor. However, McLaughlin, Cody, Kane, and Robey (1981) found that women spent more time than men as the recipients of nonaggressive storytelling and that women responded with more appreciative reactions than did men. Women appear to have some flexibility in responsiveness as they do respond when the story is not aggressive.

Second, Eakins and Eakins (1978) observed women who were assigned to tell a joke to a predominately male audience and to a predominately female audience. In the first case, the women showed hesitation, nervousness, and general anxiety; in the second instance, they were enthusiastic, expressive, and relaxed. Women who understand and conform to social norms appear to have no sense of humor when they are merely behaving in socially approved ways and discriminating between male and female audiences.

A related explanation suggests that women and men represent different groups on the basis of status and that women are similar to subordinates, while men represent superordinates. Humor is associated with persons of higher status while people with lower status are simply allowed to react to the humorous remarks. People with lesser authority tend to make fewer witticisms (Coser, 1960). The use of humor by women might be viewed as inappropriate, then, since it tends to threaten the accepted status relationship that exists between women and men.

A few investigations have looked into sex differences in the telling of jokes to determine whether women or men do, indeed, vary on this tendency. Men are credited as the source of humorous messages more frequently than are women. In a survey of 14,500 magazine readers, *Psychology Today* reported that 83% of the men surveyed and 68% of the women surveyed identified a man as the wittiest person they knew (Hassett & Houlihan, 1979). Boys tend to make more frequent verbal and behavioral attempts at humor than do girls, (McGhee, 1976), and men appear to use humor far more often than women (Coser, 1960).

Women and men may be altering their behavior in the telling of jokes, however. A recent study of the graffiti written by women and men in the late 1970s was compared to that which was written in the 1950s and 1960s and a number of changes were observed. Women wrote more graffiti in the late 1970s and their graffiti had a more sexual, hostile and issue-related tone than earlier. In the 1950s and 1960s, men wrote more; what they wrote was of a more erotic, homosexual, or pornographic nature; and women typically wrote "romantic" messages. In the late 1970s, women wrote 52% of all original graffiti, 62% of all written responses to other graffiti, and 59% of all sexual graffiti. During this same time, men wrote graffiti that was more humorous and less hostile (Greenberg, 1979). Women appear to be making more attempts at originating humorous messages.

Telling jokes is an aggressive verbal behavior. We have observed that women tend to be less aggressive than men, and we will note that men tend to speak more while women tend to listen more. It is consistent that women engage in the telling of fewer sexist jokes than men.

Sexist jokes are more often directed at women than at men. Both men and women laugh at jokes that denigrate women, but men find them more humorous. Women tell more jokes which are self-denigrating than do men. The lower status of women may cause them to be perceived as the appropriate targets for denigration. To the extent that women do not respond positively to sexist humor, they are perceived to be without a sense of humor. In fact, women's lack of responsiveness may be based on the content of the joke rather than their relationship to humor.

Sexist humor is aggressive and hurts all of us. Both men and women lose when they engage in sexist humor. Refraining from sexist humor is probably the best advice we can offer. Unfortunately, it appears that instead of refraining from such humor, women may be learning how to tell such jokes from their male counterparts. We will examine how women and men are portrayed in the media in the next section. We will observe that they are not differentiated in the aggressive manner that they are in humor; nonetheless, they are depicted differently.

Portrayal of women and men in mediated sources

We have determined that the images of women and men can be ascertained as we examine language and humor. Another valuable source of learning about women and men is the media. Busby (1975) provided an extensive review of this topic in which she determined that some aspects of sex roles are relatively unexplored, that sex roles in the mass media are traditional and do not reflect alternatives, that children model the behavior they perceive in various media, and that men serve as *gatekeepers,* or controllers of information, in most media. We will observe Busby's conclusions as we explore the literature in this area. Specifically, we will examine written media, such as newspapers and magazines; media we listen to, such as popular music; and media we watch and listen to, television. Let us begin our investigation by considering magazines.

Magazines

Magazines are written for many different groups of people. The target audience of the magazine appears to affect the stories and features that are included and the kinds of advertisements that are used. As we would expect, women and men each have some magazines written especially for them. Romance magazines, for instance, are written for women as escape literature. Adventure magazines, on the other hand, are written primarily for men, and also for escape. Romance magazines allow women to escape to fantasized relationships, while adventure magazines allow men to fantasize about being rugged individualists (Smith & Matre, 1975). Magazines in these categories tend to encourage traditional, stereotypical roles.

A number of studies have been designed to illustrate differences between working and non-working women. One such study examined the magazine reading habits of women. No significant differences were found between working and non-working women in relation to the frequency of magazine reading or the types of magazines read (Douglas, 1977). Although women's roles are broadening, women appear to maintain some of their traditional interests, including finding sufficient time to enjoy magazines.

Because of their wide readership, magazines can be effective in informing or persuading women about a variety of issues. Farley (1978) studied the coverage of the Equal Rights Amendment by women's magazines and found differences in coverage based on type of magazine, editorial policy, circulation, and social class of readership. However, she concluded that women's magazine editors appear to be attempting to change the *status quo.*

Newspapers

An extensive examination of male-centered and female-centered news stories in newspapers was completed. An equal number of male-centered and female-centered stories were selected. About 48% of the female-centered stories appeared in the first or second sections of the newspapers, while 78% of the male-centered stories were in the first or second sections. No significant differences were found in the length of the stories or in the size of the photos which were used. The occupation of the woman or man about whom the story was written was provided as frequently for one gender as for the other. Personal appearance (excluding age) was mentioned in 38% of the stories about women and in 14% of the stories about men. Marital status (disregarding the title "Mrs.") was mentioned for 64% of the women and 12% of the men (Foreit, Agor, Byers, Larue, Lakey, Palazzini, Patterson, & Smith, 1980). Sexism appears evident, in that stories about females appear to be given less importance than do narratives about males, while both personal appearance and marital status appears to be more relevant when discussing women than when discussing men.

Davis (1982) examined four Oklahoma metropolitan newspapers, two of comparable circulation from the West Coast and two from the East Coast. Of the 5,500 stories that were analyzed, only 8.6% of them had women as main characters. She questions whether newspapers can afford not to be involved in women's issues.

News photos were examined in another study. It was found that men outnumbered women in photographs by a ratio of 3 to 1 in the *Washington Post* and about 2 to 1 in the *Los Angeles Times,* the two newspapers considered here. Men clearly dominated photo coverage on the first page of both papers. Half of the women's photos were on the lifestyle page, only 10–15% of the male photos were on those pages. Women's roles were mostly as spouse and fashion models, while men were pictured as politicians, entertainers, and in a variety of other roles (Miller, 1975). The relative proportion of women and men in these newspapers suggest that men are more newsworthy than are women and that women's roles are more narrowly defined. The papers perpetuate sex role stereotyping.

The women's pages of newspapers were studied in another investigation. High circulation newspapers which were principally metropolitan had male editors for the women's pages 79% of the time. When men served as editors of the women's pages, more coverage was given to entertainment, recreation, and leisure. When women served as editors, more attention was given to club and social news as well as the women's movement (Merritt & Gross, 1978). It appears that the sex of the editor results in major differences in coverage on the women's pages.

A final study on newspapers considered the roles of women in the newsroom. It appears that reporters for the women's section are frequently associated with a contemporary, positive image of women; while the section editors are as frequently associated with traditional role images. While reporters are attempting to alter the roles of women, their superiors are attempting to maintain more stereotypical presentations. (Whitlow, 1979). As more women serve in supervisory roles in newsrooms, news reporters will be able to identify with someone other than a man as a supervisor. Differences in the treatment of women and men and differences in the coverage of gender-related topics by women and men are evident in these studies on newspapers.

Advertisements

Advertisements in the print medium have been studied extensively. Research in the early 1970s suggested that women were largely portrayed in stereotypical roles. One study stated that although 33% of the workforce was composed of females, only 12% of the workers pictured in advertisements were female. At the same time 45% of the men pictured were in working roles, but 9% of the pictured women were shown in working roles. No women were depicted as professionals or in high-level managerial positions; but they were portrayed as being entertainers, clerks, airline flight attendants, assembly line workers, airline employees engaged in food preparation, and school teachers (Courtney & Lockertz, 1971). A study which was published four years later demonstrated that the role of women in advertisements had not changed very much from 1959 to 1971. The portrayal of women as sex objects decreased from 1959 to 1971. Women were portrayed as being more concerned with physical beauty in the period 1964–1971 than they were in the period 1959–1963. Women were portrayed as being dependent upon men throughout the period from 1959–1971. Though male magazines and general circulation magazines did not reflect much change in this 12-year-period, some modifications occurred in the portrayal of women in women's magazines. (Venkatesan & Losco, 1975). Similar findings were recorded in a number of studies conducted in the 1970s (Bekaow, 1976; Culley & Bennett, 1976).

One study published in the mid-1970s considered the portrayal of women in advertisements. Among the findings were: 1) women are most concerned with their appearance and domestic duties, rather than with complex decisions; 2) women are more often portrayed in domestic settings than are men; 3) women are rarely portrayed in occupational settings; and 4) women wear pants or slacks in few of the ads, (Culley & Bennett, 1976). Smith (1977) maintains that in the past two decades women have not moved very far from their limited role; and they demonstrated that in the mid-1970s, only 16% of the women portrayed in advertisements were in non-traditional situations. Advertisers may not intend to offend women, but they may find that advertising is part of a changing society in which change sometimes takes time.

Still other studies indicate that change is occurring, albeit, slowly. One author concludes that women are being portrayed in more responsible roles (Levere, 1974), that subsequent to the study by Courtney & Lockertz, women's appearance in working roles has more than doubled (Wagner & Bunos, 1973). A more recent study offers some consolation as well. One study predicts that a larger number of women will be featured in work-related settings with men in the 1980s, and that sex will become more explicit in ads but women will be used less often as sex objects (Kerin, Lundstrom, & Sciglimpaglia, 1979). As change occurs, we must be equally sensitive to presenting men in a variety of positive roles as we are to depicting women in alternative ways.

An interesting study was conducted, comparing the portrayal of women and men in advertisements in 1958, 1970, and 1972. Employment status differences occurred in the ways that men and women were portrayed, since most women were nonworkers. Men were typically portrayed in higher income positions. Women were shown primarily in the home; and, generally, the stereotypes of women and of men did not alter during the years that were investigated (Ahmed, 1976).

More encouraging news was recently available. Mitchell Siegel, research director of Alschiller, Reitzfeld, Solvin, a New York ad agency, has investigated the roles of women and men in current advertising. He has determined that women are equally disapproving of the housewife who is in "endless pursuit of dirt" and the chauffeur-driven working woman. Judith Langer, a market researcher, states,

> What is evolving is a new kind of woman who is active, alive and out in the world. . . . She cares about her home but isn't obsessive about it. If she has a career, it isn't necessarily as a TV anchor woman. Advertisers are showing a softer woman who cares about relationships yet at the same time is strong (Bralove, 1982).

As a result of such perceptions advertisements are beginning to show multi-faceted women and men who appear to be equally proficient at managing home and career.

Should advertisements depict women in a wide variety of roles? One writer suggested, in 1971, that advertised products appear to have a strong sexual cathexis (emotional appeal or connotation), which means that some products are viewed as masculine and some products are viewed as feminine. For example, he cites automobiles as a masculine product (Stuteville, 1971). Nine years later, an article states that over ⅓ of the new cars that are purchased are bought by women for themselves, that life insurance purchased by women rose 100% in ten years, that women buy ⅔ of all wine, and that women control 80% of all spending, saving, and investing (*Advertising Age,* 1980). Another article discusses an advertising agency which grew rapidly from a $400,000 a year business to one that tops $50,000,000, based on the principle that it takes women to sell to women (Kanna, 1980). Some authors warn advertisers that they err if they misjudge the impact of the newer status of women (Belkaoui & Belkaoui, 1976), and others suggest that women are beginning to understand their own potential (Willet, 1971).

Robert F. Young, president of the world's largest women's magazine, *Family Circle,* recently discussed the double standard in advertising. Young stated, "There is no doubt in my mind that, to women, the biggest irritant of all is the widespread assumption that certain products and services are beyond their comprehension and shouldn't be advertised to them at all" (*The Messenger,* 1982, p. 6). He explained that a minority subscribed to male-female stereotypes, but persons in that minority were highly influential in the advertising industry. Young concluded,

> What does concern me—and should concern every American, inside or outside the media field—is the fact that the failure of part of the advertising community to climb aboard the bandwagon can severely impede the societal revolution that holds such great promise for the future of our country (*The Messenger,* 1982, p. 6).

What do women prefer in advertisements? They are highly critical of traditional sex roles (Witkowski, 1975; Lundstrom, 1977). About 34% of women, as opposed to 22% of men, agree that advertisers use too much sex appeal in advertisements (Sexton, 1974). Interestingly, pro-feminist, anti-feminist, and neutral-feminist women do *not* disagree about the portrayal of women in advertising (Duker, 1977).

Men and women do not appear to sharply disagree on advertising. Both men and women prefer models who are attractive to appear in ads, although men appear to prefer the model to be female and women prefer the model to be male (Baker, 1977). The preference of a group of men in another study may provide an answer for advertisers. The researcher found that men preferred ads that used a male and a female rather than males only or females only (Kanungo, 1975). A man and a woman of similar status and engaging in similar work might be most useful in minimizing sexism as well as and in selling goods and services. Or we may view women and men each living full lives which include work and home.

Popular music

Popular music has been investigated to determine how men and women are portrayed in love songs. Most of the vocalists were male, consequently, most of the songs were about women. Most of the songs included neutral words which allowed a person to sing the song about either a man or a woman. Neither men nor women were depicted as intelligent. Men were viewed as crying over love, needing or depending upon a lover, possessive, and helpless. Women were seen as controlling the relationship and active. In general, the popular music which was analyzed exchanges the stereotypic sex roles for women and men (Wilkinson, 1976). Women and men may be allowed the role flexibility that songs offer, because the stories are in song and might not be regarded as representing reality. This alteration in sex roles is useful to the extent that teenagers and young adults learn broader conceptions of sex roles.

Television

Television is widely viewed by people of all ages. Young children may view as many as forty hours of television per week (Singer & Zuckerman, 1981). Unfortunately, television appears more likely to influence lower-class individuals, younger adolescents, less-educated persons, and females than upper-class individuals, older adolescents, more educated persons and males (Christiansen, 1979).

Regrettably, television viewing is correlated with a belief in social stereotypes (Tan, 1982). That is, the more people view television, the more they tend to believe in social stereotypes. Similarly, television is capable of teaching sex-role stereotypes. One study which examined children in grades 1, 3, 5, and 7 studied the effects of light, moderate, and heavy viewing of television. The television programs that the children watched placed male role models in greater numbers than female role models. To a great extent, men were portrayed as members of the work force and had greater diversity of occupations and higher job status than women. Women were rarely shown working outside the home. As they grew older, the light viewers of television had less stereotypic views of men, while the heavy viewers' stereotypic responses increased with age (McGhee and Frueh, 1980). Sex-role stereotypes appear to be learned more easily by persons who watch television to a greater extent; consistently, people who are heavy viewers may be more conservative, home-bound individuals.

What are some of the images of men and women which are presented on television? Women are generally portrayed in roles of diminishment and subjugation (Dohrman, 1975). Women are portrayed as strong, assertive, and work-oriented; women are viewed as weak, passive, and family-oriented (Downs and Gowan, 1980). Men are depicted as possessing power and status and having a greater expectation of both rewards and punishment, while women provide and receive significantly fewer responses than men and are more likely to be involved in reinforcement (Downs & Gowan, 1980). One study demonstrated that young women associated themselves with Shirley Feeney from television's "LaVerne and Shirley" and Carol Burnett more than they did with stars like Farrah Fawcett. The author concluded that women identify more with demeaning and distorted images than with glamorous, action packed roles (Lull, 1980). At the same time, it appears that situation comedies provide a more favorable image of women and blacks than do crime dramas (Lemon, 1977). As you consider the unusual roles which both men and women portray in situation comedies and the lack of realism in such shows, the seriousness of learning roles from television becomes evident.

Altering the sex-role stereotyping which occurs on television is a complex problem. Both the image of women and the number of women who appear should be changed. In general, women are still seen as primarily in the home rather than being involved in larger political and social spheres. The primary exception to this is that women are frequently portrayed as consumers. To the extent that men dominate broadcasting and that people view the media as a way of reflecting, rather than changing, society the problems related to sex-role stereotyping will persist.

Soap operas present a view of reality and of men and women which is quite different from that shown on prime-time television. While the latter may focus on sexual themes (Greenberg, Graef, & Atkin, 1980), there is more sexual activity and more references made to sex in the afternoon soap operas (Greenberg, Abelman, & Neuendorf, 1981). In prime-time television reference to sexual intercourse is frequently suggested comically, but in soap operas the most common sexual activity is physically explicit petting. In both afternoon and evening programs, the partners for whom sexual intercourse is suggested are not likely to be married to each other. Sex is presented in the soaps by talking about it, showing erotic touching behaviors, and suggesting sexual acts. The characters in the soap operas engage in sexual acts about twice as often outside of marriage as within the bonds of marriage. "General Hospital," which has the largest total audience and the largest teenage audience, has the highest rate of sexual acts per hour (Lowry, Love, & Kirby, 1981).

Women in soap operas tend to be much younger than the general population, and they are usually acted upon, raped, divorced, abandoned, misunderstood, given drugs, and/or attacked by unusual and mysterious diseases (Soares, 1978; Kinzer, 1973; Cassata, Skill, & Boadu, 1979). Professional women are portrayed sympathetically; for housewives, the major concern is the family. Women are viewed in three categories: members of traditional professions such as airline stewardesses; persons involved in relationships with others including wives, mothers, and daughters; or individuals with undifferentiated background. Women tend to be under-represented in soap operas, just as they are under-represented in prime-time television, but they appear more frequently in the afternoon (Downing, 1974). Women often provide advice and direction on "feminine" matters, and in soap operas they relate to each other as family members. (Fine, 1981).

Men are portrayed on soap operas as more active and less tied to relationships with others than are women. Most directives, or orders of instruction, are centered on "masculine" topics and are stated by men. Men maintain control of the action through the accentuation of the role of the medical doctor. The medical profession is by far the best represented male occupation on these programs, followed by the legal profession (Downing, 1974).

Conversations in soap operas tend to center on marriage, family, romantic relationships, professional relationships, personalities, health, deviant behavior, and routine business matters. Many of the conversations are "small talk." The topics tend to be conventional and stereotypic. The conversational styles in soap operas are similar to real conversational patterns. (Fine, 1981).

Soap operas tend to appeal to people because their stories never end, they insert small dramatic scenes between the commercials, and they seldom conceal information from their audiences, but frequently withhold information from the characters (Rose, 1979). Nonetheless, social scientists have demonstrated little interest in soap opera content. Downing (1974) made a content analysis of the soaps and concluded that because soap operas are directed toward women, they are not considered seriously by critics and individuals in the entertainment world.

Soap operas present a distorted picture of behavior in the United States. Persons who regularly view soap operas with role models who engage in fornication and adultery may have an altered set of values about what is "normal" in our society. The growing audience of soap operas makes them potentially a major force in the transmission of values and lifestyles for youthful viewers. Although soap-opera plots may cause women viewers to feel secure, soap-opera settings may induce these same viewers to become dissatisfied with their own dull lives (Barthel, 1968). As long as people watch soap operas, their own lives will never seem quite right or sufficiently exciting.

Cartoons on television have also been examined. In general, women in most cartoons tend to be nonexistent or in need of help from men. The exclusion of women appears to be particularly pronounced in the chase and comic fall type of cartoon, such as "Bugs Bunny." When females are depicted on cartoons, they are usually in need of male assistance. Some cartoons, which have teaching concepts as their purpose, include active females; but the males still far outnumber the females (Streicher, 1974).

Television commercials

Television commercials have been as thoroughly examined as have advertisements in print journalism. A number of conclusions are consistent. First, *voice overs,* when a voice is heard, but no person is depicted, are predominantly male; the percentage of male voice overs ranges from 87% (Courtney, 1974) to 93% (O'Donnell, 1978). Women do not appear on commercials with the same frequency as men, but when they appear they are typically in the bathroom or the kitchen (Courtney, 1974; O'Donnell & O'Donnell, 1978; Busby, 1975). Men have a wide variety of professions, while women are typically portrayed as housewives (Verna, 1975; Busby, 1975; Schneider & Schneider, 1976; Courtney, 1974). As we observe their behavior, we might infer that the personalities of men and women are different; women are portrayed as more dependent, passive, unauthoritative, emotionally unstable, less career-oriented, less knowledgable (Verna, 1975) and ill more frequently (Mant, 1975). On the other hand, men are pictured as more ambitious, dominant, braver, and stronger (Busby, 1975). The National Organization of Women examined television advertisements and found that women were portrayed as "domestic adjuncts" (37.5%), "demeaned housewives" (22.7%), "dependent upon men" (33.9%), "submissive" (24.3%), "sex objects" (16.7%), "unintelligent" (17.1%), and "household functionaries" (42.6%) (Duker & Tucker, 1977).

Men and women tend to sell different products on television commercials. Men, in their roles as medical doctors, prescribe medicine (Mant, 1975); they also sell automobiles, travel packages, alcoholic beverages (Busby, 1975) and gas and oil (*Time Magazine,* 1973). Women sell products for women (Marecek, Piliavin, Fitzsimmons, Krogh, Leader, & Trudell, 1978): hygiene products (Courtney, 1974), female cosmetics (*Time Magazine,* 1973), and domestic products (O'Donnell & O'Donnell, 1978). In order to sell these goods, women demonstrate the use of the product by performing domestic tasks. Men simply make feature claims about their products (Courtney, 1974).

Illness is represented in an interesting manner on television commercials. As we noted above, medical doctors are always men. More often than not, the sex of the patient cannot be determined. However, when it can be determined, the patient is more likely to be female. Women are typically shown needing some kind of mood modifiers. Men's illnesses are depicted as painful interruptions of life and work, while women's illnesses are shown as an inconvenience to other people (Mant, 1975). The depiction of illness on television commercials may reflect demographic reality more than some of the other phenomena discussed in this section. The differences between male and female illness and the perceptions of it may be depressing on television and in reality.

The age of characters on television commercials has changed within the last decade. In the past, young adult characters were used to sell products. Today, there is a shift to persons of 50 years and older. At the same time, women continue to be depicted as younger than their male counterparts in the commercials in which they appear together (Schneider & Schneider, 1976).

Some changes appear to be occurring in television commercials. The traditional "gendering" of products is declining (Gentry, Doering, & O'Brian, 1978). Characters portraying women have been broadened. Fewer women are portrayed in domestic roles than was true in earlier ads (Scheibe, 1979). More women experts are selling products for women, but they still have authoritative male voices for back up in the voice overs (Maracek, Piliavin, Fitzsimmons, Krogh, Leader, & Trudell, 1978). In addition, male roles are not broadening (Scheibe, 1979). Finally Warren (1978) observes that advertisers have used the women's "liberalization" movement to sell products, but that "Advertising's liberated woman incorporates everything the women's movement has fought against" (p. 169).

Changes should be made in the roles of women and men on television commercials. First, the roles should be altered because of the negative impact on children's understanding of sex role behavior. Children view a great deal of television, as we discussed above, and from this they learn about sex roles. Young children believe that commercials are more real than do older children. Further, when children were told that the commercials were real, they had attitude changes toward women, reflecting the traditional role models they viewed (Pingree, 1978). In other words, children who believe that commercials are real begin to accept the more traditional depictions of women and men as accurate.

Second, both women and men have offered their perceptions of television commercials and both desire change. Women and men are accepting of a brand that has been advertised for the opposite sex (a particular brand of cigarettes, deodorant, soap, etc.), but women are more prone to accept an opposite-gender brand (Alreck, Settle, & Belch, 1982). Women do not mind seeing women in household roles if the roles are consistent with the product being sold. However, when the product being sold is for personal use, a nontraditional role is preferred. Male students prefer a professional role portrayal for women, while female students accept both professional and traditional role portrayals. Neither men nor women enjoy the showing of an inept woman (Courtney & Whipple, 1980).

Finally, television commercials should change because advertisers will have a larger market. Social changes are occurring that affect female and male behavior; people are becoming more open to new ideas and advertisers may be able to respond to the broadening of a market without excluding old market segments (Scheibe, 1979). For instance, depicting men drinking tea or depicting women drinking beer will probably broaden the tea and beer market without causing losses of the current patronage. As you observe the television commercials that interrupt your favorite programs in the next few days, consider some of the findings of studies presented here.

Mediated sources affect the way people view themselves. Examine a set of print media, newspapers, magazines, and other periodicals to determine how women and men are portrayed. Some of these images are probably similar to you, but others are not at all like you. Create two collages—posters with multiple pictures—from the sources you have found. One collage should pictorially represent how you view yourself and how that image is portrayed in print media. The other collage should pictorially represent how persons of your gender are represented in the print media, but it is the antithesis of how you view yourself. For instance, an athletic woman might use pictures of strong women participating in a variety of sports as one set of representations. She might use weak or submissive female pictures for the collage which represents the antithesis. A nurturing man might choose pictures of men caring for children, feeding a newborn, or listening attentively to others to represent himself; and select pictures of football players, beer drinkers, and macho men to epitomize his opposite.

After you have completed your collages, bring them to class and prepare a short talk on how you view yourself and how that self is represented in the media. You might discuss how you feel about yourself, how frequently pictures of "you" occur in the media, or how complex you feel you are compared to some of the stereotypical or simple representations of people. After each person has had an opportunity to share his or her perceptions, discuss similarities or differences in the collages. Are you surprised by some of your classmates views of themselves? How would their collages be different if you created one for them? How do others see you? To what extent do you feel that you are a "victim" of the images of women and men in the media?

Conclusions

In this chapter we considered the images of women and men in language, humor, and the media. We learned that while man-linked words and traditional generic pronouns are both widely used, they do not refer with equal precision to women and men. They may, in fact, be limiting the behavioral options of women. We determined that women are denigrated in humor more frequently than men, that people find jokes in which women are denigrated funnier than jokes which denigrate men, and that individuals will tell jokes which denigrate women to women. Women appear more willing to be the object of sexual and sexist humor than they have in the past. We learned that the portrayal of women and men in newspapers, magazines, print advertisements, and on television is not accurate. Women are generally unrepresented, and both women and men are portrayed in narrow sex roles. The images of women and men which have been determined by studies by social scientists who attempt to understand more about our society are portrayals in which men appear to dominate and women are subordinate. These images should be changed to depict women and men in their complex, ever-changing roles. Aggressiveness or bias toward or against either sex is injurious to both sexes. Stereotyping, or over-simplifying the roles which women and men play may have a variety of negative outcomes. In the following chapters we will observe that these images of women and men affect our interactions with others.

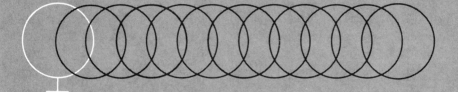

Section 2

Since communication is a process which can be divided into its components, we analyze communicative behavior by focusing attention on one or more parts or phases at a time. In this section of the text we will examine a variety of those components that are relevant to understanding the communication which occurs between and among women and men.

In chapter 4 we will learn about self-disclosure and self-assertion, two self-related

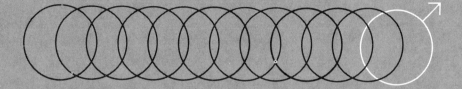

Components

communication skills. We will find that these skills have been viewed both as personality traits and as skills which are dependent upon the communication situation. In chapter 5, we will consider information-processing, which in-cludes some exciting new research on brain development. Perception, listening, and empathy are all communication skills that are related to processing information.

4 Self-disclosure and self-assertion

Introduction

The first three chapters of this text dealt with initial considerations about gender and communication which are essential to the topic. In those chapters, we explored the importance of self in communication. In this section, we begin to consider some of the components of gender and communication, based on the information in the first section.

Specifically, we will consider two self-related variables, self-disclosure and self-assertion. As we examine these topics we will emphasize the nature of communication as negotiated meaning which is transactional, and includes costs and benefits. Each of the terms will be defined, the nature of the concepts will be explored, relevant research concerning gender and the associated concepts will be examined, and conclusions will be drawn.

Self-disclosure

Self-disclosure is the process of offering verbal revelations of self to others (Jourard & Lasakow, 1958; Cozby, 1973; Pearce & Sharp, 1973). It is sometimes used synonymously with "verbal accessibility," "openness," and "social penetration" (cf. Altman, 1973; Anchor, Sandler, & Cherones, 1977; Norton, 1978; Montgomery & Norton, 1981). Self-disclosure has been analyzed in terms of the action models, interaction models, and transaction models discussed in chapter 1 (Cline, 1982). The action model suggests that self-disclosure is a trait or individual behavior in which a person engages. The interaction model suggests that self-disclosure occurs between two people who both act and react. The transaction model focuses on the relationship between the two people who are communicating, rather than concentrating on these persons as individuals.

In this text, the transactional perspective is viewed as most useful; and it is determined that self-disclosure may appropriately be viewed as a transaction. Stewart (1977) emphasized the importance of the transactional perspective of self-disclosure as he wrote, "Every time persons communicate they are continually offering definitions of themselves and responding to definitions of the other(s) which they perceive" (p. 19). Chelune (1979) supports this perspective when he adds, "Further examination of person-perception variables promise to increase our understanding of self-disclosure. . . ." Unfortunately, most of the research on self-disclosure has been completed using an action or interaction model. As a result, the findings are limited and somewhat difficult to interpret. At the same time, these studies offer the available information on the topic. We will review the research on self-disclosure and then apply it within a transactional perspective.

Self-disclosure as a trait

The earliest research on self-disclosure viewed the behavior as a trait which a person possessed. Investigators attempted to determine whether it related to other personality traits or to personal characteristics such as biological sex.

Personality factors

A number of personality factors appear to be related to levels of self-disclosure. People who score high in social poise and extroversion tend to score high in self-disclosure (cf. Ashworth, Furman, Chaikin, Derlega, 1976). This finding is not surprising; it simply means that people who are poised in social settings and who enjoy talking tend to talk about themselves.

Other personality factors have an inverse relationship to self-disclosure. For example, intimate self-disclosure is inversely related to a person's need for approval (Brundage, Derlega & Cash, 1977). In other words, when people have a high need for approval from others, they are unlikely to offer highly intimate information about themselves. When people are anxious, they decrease the amount and the intimacy level of their self-disclosures (Post, Wittmaier, & Radin, 1978). Similarly persons who are *communication apprehensive,* fearful of communicating with others, tend to avoid self-disclosure (McCroskey & Richmond, 1977). It appears that when people are generally anxious and concerned about how others perceive them, or when they are specifically anxious about communication, they will self-disclose less frequently and less intimately.

People who are depressed or feel lonely may disclose differently than those who are not depressed or do not feel lonely. Depressed women express a need to disclose information to others, but perceive their family members to be unsympathetic to them and reluctant to listen to them (Altman & Wittenborn, 1980). These women expressed a sense of helplessness and depression as a result of their need which was not being fulfilled within their families.

Loneliness also relates to self-disclosure. People who are lonely tend to disclose too much or too little in dyadic interactions, when compared to partners who are not lonely. Lonely people perceive a lack of interpersonal intimacy in their communication with others. Lonely women appear to have difficulty appropriately revealing personal information to other people, although this difficulty appears to be minimized in established relationships and in structured social situations. Lonely women may have particular difficulty establishing new relationships in novel situations (Chelune, Sultan, & Williams, 1980).

Self-esteem and self-actualization, discussed in chapter 2, also have a relationship to self-disclosure. People with high self-esteem provide more self-disclosure than do people with low self-esteem (Fitzgerald, 1963). In addition, people with high self-esteem are more attracted to others who self-disclose a great deal rather than minimally. Finally, people with high self-esteem perceive others who do not match their own high level of self-disclosure as possessing low self-esteem (Gilbert, 1977). It appears that people with high self-esteem prefer others who, like themselves, disclose a great deal.

People who are high in self-disclosure also tend to be high in self-actualization (Lombardo & Fantasia, 1976). People who self-disclose to a greater extent report that they have fulfilled their potential and are the person that they desire to be. They appear to be more satisfied with themselves than are people who are low in self-disclosure. In addition, self-disclosure is associated with feeling good (Prisbell & Andersen, 1980). Examination of self-disclosure as a trait led to the discovery of a number of related personality factors, and encouraged research on biological sex differences in self-disclosure.

Sex differences

Consistent with the trait approach to understanding self-disclosure, a number of investigations attempted to determine whether women or men self-disclosed to a greater extent. Most of these studies demonstrated that women self-disclosed more than men (cf. Littlefield, 1974; Dooley, Whalen & Flowers, 1978; Greenblatt, Hasenauer, & Freimuth, 1980; DeForest & Stone, 1980; LeVine & Franco, 1981). A smaller, but significant, number of these studies could demonstrate no difference in the amount of self-disclosure which men and women offered (cf. Brooks, 1974; Kohen, 1975; Thase & Page, 1977; Montgomery & Norton, 1981). A few studies reported that males self-disclosed more than females (cf. Sermat & Smyth, 1973; Gilbert & Whiteneck, 1976).

Men have consistently been shown to talk more than women (cf. Marlatt, 1970; Wood, 1966), a phenomenon which we shall discuss further in chapter 5. They also report the intention to self-disclose at a higher rate than do women (Gilbert & Whiteneck, 1976; Sermat & Smyth, 1973); however, these intentions are not translated into self-disclosure behavior (Wiebe & Scott, 1976). It is thus somewhat surprising that the preponderance of studies demonstrate that women self-disclose more than do men.

Factors that interact with sex differences

The conflicting findings on gender differences in self-disclosure led a number of investigators to consider whether other factors were influencing the self-disclosure process. At the same time, theorists were suggesting that self-disclosure might not be a simple, one-dimensional construct, but instead might comprise a number of varying features. Self-disclosure had been viewed as a communicative behavior which either occurred or did not occur. Writers suggested that it might be more useful to consider it as information which could be positive or negative, intimate or nonintimate, or be characterized in a number of different ways. At the present time, we have adopted this more sophisticated analysis and examine a variety of dimensions of self-disclosure. Some of the recent studies which have used this multi-dimensional approach are helpful in understanding the conflicting findings relative to gender differences in self-disclosure.

Positive or negative nature   One dimension of self-disclosure that has been examined is its positive or negative nature. In general, the disclosure of positive or desirable information results in greater attraction than disclosure of negative information (Dalto, Ajzen, & Kaplan, 1979), while positive or neutral self-disclosure result in greater communication satisfaction than does negative self-disclosure (Hecht, Sheperd, & Hall, 1979).

Do women and men disclose a similar amount of positive, negative and neutral information? Gilbert and Whiteneck (1976) found that both sexes were equally likely to disclose negative statements about themselves, but that men were less likely to disclose positive statements about themselves. Another study found that women disclosed more negative information about themselves than did men, and that women disclosed more negative than positive information (Critelli & Neumann, 1978). While these two studies appear to be contradictory, a pattern emerges. Women clearly appear to offer more negative statements (Gillis, 1978). This final study offers some explanation of the apparent contradictions in the first two investigations. The previous studies may have drawn different conclusions because the sex of the person to whom the individual was disclosing was not specified. When men and women were asked about their relative levels of disclosure, they may have been responding with a person of a particular gender in mind, and this may have influenced their responses.

Disclosing positive information about oneself is frequently discouraged. We view people who regularly provide positive self-disclosure as braggarts. Positive self-disclosure, toward which negative social sanctions exist, may be perceived to be inappropriate and the person who routinely offers positive information about himself or herself may be seen as inappropriately socialized. Would you prefer to talk with an acquaintance who routinely tells you about the success she is having with a combined program of diet and exercise in order to maintain strength and flexibility, or with an associate who sometimes expresses problems with her weight loss program? Alternatively, the person who freely offers positive information about himself or herself may be viewed to possess high self-esteem. For instance, the friend who confides that she has been accepted at a prestigious graduate school would probably be viewed positively.

Negative self-disclosure includes the problems that we are facing, aspects of ourselves with which we are displeased, and other difficulties that we have. As previously mentioned, disclosing negative information to others may be seen as more appropriate than disclosing positive information. At the same time, it may be indicative of a person who does not have high self-esteem.

Someone who regularly dismisses what he or she does as inappropriate, ineffectual, or unsuccessful is often avoided by others and viewed to be low in self-esteem. The appropriateness of offering positive or negative self-disclosure depends upon a variety of factors, including your relationship to the person to whom you are self-disclosing.

Cognitive or affective information   Self-disclosure may comprise cognitive or affective information. Cognitive information includes past history, reasoned ideas, and similar information. Affective information includes a person's feelings about a variety of topics. Two studies have examined the amount of affective information which women and men provide, and both concluded that women provide more affective information than do men (Janofsky, 1971; Highlen & Gillis, 1978). Women appear to talk more about their feelings to others, regardless of the sex of the *target person,* or the person to whom they are disclosing. In addition, they provide even more affective self-disclosure to partners of the same sex than they do to partners of the opposite sex.

Intimate or nonintimate information   The level of intimacy of disclosures has also been examined. Women report that they disclose more intimate information than do men (cf. Gitter & Black, 1973; Morgan, 1976). At the same time, men do not report differences in the extent to which they attempt to influence or control the level of disclosure (Tardy, Hosman, & Bradac, 1981). These findings occur in artificial laboratory or self-report situations; however. A different situation develops when a man and a woman interact in an acquaintance exercise. In more realistic situations, men appear to be the "architects" of the encounter and determine when intimacies should occur. In one such study, men set the pace of intimate self-disclosure. Women selected less intimate topics and matched the pace set by the males (Davis, 1978).

The conflicting results in these studies may be a result of an artificial laboratory setting as compared with a realistic situation. Women may state that they self-disclose more intimate information than men acknowledge disclosing, but actually may self-disclose less. Their intention to self-disclose intimate information may be higher, but their behavior may belie their intent. Bochner (1982) argues that self-report and behavioral studies of self-disclosure should be examined separately. The conflicting findings on gender differences may result because we have not heeded his advice. In these cases of disparate findings, we need to exercise caution in overgeneralizing or prescribing behavior on the basis of one or two studies. Research on gender and communication is in an embryonic stage, and few firm conclusions have been made. We will observe, however, as we examine the literature in a number of areas, that women and men frequently report differences in their communicative behavior, but actually the behavioral manifestations of differences are minimal. We may feel obligated to report communicative differences, but, in fact, communicate in a similar manner with persons of the opposite sex.

Topics under discussion   Closely related to the level of intimacy of self-disclosure are the topics about which men and women self-disclose. Men and women do not differ in the amount that they self-disclose on politics, but women self-disclose more on more intimate topics such as religion and sex (Lombardo & Berzonsky, 1979). The level of intimacy of the topic may be considered, then, for self-disclosure differences between women and men.

The gender of the target person   The sex of the target person may cause differences in the levels of disclosure that occur in interactions. Some investigations seem to indicate that the target's gender affects the self-disclosure process. Females select other females as their preferred target of disclosure. These target people were alternatively identified as best-friends or mothers (Littlefield, 1974). When opposite-sex dyads interacted, rather than same-sexed dyads, women did not self-disclose more than men (Kohen, 1975). Early studies which demonstrated that women disclosed more than men might be due to the pairing of same-sex partners rather than opposite-sex partners. This study also confirms the research, reported above, in which women allowed men to serve as the "architects" of interaction in determining the intimacy level to be established in a conversation with an opposite-sex acquaintance.

Attractiveness of the target person   Attractiveness is another factor which appears to confound the sex differences that are observed in self-disclosive behavior. In general, people appear to self-disclose more to attractive than to unattractive persons (Pellegrini, 1978; Young, 1980). Some research has indicated that the attractiveness of the target, or person to whom the disclosure is made, is relevant in the disclosure of women, but is not an important feature for men (Robison, 1976; Kohen, 1975; Sote & Good, 1974).

Attractiveness and the gender of the target person   Two studies demonstrate that the interaction of the sex of the discloser and the sex of the target person is an important consideration when attractiveness is examined as a predictor of self-disclosive behavior. Men appear to self-disclose more to attractive women (Harrel, 1978). In general, individuals self-disclose more to attractive individuals of the same sex, while they provide less negative self-disclosure to attractive individuals of the opposite sex (Cash, 1975). Men may self-disclose more to attractive persons of the same sex in order to attempt to establish a relationship with them. They may wish to interact further with an attractive woman and attempt to do so by disclosing to her. Similarly, people may self-disclose more to same-sexed partners in order to establish or continue a relationship. People may provide less negative self-disclosure to attractive members of the opposite sex in order to present a positive side of themselves. They may feel that negative information will result in their being perceived as unattractive to the attractive person of the opposite-sex.

The attractiveness of the discloser   The attractiveness of the discloser also affects his or her self-disclosure. Men who perceive themselves as attractive self-disclose more than do men who perceive themselves as unattractive. Women who perceive themselves as attractive self-disclose less than do women who perceive themselves as unattractive (Cash & Soloway, 1975; Pellegrini, 1978). Men who perceive themselves as attractive may feel confident about their communication and self-disclosive skills and offer self-disclosure freely. Unattractive men may not feel the same sense of confidence.

The physical appearance of women is more important than the physical appearance of men in our culture. Women who are attractive have an advantage over women who are not attractive, as we shall discuss in chapter 7, and this is a greater advantage for women than for men. Attractive women may thus have more opportunities to interact with others than do unattractive women. As a consequence, they may not have to disclose as much with others in order to have sufficient conversational opportunities or satisfying interactions with others. Unattractive women, by contrast, may find that self-disclosure is an effective strategy for initiating interactions which might not otherwise occur. In addition, attractive women may feel more vulnerable or accessible than do unattractive women and may avoid self-disclosure in order to protect themselves from increased interactions.

The age of the discloser   Age also is associated with male-female self-disclosure differences. Among children, 6 through 12 years of age, girls self-disclose more than boys, they self-disclose more intimate information than do boys, and they self-disclose more about their feelings than do boys (O'Neil, Fein, Velit, & Frank, 1976). Among ninth grade students, females appear to disclose more than do males (Klos & Loomis, 1978; Littlefield, 1974), but females appear to be more selective with respect to confidants, or the targets of self-disclosure, while boys show greater concern with the content of self-disclosure than do girls (West, 1970). These findings are generally consistent with self-disclosure differences found for adult males and females, although the relative importance of the target person or the content of the self-disclosure is new information.

In general, adolescent girls appear to self-disclose more than adolescent boys (Rivenbank, 1971), with self-disclosure increasing among boys as they grow older. For example, a comparison of ninth grade and twelfth grade students was made. Low self-disclosure occurred when ninth grade males self-disclosed to other ninth grade males. Moderate self-disclosure occurred among ninth grade males to ninth grade females, and moderate self-disclosure occurred from twelfth grade males to other twelfth grade males. High levels of self-disclosure occurred among twelfth grade males to twelfth grade females; high levels of self-disclosure occurred among ninth grade females to ninth grade females; and high levels of self-disclosure occurred when twelfth grade females disclosed to other twelfth grade females (Klos & Loomis, 1978).

Self-disclosure appears to increase as individuals mature and become older. High school students self-disclose less than college students (Snoek & Rothblum, 1979). High school males are less intimate than are college males (Mark, 1976). Similarly, self-disclosure to peer targets appears to increase with age for adolescents (Rivenback, 1971). In general, both boys and girls tend to self-disclose more as they become older.

The sex of the discloser appears to affect the rate of increase of self-disclosure as persons mature. Females, during adolescence, appear to disclose more to same-sex friends than males disclose to same-sex friends (Mulcahy, 1973). We see, then, that both age and biological sex affect the disclosure process with females disclosing more than males and older people disclosing more than younger people.

The self-disclosure of older adults, persons over sixty years of age, has been studied as well. In this age group, women self-disclose more than men and over 75% of the disclosers identified other women as their confidants. People who were between 70 and 80 years of age self-disclosed less than people between 60 and 70 (Henkin, 1980). Self-disclosure may decrease among people in their 70's because of ill-health, limited opportunities to interact with others, or other causes outside the individual's control.

Self-disclosure and nonverbal behaviors   Another entire area of research has considered the impact of nonverbal behaviors on self-disclosure between women and men. The research in this area suggests that differences occur, expressed in such terms as eye contact, personal space, touch, and bodily movement. Eye contact has a different effect on self-disclosure for women and for men. Direct gazing appears to promote the intimacy of self-disclosure between women; direct gazing decreases the self-disclosure between males (Ellsworth & Ross, 1975). This finding was confirmed in a more recent study in which high verbal intimacy in male dyads was associated with low eye contact, and low verbal intimacy was accompanied by high eye contact (Amerikaner, 1980). We shall see in chapter 8 that women and men exhibit a variety of differences in their eye contact behavior. This finding suggests behavior which we will see repeated in other interactions, e.g., women tend to look at each other more than men tend to look at each other; women are inclined to watch the speaker while the other person is speaking; and they avert their eyes or look away when they are being stared at. Men tend to stare at others, but they do not watch the speaker as carefully when she or he is speaking to them. As a consequence of these findings, it is not surprising that self-disclosure and eye contact have a positive correlation for women and a negative one for men.

Personal space appears to affect self-disclosure. Most studies demonstrate that women self-disclose more as the amount of personal space decreases and men self-disclose less (cf. Sundstrom, 1975; Skotko & Langmeyer, 1977). Only one exception occurs in the literature, a situation in which no correlation was found between or among the amount of self-disclosure, the gender of the discloser, and the amount of personal space available (Johnson, 1973). Most of the studies confirm a positive correlation between self-disclosure and physical closeness for women, but a negative correlation between self-disclosure and physical closeness among men. This finding is consistent with the research on eye contact. Women appear to establish closeness with eye contact, physical space, and self-disclosure behavior. Men appear to distance themselves from others through lack of eye contact and increased physical space as they self-disclose. The significance of these findings will become apparent later in this chapter when we consider the reasons why women and men self-disclose differently.

Touch intervenes in the self-disclosure of women and men; moreover, touch is viewed as a positive indicator of self-disclosure for both women and men. As touch increases, so does self-disclosure (Lomranz & Shapira, 1974). Touch, unlike eye contact or physical space, appears to be positively related to increased intimacy and self-disclosure.

Bodily movement also plays a role in self-disclosure. When male counselors moved more, self-disclosure by a client tended to increase; conversely, when female counselors moved less, the self-disclosure of the clients increased (Gardner, 1973). The typical larger movements of men and smaller movements of women (which we shall consider in chapter 8) suggest that men may be perceived to move more than do women. Consequently, a client may perceive the male counselor's increased movement and the female counselor's decreased movement as appropriate and conducive to self-disclosure. Or the client may perceive the male counselor to be distracted and may attempt to win his attention, although he or she will not attempt to compete in the same way for the female counselor's attention. The client may perceive the female counselor's lack of movement as indicating attentiveness and concern, and may disclose more to her, whereas the male counselor's lack of movement is not interpreted the same way. The information presented in chapter 8 will amplify this discussion.

Sex-related variables   Finally, we need to consider sex-role orientation and sexual affectional orientation or preference, as they relate to self-disclosure. Sex role orientation and sexual affectional orientation, or sexual preference, both help explain the conflicting findings on biological sex differences in self-disclosure. Sex role orientation was introduced in chapter 1 of this text, and described as an individual's adoption or rejection of masculine and feminine descriptors. You will recall that a feminine person accepts feminine descriptors and rejects masculine ones, a masculine person accepts masculine descriptors and rejects feminine ones, an androgynous person accepts both masculine and feminine descriptors, while an undifferentiated person rejects both.

Three studies demonstrate a relationship between biological sex and psychological sex type as they affect self-disclosing communication. Greenblatt, Hasenauer & Freimuth (1980) showed that masculine men have lower total disclosure scores than do androgynous men, but feminine females do not report higher total disclosure scores than do androgynous women. Pearson (1980) demonstrated that masculine females disclosed more than did feminine females, and feminine males disclosed more than masculine males.

Women who identified with their fathers and women who identified with their mothers were compared. Women who identified with their fathers might view them as role models and may behave in more masculine ways while women who viewed their mothers as their role models might behave in more feminine ways. Women who identified with their fathers tended to engage in longer conversations on private topics. Women who identified with their mothers showed more discomfort as they talked about themselves. At the same time, no differences in self-disclosure were identified between females who identified with conventional parental models and those who identified with sex-role-reversed parents (Doster, 1976).

The relationship between self-disclosure and gender variables is not a simplistic linear one. For men, both increasing levels of femininity and decreasing levels of masculinity are associated with increased self-disclosure. For

Table 4.1 Gender differences in self-disclosure are dependent upon a variety of factors

Positive or negative nature	*Both sexes are equally likely to offer negative information. *Men are less likely to disclose positive information than are women. *Women offer more negative than positive information.
Cognitive or affective information	*Women offer more affective information than do men.
Intimate or nonintimate information	*Women report that they disclose more intimate information than men report. *In interactions, men set the pace of intimacies and women match the pace set by men.
Topics under discussion	*Men and women do not differ on the amount they self-disclose on nonintimate topics, such as politics. *Women self-disclose more on intimate topics such as sex and religion.
Gender of the target person	*Females prefer other females to whom to self-disclose. *In mixed-sex dyads, females and males do not self-disclose to a different extent.
Attractiveness of the target person	*In general, both women and men self-disclose more to an attractive person than to an unattractive person. *Attractiveness may be a more relevant variable for women than for men.
Interaction of attractiveness and the gender of the target person	*Both women and men self-disclose more to attractive individuals of the same sex. *Both women and men provide less negative self-disclosure to attractive persons of the opposite sex.
Attractiveness of the discloser	*Men who perceive themselves as attractive self-disclose more than men who perceive themselves as unattractive.

women, increasing levels of masculinity coupled with decreasing levels of femininity are similarly associated with increasing levels of self-disclosure; however, the addition of increased masculinity to stationary levels of femininity are not.

You will recall that in chapter 1, people who were identified as androgynous appear to be more flexible than do people who are sex-typed as masculine, feminine, or undifferentiated. Androgynous individuals tend to be more flexible in their self-disclosure behavior than are masculine, feminine, or undifferentiated people (Parrish, 1981). Androgynous people alter their self-disclosure, depending upon other factors in the communication setting.

Table 4.1—*Continued*

	• Women who perceive themselves as attractive self-disclose less than do women who perceive themselves as unattractive.
Age of the discloser	• In general, women self-disclose more than men at all ages. • For both women and men, self-disclosure increases as they mature and become older.
Nonverbal behaviors	• Increased eye contact encourages self-disclosure in women, but inhibits self-disclosure in men. • As the amount of personal space decreases among interactants, women self-disclose more while men self-disclose less. • For both women and men, increased touch is associated with increased self-disclosure. • Increased movement on the part of a male target of disclosure and decreased movement on the part of a female target of disclosure resulted in increased self-disclosure on the part of clients in a counseling setting.
Influence of sex-related variables	• For men, increasing levels of femininity and decreasing levels of masculinity are associated with an increasing level of self-disclosure. • For women, increasing levels of masculinity coupled with decreasing levels of femininity are associated with increasing levels of self-disclosure; however the addition of masculinity to stationary levels of femininity is not associated with increased self-disclosure. • Homosexual men and heterosexual women are similar in self-disclosive behavior while homosexual women and heterosexual men are not.

Sexual affectional orientation, or sexual preference, has also been examined in terms of self-disclosure behavior. Homosexual men and heterosexual women are similar in their self-disclosure behavior. Homosexual females and heterosexual males are not similar, however (Bender, Davis, Glover, & Stapp, 1976). Self-disclosure appears to have some relationship to sexuality. Homosexual men may be adopting heterosexual female behavior. Or they may be behaviorally more flexible as they adopt increased levels of self-disclosure when appropriate, and decreased levels when appropriate, resulting in a total increase of self-disclosure over their heterosexual male counterparts. The factors which interact with sex differences are summarized in Table 4.1.

Perhaps you have not thought as much about sex roles in our society as you have while you were reading this text. Sex roles are sometimes so integral to people that they do not think about them. In this exercise, you will have an opportunity to think about your own sex roles and to share that information with others. Spend about thirty minutes reflecting upon reasons that you are pleased that you are a woman (or man), and reasons that you are not pleased to be a woman (or man). After you have compiled your lists, spend about one hour with a group of people of the same sex and share your feelings. After each person in your group has had an opportunity to share his or her feelings, put the two groups together so the men and women can hear the perceptions of opposite-sex people.

After you have engaged in this interaction with others of the same sex, write a short essay on the experience. In your essay, consider how much you were willing to self-disclose about your feelings in the two groups. You are more likely to have disclosed more with people of the same sex than with people of the opposite sex. Was this true for you? Why or why not? Did you write down some feelings which you were unwilling to share in either group? Why or why not? Does this exercise demonstrate any of the research findings reported above on self-disclosure? Explain. What have you learned about sex roles in this exercise?

Self-disclosure in the dyad

Most of the studies that we examined in the section above focused on individual traits of the discloser, including personality traits, personal characteristics, and other variables which seemed to correlate with them. Some of the variables which interact with sex, for example, take into consideration the characteristics of the other person. These studies based on two people in an interaction rely upon the interaction model of self-disclosure which was discussed at the beginning of this chapter. In this section of the chapter, we will further consider the notion of self-disclosure as an interaction.

The basic characteristic of self-disclosure as an interaction is that it occurs in a dyad, or two person group, and that both people send and receive disclosures. The earliest literature on self-disclosure treats it as a "dyadic effect." This reference by Jourard suggests that self-disclosure occurs most frequently in the two-person group. The predominance of self-disclosure in the dyad is evidenced by the large number of studies which have investigated it in this setting (cf. Burke, Weir, & Harrison, 1976; Casciani, 1978).

Self-disclosure may occur in the dyad or in a larger group; however Jourard (1971) believes that the presence of a "third party" may inhibit disclosure. People appear to continually manage an appropriate level of self-disclosure in the dyad, rather than in a larger group (Derlega & Chaikin, 1977; Davis, 1977). Individuals are more willing to disclose personal information in a dyad than in a triad. The necessary level of confidentiality, which appears to be more attainable in a dyad than in a triad, may be responsible for the difference (Taylor, DeSoto, & Lieb, 1979). Although disclosure may occur in larger groups, the dyad appears to be the optimum group in which it can occur.

Gender differences in the dyad and triad were examined. Men self-disclose more in dyads than they do in small groups of three or more; females not only self-disclose significantly more in a small group setting than do men, but they also self-disclose more in the small group than they do in the dyad (Pearson, 1981). The people in the dyads and small groups included individuals who were known to the disclosers as well as persons who were previously unknown to them. While self-disclosure may be maximized in the dyad rather than in the small group, it appears that other factors, including gender, may affect the outcome of self-disclosure that is viewed as appropriate.

Researchers who have studied self-disclosure within the dyad have concluded that self-disclosure is generally reciprocal; that is, as the disclosure of one person increases, so does that of the other person. (Feigenbaum, 1977; Cozby, 1972, 1973; Erlich & Graeven, 1971). In addition, when individuals do not reciprocate, they are generally viewed as incompetent (Hosman & Tardy, 1980; Bradac, Tardy, & Hosman, 1980). Patterns of reciprocity appear to occur within the first five minutes of interaction in opposite-sex dyads (Kohen, 1975). It appears that a person may be well advised to offer disclosures similar to those which she or he is receiving.

The only limitation on reciprocity which has emerged occurs with men in high self-disclosure situations. In a laboratory situation, experimenters moved from low through moderate and high self-disclosure. In each case, women reciprocated the level of disclosure; men reciprocated in the low and moderate conditions, but did not reciprocate in the high disclosure situation (Archer & Berg, 1978). Men may feel discomfort in offering high self-disclosure in an experimental setting, or they may be unaware of any demands that disclosure by the other person places on them. In any case, they do not offer reciprocal high levels of self-disclosure.

Closely related to the reciprocal nature of self-disclosure is the relationship between self-disclosure and trust (cf. McAllister, 1980). Individuals who trust each other are more likely to self-disclose than are individuals who do not. Similarly, self-disclosure frequently results in trust among persons (Wheeless & Grotz, 1977; Ellison & Firestone, 1973). Trust exerts a strong influence on the willingness of both persons to disclose in a dyad. Moreover, trust is an important factor in developing a sense of interpersonal solidarity, or "oneness" between the members of the dyad (Wheeless, 1978). This feeling of trust may have roots in early childhood: people who felt that their parents were nurturing or high in affection tend to be more trusting and higher in self-disclosure (cf. Pederson & Higbee, 1969; Snoek & Rothblum, 1979).

Self-disclosure and the relationship

The stage of the communicator's relationship also affects self-disclosure. Early acquaintanceship, friendship, or intimacy all affect the levels of self-disclosure which are likely to occur. One area of particular interest is the self-disclosure which occurs between strangers who never expect to see each other again. In these situations, which may occur on public transportation, in public places, or in disastrous conditions, self-disclosure frequently occurs quickly (cf. Murdock, Chenowith, & Rissman, 1969). People may feel more freedom to offer high levels of self-disclosure, since they are unlikely to interact on any future occasion. Unlike other situations, self-disclosure in these situations is relatively risk-free. Long-term difficulties are generally not possible.

Developing relationships

In relationships which appear to have some endurance, a pattern which can be generalized seems to emerge. First, a relatively high level of nonintimate information is disclosed, and then intimate information is disclosed at a gradually increasing rate (Taylor, 1965). A curvilinear relationship between communicators and the amount of self-disclosure that occurs seems to exist (Pearce & Sharp, 1973). This appears to indicate that the least amount of self-disclosure may occur between acquaintances who do not know each other very well, but between whom future interactions are likely to occur.

Self-disclosure among strangers who expect to see each other again is generally not preferred by the targets of disclosure. People who are strangers have indicated a preference for those who disclose very little rather than for those who disclose a great deal (Culbert, 1968; Archer & Burleson, 1980). When intimate disclosures are inappropriately timed; that is, when they occur too early, others may perceive the person who is disclosing as suffering from maladjustment or inappropriate socialization (Kiesler, Kiesler, & Pallack, 1967). Two researchers wrote, "Intimate disclosure to a stranger or an acquaintance was seen by observers as less appropriate and more maladjusted than nondisclosure" (Chaikin & Derlega, 1974).

More specific information has been gleaned concerning the effect of the length of a relationship on self-disclosure. Persons appear to first disclose nonintimate information in the order of positive statements, neutral statements, and negative statements. They then disclose intimate information beginning with negative statements, followed by positive, and concluding with neutral statements (Gilbert & Whiteneck, 1976).

Timing appears to interact with the sex of the discloser. Although one study demonstrated that low male disclosure was seen as significantly more appropriate when talking to a stranger than was low female disclosure (Chelune, 1976), men appear to self-disclose more to strangers than do women (Rosenfeld, Civikly, & Herron, 1979; Stokes, Fuehrer, & Childs, 1980). A number of studies have demonstrated that men generally disclose information earlier in the development of a relationship than do women (Gilbert & Whiteneck, 1976; Berger, Gardner, Clatterbuck, & Schalman, 1976). Men self-disclose more to acquaintances (Stokes, Fuehrer, & Childs, 1980) and to casual friends (Woodyard & Hines, 1973) than do women. Women, on the other hand, are more likely to self-disclose to close friends or intimates (Woodyard & Hines, 1973; Stokes, Fuehrer, & Childs, 1980; Highlen, 1978; Littlefield, 1974; Rubin & Shenker, 1978).

Friends

Studies on the influence of the kind of relationship on self-disclosure have considered the gender of the target person. Let us examine findings on the target's gender when that person is a friend or family member. Women appear to select female best friends with whom to self-disclose. Men tend to self-disclose least to female friends (Diamond & Hillkamp, 1969). Men who are more meditative and emotionally unstable tend to disclose more to their best male friend than do men who do not have these characteristics (Pederson & Higbee, 1969).

Family

Similarly, family relationship has been examined for patterns of self-disclosure. The findings on self-disclosure in this context are fairly consistent. In general, children of either sex tend to self-disclose more to their mothers than to their fathers (Balswick & Balkwell, 1977; Ryckman, Sherman, & Burgess, 1973; Littlefield, 1974; Jourard & Lasakow, 1958; Morgan, 1976; Pederson & Higbee, 1969). Fathers appear to be the recipients of more inaccurate information while mothers are the recipients of more accurate disclosures. (Woodyard & Hines, 1973). As a rule, mothers receive more extensive and accurate information than do fathers.

Does any group disclose more to their fathers than to their mothers? Women who are emotionally more stable select their fathers rather than their mothers as the target of their disclosure (Pederson & Higbee, 1969); they may also have a closer relationship to their fathers, may be "androgynous" or "masculine," using the psychological sex role orientation distinction, or they may view their fathers as role models for their own behavior.

Courtship

The dating relationship provides an interesting context in which to study self-disclosure, behavior which is related to the self-report statements of loving for dating couples (Critelli & Dupre, 1980). People who report that they love each other strongly also enjoy high levels of self-disclosure. This finding is not surprising and is probably related to the idea that we self-disclose more when we trust the other person.

The attitudes that couples express appear to be related to their levels of self-disclosure. Those who expressed egalitarian ideals (that both persons should be involved in decision-making, that both persons had the opportunities of making money and spending it, that either person could initiate sexual activity, etc.), rather than traditional ideals (that the male initiated sexual activity, earned the living for the couple, was the primary decision maker while the female was primarily a homemaker, that the female was to be responsive to her mate's decisions), appeared to be more disclosive. Both partners of the couple tended to disclose more when egalitarian ideals were expressed than did members of the couple who expressed traditional ideals (Hill, Peplau, & Dunkel-Schetter, 1980).

In developing heterosexual relationships men and women tend to disclose differently. Men appear more likely to define their relationships in a romantic-dating-sexual framework, regardless of the cues which are offered, to anticipate more sexual activity, to be less selective in making disclosures, and tend to be less selective in making sexual decisions. Females, on the other hand, are more likely to make distinctions between friendly and romantic relationships, more discriminating in their self-disclosure and their sexual behavior (Rytting, 1976). We will note in chapter 8 that women tend to be more observant of nonverbal cues than are men; the current study suggests that women may be more observant of a variety of cues than are men.

Marriage

Marital couples show similar trends: those couples who disclose more frequently express greater marital satisfaction (Fiore & Swenson, 1977; Jorgenson & Gaudy, 1980; Burke, Weir, & Harrison, 1976). Just as dating couples who disclose more, report higher levels of love; marital couples with high levels of disclosure report greater marital satisfaction.

While marital couples who self-disclose more, generally report higher levels of marital satisfaction, other factors may intervene. For instance, Phillips and Goodall (1983) found that marital satisfaction was not a function of self-disclosure. They maintain that the contribution of self-disclosure to marital satisfaction lies in the history of the relationship and the goals for the self-disclosing talk. For example, the spouse who overhears some negative information about his or her partner's occupational performance may find that marital satisfaction is enhanced by keeping the information confidential, rather than by sharing it. Or, if a couple has never shared minute, day-to-day problems at work when they are at home, initiating such an activity may actually interfere with marital satisfaction.

Other studies report similar findings. Levinger and Senn (1967) and Voss (1969) demonstrate that marital satisfaction may be more affected by the communicators' favorable attitudes toward the information disclosed than by the amount of self-disclosure. In addition, they found that only two of seventeen topics were important in predicting marital satisfaction. These two topics were identified as "shared activities" and "children and careers." In other words, the couples may disclose about a variety of other topics, but the levels and amount of disclosure do not affect the amount of marital satisfaction they report.

The topics of self-disclosure were also examined with regard to differences in attitude between men and women, in connection with the topics about which people need to disclose. The most significant areas for women were identified as "body" and "personality;" for men, the most significant areas were "attitudes," "opinions," and "money" (Farber, 1979). These differences may modify the findings on the relationship between self-disclosure and marital satisfaction. For instance, if two people disclose their feelings on money and economic matters, the male may feel greater satisfaction while the female may not. Or if they discuss their perceptions of their own or other's, bodies or personalities, the woman may feel more satisfied, but the man may not.

Deteriorating relationships

What happens to levels of self-disclosure when couples are in the process of terminating their relationship? Since higher levels of self-disclosure are related to higher levels of marital satisfaction, we would probably expect that couples who are separating, divorcing, or ending their relationship in other ways, would disclose less. Indeed, this is the conclusion of a study which considered relationship disengagement, or termination. People are less willing to disclose when they are attempting to disengage themselves from a relationship (Baxter, 1979).

We might note, however, that the alterations in behavior that occur when couples terminate a relationship are analogically significant in the self-disclosure process (cf. Haley, 1976; Goodall, 1983). In other words, the act of providing less personal self-disclosure to one's partner provides a message, or discloses one's feelings. Just as it is difficult to avoid communicating with others, it is difficult to avoid self-disclosure to intimates. Relational differences in self-disclosure are summarized in Table 4.2.

Table 4.2   Self-disclosure in relationships

In developing relationships	*A high level of non-intimate information is disclosed early, followed by intimate information which is disclosed at a gradually increasing rate.
Among friends	*Women prefer to self-disclose to female best friends. *Men self-disclose least to female friends. *Men who are emotionally unstable or meditative disclose more to male best friends than do men who are emotionally stable or not meditative.
In the family	*In general, children of both sexes self-disclose more to their mothers than to their fathers. *Women who are emotionally stable self-disclose more to their fathers than to their mothers.
In courtship	*In dating, a couples self-disclosure is associated with self-report statements of loving. *Self-disclosure is associated with egalitarian ideals in couples. *Women self-disclose more discriminately than do men in their relationships.
In marriage	*Frequently, married couples who disclose more also express greater marital satisfaction; however, the history of the relationship, the nature of the disclosure, and the intent of the disclosure may intervene.
In deteriorating relationships	*Deteriorating relationships are marked by decreased levels of self-disclosure.

Explaining gender differences in self-disclosure

As we have examined various aspects of self-disclosure in this chapter, we have observed a general pattern of women self-disclosing more, being more aware of cues that affect their self-disclosure, and of women and men disclosing on different topics or in different ways. Let us consider some explanations for the differences in disclosure. First, women may self-disclose more because they are socialized to be open and expressive. Women, as we viewed in chapters 1 and 2, tend to be more oriented to relationships. They tend to devote more energy when engaged in, maintaining and nurturing relationships with others. Women may view self-disclosure as an opportunity to be closer to another person. Intimate interpersonal relationships may be more essential to women than to men.

There may be other explanations for gender differences in self-disclosure. Women may feel that they are of lower status and therefore are obligated to provide more information about themselves to others. Just as the dean of the college can ask the janitor about his or her family while the janitor does not have the same privilege of inquiring about the dean's family, persons of lower status frequently feel obliged to provide information to individuals of higher status, while expecting little or no information in return. In our culture, information about ourselves, like other behavior which denotes respect, may flow from the less powerful to the more powerful.

Finally, male socialization may explain the gender differences that we have observed in self-disclosure. The masculine sex role may include elements which inhibit men from developing an intimacy motivation. In other words, men may not feel encouraged to develop close interpersonal relationships with other men in the same way that women find relationships with those of their sex to be gratifying. Confiding in others might not hold the same positive outcome for men as it does for women; men may perceive communication to be more task-oriented than relationally-oriented.

More intriguing explanations for gender differences have been offered. Earlier in this chapter, we noted that women are more willing to disclose to intimates, while men are more willing to disclose to strangers and casual acquaintances (Stokes, Fuehrer, & Childs, 1980). These authors suggest that stereotypically successful men are expected to compete and win, and that competitiveness is not conducive to intimacy. They conclude that one form of winning is exploiting another person's weakness and hence, that men may cut themselves off from others in order not to expose their vulnerabilities.

A second author supports this explanation when he maintains that men avoid self-disclosure so as to maintain control over their relationships, whereas women avoid self-disclosure in order to escape personal hurt and difficulties with interpersonal relationships (Rosenfeld, 1979). These theoretical explanations offer some ideas for the differences presented in this chapter.

The desirability of self-disclosure in communication

We have examined a great deal of information on self-disclosure, and learned about different patterns of self-disclosure for men and women, and have proposed some explanations for those differences. The question which remains is the extent to which we should attempt to include self-disclosive communication in our interactions with others. In other words, is self-disclosure desirable behavior which we should encourage in ourselves and in others, or is it an undesirable behavior which should be discouraged?

The early writings on self-disclosure implied that this skill was related to a "healthy interpersonal relationship" in which people were willing and able to communicate all of their real selves to others (Jourard, 1958). Open communication promotes growth, according to Jourard. Other writers, following Jourard's lead, similarly contended that self-disclosure is a positive skill which is related to personal growth, attraction, liking, trust, and facilitative conditions.

As a consequence of the positive attitude toward self-disclosure, practitioners encouraged the communicative behavior in a variety of ways. Self-disclosure was identified as a dimension of interpersonal competence (Bochner & Kelly, 1974), as a component of dialogue (Johannesen, 1971), and was taught in workshop settings (Lewis, 1978).

Today, researchers are less enthusiastic about prescribing self-disclosure for all interpersonal relationships. Gilbert and Horenstein, for instance, write, ". . . the communication of intimacies is a behavior which has positive effects only in limited, appropriate circumstances. . . . 'the transparent self' is not, perhaps, the ideal model for all people (Gilbert & Horenstein, 1975). Other authors enumerated potential problems of disclosure (cf. Archer & Berg, 1978; Flaherty, 1979).

An examination of some of the outcomes of disclosure is helpful in presenting recommendations about self-disclosure, since the theorists appear to disagree on the usefulness of this communicative behavior. Moderate self-disclosure to others generally results in positive outcomes. A great deal of self-disclosure by a person causes him or her to be perceived as acting inappropriately (Lombardo & Wood, 1979) and as unattractive (Gilbert, 1977). Moderate self-disclosure leads to successful relationships (Lombardo, 1979), inasmuch as a person is perceived as well adjusted (Derlega & Chaikin, 1976), and attractive (Gilbert, 1977). As we have observed in this chapter, disclosure appears to result in an increase in general satisfaction (Hecht, Shephard, & Hall, 1974), loving (Critelli & Dupre), and personal solidarity (Wheeless, 1976). In addition, persons who offer positive self-disclosure are viewed as attractive (Gilbert & Horenstein, 1975). It appears that moderate self-disclosure is preferred over high levels of self-disclosure and that self-disclosure tends to have positive effects.

Though self-disclosure appears to be generally useful, variables in the communication process can affect its utility. The gender of the communicators can make a difference. Women who disclose are liked more than are women who do not disclose; however, men are liked equally well, whether or not they disclose (Derlega & Chaikin, 1976). We have observed other variables which appear to affect the communication of personal information.

Similarity in self-disclosure generally results in positive outcomes. Strangers who self-disclose to a similar extent with each other are perceived as more attractive (Gelman & McGinley, 1978). The idea of reciprocity in self-disclosure behavior is consistent with the concept of communication as a negotiated transaction. The most accurate prescription which can be offered, then, is that self-disclosure should be negotiated within an individual transaction. An individual's sensitivity to the cues that are offered to him or her, the level of disclosure of the other person, and the information which is available in this chapter, are all useful in disclosing at appropriate levels in an interaction with another person. You may wish to review this material so that you understand what normally occurs when people self-disclose to a certain extent, with specific people, and under prescribed conditions. Keep in mind, however, that the research findings reported here should not limit your behavior; these studies simply report typical self-disclosure patterns and the outcomes that normally result. Your sensitivity as a communicator and your ability to "bargain" concerning an appropriate level of self-disclosure, will be keys to interacting successfully with others. Let us consider, now, a second communication skill which also deals with the centrality of self in communication, self-assertion.

Self-assertion

Self-assertion, the ability to communicate your own feelings, beliefs and desires honestly and directly while allowing others to communicate their own feelings, beliefs, and desires (Pearson, 1983), is another skill which is needed in a complete behavioral repertoire. Self-assertion relies on a negotiation process in which each person states his or her own feelings while allowing the other person to engage in the same behavior; self-assertion is thus a give-and-take process.

Paralleling the original research on self-disclosure which is credited to Sidney Jourard, Andrew Salter conceived the idea of assertiveness training. In *Conditioned Reflex Therapy* (1949), Salter distinguished between nonassertiveness and assertiveness. Largely as a response to Salter's work, therapists began offering assertiveness training. In the late 1960's, the concept became popularized and assertiveness training groups became widespread among lay audiences.

Distinguishing among assertiveness, nonassertiveness, and aggressiveness

Assertiveness is variously defined by different authors, but most specialists agree that the concept lies on a continuum somewhere between nonassertiveness, shyness, or passivity at one end and aggressiveness at the other. Nonassertiveness occurs when people are unable to communicate their own feelings, beliefs and desires to others. Nonassertive individuals tend to be quiet or they may attempt to be assertive, but in dysfunctional ways, i.e., unsuccessfully. Suppose you ask a nonassertive person whether she or he would like to accompany you to a particular movie. Suppose, further, that this person has already seen the movie and did not enjoy it. While an assertive person would probably state that he or she had already seen it and did not enjoy it, the nonassertive person probably would not. Instead, he or she would say nothing, would stammer and stutter in an unclear way, or would say something *after* viewing the movie a second time. Nonassertive people frequently choose to appease others rather than satisfy themselves. Although they may appease others, they rarely are personally satisfied. Nonassertive people are often viewed

"The Supreme Court may have decided it was OK to publish H-Bomb plans, but I'm sure they'd agree this recipe isn't covered by the First Amendment."

sympathetically by others, or may be the victims of anger from others who feel that they cannot enter into honest discussions with them. Nonassertive people are often depressed and anxious, and rarely achieve their goals. Nonassertiveness, in our culture, appears to occur more frequently with women than it does with men. Though observational work does not reveal any tendency for women to be more timid than men, females report themselves to be less assertive (Chandler, Cook, & Dugovics, 1978).

Aggressiveness has been more widely studied than nonassertion. It involves communicating your own feelings, beliefs, and desires honestly and directly without allowing others to communicate their own feelings, beliefs, and desires. This person disregards the rights of others in an effort to assure that his or her rights are protected. The aggressive person frequently hurts others; targets of their aggression often feel defensive or humiliated when dealing with such a person. Aggressive people want to win, but they often "win the battle and lose the war." In other words, they may coerce the other person and be allowed to select the movie they see, the restaurant in which they eat, and the bar to which they go for a drink; however, they may interact with the other person on few, if any, other occasions.

An example of aggressive behavior is frequently supplied by the cartoon, "The Other Half." In this example, the husband is behaving in an aggressive manner. He uses sarcastic humor rather than an assertive statement to express his feelings about the particular recipe. The wife appears to be humiliated and angry by his behavior. We will observe in the next section on gender differences that this pattern in male-female interactions is not atypical.

Gender differences in assertiveness, nonassertiveness, and aggressiveness

Men are more frequently aggressive than women. People were asked to determine the level of physical shock to administer to an opponent in one study. Masculine subjects facing a male opponent recommended the highest level of shock more often than did any other combination of persons (female subject with a female opponent, female subject with a male opponent, or male subject with a female opponent). Males were far more aggressive with other males than they were with females; female subjects did not vary the amount of physical shock they recommended on the basis of the opponent's sex (Hoppe, 1979). This study suggests that men are generally more aggressive than women. Furthermore, men are particularly aggressive with other men rather than with women.

Gender differences in self-assertion were examined in a study which considered performance self-esteem and dominance behavior in mixed-sex dyads. Men are more assertive than women during the process of decision-making, and people perceive men to be more assertive than women in these situations. Nonetheless, this study suggests that the differences in assertiveness are not the result of differences in overall self-esteem, but rather the result of females' behavior being mediated by self-evaluations. When women have confidence in themselves, they assert themselves (Stake & Stake, 1979). In other words, women may be unassertive in problem-solving because they do not have high regard for their own ability to perform or to contribute to the specific topic under discussion; however, when they have confidence in their ability to contribute or add to the discussion, they demonstrate assertiveness.

Another significant aspect of gender differences is other people's perceptions of assertiveness and aggressiveness. Stereotypically, men are perceived to be assertive while women are not. Further, any specific instance of assertive behavior on the part of a woman is less likely to elicit the inference that she is assertive in general than is a particular instance of assertive behavior of the part of a man. Since women are presumed to be unassertive, specific assertive behaviors are probably perceived to be isolated, unique events rather than part of a general behavioral response. For instance, if a woman would send back food in a restaurant, onlookers might not conclude that she is an assertive person, but if her male partner sent back his food, they would probably conclude that he was assertive. The woman's behavior would be viewed as unique or exceptional for her, while the man's conduct would be seen as part of a consistent assertive response.

Not only are men perceived to be aggressive and women nonassertive; aggressive people are viewed to be male and nonassertive people are thought to be women (Hess, Bridgewater, Bornstein & Sweeney, 1980). When people do not know the sex of the person who is behaving in either an aggressive or nonassertive manner, they generally assume that the person who is behaving aggressively is male while the person behaving nonassertively is female.

Are women and men judged positively or negatively when they behave differently than anticipated? In a written role-playing situation, people offered positive assessments of women behaving assertively, and even aggressively. College students demonstrated that even though nonassertiveness in women is more acceptable than nonassertiveness in men, they have an increasing tolerance of women exhibiting assertive and aggressive communication behavior (Sereno & Weathers, 1981).

However, these same results did not occur in an actual discussion. In this instance, females tended to be judged negatively when they behaved in an aggressive manner. When women behaved aggressively, in what appears to be stereotypical male behavior, other women provided negative sanctions. Specifically, when women discussed feminism in either an assertive or an aggressive manner, females observing the discussion provided negative responses to the aggressive women. Men who observed the conversation did not (Hall & Black, 1979). Men were less influenced by the aggressive woman than were the women.

These conflicting results are probably accurate reflections of the changes occurring in our contemporary culture. In some instances, both men and women may find that they are judged negatively for communicating in alternative ways. On other occasions, they may find acceptance for communication strategies which are appropriate for the situation, even though they violate traditional sex role expectations.

Explaining gender differences in self-assertion

We have observed that assertiveness appears to be related to gender. Women tend to fall in the range from nonassertive to assertive, while men tend to fall in the range from aggressive to assertive. Interesting explanations for these gender differences have been offered.

One author suggests that a "threshold of assertiveness" may exist for people, especially for women, allowing them to behave in an assertive way up to a point, but then not allowing them to go any further (Lane, 1981). Two other authors hint at this "threshold effect" when they explain that when a person's "polite restraint" is too well developed, he or she may eventually become incapable of making assertive responses (Alberti & Emmons, 1974). These enlightening notions are consistent with the socialization processes which we discussed in the first two chapters. The encouragement of women to be polite, quiet, and considerate of other peoples' feelings, while men are not provided with the same encouragement, offer some explanation for the differences. We will observe that "politeness" runs through a variety of female behaviors, as we continue to examine gender differences in communication in this text. At this point, we should note that people may be able to be assertive to some degree, but because of socialization they may be limited in moving beyond a particular level of assertiveness.

The desirability of self-assertion

Self-assertion appears to be a positive skill and is related to other positive outcomes. Assertiveness is related to positive self-concept. In chapter 2, we discussed the importance of accepting oneself. In addition to the reasons offered earlier, self-acceptance appears to be related to assertiveness. A recent report showed that assertiveness is related to self-acceptance in both men and women (Currant, Dickson, Anderson, & Faulkender, 1979).

Assertiveness is related to a number of communication skills. Verbal intensity, talkativeness, and a good communicator style are all correlated with assertive behavior (Norton & Warnick, 1976). Among the verbal characteristics of assertive people is their tendency to talk more than others, to be more intense, and to have a direct, open style of communication. People who are assertive tend to be enthusiastic about communication and interactional opportunities.

Interpersonal relationships appear to be superior for assertive people. In the area of marital relationships, for example, assertiveness is related to satisfying marriages. Marital problems are frequently caused by one of the partners being dominant and exhibiting aggressive behavior or by both of the partners behaving in a nonassertive manner (Alberti & Emmons, 1978). When one person is aggressive, the other experiences fear and anger. If the second person is nonassertive, she or he may remain in the marriage, but be highly dissatisfied; if the second person is assertive, she or he may leave the marriage; if she or he is aggressive, open conflict may ensue. When both partners are nonassertive, a lack of understanding often occurs, with neither partner communicating openly and honestly with the other. Marriages with two nonassertive people may withstand the test of time, but they are frequently reported to be unsatisfying.

Assertive people also seem to fare better at the workplace. College recruiters were presented with videotapes of male and female applicants who would either display nonassertive or assertive/moderately aggressive self-presentation styles. Recruiters evaluated the nonassertive candidates as less suited for supervisory positions than the assertive candidate, regardless of the candidate's sex. The assertive candidates were more frequently invited for a second interview than were the nonassertive candidates, and the qualifications of the assertive candidates were viewed more positively, even though they were actually the same in all other ways (Dipboyle & Wiley, 1978). Assertiveness may result in being hired, in preference to a less assertive person. However, achievement motivation, the desire to achieve, does not appear to be related to assertiveness (Borges & Laning, 1979). People appear to be motivated to accomplish goals independently of their assertive or nonassertive styles.

Assertiveness is negatively related to anxiety. The large number of studies in this area demonstrate that high levels of anxiety are incompatible with assertive behavior (Ferrell, 1977; Warren, 1977; Wolpe & Lazarus, 1966).

Sometimes it is easier to be assertive with people we hardly know than it is to behave assertively with our friends. Consider the following two situations and write down your response to each, how you felt during the time you were waiting in each case, and what you felt when your friend arrived. Imagine that you and a friend both enjoy a particular musical group. You learn that the group is on tour and will be performing in a nearby city. As a gift, you buy tickets for yourself and your friend, even though the price is quite high. You tell your friend, and she or he is very enthusiastic about the concert and agrees to drive to the concert as a way of thanking you for the tickets. The night of the concert arrives, but your friend does not. Finally, half an hour late, he or she shows up, but offers no explanation. Provide answers to the following questions:

1. If your friend was the same sex as you,
   a. What would you say or do when he or she arrived?
   b. How would you feel while you were waiting?
   c. How would you feel when he or she finally showed up?

2. If your friend was the opposite sex from you,
   a. What would you say or do when he or she arrived?
   b. How would you feel while you were waiting?
   c. How would you feel when he or she finally showed up?

Do you have different responses to the situation if the friend was the same or opposite sex from you? Why or why not? Would you characterize your response as nonassertive, assertive, or aggressive? Compare your answers with those of others to determine how most people would respond. What have you discovered about assertiveness in this exercise?

Behaving Assertively

Men tend to err by behaving too aggressively at times, while women may err in behaving too nonassertively. Each of us has difficulty in saying "no" to unwanted requests. Five situations are listed below. If you are a man, provide a nonassertive response in which you attempt to say "no" to the other person; if you are a woman, provide an aggressive response in which you attempt to say "no" to the other person. Then, write an appropriate assertive response. How would you feel if you offered the aggressive or nonassertive response you suggested? How would the other person feel? How would you and the other person feel if the assertive response was provided? What would you be most likely to do in each of the situations: provide a nonassertive response, an assertive response, or an aggressive response? Why?

1. **Friend**   I've been studying all week and I need a break. Let's go barhopping tonight.
    NONASSERTIVE OR AGGRESSIVE RESPONSE: _____

    ASSERTIVE RESPONSE: _____

2. **Instructor**   I know that I forgot to tell you that your paper needed to be typed, but I would like to receive it in typed form. Would you take it home tonight and type it for me—it's only 20 pages.
    NONASSERTIVE *OR* AGGRESSIVE RESPONSE: _____

    ASSERTIVE RESPONSE: _____

3. **Roommate**   I hope you don't mind—I have a big exam to study for and I've invited a few friends over to study in our room tonight. We'll probably stay up until 2 or 3.
    NONASSERTIVE OR AGGRESSIVE RESPONSE: _____

    ASSERTIVE RESPONSE: _____

4. **Parent**   I hope you can come home early during final exam week— your grandparents will be here.
    NONASSERTIVE OR AGGRESSIVE RESPONSE: _____

    ASSERTIVE RESPONSE: _____

5. **Opposite-sex Friend**   We've gone out three times—don't you think it's about time we slept together?
    NONASSERTIVE OR AGGRESSIVE RESPONSE: _____

    ASSERTIVE RESPONSE: _____

"I've been a housewife for twenty-five years now, and I've decided to retire next month."

Assertiveness is inversely related to trait anxiety, neuroticism, interpersonal anxiety (Orenstein, Orenstein, & Carr, 1975), communication apprehension (Pearson, 1979), and the fear of social situations (Hollandsworth, 1979). Conversely, then, we can summarize by stating that assertive people tend to be low in anxiety, neuroticism, in the fear of interpersonal interaction, fear of speaking with others, and fear of interacting in social situations. People who are more assertive tend to be less impulsive (Green, Burkhart, & Harrison, 1979). Impulsiveness may be related to anxiety or lack of clear and consistent planning. In general, then, assertiveness appears to be related to positive outcomes.

Altering assertive behavior

Self-assertion can be altered. First, situational and circumstantial changes may lead to modify assertiveness. For instance, people appear more able to behave assertively as they engage in less personal situations (Nesbitt, 1979). In other words, people may behave assertively at work, but be less assertive when they are at home. The woman in this cartoon demonstrates that assertiveness skills can be transferred to the home. She has determined that twenty-five years of housework entitles her to retirement.

Second, self-assertion can be learned. Women who engage in assertiveness training frequently learn new behaviors which affect their interpersonal relationships. An examination of women who participated in an assertiveness training workshop revealed that women not only became more assertive through the training; they also became more receptive of stereotypical masculine characteristics in themselves (Wheelan, 1978). The increase in assertiveness appears to have some lasting results. Thus, middle-aged women who participated in an intervention program showed significant increases in assertiveness and self-actualization immediately after the program and when tested five months later (McVicar & Herman, 1983). Assertiveness can be altered throughout a person's lifetime.

Conclusions

In this chapter, we considered two components of communication: self-disclosure and self-assertion. Self-disclosure, the process of offering verbal revelations of ourselves to other people, has been examined in a great deal of research during the past twenty-five years. The concept has been considered from the perspectives of an action, interaction, and transaction. In this text, the transactional approach is recommended. Self-disclosure appears to be related to a number of personality traits and to gender differences. The conflicting findings on gender differences are probably due to an oversimplification of the communication process. As newer research stresses negotiated meanings among people, we will probably find more consistent findings in the literature. The best advice that can be offered on self-disclosure is that communicators become aware of the findings in this area, that they develop sensitivity to the other persons with whom they are communicating, and that they respond to all of the cues in the environment as they determine the amount and level of self-disclosure in which to engage. Self-disclosure appears to be a generally positive communication skill, when it is understood and is used in moderation.

Self-assertion is an equally intriguing communicative behavior, but fewer studies of this trait have been conducted. Assertiveness, by definition, is a behavior that can occur best in a negotiated transaction. Assertiveness requires that both individuals be able to communicate openly and freely about their feelings, needs, and desires. Stereotypical and behavioral gender differences occur on the assertiveness dimension, with women tending to behave more nonassertively and men tending to behave more aggressively. Both women and men need to broaden their behavioral options to include assertiveness more routinely. Fortunately, change in this area appears possible.

5 Information processing

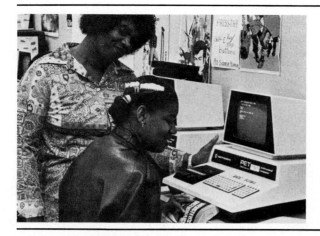

2. Organization
   a. Figures and background
   b. Proximity
   c. Similarity
   d. Perceptual constancy
3. Interpretation
   a. Context
   b. Comparison

IV. Listening
   A. The nature of listening
      1. Listening is a complex activity
      2. Poor listening skills
      3. Listening is an essential
         communication activity

4. Types of listening behaviors
   a. Critical listening
   b. Active listening
   c. Feedback
   B. Gender differences in listening

V. Empathy
   A. The nature of empathy
   B. Gender differences in empathy

VI. Conclusions

Introduction

Information processing, or giving meaning to that which comes to us through our senses, is the topic of this chapter. Information processing is a complex process which consists of a number of interrelated activities. When we consider information processing in communication, we usually discuss communication components like perception, listening, and empathy. As we shall determine, these topics are relevant to a consideration of gender and communication, since men and women differ in the way they process information. One of the most interesting developments in the area of information processing is the recent research on the influence of brain development. In the past decade, a great deal of research has investigated the neurophysiological basis of communicative and other behavior. We shall begin our consideration of information processing with this intriguing area of study, and will consider the implications for women and men.

Brain development

In the second chapter of this text, we examined both the biological and sociological influences which cause people to perceive themselves as women or men. We noted that both biology and sociology affect people's behavior. The relative importance of physiological and psychological factors has been the subject of a great deal of debate. Often, people who believe that women and men are more different than alike rely upon a physiological explanation of differences. Those who believe that women and men are more similar than different emphasize the importance of socialization and psychological differences which are learned rather than "natural." Both "nature" and "nurture" affect our behavior; hence it is unreasonable for us to deny either perspective and its potential for explaining behavior.

The nature of brain development

An examination of brain development involves physiology rather than sociology or psychology. Research concerning the development of the human brain has provided a wealth of information which is highly useful in understanding communicative behavior. During the past decade at least two lines of research have been expanded, both of which have implications for communication. One startling finding was that brain growth in children, as measured by head circumference, occurs in spurts rather than at a regular, steady rate. (cf. Eichorn & Bayley, 1961; Epstein, 1978; Telzrow, 1981). Sometimes periods of rapid growth are followed by periods of slow growth, and occasionally by plateau periods. It appears that male and female children experience different patterns of brain growth. For example, between the ages of ten and twelve, girls' head growth is about twice that of boys, but the situation is reversed in the incidence of the growth spurt which occurs around fifteen years of age (Epstein, 1978). These developmental differences have proven to be highly useful to persons in speech pathology, language development, and educational curricular decision-making (cf. Tezrow, 1981; Sonnier, 1982).

The second area of special interest on brain development is of greater importance to a consideration of gender and communication. This area of research concerns differentiating the functions of the right and left brain hemispheres of the cerebral cortex. Since the mid-nineteenth century, when language was tentatively localized in the left hemisphere of the brain (Walsh, 1978), attempts have been made to identify areas of the brain which serve specific functions. Until recent times, the implications of such research were relatively unexplored.

Left brain versus right brain

The two sides of the cerebral cortex, the left brain and the right brain, or the left side and the right side, are connected by a large set of associate fibers known as the *corpus callosum*. Each side of the brain serves different functions, so that the two hemispheres contribute differently to the perception of organization of information. The purpose of the hemispheric specialization is thought to be an improvement in the efficiency of the human organism, since information may be processed more expediently because of the "division of labor" of the brain (Dimond, 1978).

What are the two sets of functions of the brain? The left side of the brain processes information in a logical, sequential, analytic way which is particularly well suited to language-related functions (Wittrock, 1978). Thus, the left hemisphere is known as the "verbal" hemisphere. Consistent with this explanation, persons who experience stroke, tumor, or other left hemisphere trauma frequently lose their ability to comprehend or produce language, to read or interpret written symbols (Lesak, 1976).

The right side of the brain interprets information in an holistic, gestalt manner, frequently involving a visual-spatial structure of organization. Persons who experience right hemisphere damage do not experience the same debilitating effects as do those who have left hemisphere damage. Nonetheless, they may experience difficulty in perceiving wholes, in locating their position in space, such as that involved in map reading, or in copying figures accurately. It is commonly believed that the right hemisphere is considered the location of aesthetics, including art and music appreciation (Lesak, 1976). A summary of the processes of the left and right hemispheres is provided in table 5.1.

In some people the two hemispheres of the brain do not develop to the same extent. Some persons have larger left hemispheres while others have larger right hemispheres. Investigations of elementary school children demonstrate that some are "left hemisphere learners" who demonstrate verbal

Table 5.1 Hemispheric processes

Left Hemisphere	Right Hemisphere
Analytical	Analogical
Abstract	Appositional
Convergent	Artistic
Causal	Coincidental
Deductive	Divergent
Exclusive	Depressive
Linear	Holistic
Logical	Idealistic
Manic	Imaginative
Mathematical	Inclusive
Propositional	Inductive
Rational	Intuitive
Realistic	Multiple
Sequential	Simultaneous
Singular	Synthetic
Symbolic	Temporally cyclic
Temporally linear	Visually imaginative
Verbal	Visuo-spatial

proficiency, but may be awkward, have low visual-spatial skills, and experience some difficulty in generating images. At the same time, "right hemisphere learners" have delayed language development, may demonstrate reading and spelling problems, but have average or superior visual-spatial skills (Hartlage, 1980). In research on dyslexia and other brain-related disorders, evidence has appeared which seems to indicate that the larger hemisphere of the brain frequently takes over and minimizes the contribution of the other hemisphere (Witelson, 1977).

Gender differences in brain development

Males and females do not have similar brain development. We have already stated that the brains of male and female children develop differently and experience growth spurts at different times. In addition, the two sexes have hemispheric differences (Elias, Wright, & Winn, 1977). Levy and Levy (1978) postulate that fetal sex hormones may influence the asymetrical development of the brain's hemispheres. Bannatyne (1971) relates differences in males and females in such areas as verbal, spatial, mathematical and mechanical tasks to this difference in brain development. Similarly, Restak (1979) asserts that boys and girls think differently. He maintains that research on brain behavior is essential, and that behavioral differences between men and women are based on differences in brain functioning. Men are more inclined to rely on the right hemisphere of the brain, and women tend to use both hemispheres. Recent research supports Restak's position, as it indicates that men demonstrate more hemispheric specialization, while women employed a method of integrating their left and right hemispheres in learning and thinking (Tan-Willman, 1981). In sum, the data indicate that biological differences occur between the male and female brain.

Minimizing differences

Teilhard de Chardin wrote,

> What we need most, if we are to recognize the convergence of the universe, is not so much new facts (there are enough, and even embarrassingly more than enough, of these everywhere) as a new way of looking at and handling the facts. A new way of seeing, combined with a new way of acting; that is what we need (Mortier & Aboux, 1966).

He may have been writing an idealized prescription for minimizing the information processing differences that occur between men and women based on differences in brain development. A variety of theorists and educators have offered similar statements. It appears that the development of either hemisphere of the brain can be stimulated. Some writers have proposed methods of developing the right brain in isolation (Watzlawick, 1978), while most have encouraged the development of both hemispheres, thus facilitating hemispheric interaction (cf. Ornstein, 1972; Ommaya, 1978; Sonnier, 1982).

What advantages accrue when differences are minimized, when men are encouraged to develop their right brain as well as their left, and women are further encouraged to enhance an interactive system? De Chardin's words are instructive as he suggests that a new perspective is useful. On a more practical level, researchers have determined that a hemispheric balance is associated with optimal cognitive functioning (Fischer & Rhead, 1974), optimal memory (Zaidel & Sperry, 1974), increased creativity (Bogen & Bogen, 1969); formal operational thinking (Brooks, 1979), and even mental health (Galin, 1974). Gardner writes, "Only when the brain's two hemispheres are working together can we appreciate the moral of a story, the meaning of a metaphor, words describing an emotion, and the punch lines of jokes" (Gardner, 1981, p. 74). The development of both hemispheres of the brain and the minimization of biological differences between the brains of women and men appear to be well worth the effort that is currently being expended. Let us consider one of the more traditional areas of interest in information processing: the influence of perception on communication.

Perception

The nature of perception

Perception, the way we see, hear, smell, taste, or feel a specific stimulus, is one of the activities involved in information processing. Differences in the way people perceive the world are well known. Our experiences are not the same as another person's nor are our perceptions of these experiences. Perception is subjective, active, and creative. Events and objects do not have inherent meaning which is observed in exactly the same way by everyone. We do not passively receive and record the stimuli that occurs around us. Instead, each of us is actively engaged in observing our world, and we experience it in different and unique ways.

Differences in perception

Why do people have different perceptions of the same phenomenon? At least three reasons have been provided for the differences in perception. First, physiological factors, as we have been discussing, intervene in the perceptual process. Second, past experiences affect how we perceive the world. Finally, our feelings and the circumstances in the situation affect how we perceive phenomenon. Let us consider each of these reasons for differences in perception in more detail.

Physiological differences
We have already discussed the influence of brain development on perception. As one example of the impact of a different hemispheric growth of the brain in women and men, consider a task like map reading. It is claimed by some writers that women are not as adept as men at reading charts, maps, or graphs because they are less able than men to organize and conceptualize holistic, visual-spatial data (cf. Bannatyne, 1971). In a variety of other ways the brain influences peoples' perception.

Other physiological factors also affect the perception process. Obvious physiological differences such as height affect how well you can see. Less obvious differences such as your own physical fitness will modify or determine how you perceive the idea of a marathon run. Twenty-six miles is an attainable goal for some people; for others, the distance appears unrealistic. Physical abilities and disabilities, acuity in your senses, or sensory loss, all influence how you perceive the stimuli in your environment.

Past experience

In many ways our past experiences affect our future perceptions. We will consider the processes of perception in another section of this chapter, noting how our attitudes, personality, and other factors affect perception. At this point, we might note that the experiences we have with the world encourage us to attend to and consider some phenomena and neglect others. For instance, we tend to focus attention on familiar stimuli. Recall how you may have been eavesdropping on a conversation and actually heard nothing until the people talking mentioned your name. Or you are studying while you listen to the radio, but you can only recall one song, a lyric which has special meaning for you.

In many ways, we are inclined to focus on certain stimuli in our environment and to ignore others. For example, if you are involved in a committed relationship with another person, but you rarely respond to that individual's feelings of frustration, you may find that the relationship terminates. You are, in a sense, punished for ignoring cues which the other person feels is important. If you are a sensitive communicator, you learn from the experience, begin to focus on other people's moods and feelings, then attempt to respond to them.

If you grew up in a home where cleanliness and order were highly important, you may notice messiness and debris to a greater extent than someone who grew up in a more relaxed environment. If you have been teased or tormented about your weight, you may observe the shape of most of the people you encounter. If you are a male who has been taught that women are to be valued for their bodies, you may attend to women with attractive bodies and ignore those who are bright, but less physically beautiful. If you are a female who has been told that men are to be selected on the basis of their ability to earn money, you may not interact with men who are interesting, attractive, or bright. The values which we hold affect our perceptions.

Similarly, the cultural and subcultural expectations which we learn affect our perception. If we are taught to value analytical, deductive, linear, logical, rational, mathematical skills but ignore analogical, artistic, imaginative, and inductive abilities, we will view the work of people differently. We may have high regard for the computer specialist who can speak to us about the different functions of personal computers and word processors, but have little appreciation for the struggling artisan who creates stained glass windows. In addition, we may spend our money on home computers, but deny ourselves artistic additions to our homes. We would view the $3,000 we spend on a computer a "good investment," but a $500 print would be a "waste of money."

Throughout this text we qualify some of the observations with the phrase, "in this culture." Our culture is different from those of others and our experiences are not shared in other regions of the world. Sometimes *xenophobia,* our fear of strangers or other cultures, blinds us to examining our own cultural values critically, or even recognizing that the values of our culture are not shared by all inhabitants of our planet. For example, our culture stresses different values than cultures in the Far East. Our cultural milieu stresses the analytical, deductive, linear thinking that was mentioned above, while Eastern cultures tend to stress artistic, imaginative, temporally cyclic perspectives. These differences between cultures strongly influence the way persons from the West and from the East perceive the world.

Subcultural differences should be obvious to each of us. As you have read the first four chapters of this text, you have learned about many of the differences between women and men in our culture. Little girls and little boys do not experience the same world. Women and men have learned to perceive phenomenon differently. In the same way, people of other subcultural groups learn different attitudes, values, and beliefs which affect their perceptions. For example, the traditional black family may have a mother at its head, and an absent father. The matriarchal nature of many black families is in contrast to the traditionally patriarchal nature of most white families in the United States. Differences of age, race, gender, and other subcultural group differences affect our perceptions of the world.

Present feelings and current circumstances

None of us has totally unchanging moods, identical feelings, similar physical health or illness; nor do we experience identical circumstances throughout our lives. Instead, we experience periods of time in which we feel ill, depressed, worried, frustrated, or when we are fearful of losing a relationship with another person. Any of these factors can influence our perceptions. If you are experiencing any of these negative states, you may be less patient, less understanding, less effective, and less efficient. We simply do not perceive people or events in the same way when we are experiencing strong negative or positive changes.

Variations in your current circumstances or situation also affect your perceptions. If you are late for an appointment, you may look at the time on the clock that stands before a local bank; if you are dieting, you may notice every morsel of food that comes into sight; and if you are worried about an exam, you might become more observant of other students who are studying. In order better to understand how these differences come to influence our perceptual processes, let us consider some of the activities that are involved in the process of perception.

Activities of perception

Perception is a highly complicated process which is affected by a number of factors, as we have discussed. We appear to engage in at least three activities when we perceive a phenomenon, though we are generally not aware that we are engaging in separate activities because they occur quickly, almost simultaneously. Nor do they necessarily appear in a neat, linear manner, as they are presented here. However, each of these activities is involved in our perceptions of people and events.

Selection

As we observed earlier, we do not perceive all of the phenomenon in our environment. Instead, we select some stimuli on which we concentrate our attention, but we ignore other stimuli. The examples cited above, the conversation in which you hear only your name, or the radio broadcast from which you can only recall one song, demonstrate our selectivity in perception. We appear to attend selectively to stimuli, selectively to retain or recollect stimuli, and selectively to expose ourselves to stimuli.

Selective attention   refers to our tendency to focus on some stimuli and to ignore others. If you are in a room in which a number of people are conversing, you may hear only what your conversational partner says, although the voices of the others are loud enough for you to hear. You may hear part of a news broadcast, but miss what a friend tells you at the same time.

Selective retention   means that we categorize, store, and retrieve some information, but fail to categorize, store, or retrieve other information. Consider the first memory you have in your childhood. For many people, the event may have occurred when they were as young as three or four years of age; for others, it may be earlier or later. However, in almost every case, the occurrence was one of significance. You may recall the birth of a baby brother or sister, an accident that occurred, or some other traumatic event.

Why do we remember some occurrences but not others? Why do we ignore the stated attitudes of our parents and respond and recall the attitudes of our peers? Does a message on television have more impact on you than a statement made by one of your instructors? To a large extent, some of the factors that we have already discussed, our physiological differences, past experiences, and present feelings and circumstances, determine the stimuli which we recall and those which we forget. Additional factors such as the credibility of the source of the message, the medium from which it originated, our personality and belief structure, as well as other variables beyond the scope of this text, similarly influence selective retention.

An example of one factor which appears to affect selective retention is the agreement or disagreement of a speaker's message with our own beliefs. Nor do we recall all messages at the same level or to the same extent. Buchli and Pearce (1974) determined that people do not listen as well when they are told beforehand that a speaker will endorse a position, in which they believe.

The highest retention scores were achieved by those people who were told that the speaker would present a message with which the listeners disagreed, especially when the speaker did indeed present such a message. The combination of predictability and disagreement, then, appears to result in the highest level of retention. For our present purposes, we need to recognize that some stimuli do not have the same probability of being recalled as do others.

Selective exposure   means that we tend to seek out stimuli to which we wish to be exposed, and to avoid coming into contact with stimuli which we do not wish to experience. Suppose you weigh ten to twenty pounds more than the ideal weight for your height. It is likely that you will put yourself in situations in which you observe other people who are as heavy as yourself or even heavier, while you will avoid interacting with people who are at their ideal weight or lower. People who work out each day do not tend to socialize with heavy drinkers who spend a great deal of their time in bars. High school dropouts do not seek out people with Ph.D.'s with whom to interact.

Most investigations which considered selective exposure have demonstrated that persons tend to expose themselves to messages that are consistent with their own attitudes and interests. Klapper (1960) writes that "Consciously or unconsciously, [people] avoid communications of opposite hue (p. 19)" in their selection of mass communication. Sears and Friedman (1967) state that "communication audiences usually share, to an extraordinary degree, the viewpoints of the communicator (p. 202)." Political campaigns, then, are often viewed as reinforcing voters' pre-existing preferences or predispositions, rather than presenting new alternatives (Lazarsfeld, Berelson, & Guadet, 1948).

More recent research indicates that the effects of selective exposure are not as easily interpreted as we may have thought. Our assumption is that selective exposure serves to reinforce the relevant existing attitudes which people hold. One investigation emphasizes that major criticisms of earlier studies calls this assumption into question for at least two reasons. First, the earlier studies measured individuals' interests in certain types of materials, rather than their tendency to avoid or seek out information. Second, in these earlier studies no measurement was made of disagreement, dissonance, or stress which might have been produced by stimulus materials. This investigation proposes alternative methods for measuring the effects of selective exposure (Donohew, Parker, & McDermott, 1972).

"Boomerang effects" may occur when people expose themselves to information that is consistent with their beliefs and attitudes. Paletz, Koon, Whitehead and Hagens (1972) demonstrated that people who listened to messages that were consistent with their previously stated attitudes actually became less committed to them than they were before they heard them. In other words, continual exposure to messages with which we agree may result in questioning that agreement. For instance, if you feel that abortions should be available to all women and you regularly attend meetings in which speakers espouse this position, you may begin to question your own attitude. You may, for example, begin to examine cases of very young women, or you may consider the woman who has experienced multiple abortions. You may come to question your previously firm commitment to abortion for all. The differing expectations which people hold, as well as other variables, may influence the effects of selective exposure.

Organization

A second activity in perception is organization. First, we select the stimuli to which we will attend; next, we attempt to organize it in some way. Some of us are prone to organize stimuli in a linear, logical way, while others will organize stimuli in an holistic manner. To the extent that we organize phenomena differently, we perceive them differently. Some examples will help to clarify this point.

Figure and background method of organization means that we may perceive one thing as the figure, or most important part, and the rest of the stimuli as the background, or less important part. If you glance into a physician's waiting room and observe that the receptionist is not at his or her window, but do not notice that one of your friends is sitting in the room, you are perceiving the receptionist as the figure and the rest of the stimuli in the room as background. Another person, who was less task-oriented and more relationally-oriented, might notice the friend but not observe that the receptionist was temporarily absent.

Closure occurs when we fill in missing elements or parts. Suppose you sit down in the physician's waiting room and decide to strike up a conversation with one of the other people in the room. You observe that the other person is favoring his or her left arm. You might ask whether the person is seeing the physician about the arm. While you cannot be sure that the arm is injured, you observe the cues and fill in what you believe to be true. Or, you perceive an older couple sitting together and touching each other in a familiar way. Your conclusion? The couple has had a long and happy married life. We risk error when we organize stimuli. Thus, we may find that the person who was favoring his or her arm just bumped it, had just received an allergy injection in the arm and is waiting to determine that he or she has no reaction, or has a congenital birth defect. The couple may have only recently met; may be living together, but not be married; or may be siblings rather than a married couple.

Proximity is another method of organizing stimuli and refers to the fact that we group together things which appear close together. The couple was perceived to be together because of their physical proximity to each other.

Three children playing in the corner in the waiting room are perceived to be siblings because of their grouping together. We might conjecture that a man who is listening intently to another man discussing the merits of a particular political candidate favors the person, because of the speaker's level of interest and our assumption that "birds of a feather flock together."

Similarity in perception means that we group stimuli together because of resemblance in size, color, shape, or other attributes. You may believe that all college athletes are in a group of people with brawn, but have little else to offer. You may notice that the little children who are playing together in the waiting room are all blonde and brown-eyed and conclude that this is further evidence that they are siblings. When you meet someone who shares your economic views, you may assume that person will also appreciate your taste in music or clothing.

Perceptual Constancy as an organizational principle refers to the idea that we tend to maintain the same perception of a phenomenon once we have gained it. You might have a view of your parents when they were ten years younger or have a picture of the house that you grew up in, which is quite different from the actual house. This principle explains why it is so difficult for us to change our perception of another person even when that individual has changed. If you have a friend who was chemically dependent, on alcohol or drugs, and if the person has behaved in inconsistent ways, you may have trouble adapting to his new, consistent behavior, even though the new behavior is preferable.

You may still worry about whether he will show up when he states that he will; whether he will go to work, attend classes, and fulfill other commitments. A long period of time may pass before you trust him to behave consistently.

Interpretation

After we have selected and organized stimuli, we interpret it. Interpretation is perhaps more creative than is selection and organization; the more ambiguous the stimuli, the more room there is for creativity in our interpretation of it. When we meet a new person in an unfamiliar place, we have more freedom to interpret what the person may be like than we do when she or he is introduced to us by a friend who provides information about this individual.

Both context and comparison are used in our interpretation of stimuli. If we meet a new person in a class, we assume that he or she is a student, is interested in the subject matter of the course (unless it simply fulfills a requirement), and has certain attitudes and beliefs which are shared by many college students. The context of the classroom helps you to draw these conclusions, although they may be incorrect. Similarly, you use the method of comparison to draw conclusions about the person, observing whether she or he looks older than the other students, appears to be more alert, and is more talkative. You may decide that she or he is a returning student, intelligent, and friendly. Again, you could be wrong, but you are using the method of comparison to draw these conclusions. In studying the highly complex process of perception in the field of communication, we have paid particular attention to one kind of perception, listening. Let us consider this topic in greater detail.

Listening

The nature of listening

We defined perception as the process of experiencing stimuli through any one of our five senses. *Listening* focuses exclusively on hearing; it is defined as the process of receiving and interpreting aural stimuli. All the factors discussed as being relevant to perception are equally applicable to our understanding of listening. In listening, we attend selectively to some sounds and ignore others; we recall some things that we have heard and we forget others; we expose ourselves to particular aural messages and avoid others. We organize the sounds that we hear into meaningful units. For instance, when someone asks, "Are you going?" we may fill in the object of the sentence and conclude that they are asking whether we are going to the football game, thus using the principle of "closure." Or, we may use figure and background to determine that the words, "Are you going" is not as relevant as the frustrated manner in which they state the question. Finally, we interpret what we hear in creative ways.

Differences in perception occur for a variety of reasons. In this exercise, you will determine some differences between yourself and other members of your class. For each of the following descriptions, list, as specifically as you can, your own response.

_____ 1. The amount of money that you will be earning in ten years.

_____ 2. The most important personality characteristic that an attractive member of the opposite sex possesses.

_____ 3. The most important personality characteristic which a friend of the same sex possesses.

_____ 4. The one thing that you must have in order to be happy.

_____ 5. The best politician who is currently serving in the government.

_____ 6. The most interesting male actor who has ever performed.

_____ 7. The most beautiful woman of all time.

_____ 8. The most handsome man of all time.

_____ 9. The best food in the world.

_____ 10. The worst food in the world.

_____ 11. How many children should people have?

_____ 12. How many times should a person marry?

_____ 13. How much daily exercise should a person engage in?

_____ 14. What kind of automobile is best?

_____ 15. What kind of sexual activity should be avoided?

After you have completed answering these fifteen questions, compare your responses with a partner. Determine the areas of similarity and the areas of greatest difference. Discuss with your partner the rationale for your respective answers. Explain the physiological factors, past experiences, and present feelings and circumstances which may have affected your answer. Listen to the other person as he or she explains the reasons for his or her answers.

Your instructor may wish to place the answers to selected questions on the board to determine general patterns within the group. The responses may be divided up into male and female replies in order to determine whether any variations on specific questions appear because of sex differences. For example, women and men may have a different notion of attractiveness in other men and women, women and men may differ about the ideal number of children a couple should have, and they may disagree about what kind of sexual activity should be avoided. Questions about food (do real men eat quiche?), exercise, and money may elicit different answers from women and men. What implications do these differences have for communication between the sexes? How can problems in communication between people with different perceptions be overcome?

Listening is a complex activity

As you can see, listening is just as complex as other types of perception, and it involves far more than simply hearing a sound. Hearing is a natural, physiological function which we can perform unless we suffer a physiological loss. Listening is a selective activity which involves both the reception and the interpretation of aural stimuli. Contemporary researchers are engaged in trying to determine the specific skills involved in listening (cf. Bostrom & Bryant, 1980). The complexity of listening is apparent as you consider your own experiences. You may have heard a popular song a dozen times, but never have listened to the words. You may hear what another person has to say, but not listen to the content or intent of his/her message. Listening is also complex because we engage in it for a variety of reasons: appreciation, discrimination, comprehension, evaluation, empathy, and therapy (cf. Wolvin & Coakley, 1982; Wolff, Marsnik, Tacey, & Nichols, 1983).

Poor listening skills

Although we commonly believe that we listen quite well, most of the evidence contradicts this assumption. In general, people appear to recall about one-half of what they have heard, when tested immediately after a message, even when they are informed that they will be tested on the information. When they are tested two months later, they recall only about one quarter of the information (Nichols & Stevens, 1957).

Why do people listen so poorly? First, as we have discussed, listening is a complex activity. It involves hearing, selecting, organizing, interpreting, and recalling aural symbols. An individual can fail in any one of these activities.

For instance, a person may not listen well simply because she or he was not attending to what another person was offering. Or, the meaning of the aural message may be interpreted differently than was intended by the speaker. Perhaps an individual listens poorly because he/she cannot recall the first ideas the speaker presented and therefore cannot apply them to the last suggestions that were made. Listening can break down at a variety of different points.

People may also appear as poor listeners because of the methods by which we determine their listening abilities. In the study cited above, and in most research on listening, the operational, or working, definition of the term relies on a "lecture-test" method. In other words, people who are perceived to be effective listeners are those who do well on paper-and-pencil tests which formulate questions about the material that was discussed. This method of determining listening ability is limiting and certainly does not take into consideration all the nuances of the listening process. For example, a person may be a poor test-taker, may be of below-average intelligence, or may speak English as a second language. In all of these instances, she or he would do poorly on the "listening test." At the same time, she or he may have understood the message. In addition, the "listening test" may be measuring the cognitive material or "facts" which were presented, but ignore the subtleties in language, emotional tone, and other nonverbal features. The listener may have gained a great deal of information, but the test focuses only on facts and figures. We will observe how both these issues, being skilled in some ways in the listening process, but not in all, and being tested for listening ability on the basis of written tests, contribute to the confusion in gender differences in listening.

Listening is an essential communication activity

No matter how well or poorly we listen, listening is an essential communicative activity. Listening is a fundamental component of communication; and we spend a great deal of time engaged in the activity. A classic study stated that we spend more than 40% of our time engaged in listening (Rankin, 1926). Similarly, contemporary studies demonstrate that we listen to a greater extent than we engage in any other form of verbal communication. Weinrauch and Swanda (1974) found that business personnel, including those with and without managerial responsibilities, spent nearly 33% of their time listening, almost 26% of their time speaking, nearly 23% of their time writing, and almost 19% of their time reading. When Werner (1975) investigated the communication activities of high school and college students, homemakers, and employees in a variety of other occupations, he determined that they spent 55% of their time listening and only 23% speaking, 13% reading, and 8% writing.

If these studies were to be repeated today, with the addition of various forms of mass communication, an even larger percentage might result. We spend time listening to people in social situations, classrooms, and at work; we listen to the radio, the television, records, cassette tapes, movies, cable programs, and word synthesizers. Thus, a large portion of our time is spent engaged in listening.

Types of listening behaviors

We engage in a variety of listening behaviors. The behavior of the speaker, the nature of the information under discussion, and the communication setting all affect our listening behavior. Critical listening and active listening are two types of listening behavior which may be relevant to a consideration of gender and communication.

Critical listening   occurs when you are attempting to discriminate among the information and ideas which are presented, then seek to make analytical judgments about the validity and usefulness of the information. You may engage in critical listening in a public speaking setting or in smaller groups. When you listen critically, you attempt to distinguish between facts and inferences, to categorize arguments as emotional or logical, to understand the lines of reasoning the speaker uses, to determine the speaker's unique perception, and to identify the key points of his or her message.

Active listening,   defined as "involved listening with a purpose" (Barker, 1971), has been distinguished from passive listening. One person distinguished between active and passive listening, as follows:

> In the former, the individual listens with more or less his [her] total self—including his [her] special senses, attitudes, beliefs, feelings and intuitions. In the latter, the listener becomes mainly an organ for the passive reception of sound, with little self-perception, personal involvement, Gestalt discrimination, or alive curiosity (Barbara, 1957).

Active listening is so labeled because a certain amount of activity is required on the part of the listeners. When you listen actively to another person, you do not lethargically sit or stand; instead, you respond through movement and change.

Feedback is a distinguishing characteristic of active listening. *Feedback* is defined as the verbal and nonverbal responses to a message, as these responses are received and understood by the speaker. Feedback allows you to monitor your communication with others. If you are effective in using and receiving feedback, you can avoid misunderstandings. You can alter, correct, or reinforce your original message to others as you observe and interpret the feedback which they provide.

Feedback may be differentiated on a number of dimensions. It may be positive or negative, immediate or delayed, verbal or nonverbal. When you provide encouragement, reinforcement, or allow the other person to know that you understand, you are providing *positive feedback*. When you discourage the speaker, do not reinforce him or her, or let him or her know that you do not understand, you are providing *negative feedback*. Examples of positive feedback are smiles, nodding your head in agreement, or restating the other person's message. Negative feedback would include frowning, looking away, appearing uncomfortable, or commenting that you do not understand what the other person is saying.

Immediate feedback occurs simultaneously with the message or soon thereafter. Your nonverbal responses as the speaker is talking, or your almost unconscious vocalizations such as "mmh," or "uh-huh," which may occur at almost the same time as the speaker is talking, are examples of immediate feedback. Questions or comments which you formulate after the speaker has finished are similarly categorized as immediate feedback. *Delayed feedback* occurs much later. If someone makes a highly unusual self-disclosure to you, you may not respond immediately. Perhaps later in the day, or even later in the week, you may tell him or her about your feelings about this self-disclosure. Or you may use delayed feedback when you find it uncomfortable to tell a person how you feel in a particular setting. If you are with a group of people and your spouse says something which is offensive or upsetting to you, you may choose to wait until you are alone with him or her to tell him or her your feelings.

Verbal feedback includes any response in words. If you state, "Go on," "Tell me more," "Then what did she say?" "I see," "I understand," "I really like your comment—it sums up the situation perfectly," or "Do you mean that you never made it to class?" you are offering verbal feedback. *Nonverbal feedback* includes responses which are not verbal. When you shake your head, move away from the speaker, use facial expression, gesture, point, lean toward the speaker, or offer sounds which are not words like "oooooh," "whew," or "mmmmmh," you are providing nonverbal feedback.

Gender differences in listening

We have considered the complexity of listening, how listening has been measured, two kinds of listening behavior, and the role of feedback in listening. We are now prepared to consider gender differences which have been uncovered in the research on listening. At this time, the research evidence is inconclusive as to whether men or women are better listeners. Some studies have

Personal Feedback

We provide feedback to speakers about their messages, but we also furnish feedback to people about our perceptions of them. If you do not like someone, you typically spend little or no time with them. When you are highly attracted to another person, you tend to sit and stand more closely to that individual than you do to someone to whom you are not attracted. This exercise will give you an opportunity to elicit feedback from other members of your class and permit you to provide them with feedback.

By yourself, write down the name of one other person in your class whom you would choose for each of the following categories:

1. The person whom you would most like to be dating.

2. The person whom you would most like to have as a partner for an assignment in this class.

3. The person whom you would most like to introduce to your parents.

4. The person with whom you would most like to discuss a new idea.

5. The person whom you would most like to be your boss.

6. The person whom you would most like to have work for you.

7. The person whom you would most likely ask for help if you were in great danger.

8. The person whom you would most like to help if all your classmates were in danger.

9. The person whom you would most likely trust with some object of great value that belongs to you.

10. The person whom you would most like to be stranded with, in a deserted cabin, on a hike in the mountains, or in a home during a severe snowstorm.

Your instructor may wish to place some of the ten categories on the board and write down responses to the categories from your lists. You should observe the number of times that certain people's names appear. Why are some people mentioned more frequently than others? Are men listed in some categories more frequently than women? Are women listed in some categories to the near exclusion of men? What are the bases of the choices? What kind of feedback are you providing the other members of your class? What kind of feedback have they provided you?

demonstrated no significant differences in the listening skills of males and females (cf. Hollow, 1956; King, 1959; Buchli & Barnett, 1974), a few studies have reported that females are better than males at listening (cf. Lundsteen, 1963; Winter, 1966; Palmatier & McNinch, 1972), but most of the studies have suggested that males are better than females at listening (cf. Caffrey, 1955; Goldhaber & Weaver, 1968; Irwin, 1953; Winter, 1966; Hampleman, 1958; King, 1959; Nichols, 1948).

The studies that have sought to determine gender differences in listening skills have not demonstrated that men or women are superior. For a number of reasons, little speculation has been offered about differential listening ability. First, of course, studies demonstrate no consistent differences. Second, most of the studies have relied upon paper-and-pencil recall tests, the results of which have been challenged. (cf. Bostrom & Waldhart, 1980). These "listening tests" were shown to be more a measure of general mental ability than of listening (Kelly, 1965, 1967). Third, researchers have contended that the differences may be a result of aberrant populations. (Some of the studies used elementary school children, others used high school students, and some used first year college students.)

Though neither sex may listen "better," it appears that women and men listen differently. Men may select and attend to different data in their environments because of their attentional style, which has been identified as "continually shaping, forming, observing, inquiring, and directing energy toward a chosen goal, a new structure" (Weaver, 1972). The female attentional style, on the other hand, is characterized as one which searches for "relatedness of parts of a pattern, of intuitive perceptions of feeling situations, of openness of images of the unconsciousness as well as to the external environment" (Weaver, 1972).

We observed earlier that men and women have different hemispheric development of their brains, and that men tend to be more right brain oriented while women tend to integrate the two hemispheres of the brain. A writer explaining information processing recently stated,

> . . . it is hypothesized that three modes of data processing are possible within the brain. One mode is analytical processing which is essentially left hemisphere, one mode is Gestalt processing which is essentially right hemisphere, and a third mode is holistic which involves an interaction between the two hemispheres (Powers-Ross, 1978).

The three modes of information processing are summarized in Table 5.2 (Howell, 1982).

Understanding differences in brain development enhances our understanding of the literature on listening skills. While the female is more easily distracted by competing details, the male finds segments of configurations and ignores most parts of the configuration. Males tend to restructure observation in terms of their own goals, whereas females tend to accept the pattern as it

Table 5.2 Modes of information processing

Analytic	Holistic	Gestalt
1. Predominantly left brain	1. Combined left and right brain	1. Predominantly right brain.
2. Data are processed sequentially	2. Data are processed sequentially and simultaneously	2. Data are processed simultaneously
3. Process is within awareness	3. Process is out of awareness	3. Process may be in or out of awareness
4. Process is symbolic, partial, and quantitative	4. Process combines symbolic and signal functions	4. Process is nonsymbolic and nonquantitative
5. Data are processed systematically	5. Products of random right brain activity are systematized	5. Data are processed randomly

From THE EMPATHIC COMMUNICATOR by William S. Howell. © 1982 by Wadsworth, Inc. Reprinted by permission of Wadsworth Publishing Company, Belmont, California 94002.

is in order to determine relationships. The female hears more of a message because she rejects less of it, while the male derives more coherent meaning of the message, because he is building a general structure of the overall message as he listens. In addition, the female style allows emotions and unclear impressions to govern selective attention more than does the male style.

A recent study validates this conclusion. College students were told to listen to one of two stories presented simultaneously. They were then tested on their assigned story, and males were found to extract more information than were females (Halley, 1975). The study shows that females were more easily distracted by the irrelevant story, but males were more goal-oriented. It appears that the different hemispheric development in males and females combined with differences in sex role socialization helps us understand differences in listening.

How do these differences in listening behavior affect our interactions? Two situations which recently occurred illustrate the effect. One evening a couple was sitting in our family room watching television with us. The woman was doing some needlepoint which she always carried with her in her oversized bag. She was also "listening for" our front door to open, which would mean that some of the children from their family or some of ours had come back from a neighborhood park. She also "heard" the sound our coffee pot makes when it is done brewing, since she immediately asked if anyone wanted a second cup of coffee. After she returned with the coffee, she asked her husband about the plot of the movie. He seemed annoyed and suggested that she watch the movie if she wanted to follow the fairly complex plotline. A little later she seemed exasperated when he did not hear the children return from the park. Was either member of the couple at fault? No, they were simply demonstrating the listening differences between women and men which occur each day.

A second example occurred with another couple. These friends, Mark and Sue, and another couple, Len and Carol, often socialized with each other. Both couples were mutual friends of ours, as well. Over drinks and dinner one evening, Sue remarked that she would not be surprised if Len and Carol separated. The two men disagreed. They pointed out the beautiful house in which Len and Carol lived, their new mobile home, their recent vacation to Florida, their commitment to equal rights and job sharing in the home, and their two children. Although I had not thought about it before, I knew that Sue was probably correct. Neither Sue nor I could point to "hard facts," as the men did; instead, we observed the aggressive remarks, the hostile looks, the physical distance that seemed to separate Len and Carol when they sat in a room or walked together, and we noted a general level of indifference between them. Len and Carol separated less than a month after our discussion of the probable success or failure of their marriage. Were the men poorer judges of human behavior? Probably not; they were simply focusing on data which they believed to be relevant. Again, the women and men in this example illustrate different styles of attention.

Differing attentional styles and diverse socialized expectations result in differences in listening skills. Studies which have been conducted concerning which sex is listened *to,* demonstrate that men have an advantage. Bridgewater (1980) demonstrated that we listen more carefully to men than we do to women. The traditionally higher status of men in our culture may account for this difference. Let us consider, next, an area of information processing in which women appear to have an advantage.

Empathy

The nature of empathy

Empathy is defined as the ability to perceive the other person's view of the world as though it were our own. When someone asks you to put yourself "in his or her shoes," that person is figuratively asking you to empathize with him or her. In the 1920's, research on empathy was performed by physiological measures of muscle tensions and movements. The concept changed from that time to now, when empathy is regarded as a perceptual variable.

Our ability to measure empathy has changed as the meaning of the term has been altered. When empathy was defined as a physical response to stimuli, it was a relatively easy matter to measure. But when we define it as a perceptual variable, we encounter the same problems in measurement which we observed in the listening literature. Pearson (1983) explained the complexity of empathy, as it is currently conceptualized, as a set of interrelated steps.

First, you must be sensitive to yourself, and be able to vividly recall your past experiences. Empathy involves the process of recalling our past emotions and feelings in order to see common experiences with others. Second, you must be able to recall how particular feelings were translated into behaviors for you. To the extent that we can relate particular behaviors to specific feeling states within ourselves, we can recognize the same or similar behaviors suggesting shared feelings. Third, you must be a sensitive perceiver of those cues offered to you by another person. The empathic person is alert to subtle, as well as blatant, cues in the environment. An empathic person possesses insight, perceptiveness, and social acuity. Fourth, you must be able to separate your own intellectually reflective response and your emotional or feeling response from those of the person with whom you are empathizing and hold your responses in temporary suspension. In other words, judgments and the drawing of inferences are withheld. Fifth, you must interpret the available cues assisted by your past knowledge of the other person, similar experiences, and cognitive ability. The empathic person is able to generate creative hunches, adequate explanations, and correct inferences. Finally, you must communicate your understanding to the other person through clear and specific feedback.

As you examine this list of skills, you begin to understand the complexity and difficulty of responding empathically to others. Your ability to respond empathically may be impaired if you are unable to focus on yourself and to recall your own past experiences. The relationships between feelings and behaviors must be understood. Ability to be a sensitive perceiver of other's behaviors is required. Persons who wish to respond empathically must understand the differences that might occur between their own feelings and behaviors and the feelings and behaviors of other persons. You are called upon to be skilled in understanding people. In addition, you must be able to communicate that which you understand in a manner which is clear to the other person.

Too often, we assume that other people perceive the world in exactly the same way that we do, or, at least, in a very similar way. Great variations in perception exist, however, particularly between people of different subcultures. We have viewed countless ways in which women and men socialize differently in our culture, and how the two sexes consequently perceive the world differently. At the same time, empathy is a particularly important skill when we wish to communicate effectively with a person with different perceptions, and/or a person of the opposite sex. Let us consider some of the differences in empathic ability that have been identified in the literature.

The goals of empathy include accepting ourselves and accepting others. However, stereotypes affect our ability to empathize with others. For instance, if you believe that men are insensitive, you may never express intimate feelings because you think that they won't understand them. Or if you think that women are overly emotional, you may refrain from sharing highly emotional information with them for fear that they cannot cope with it adequately.

This exercise will help you understand stereotypes about sex which you may have, and will provide an opportunity to demonstrate empathy to another person. Before you are paired off, write down at least five sex-typical behaviors in which you engage and at least five sex-atypical behaviors in which you engage. For instance, you might include knitting, sewing, or cooking as sex-typical behavior if you are a woman, and weight-lifting, sports car racing, and bartending as sex-atypical behavior. Men might include jogging, motorcycle racing, and small motor repair as sex-typical behavior, and babysitting, crocheting, and baking as sex-atypical behaviors. With your partner, take turns sharing your lists of activities. You will probably find that your partner can easily understand why you participate in the sex-typical behaviors, but may have some difficulty understanding why you pursue some of the sex-atypical activities. Try to explain why you engage in the sex-atypical behaviors to your partner's satisfaction, until you feel that he or she genuinely understands your behavior. As you listen to your partner discuss his or her behaviors, try to demonstrate empathy. Consider the complexity of empathy and the number of steps involved. Consciously attempt to go through these steps, demonstrating sincere and honest understanding for the other person's behaviors.

With the entire class, discuss your feelings about this exercise. Did you find it relatively easy or difficult to demonstrate empathy? Why or why not? Did you learn anything about your own communication skills? What stereotypes tended to interfere in your ability to understand the other person? What steps in the empathy process seemed particularly difficult for you? Which steps were relatively easy? How can you improve your ability to empathize with others of the same- and opposite-sex? This exercise can be repeated, so that each person has an opportunity to interact with members of the same-sex and members of the opposite-sex. Results can be compared and contrasted to determine whether empathy is more difficult or easier when discussing sex-atypical behaviors with people of your own gender or those of the opposite sex.

"I'm married. I have three sons. My boss is a man. I sell Jockey shorts. And I just need a woman to talk to!"

Gender differences in empathy

If you surmised that women are more empathic than are men, your conjecture would fit the traditional perspective on gender differences in empathy. James Stephens wrote that "Women are wiser than men because they know less and understand more." Such stereotypical representations of women and men imply that women are more sensitive than men in perceiving other people's feelings and subtle nuances of behavior. The implication in this cartoon is that a woman would be more empathic than the men with whom this woman typically interacts.

The literature does not offer conclusive evidence that women are superior to men in empathic ability. Maccoby and Jacklin (1974) determined that this assumption was incorrect, when they wrote that the two sexes "are equally adept at understanding the emotional reactions and needs of others, although measures of this ability have been narrow." No significant differences in the empathic ability of one sex over the other were found in two different studies (Olesker & Balter, 1972; Breisinger, 1976). In addition, an investigation in which the empathic skills of male and female nursing students were examined, produced interesting results. Male nurses scored highest in empathy, followed by female non-nursing students, female nurses, and finally, male non-nursing students (MacDonald, 1977). Factors other than gender seem to appear in the area of empathy.

Hoffman examined the notion of traditional thought on sex differences in empathy, i.e., that women are superior to men, and suggested an alternative explanation. He felt that women might not be more empathic, but rather, that they may be overly concerned about hurting other people (Hoffman, 1977). In other words, empathy in women may be a result of a prosocial affective orientation which includes experiencing guilt when they harm other people. This perspective suggests that women are not more successful in assessing other people's affective, cognitive, or spatial perspectives than are men. In addition, empathy does not appear to be part of a larger interpersonal sensitivity which includes egocentric concerns about the feelings of others toward self.

Because it is difficult to isolate empathy in the laboratory, the issue may remain undecided. Women may not be "naturally" more empathic than men, but empathy is associated with the traditional feminine role in our culture and may be encouraged in women. Bem (1975) asked students to listen to the apparently spontaneous conversation of another person (who was actually a confederate delivering a prepared statement). The confederate disclosed personal problems and the investigators recorded the number of times each student listener nodded or made sympathetic comments. The women who were more traditionally feminine reacted with more concern than did men or less traditional women.

Another study similarly examined empathy in terms of sex roles, and further clarified the findings in this area. Watson (1976) found that empathy is limited by the degree to which the self-concepts of men and women are restricted by masculine and feminine roles. Persons who combine characteristics of male and female roles, that is, androgynous persons, appear to have a broader self-concept and greater flexibility in their behavior than do persons with conventional sex roles. In this study, women whose ideal sex role index was most radically different from the feminine stereotype (cross-sexed females) appeared to be the most empathic.

Let us consider these conflicting findings. Women are stereotypically believed to demonstrate more empathy than men, and yet the studies are equivocal. Traditional female roles may have encouraged empathic responses. For instance, the nurturing of children is often identified as an area in which empathic skill is important. The inability of infants to verbalize their feelings, and their heavy reliance for survival on their caretaker's ability to understand their needs, is one example. Mothers of young children appear to be particularly capable of deciphering the speech of the young children even when the words are blurred.

Another explanation of differences in empathy lies in the notion of status differences. People with less status are generally required to read the signs and signals of people who are high in status. The secretary must learn to "read" his or her boss; the nurse must learn to "read" his or her physician; and the student must learn to "read" his or her professor! Women may have been required to understand the expressions of others with greater accuracy in order to advance or even survive. Subtlety is in order when people are powerless.

The kind of occupation or training of an individual also may affect his or her ability to sensitively read the cues of others. In the study of nurses reported above, the male nurses exceeded all other groups in their ability to empathize with others. Similarly, men who were in training for, or working in, occupations which required nurturing, expressiveness, or artistic skill, performed as well as women in tests of decoding nonverbal signs of other people's feelings (Rosenthal, Archer, DiMatteo, Koivumaki & Rogers, 1974). It is not clear whether people in fields such as psychiatry, acting, art, mental health, and teaching grow in social sensitivity because of their positions or whether sensitive men are drawn to these professions.

Finally, people may be able to demonstrate more empathy when they are cross-sexed (women who indicate a masculine psychological sex type and men who indicate a feminine psychological sex type), because they have experienced some of the feelings of both sexes. In one of the studies reported above, masculine women, for instance, were found to be highly empathic. These women may understand the feelings of women, since they are biologically female, and may also understand the feelings of men, because they have psychological characteristics such as aggressiveness, independence, and goal-orientation which are similar to men. As we consider this variety of explanations, we are again impressed by the complexity of information processing. Perception, listening, and empathy are all processes which are highly complicated. Simple gender differences do not explain the divergences. At the same time, we have uncovered some significant patterns postulating the manner in which women and men process information.

Conclusions

In this chapter, we examined the role of information processing in the communication of women and men. We discussed both biological and psychological differences between women and men which may contribute to their diverse ways of processing information. We learned about brain development and found that women and men differ in this area. Males and females experience different growth spurts in the development of their brains, and differences also occur in hemispheric specialization. Men tend to develop right brain hemispheric specialization while women tend to integrate their left and right hemispheres.

Perception includes the selection, organization, and interpretation of stimuli. We selectively attend to, recall, and expose ourselves to stimuli in our environment. We organize the stimuli in a variety of ways, including processes such as figure and ground, closure, perceptual constancy, proximity, and similarity. Interpretation frequently relies upon context and comparison. We may make errors at any of these stages in the perceptual process. Perception varies as a result of physiological factors, including gender, past experiences, present feelings, and circumstances.

Listening is an area of perception which is equally complex. Studies which have considered listening differences between women and men have been impaired or invalidated by questionable definitions of the concept and by even more doubtful ways of measuring performance. It appears that women and men listen differently; but no conclusions can be drawn as to whether one sex or the other listens better.

Empathy is believed to be an area in which women excel. Traditionally female occupations like nursing, teaching, and parenting require high levels of empathy. Socialization and training rather than biological sex differences may account for variations in empathy which have appeared. It is clear from the current literature that men can be as empathic, and even more empathic, than can women. The area of information processing is complex, but essential to our consideration of gender and communication.

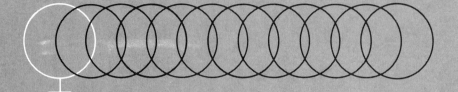

Section 3

In this section, the specific codes which are used to communicate with others are detailed. You will learn about language usage in chapter 6. Women and men are perceived to employ more language differences than they actually use, and they disclose some differences which are not perceived. The provocative topics of interpersonal attraction and physical allurement are the subject of chapter 7. You will learn of the causes of interpersonal attraction, of the importance of physical appeal, and of gender

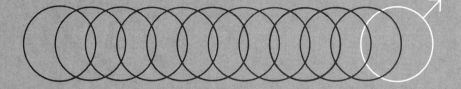

Codes

differences that exist in this area. Chapter 8 summarizes the innumerable studies that have been conducted on nonverbal communication. The codes of nonverbal communication, including proxemics, kinesics, tactile communication, paralanguage, artifactual communication, and nonverbal sensitivity, are all included in this chapter.

6 Language usage of women and men

Introduction

We have dealt with some initial considerations about gender and communication and we have learned about the components of communication between and among women and men. In this section, we begin to examine the codes that are used in that communication, exploring the verbal code, language. In the next two chapters, we will determine the role of nonverbal codes in communication by examining interpersonal attraction and physical allurement in chapter 7, and such codes as kinesics, proxemics, paralinguistics, tactile communication, and artifactual communication in chapter 8.

In the first chapter, we stated that communication involves codes and consists of encoding and decoding. The codes that people use may be categorized as verbal and nonverbal. Verbal codes are generally viewed as the language or words that we use, and nonverbal codes are the communicative behaviors which are "non-words," such as touch and movement. We have already considered how language is used to discriminate against women and men, that is, how the terms that we choose demonstrate a bias against one sex and in favor of the other. Our purpose in this chapter is to examine how women and men are perceived to differ in their conversational styles and in the substance of their conversations, how they actually differ in these two modes, the explanations which exist for these differences, and a proposal for how women and men might communicate in the future.

Stereotyped perceptions of language differences

When the topic of "sex and communication" emerges in conversations, nearly everyone has an opinion on how women and men differ in their communication styles. Adults attach linguistic variables to men and women, thereby stereotyping them; and children also learn these stereotypes (Edelsky, 1976). Since most stereotyping hurts women more than it hurts men, it is particularly surprising that a recent study demonstrated that women tend to perceive greater differences between the sexes in their use of language than do men. Kramer (1977) found that women perceived four times as many differences as did men. Stereotypes about men and women abound, as we have already noted. Let us examine some of the specific ways that we stereotype the language of women and men.

One of the most prevalent notions about women's and men's speech is that women talk more than men. People perceive women, rather than men, to gossip, to "gab," "to cackle like a group of old hens," and they characterize people who talk a great deal as sounding like a "bunch of old women." This stereotype is illustrated in "The Wizard of Id." Later in this chapter we will see that this stereotype is incorrect. At this point, we will simply note that both men and women believe it.

Before you begin to examine the material in this chapter, compile a list of language differences you believe exist between women and men. Include such features as which sex talks more, which sex uses assertive language, which sex is more "proper" in language usage, which words are used by men and which by women, what topics are typically discussed by men and which are generally reserved for women, and which sex uses more expressiveness or feeling communication as contrasted with goal-oriented communication. After you have compiled your list, read the chapter. Then, mark those statements which are consistent with other people's stereotyped notions of female/male differences in language usage. Finally, write a short response to each of your statements in which you identify it as true, false, or limited in some manner by the research which has been completed.

Related to the amount of talking attributed to men and women is the stereotype that women use empty talk, that they seldom say anything of importance, that they deal in the trivial and the unimportant. People believe that more emotional speech and more extensive use of details characterize women's speech (Kramer, 1977). Male's speech, on the other hand, is viewed as bold and straightforward, focusing on important subjects (Fillmer & Haswell, 1977).

In addition, women's speech is viewed as unassertive and lacking in power (Siegler & Siegler, 1976). Male language is viewed as aggressive, contrasting with female language, which is seen as passive (Fillmer & Haswell, 1977; Fitzpatrick & Bochner, 1981). Women are characterized as more submissive, more susceptible to social pressure, more responsive to the needs of others in their language, while the opposite traits are ascribed to men (Shuy, 1969; Strainchamps, 1971; Kramer, 1974, 1975; Markel, Long and Saine, 1976).

In general, women are perceived as more "proper" and "polite" than are men. Some people have contended that women's reliance on more polite terms may indicate their relative lack of self-confidence and power in a society which does not take women seriously (Lakoff, 1973). A cross-cultural study presents the same finding. British studies show a greater use of "prestige" (upper class) forms by females, which is interpreted as an overt attempt to make up for social inferiority with linguistic superiority (Kramer, 1974). However, Beck (1978) examined one aspect of verbal ability, grammatical structure, and found that females displayed inferior codes. She observed that men and women not only had sex differentiated codes, but that women employed language similar to the lower class. Men tend to use profanity and harsh language, while women avoid harshness and anger in their speech (Kramer, 1978).

Another stereotype about men and women is that they use different words and discuss different topics. This is closely related to the idea of women and men differing in the "politeness" of their speech, but actually it goes beyond this notion. For example, men are perceived to use more jargon and also tend to claim authority in areas such as business, politics, baseball, and women's speech. Women, on the other hand, in addition to avoiding harsh language, are viewed as discussing social life, books, food and drinks, caring for their husbands, and social work (Kramer, 1978).

As we shall see in the following sections, the clichés about the language of women and men appear to be stronger than are the actual differences (Kramer, Thorne, & Henley, 1978). We perceive men and women to be more different than alike. But we have not demonstrated these differences in behavioral studies. Many of our assumptions about male/female language differences are based on introspection (Lakoff, 1972, 1973, 1974, 1975, 1978) and personal observation (Lakoff, 1975; Parlee, 1979; Eakins & Eakins, 1978). In the next sections, we will limit our statements about male/female differences to those which have been substantiated in systematic studies that have achieved empirical verification. For a variety of reasons, because of the influence of subcultural differences on our perception, because we live in a society which stresses differences between women and men rather than similarities, because of the nature of our culture which is based on competitiveness and power, we tend to perceive exaggerated differences in the verbalizations of women and men.

Actual language differences of women and men

As we stated earlier in this chapter, people have immediate responses to the kinds and types of differences which exist between the language of women and men. Some of those perceptions concern the structure of talk, for instance, whether men or women talk more, while other perceptions concern the substance of conversations, for example, whether men or women use more hostile language. In this section of the chapter, we will consider the empirical findings relative to male/female language differences examined from a general point of view, from a substantive perspective, and from a structural view point. We will begin our consideration by discussing general differences in the language of women and men.

General language differences

The same stereotypes that guide our thinking about women and men, thoroughly discussed in chapters one and two, are equally relevant here. You will recall that women are viewed as more expressive, supportive, affiliative, compliant, and conforming, while men are perceived as more aggressive, instrumental, and task-oriented. These clichés of women and men may be accounted for, at least in part, by the language patterns which appear to emerge from the two sexes.

Women show more affiliating and socially expressive responses than do men. For instance, in mock jury deliberations, two researchers found that females scored significantly higher than males in positive reactions, i.e., utterances which exhibited solidarity, released tension, or agreement. Men scored higher than women in the aggressive category of attempted answers, i.e., utterances that expressed a suggestion, an opinion, or an orientation (Strodtbeck & Mann, 1956). Similarly, in the small group setting, women initiate more verbal acts; men provide more suggestions, opinions, or information; and women offer more reactions including agreements or disagreements (Aries, 1982). In a study which sought to determine behaviors that would predict male and female democratic leadership, females contributed a significantly greater percentage of positive socio-emotional communication acts than male democratic leaders (Fowler & Rosenfeld, 1979).

In an investigation of preschoolers which indicates that girls develop language strategies earlier than boys, Haslett (1983) observes that "Females are reinforced more than males for being other-directed and nurturant" (p. 128). There is no doubt that this reinforcement encourages some of the linguistic differences which have been identified.

Apparently men and women differ in the number of requests each makes. In a study of preschool children, boys made more requests for help in completing a puzzle than did girls (Pellegrini, 1982). Another investigation demonstrated that boys who were 4, 8, and 12 years of age all made more direct requests than did girls of the same ages (Haas, 1981). In general, girls try to solve problems themselves rather than request help, while boys tend to seek help when presented with a problem. This difference may be associated with the female tendency to be supportive and compliant, as compared with the male tendency to be instrumental and task-oriented. The girls may not wish to question their task or create problems for others, whereas the boys might feel more motivated to complete the task as quickly as possible. We must take care to state that we do not know whether these results apply generally to adult females and males.

A study which examined exploitative behavior versus accomodative behavior of male and female managers revealed that females scored significantly higher on accomodative behavior and lower on exploitative behavior than did males (Brenner & Vinacke, 1979). Similarly, another study demonstrated that males were found to be more aggressive but females were found to be more compliant (Leary, 1979). In an examination of 4, 8, and 12 year-old boys and girls, the girls demonstrated more compliance than the boys (Haas, 1981). Two psychologists pointed out that many of the ideas that we have about male/female language differences are based on myths, but that differences do indeed occur which clearly indicate that male language is more aggressive than that of females (Maccoby & Jacklin, 1974).

Women are more expressive in conversations, and they appear to be particularly expressive of love, sadness, and happiness. In addition, women's abilities to be expressive appear to correlate with their parents' ability to express emotions. Expressiveness in conversations, then, may be learned through sex role modeling (Balswick & Avertt, 1977). We will observe in the next few chapters on nonverbal communication that women actually use more expressive facial gestures than do men. In this case, the nonverbal mode complements the verbal.

Women are more supportive conversationalists (Thorne & Henley, 1977). In a study which used male-male dyads and female-female dyads, the researchers determined that the female dyads were more affiliative and socially expressive than were the male dyads. The women used more expressions of positive affect and laughed more than did the men (Ickes, Schermer & Steeno, 1979). A number of studies have implied that women are far more concerned with the internal psychological states of the other communicators than are men (McMillan, Clifton, McGrath, & Gale, 1977). Female supportiveness and compliance also reveals itself in women's perceptions of their communication. In a study of mixed-sex dyads, women expressed satisfaction with their interactions even though they contributed less (Hilpert, Kramer, & Clark, 1975).

An interesting investigation of adolescents on a co-ed 3 week bicycle trip was conducted. In this study, females were more likely than males to offer verbal support and comfort; however, males were more responsive when the situation required physical assistance. Although it was not observed that the males and females actually differed in their camping abilities, males were perceived as the more competent campers. The researchers concluded that in tasks requiring physical assistance, males may have taken the initiative and females may have deferred because they shared the perception that males were more competent (Zeldin, Small, & Savin-Williams, 1982).

Women and men have different perceptions of their own communicator style. Women perceive themselves to have higher levels of animation than do men, while men perceive themselves to be more precise than do women. Men and women do not differ in their perceptions of their levels of being open, contentious, dramatic, dominant, relaxed, friendly, attentive, or in their leaving impressions (Montgomery & Norton, 1981). Similarly, communicator style appears to be related to psychological sex-type, although some questions about the meaningfulness of this relationship have been raised (Talley & Richmond, 1980).

Differences also occur in the perception of the communication behaviors of female and male managers. Female managers were viewed as more receptive to employees, more encouraging, more willing to give information and more concerned with happy interpersonal relationships than were male managers. The female communication style was perceived as more attentive than that of the males who appeared as more dominant, directive and quicker to challenge the ideas of other people. The researchers who conducted this study believe that female management style is hypothetically more conducive to good employee morale. They conclude that the female managers in this study are perceived as more effective than the male managers (Baird & Bradley, 1979), but we should observe that the research does not suggest that the female style is *actually* superior.

We stated above that females tend to be more compliant in their communication behavior than are men; similarly, women are higher in conformity. Women appear to be more concerned with the other person's feelings than with holding and stating a position on a specific issue. Some researchers have stated that differences between women and men in language usage imply that women are less secure than men, not that they are more responsive to feelings (Brower, Gerritsen, & DeHaan, 1979). Later in this chapter, we will discuss some of the reasons which may account for male/female language differences.

Substantive differences

In order to organize the language differences that appear to occur between women and men in a useful way, we have categorized them into substantive differences, structural differences, and a category of differences which appear to be hybrids of these two. We will call this third category substantive differences merging into structural differences and will consider it between the other two categories for proper placement. Substantive differences are those modifications or variations that occur within messages; they may be thought of as the differing words or vocabularies used by men and women. Structural differences include the frequency of times that someone talks, how long each person talks, how willing an individual is to yield the floor, and how each person was able to secure his or her turn to talk. When we refer to substantive differences merging into structural differences, we include such features of a conversation as questioning, controlling the topic of the conversation, and offering compound requests. Let us first consider substantive differences.

Vocabularies

Women and men appear to have different working vocabularies as they make distinctive lexical choices. A recent study added behavioral verification to Lakoff's (1975) hypothesis that men and women make differing lexical choices (Crosby & Nyquist, 1977). Men use more colloquial or nonstandard forms than do women (cf. Graves & Price, 1980).

Another difference in the language of women and men concerns color terms. Before you continue reading this chapter, ask a friend of the opposite sex to name the colors of ten items in the room. At the same time, when she or he is writing down her or his perceptions, write down your own color descriptors for the same items. Compare your lists. You may find that they conform to the research findings in this area. Lakoff (1975) noticed that women appear to have a far more discriminating set of names for colors than do men. Words like "puce," "chartreuse," "mauve," "ecru," and "teal" are more likely to show up in a conversation among women than among men. Specific career lines make great use of color, however, and it would not be surprising for a person in interior design, painting, or other creative fields to be sharply aware of these colors, regardless of this individual's sex. We may also see an alteration in the awareness of colors by men in the future. While women use more exotic or "fancy" words for colors than do men, younger men tend to use more discriminating or elegant words than do older men (Rich, 1977). In other words, younger men who at this time do not have the same vocabulary for colors as do women are making strides in learning and becoming aware of far more than were their predecessors.

Men and women do not discuss male and female body parts nor intercourse in similar language. Two researchers asked respondents to identify the terms that they would use to describe male genitals, female genitals, and copulation in each of four contexts—in informal conversation in a mixed-sex group, in informal conversation in a same-sex group, in private conversations with their parents, and in private conversations with a lover or spouse. They found that norms concerning sexual terminology did differ according to the context, with the most limited, most "clinical," terminology being used by both sexes in the "parent" context. Female subjects used a more limited vocabulary in all contexts than male subjects. Both sexes were more hesitant to name female than male genitals. Males used more "power slang" in discussing genitals and copulation, such as "my weapon," "my pistol," and "bolt action;" they were more verbal and employed greater variety in terms. Females used more clinical terms and more often manifested vagueness or made no response. The researchers speculate that the differences in terms between the two sexes may lead to confusion. In addition, women may feel more discomfort about their own sexuality and that of others than do men (Sanders & Robinson, 1979).

A more recent study replicated this investigation and provided more information. Simkins (1982) asked undergraduate students the terms they would use to describe female genitalia, male genitalia, and sexual intercourse in the same four settings used by Sanders and Robinson. Simpkins found that men and women tended to use formal terminology in mixed company and with parents. With same-sexed friends, males used colloquial terms for all three concepts, while females retained more formal terminology. In discussion with a spouse or lover, both males and females used formal terminology for the female genitalia; females retained a preference for formal terminology for male genitalia while men used more colloquial terms; both males and females used colloquial terminology for sexual intercourse.

A useful sidenote to this research is provided by Otto Jespersen, who wrote a classic text on language in 1922. Jespersen included a chapter on sex differences in language. Excerpts from the chapter are quoted, sometimes out of context, to illustrate how far we have come in eradicating language differences between women and men, or how little distance we have traveled in altering linguistic patterns between the sexes. Jespersen contends that men are the innovators of language and that they have far more words than do women. Although we can only speculate on the number of words which men and women each "possess," it is apparent that the two sexes tend to use different words.

Hostility, profanity, and expletives

Men appear more likely than women to use hostile words, profanity, and expletives. In 1975, Lakoff speculated that women are less likely to use profanity than are men. More recently Staley tested Lakoff's assertion and found significant results. She asked students who were ages 18–47 to respond to a questionnaire listing a series of emotional situations. For each situation, the respondents were to report the expletive they would use, the expletive which they predicted a member of the opposite sex would use, and to define each expletive they provided. Males and females averaged about the same number of expletives per questionnaire. A great difference in predicted response was observed; however, men predicted fewer expletives for women and women predicted more expletives for men. In addition, men predicted weaker expletive use by women. Both sexes judged female expletive use as weaker than male expletive use, even when the terms were identical. Both sexes viewed the expletives as devoid of literal meaning (Staley, 1978).

In the case of expletives, our stereotypes are not keeping pace with our behavioral practices. Men and women engage in similar behavior, yet they are judged to behave differently. The same situation may be true for modifications in hostile language since the most recent study was done in the early 1970's. At that time, females were found to use fewer hostile verbs than males. The researchers concluded that males are less inhibited in expressing hostility, although group pressure or social context may also influence the use of hostile

For each of the following words or groups of words, write at least one *euphemism,* a substitute word or phrase which is less offensive, and one *dysphemism,* or substitute word or phrase which is considered to be more offensive. Circle those euphemisms and dysphemisms that you are likely to use in conversations with others. Compare those terms that you have circled with others. Do you perceive any female/male differences? For instance, did the men tend to circle more *dysphemisms* than the women or did the women tend to circle more euphemisms than the men? What conclusions can you draw?

Word or Phrase	Euphemism	Dysphemism
1. Old person		
2. Poor person		
3. Woman		
4. Man		
5. Child		
6. Housecleaner		
7. Father		
8. Mother		
9. Professional athlete		
10. Secretary		
11. Old woman		
12. Old man		
13. Cab driver		
14. Female teacher		
15. Male teacher		
16. Waitress		
17. Waiter		
18. Female date		
19. Male date		
20. Black person		

verbs by men (Gilley & Summers, 1970). In the intervening 15 years since this study was completed, females may have increased their use of hostile language.

At the same time that Jespersen (1922) was describing male language as consisting of more vocabulary than female language, he was describing female language as that which included the most "decent words" and frequently included euphemisms. The notion that women would use more *euphemisms,* inoffensive words which are substituted for offensive terms, than men is parallel to the idea that men use more *dysphemisms,* offensive words which are substituted for inoffensive words. Although this conclusion is consistent with men using more expletives, more slang terms, and perhaps more hostile verbs, these findings are not stable. Instead, language may be changing in these areas for both men and women; in any case, we have little empirical verification for concluding that women do indeed use more euphemisms than do men.

Hypercorrection

Lakoff (1975) also hypothesized that women engage in *hypercorrection,* or reminding people of correct forms when they make errors. For instance, hypercorrection would occur if a person asked another, "You mean 'lie' instead of 'lay,' don't you?" "Do you mean *set* the glass on the table?" or "When are *she* and *he* coming?" Crosby and Nyquist (1977) demonstrated that women do tend to engage in hypercorrection more than men. We will note in chapter 8 that women are more likely than men to pronounce words correctly and to use the complete "ing" ending of a word while men are more likely to mispronounce words and drop the final "g" of words which end with "ing." This correctness in pronunciation is parallel to women's greater likelihood to correct others; men's incorrectness in pronunciation makes them more likely candidates for correction.

Intensifiers, hedges, fillers and qualifiers

Women appear to use more intensifiers, hedges, fillers, and qualifiers than do men. Adverbs like "so," "such," "quite," and "awfully" are examples of *intensifiers* which women appear to use more than men (Key, 1972; Lakoff, 1975; Jespersen, 1922). One behavioral study which employed small groups of five to seven people found that women in all-female groups used six times more intensifiers than did men. In mixed sex groups, women used fewer intensifiers than women in same sex groups; however, in mixed sex groups, women used five times as many intensifiers than men in the mixed sex groups (McMillan, Clifton, McGrath, & Gale, 1977).

Hedges, or *qualifiers,* are words which modify, soften, or weaken other words or phrases. Hewitt and Stokes (1975) explain that hedges indicate the tentative nature of a statement or indicate some measure of uncertainty about the other person's response to it. Examples of such words and phrases are "maybe," "perhaps," "somewhat," "you know," "in my opinion," "it seems to me," and "let's see." When qualifiers or hedges are added to otherwise direct statements, such assertions become weakened and sound more tentative. For instance, imagine a parent scolding a child, "You should never touch a hot stove," compared to "Possibly you should never touch a hot stove." Or, contrast the woman who tells her date, "It's time to go," with her friend who states, "I guess it's time to go." Would you respond differently to your supervisor if she or he directed you to "Come into my office," than if the message was "Perhaps you could come into my office." Crosby and Nyquist (1977) found that adult women use more hedges or qualifiers than do men, but Staley (1982) did not find any gender differences in the use of hedges by children aged 4, 8, 12, and 16. Staley observes that language behavior in society may be in the process of change and that linguistic sex role stereotyping may not be as predictable as it has been.

Disclaimers are a special class of hedges. Disclaimers are words or phrases which weaken or disparage the speaker's request or statement. The disclaimer suggests that the speaker is not serious, sincere, or very interested in his or her request. For instance, a person might say, "If you don't mind, could we . . . ," "I know this will sound unreasonable, but would you . . . ," "I hope you don't think I'm being unreasonable, but would you . . . ," or "Of course I don't know anything about politics, but I think. . . ." Persons who use disclaimers put the other person in an awkward position. The respondent does not know how he or she is to respond to the request or the information. If one acts upon it, he or she may be told later that the speaker said that it was unimportant or that one was being unreasonable; if the listener fail to act upon it, the speaker might say that he or she had made a request. Disclaimers confuse communication between two people and weaken the messages we send to others.

Verbal fillers and *vocal fluencies* frequently occur in our communication with others. Verbal fillers are those words or phrases that we use to fill in silences such as "like," "right," "okay," "well," and "you know." Vocal fluencies include uncodified sounds like "mmh," "ahh," and "eh" which are used for the same purpose. We are sometimes afraid of allowing a silence to occur when we are talking, so that we fill in the blanks with fillers or fluencies. Hirschman (1975) found that when women talk to men in two-person interactions, women use more fillers than do men. Women used fewest fillers when they were engaged in conversations with other women, although even here they used more fillers than did males in same-sex pairs.

Let us summarize the substantive language differences between women and men. First, they make different lexical choices or use different vocabularies. Women tend to use more formal terms, while men use more colloquial forms. Men use more hostile words, profanity, and expletives. Women engage in more hypercorrection than men. Women use more intensifying modifiers than do men, as well as more verbal fillers. In general, women appear to be more precise, more proper, and more polite than men. Although men and women exhibit substantive language differences, we may be perceiving far greater differences than those which actually occur. Our usage of language is constantly in flux, and men and women appear to be using more similar forms; at the same time, our perceptions of those forms tend to be somewhat outdated and stereotypical. Thus, our perceptions of language differences do not appear to be keeping pace with actual practice.

Substantive differences merging into structural differences

When we discuss structural differences in conversations, we are referring to a number of different components. Zimmerman and West (1975), for example, thought that the basic structure in a conversation must include the assumptions that usually one person speaks at a time and that generally people alternate as speaker and listener. We can thus discuss conversations from the point of view of "taking turns": how many turns each person took, how long each one's turn lasted, how willing each individual was to allow another to have a turn, and how each was able to secure his or her turn.

The notion of turns and taking turns is neither complex nor difficult to understand. At a noisy dinner table it is not unusual for children as young as two or three to tell others to be quiet because it is their turn. One of our children remarked to his garrulous grandmother that she had taken two turns when she had spoken and now was required to listen to him for two turns before she could again proceed. Although the notion of dividing conversations into turns is elementary, it is very useful.

When we examine taking turns in conversations, we find that all people do not take the same number of turns, that some tend to take far longer turns than others, that people challenge each other for turns, and that some people have definite ideas about who has the right to take a turn. Turns alternate very quickly. Anyone who has been associated with the threatre, radio, or television knows that silences generally do not occur after one person has spoken and before the next person begins to speak. When we are engaged in a conversation, we are typically ready to speak the moment the other person stops. Speakers generally provide us with transition cues which indicate that they are about to conclude their message and we can begin ours. Sometimes those cues are not present, however, or we do not notice them, so that two people are speaking at once, or no one is speaking.

When we examine language differences between women and men, we find that some variations are easily categorized as substantive differences while others are as readily classified as structural differences. At the same time, some differences appear to fall between these two categories. Substantive differences appear to merge into structural differences. For example, when sex differences are found on questioning-asking, are we considering structural or substantive differences? The substance of a comment is changed if it is phrased as a question rather than as a declarative statement; but the structure of the interaction is also affected as it calls for a comment from the other communicator. In this section of the chapter, we will consider a number of such sex differences in communication, including compound requests, tag questions, the use of questions, the final word, and the control of the topic of conversation.

Compound requests

When we make a request of another person, we may do so in a direct manner or we may add qualifiers and other terms to soften the request. If you wish to have someone come closer to you, you may simply say, "Come here." On the other hand, you may add, "Please come here," or "Would you please come here," or "If you don't mind, would you please come here." In each case, you are adding words and phrases which soften the request. If you use the command, "Come here," you are making a direct request or giving a direct order; if you use any of the other longer forms, you are making a *compound request*.

What are the effects of compound requests? They tend to sound more polite and less demanding than direct requests. At the same time, they sound tentative. If you ask someone to behave in a certain way, "If you do not mind," "If you would," or "If it would not inconvenience you," you appear to be asking them a question in which a choice is possible, rather than making a request of some action that you wish to have accomplished. Propriety and politeness are acquired at the expense of being misunderstood or not achieving your goal.

Compound requests are viewed as less assertive than direct requests or orders, and they are viewed as feminine linguistic forms (Newcombe & Arnkoff, 1979). Apparently women use compound requests more frequently than do men (Thorne & Henley, 1975; Zimmerman & West, 1975). Women are more likely to ask others to do things for them with more words than their male counterparts would use. Though women may be viewed as more polite in their requests, they may find that they do not always obtain the action or response which they are seeking.

Tag questions

Tag questions occur when we make a declarative statement, then follow it with a question relating to the same statement. For example, "It's really hot in here, isn't it?" "This is a good movie, don't you think?" and "They are all going out to dinner, aren't they?" are all tag questions. We sometimes use tag questions when we are not sure of information. If someone has told you something that you did not hear completely, or if you have reason to believe that a situation has changed, you might inquire, "You're going to attend U.S.C. this fall, aren't you?" We also use tag questions when we are trying to elicit information from another person, when we are attempting to obtain an answer to a question, or when we are trying to strike up a conversation. We might ask, "Texas is really lovely at this time of the year, isn't it?" "The game between Michigan State and Iowa was interesting, wasn't it?" or "This party is pretty dull, don't you think?" Finally, we use tag questions when we are attempting to persuade someone to accept or share a belief which we hold. You might suggest to your spouse, "Playing cards with the Millers tonight sounds like fun, doesn't it?" You might ask one of your parents, "The tuition at Georgetown is really expensive compared to Princeton, where I want to go, isn't it?" To a friend you might say, "I can borrow your brown suit for my job interview tomorrow, can't I?"

Tag questions are clearly less assertive than declarative statements; moreover, tag questions are viewed as being part of the female's linguistic repertoire rather than the male's language usage (Newcombe & Arnkoff, 1979). Early research in this area indicates that women make more frequent use of tag questions than do men (Zimmerman & West, 1975). In actual communication situations, women use twice as many tag questions as do men. In mixed sex groups, women use three times as many tag questions as men. Women in mixed sex groups also used three times as many tag questions as women in all female groups (McMillan, Clifton, McGrath, & Gale, 1977).

Men in a professional meeting used far more tag questions than did the women who were in attendance. The context in which such questions are used should be considered in order to determine whether they are more likely to be used by men or by women. Tag questions do not necessarily indicate condescension; they may indicate simple requests, be used to forestall opposition to the speaker's statement, or function as requests for agreement or confirmation (Dubois & Crouch, 1975). Thorne (1981) also views tag questions as a contextual variable. She suggests that women may use tag questions in conversations with men in order to draw men out. Men are somewhat uncommunicative so that women may feel obligated to do the "embroidery" or "dirty work" in conversations. In other words, tag questions may not be a sign of uncertainty, but rather may indicate an interest in continuing a conversation.

Women may ask tag questions in order to engage the other person in talking to them and give them an opportunity to look at the other person, listen actively, and contribute feedback.

A recent examination of tag questions yielded some disturbing results. In this investigation, tag questions were detrimental only when they were used by women. In general, women who used certain devices, including tag questions and disclaimers, were perceived to have little knowledge, little intelligence, and little influence. The same negative effect was not produced by men who used tag questions and disclaimers (Bradley, 1981). This study implies that the linguistic devices which women have traditionally used may not be the significant elements in the devaluation of women's language; rather, the lower status of the women may be the relevant factor. Women who use tag questions are underestimated because of their biological sex rather than because of their linguistic style.

Tag questions may place the speaker in a subservient position or they may be functional in a conversation. Sometimes women appear to use tag questions to demonstrate concern for another person, and not because they perceive themselves as subservient. Nonetheless, others may perceive them to be subservient, even though this is not their intent.

Another linguistic style which is sometimes an appropriate, effective substitute for the tag question is the statement followed by a question relating to the other person's perceptions. Instead of using the tag question, "The University of Kansas really has a great number of courses in interpersonal communication, doesn't it?" a person may say, "The University of Kansas really has a great number of courses in interpersonal communication. Were you aware of that?" Instead of stating, "This is delicious lasagna, isn't it?" you might assert, "I think this lasagna is delicious. What's your opinion?" In each case, you clarify your own perceptions and still invite the opinion of the other person. At the same time, you are not compromising your own point of view; in other words, your perception of the university or of food may be different from that of your partners. The use of the statement followed by a question may be considered a useful addition to your behavioral repertoire. It is especially helpful when you are actually using tag questions to express your own opinions or feelings.

Questioning

Do women or men ask each other more questions? Sometimes men ask women more questions than women ask men. For instance, in a study of interaction among male-male dyads and female-female dyads, a greater proportion of the women's comments consisted of answers to questions than did the men's comments (Rosenfeld, 1966). In an analysis of the conversations of three middle-class couples between the ages of twenty-five and thirty-five, the women used three times more questions than did the men (Fishman, 1978). Thus, it is not clear which sex asks the other more questions.

Perhaps more useful than merely trying to determine whether questions are asked more frequently by one sex than the other is consideration of the rationale for asking questions. Eakins and Eakins (1978) state that asking questions and interrogating people are associated with behavior of the superior, while acquiescing or replying is often considered to be the behavior of a subordinate. We know that sharing personal information about ourselves, self-disclosure, which we discussed in chapter four, can be perceived as the loss of a resource, when viewed negatively. In other words, when we tell others about ourselves, we are providing them with information which they can use. As we discussed in chapter four, women tend to provide more information about themselves than do men. The idea that women disclose morethan men is related to the fact that they are asked more questions.

In those instances in which we determine that men ask more questions, we may hypothesize that this is done to gain information, and in a sense, to acquire power. On the other hand, men may be asking questions because they are interested in the other person. Similarly, either consciously or subconsciously women may answer questions in order to demonstrate subservience, or they may reply to questions because they enjoy interacting with others. Question asking and answering can be part of a power struggle in conversational interaction, or it may be a functional method of communicating, as in the interviewing process.

How can we explain the large number of questions women ask in established relationships compared to men? Fishman (1978) theorizes that women ask questions in order to elicit verbal responses from men. Frequently women preface their comments with phrases such as "Do you know what?" in order to gain a response from men. In these instances, they may be attempting to gain a "What?" or similar response which serves, in effect, as permission to speak.

The inconsistent findings on questioning and the alternative explanations for these differences disallow clear prescriptions regarding the use of questions in interactions. Nonetheless, to the extent that differences occur between men and women, we need to be cautious about behaving in traditional, stereotyped ways. If you are a woman, consider the questions you are asked before responding freely, then try to determine the purpose of prefacing comments with a question. If you are a man, consider the appropriateness of the questions which you would like to ask, and your own sensitivity in responding to the questions asked of you.

In order to give you the opportunity of developing alternatives to some of the linguistic forms discussed in this section, complete the following exercise. Enter the requested response in each of the spaces provided:

1. Imagine that another person has entered the room and left the door open rather than shutting it (as it was before he or she entered). You wish to have the door closed.

    DIRECT REQUEST: _____

    _____

    COMPOUND REQUEST: _____

    _____

2. You are seated at dinner and no one has passed the salt and pepper. You would like to season your food.

    DIRECT REQUEST: _____

    _____

    COMPOUND REQUEST: _____

    _____

3. You are attempting to maintain a conversation with another person who is quiet. You know that the other person attends an out of state college and you decide to discuss college life.

    TAG QUESTION: _____

    _____

    DECLARATIVE STATEMENT: _____

    _____

    DECLARATIVE STATEMENT FOLLOWED BY A DIRECT QUESTION: _____

    _____

4. The person with whom you are speaking has made a very negative statement about people with your ancestry. She or he does not know that you are a member of the group and you do not wish to disclose the information. However, you do want to indicate to this person that his or her perceptions may be incorrect.

    TAG QUESTION: _____

    _____

    DECLARATIVE STATEMENT: _____

    _____

    DECLARATIVE STATEMENT FOLLOWED BY A DIRECT QUESTION: _____

    _____

5. The other person in a conversation has asked you a highly personal question which you feel uncomfortable answering. Provide a response which would allow you to refuse to answer the question without offending the other person:
DIRECT STATEMENT: _____

DIRECT STATEMENT PREFACED BY A QUESTION OR QUESTION FORM SUCH AS "DID YOU KNOW?" _____

_____

6. You are attempting to talk to a new acquaintance about a matter of importance to you, but he or she is not responding to you. Your desire is to continue the conversation.
DIRECT QUESTION: _____

DECLARATIVE STATEMENT FOLLOWED BY A DIRECT QUESTION: _____

DIRECT STATEMENT PREFACED BY A QUESTION OR QUESTION FORM SUCH AS "DID YOU KNOW?" "DID YOU HEAR?" OR "GUESS WHAT?" _____

7. You are interviewing a potential employee. You need to ask this person about his or her experience.
DIRECT QUESTION: _____

TAG QUESTION: _____

DECLARATIVE STATEMENT FOLLOWED BY A DIRECT QUESTION: _____

8. You are talking with someone you recently met and she or he tells you about something that is unfamiliar to you, but which you would like to learn about.
DIRECT QUESTION: _____

TAG QUESTION: _____

Control of the topic

In *Through the Looking Glass,* this conversation between Alice and Humpty Dumpty occurs:

> "I don't know what you mean by 'glory'," Alice said.
>
> Humpty Dumpty smiled contemptuously. "Of course you don't—till I tell you. I meant there's a nice knockdown argument for you!"
>
> "But 'glory' doesn't mean 'a nice knockdown argument'," Alice objected.
>
> "When I use a word," Humpty Dumpty said, in a rather scornful tone, "it means just what I choose it to mean—neither more nor less."
>
> "The question is," said Alice, "whether you can make words mean so many different things."
>
> "The question is," said Humpty Dumpty, "which is to be master—that's all" (Carroll, 1965).

Although Humpty Dumpty was referring to the definition of words, his point is useful as we consider topic selection in conversations. Thorne (1981) asserts that the real power in controlling the topic of a conversation is the power to define reality.

Male-male, female-female, and male-female dyads have been investigated to determine patterns of topic change. Males, in male-female conversations, appear to assert strongly their claim to control topics (Zimmerman & West, 1975; Fishman, 1977, 1978). Male-female dyads in developing relationships do not talk as long about a topic as do two people of the same sex. In addition, male-female dyads use different strategies to change the topic. They tend to use more abrupt and direct methods, which may indicate that they are attempting to avoid over-commitment. Men, in male-male dyads, tend to use more indirect and gradual methods of topic change, that is, procedures which could be associated with a relational control process. Men may wish to avoid confronting the issue of who is to control the change of topics within conversation in male-male dyads (Ayres, 1980).

Associated with topic changes are the topics to which the conversation is changed. Four, 8, and 12 year-old males make more references to sports and specific locations while females of the same ages make more references to school, items they wish for, their needs, and their identity (Haas, 1981). Kelly, Wildman, and Ural (1982) contend that the use of male stereotypical topics may inhibit females from participating in conversations. Thus, both the content and the structure of the interaction encourage male control of the conversation.

Topic control is accomplished in a variety of ways. Among the more common are minimal responses to the other person's comment, silence, and interruptions. Delayed responses are also used to bring a topic to its conclusion, and if a theme is repeated too aggressively, you may decide to stop communicating with the other person: Walk away, say nothing, or look away from the other individual. In any event, keep in mind that in order for another person to control the topic, you must be willing to "relinquish the floor." The other person cannot control the subject of conversation unless you allow it to occur.

We can now summarize the material in this section on substantive differences merging into structural differences. Women make more compound requests than do men. Women tend to use more tag questions than men; although in some contexts, men tend to use this construction to a greater extent. Both women and men ask questions, but they appear to do so for different reasons. Males control the topics of conversations in male-female dyads, and may use abrupt and direct methods to do so. In male-male dyads, men use less abrupt and direct strategies to change the topic.

These linguistic forms tend to weaken or minimize women's statements, but they do not lessen or impair men's statements. At the same time, many of these forms serve necessary functions in the management of conversations. For instance, tag questions result in a woman being viewed as less knowledgable and less influential; however, tag questions may encourage another communicator to continue a conversation. When men use tag questions, they are not perceived as lacking in knowledge or influence. More than in the past, men and women may be using these linguistic forms in a similar way. Nevertheless, women are provided with negative sanctions when they use these forms, but men are not.

Structural differences

We have considered substantive differences and the hybrid category of substantive distinctions merging into structural differences. In this section of the chapter, we will consider those language differences between men and women which appear to be purely structural. These include who dominates or talks more in a conversation, who interrupts, who overlaps, and how silence is used in conversational interactions.

Talk time

Who talks more, men or women? If you ask people on the street their opinion on this question, you are more likely to receive consistently incorrect responses to this than to any other question discussed in this book. One of the most popular myths surrounding male/female communication is the notion that women talk more than men. In fact, men talk more than women (Eakins & Eakins, 1976; Wood, 1966; Swacker, 1975). In a summary of the research in this area, Thorne (1981) stated that most studies demonstrate that men either talk more than women, or there are no differences between the amount of talking men and women do. She points out that no studies have demonstrated that women talk more than men. Higher status women tend to talk more than lower status women. Boys are involved in more interactions than are girls. Male students talk more than female students, particularly when the teacher is female.

Thorne's summary demonstrates that in a variety of contexts, and at various ages, men talk more than women.

An interesting study of parental interaction shows similar findings. This study investigated mothers and fathers talking with their children. The parents and their children were placed in a room and told to play with each other. At first they were told to simply interact, but after a period of time a complex toy was introduced to the situation and the parents were told to explain it to the child. Women tended to adjust their speech when talking to the children, reducing their sentence length, making their ideas less complex, including more redundancy, and offering more pauses. When the parents were free to interact with the children, before the toy was introduced, the mothers and fathers talked about the same amount. When the toy was added to the situation, the women allowed the men to talk far more. The men were treated as "experts," even though they had no more information about the toy than did the women (Golinkoff & Ames, 1979). This study implies that one of the reasons that men may be allowed to talk more than women is that they are perceived as more knowledgeable, more competent, or in some way more credible.

Interruptions

Interruptions occur when the person who is listening begins to speak before the last word that could suggest the end of the speaker's statement, question, or comment. For instance, if one person were to state, "I can't wait to tell you what my mother said", and the second person began his or her comment, "Did you talk to Professor Fisher?" on the third word of the first person's statement, "wait," we would call the second person's comment an interruption.

Why do people interrupt each other? Some persons may interrupt because they are unaware of the implicit conversational rules which imply that one person waits for the other to complete expressing his or her thought before beginning to respond. Few people, however, are really unaware of this rule. More often, individuals interrupt because they are enthusiastic about something they have to share and are impatient about "waiting their turn," because they believe that what they have to offer is more important than the first person's message, or because they feel that they are personally more important than the other speaker.

Men interrupt others more than women do, and women are more frequently interrupted by others than men are interrupted by others (Zimmerman & West, 1975; Thorne & Henley, 1975; Baird, 1976; Kramer, 1974; Eakins & Eakins, 1978). Women appear to be less obtrusive and less forceful than men in conversational dominance (Frost & Wilmot, 1978; McMillan, Clifton, McGrath, & Gale, 1977). The pattern of interruptions between men and women might be anticipated, in view of our discussion of topic control. We noted that topic control occurs, to some extent, because people interrupt the speaker. We will see that this pattern is also consistent with overlaps which we will discuss in the next section.

The unequal distribution of interruptions between women and men should immediately cause us to be suspicious. Interruptions are generally perceived as attempts at conversational dominance, since they minimize the communicative role of the person being interrupted (Markel, Long, & Saine, 1976). Whether or not the interruptor is aware of this behavior, this individual is asserting relational dominance over the other person. Less pejoratively, interruptions are sometimes perceived as methods of controlling the interaction. In the same way that people control the topic of a conversation by "breaking in," they maintain control over the structure of the conversation by interrupting. Brandt (1980) demonstrated that the frequency of interruptions is often correlated with a person's control over the direction of the conversation. In either case, interruptions serve to manage the interaction.

The same kinds of suggestions that were offered at the end of the section on topic changes apply here. If you are a person who is regularly interrupted, you should consider possible options. You can continue to talk even after you have been interrupted, you can ignore the interruption, or you can increase your volume. You can use the same tactics as the person who has interrupted you and allow him or her to talk but begin a new thought in the middle of his or her discourse. You can decide that you will not communicate with someone who continually interrupts you, say nothing, look away, or walk away from the other person. You can stop in order for the other person to present his or her message, then continue from the same point that you were interrupted, without responding to the interruption. You can describe to the other individual, in a non-evaluative manner what has occurred: "You have interrupted me three times in the last five minutes." Interruptions involve two people: the person who is doing the interrupting and the person whose statement or presentation is being interrupted. You are susceptible to being interrupted by others if you choose, or can indicate clearly that you will not be regularly interrupted by them if you find the practice dissatisfying to you. At the same time, you need to understand that your behavior will have consequences. To the extent that your communicative behavior is altered, the relationship between yourself and the other communicator is changed.

Overlaps

Overlaps occur when the individual who is listening makes a statement before the other person has finished speaking, but about the same time as the speaker's last word is uttered, or a word which could be perceived as his or her last word. For example, if someone states, "I would like to go to the movie at the Varsity tonight," and the second person responds, "Yes, me, too!" while the first person is verbalizing "tonight," the respondent's act would be considered an overlap.

Overlaps may occur for the same reason that interruptions occur: the second person believes what she or he has to add is more important than the message of the first person, or she or he is very enthusiastic about talking. Overlaps can be more easily justified than can interruptions. Often, the second speaker senses that the first speaker has about finished expressing his or her thought, and has simply begun talking a moment too soon. On the other hand, the person who overlaps may be attempting to shorten the first person's statement or may be competing for a role as speaker if a number of people are trying to "gain the floor." Dominance and control are also possible reasons why people overlap each other. Whatever the rationale, men overlap women more than women overlap men (Zimmerman & West, 1975).

Silence

A final area in which sex differences occur is in the use of silences. Zimmerman and West (1975) examined the use of silence in female-female, male-male, and male-female dyads. They found that females in female-male conversations were silent more than any other person in the various combinations.

In male-male and female-female conversations, the silences were scattered among the comments in a relatively equal manner. These researchers explained their findings by noting that most often the females who fell silent in the female-male dyads did so after one of three occurrences: a delayed minimal response by the male, an overlap by the male, or an interruption by the male. In these instances the female may have been uncertain about her partner's reaction to her comment or about the other person's feeling concerning the conversation. The less-than-positive response from the male partner appeared to affect the female's approval or enthusiasm about communicating.

Let us summarize these research findings. Men and persons of high status talk more than do women and low status persons. Men interrupt others more than women do, and women are the victims of more interruptions than are men. Men overlap women more than women overlap men. Women fall silent more often when they are interacting with men than do women or men in same-sex dyads, or than men do in mixed-sex dyads. The communicative patterns in this area imply that women are less competitive and aggressive in interactions; men appear to compete and win. Men talk, interrupt, and overlap more frequently, while women respond with silence.

Explaining differences in language usage of women and men

In our discussion of the language differences which exist between women and men, we have presented a rationale and explanations for the differences. In this section of the chapter, we will attempt to delineate three major categories of explanations that appear to run through many of them. We will consider dominance and control by men, compare men's task orientation with women's relational orientation, and then cite some other possible explanations.

Dominance and control by men

One of the most prevalent theories about male/female differences is the notion that men dominate and control in our culture. You observed in chapter three that the language that is used to discuss women and men illustrates this point very well. Researchers in other fields have observed the importance of learning about dominance and submission from our symbolic systems. Sociologist Hugh Duncan (1968) states it is axiomatic that "Hierarchy is expressed through the symbolization of superiority, inferiority, and equality, and of passage from one to another (p. 52)." He explains that individuals learn the role behaviors associated with being a superior, an inferior, and an equal. Further, he proposes that individuals move in and out of these roles throughout their lifetimes.

Interruptions, overlaps, silence, and other structural differences that we discussed in this section are difficult to deal with in conversations. In order to gain some practice in dealing with these strategies, complete the following exercise.

1. You have been talking to another person, but he or she has interrupted you three or four times. You begin again, but she or he interrupts once more. After he or she has completed his or her thought, you state:

   _____

   _____

   What do you think the other person's response would be if you made this statement: _____

   _____

2. You are disclosing some very exciting news to a friend who is uncharacteristically quiet. Each time you express excitement or enthusiasm, the friend is silent. You try once more, but again he or she is silent. You say:

   _____

   _____

   What do you think your friend would say or do in response?

   _____

   _____

3. You have met a new person and you are engaged in your first extended conversation with him or her. During the conversation, the

Although women and men do not play static roles of the inferior and the superior, a great deal of verbalization fits the model of submission and dominance. Well-known and respected writers on sex differences such as Thorne and Henley (1975), Lakoff (1973), and Kramarae (1981) have stated that the language used by women and men demonstrates a superior-subordinate relationship between men and women. For example Lakoff writes that "women's language" stems from the idea that women are marginal to the serious concerns of life. She hypothesizes that sex variations in language patterns reflect and support the different and unequal roles of males and females in our culture. Thorne and Henley (1975) write that there is an assumption that male speech is the norm, adding that male dominance is apparent in the content of the words that each sex is expected to use. Even Jesperson (1922) noted that men are the "chief renovators" of language.

other person regularly overlaps you. How do you feel about his or her overlaps? _____

What would you say or do in this situation? _____

4. In a conversation with someone you are dating, you observe that your level of enthusiasm has caused you to overlap or interrupt the other person several times. The other person finally responds by stating that she or he does not believe how rudely you are acting. How do you feel?

What do you say to him or her? _____

5. You are feeling very upset by a personal problem, and your employer initiates a conversation with you. During the conversation, you tend to be unresponsive because you are focusing on your problem. After a period of time, she or he begins to use tag questions, direct questions, and questioning prefaces to her or his direct statements. How do you respond to these questions? _____

After you observed that you were falling into silence rather than responding, would you explain your situation? _____ Why or why not? _____

Communication, we stated in chapter one, consists of bargaining, includes costs and benefits, and occurs in interactions which are either complementary or symmetrical. At this point we should add that communication allows us to control ourselves, our physical environment, and sometimes other people. During conversations, we decide to make some statements and avoid others in order that the communication will progress in the direction which is relevant to us. A number of communication theorists and researchers have dealt with the concept of control in conversations. The literature stems from psychotherapeutic sources (Bateson, 1972; Haley, 1965; Watzlawick, Jackson, & Beavin, 1967), and from analysis of on-going conversations by using behavioral category schemes (Bales, 1950; Mark, 1970).

Dominance has been investigated. *Dominance* refers to the extent to which one person in a conversation is able to control and define the position of the other person relative to himself or herself. In chapter nine, we will distinguish between dominance and domineeringness, considering the importance of these two concepts in the communication which occurs between married couples. At this point we should note that the dominance dimension of relationships has been explicated by a number of authors (Courtright, Millar, Rogers-Millar, 1979; Watzlawick, Beavin & Jackson, 1967). Zimmerman and West (1975) note that in their conversational interactions with women, men display the power and dominance which they enjoy in other contexts of their lives.

A recent investigation takes issue with this explanation of language differences. Martin and Craig (1983) coded the acquaintance conversations of 20 dyads. Their results did not clearly support dominance and submission by males and females in the mixed-sex dyads. They indicated, instead, that men and women communicate differently, depending upon the sex of the dyadic partner. Martin and Craig's research may be predictive of a new mode of communication for women and men in our culture.

Masculine and feminine behaviors

In chapter one, we considered the different notions of masculinity and femininity which we have identified in our culture. Men are viewed as instrumental, task-oriented, aggressive, assertive, ambitious, and achievement-oriented. Women, on the other hand, are seen as relational, socio-emotional, caring, nurturing, affiliative, and expressive. As we reviewed the literature on male/female differences in language, we noted that women tend to be more affiliative in their language usage (Ickes, Schermer, & Steeno, 1979), more accomodative (Brenner & Vinacke, 1979), more expressive (Balswick & Averti, 1977), more receptive to subordinates, more encouraging, more willing to provide information, and more concerned with pleasant interpersonal relationships (Baird & Bradley, 1979). These differences conform to an explanation of male/female differences based on psychological orientations.

An additional study on male/female differences also supports this conclusion. Camden and Kennedy (1982) found that graduate student women were more likely to interrupt in group settings than were graduate student men, and that interruptions were found to be an index of inadequate communication dominance. The authors concluded that interruptions may serve a healthy, functional, and confirming communication role. This study, which differs from other findings on interruptions, stresses the idea that men and women may be playing different, but significant roles in communication settings. The male style of communication may thus be indicative of a specific behavioral role rather than dominance.

A number of studies have shown that there are pervasive societal expectancies for females and appropriate role models for men (Tyler, 1965; Hilgard & Atkinson, 1967; Spence, Helmreich, & Stapp, 1975; Bem, 1974). Berryman and Wilcox (1980) remind us that societal expectations and stereotypical beliefs are relevant because of their potential prescriptive nature in determining sex role related communication behavior. Broverman, Vogel, Broverman, Clarkson and Rosenkrantz (1972) posited that sex role standards exert real influence which induce people to behave in specific ways. Rubble and Higgins (1976) maintained that sex role norms are so pervasive that in our interactions with others we are disposed to behave in sex-appropriate ways. These researchers imply that our beliefs and mythology about sex role differences in language are as important as actual differences, since the beliefs may *cause* female/male differences in behavior.

The explanation of power and dominance which we presented above has value for evaluating individuals and situations. Most people would object to one sex having access to resources or being in a position to dominate the other sex, simply by virtue of biology. This explanation is not as unequivocal as it may first appear. For instance, a person could argue that sex differences exist in language by men and women, and *vive la difference!* They may contend that an instrumental style and an expressive style are both useful in interactions. We should be careful, however, in accepting this perspective. In many ways, the stereotyped picture of women's speech and the actual differences between women and men do not help women in our culture. At this time, women do not have the same access to power in our country, such as political office, economic power, and occupational prestige. Contemporary linguistic forms are unlikely to result in gains in any of these areas. To the extent that instrumentality is highly correlated with men, and relationality is associated with women, women tend to lose.

On the other hand, some experts contend that there exists a significant subculture in our country which has a powerful system of alternative values. This subculture stresses the goals and welfare of the group, self-realization, and the importance of *who* a person is rather than *what* she or he has accomplished (Eakins & Eakins, 1978). We can argue that relational satisfaction is as important, or more important, than accomplishments and achievements. The female language style fits very well into this model, a conclusion which is supported by an investigation. Kramer (1978) found that many characteristics associated with female speech are not disparaged or rejected by women and men, but rather include numerous characteristics perceived as close to ideal speech. She contends that women's method of communicating should be viewed positively and defined as useful, rather than as the undesirable opposite of men's speech.

Alternative explanations

Biological causes

Other explanations have been offered to account for differences between women and men in their use of language. Several studies have considered physical development, biology, and genetic differences, and postulated that "nature, not nurture" causes the differences that emerge (Jonas & Jonas, 1975; Dibble, 1976). Another research study concludes by asserting that women may be superior in performing tasks which involve understanding and producing language (Maccoby & Jacklin, 1974). In other words, women are better suited to engage in interaction. Lower self-esteem on the part of women has been posited as a possible explanation for differences which place men in a dominant role and women in a subordinate one (Stake & Stake, 1979).

Can biological differences be substantiated as an explanation for linguistic differences? Hirst (1982) responds to the claims that innate sex differences exist in linguistic ability and that these differences are due to brain organization. This investigator reviews literature in the area and observes that many other predictors are more powerful than biological sex, including age of maturity and psychological sex type. The article concludes,

> It is important that researchers keep in mind the social implications of sex difference research; experiments that could needlessly produce results open to popular misinterpretation should be avoided. For example, a finding that less physically androgynous females had superior verbal ability could have easily been distorted in the press as, say, breast size determining a female's verbal ability, or worse yet, her secretarial abilities. Scientific research is not done in a social vacuum (p. 111).

Neer and Hudson (1983) demonstrate behaviorally that gender differences are not consistently evident in the communication role preferences of women and men, a conclusion which provides further evidence against biology offering a parsimonious explanation for linguistic differences.

Thorne (1981) also disagrees with the biological explanations of linguistic differences between women and men. She asserts that women are always devalued and that the differential findings on male/female communication styles are caused by differences in evaluation. In other words, even when women and men behavior *similarly* in conversations, people perceive them as behaving differently simply because they are women *or* men. Thorne's statement suggests that regardless of research findings, women and men may, in fact, be more similar than they are different.

Understanding and conforming to communication rules

Women and men may exhibit differences in their verbal communication because of a difference in the way they understand and are willing to conform to communication rules. Shimanoff (1980) proposes that communication can best be understood as consisting of rules. She explains that some communication rules are explicitly stated, while others are unstated and implicit. The implicit rules are identified by observing communicative behavior. In order for a person to behave in accordance with a communicative rule, she or he must know the rule, that is, be able to distinguish between behavior which would conform to it and behavior that would be inconsistent with it; moreover, she or he must be willing to comply with it. Women may be both more conscious of the "rules" of communication and more compliant in conforming to them.

Natale (1975) notes that women are more highly conforming. She explains that a person high in conformity is seeking to satisfy a need for approval and is willing to give up her or his own idiosyncratic speech behavior and adopt the speech behavior of her or his dyadic speaking partner. The more socially desirable a person wishes to become, the more willing she or he is to yield the floor to another speaker. To the extent that women offer men talking turns, for instance, they are demonstrating their conformity. Sensitivity to the situation, a willingness to conform, and similar traits appear to hold some explanatory value.

Contextual variables

The situation in which communicators find themselves may be of more importance than their gender. Fisher (1983) observed that research on gender differences had been distorted by the use of perceptual measures rather than behavioral observations, by the observation of isolated behaviors rather than more universal behaviors, and by the lack of control of the same-sex or mixed-sex composition of the groups studied. He examined the impact of sexual composition and interactional context on interaction patterns in both same-sex and mixed-sex dyads. Fisher determined that the interactional context exerted an impact on the patterns of interaction, but that the sexual composition of the dyads did not. Similarly, Camden and Kennedy (1982) found that the context altered the patterns of interaction between male and female graduate students.

Finally, variables such as the person being addressed have been cited as explanations for differences in male/female language. The sex of the addressee affects the utterances used by speakers (Brouwer, Gerritsen & DeHaan, 1979; Martin & Craig, 1983). These studies indicate that we should consider contextual variables and such factors as intimacy of the topic, duration of the relationship between the two speakers, the environment, and the speaker's ability to predict the response of the listener in order to fully understand male/female communication.

Taking corrective action

We have determined in this chapter that far more restrictions and limitations are placed on women than on men in language usage, but men, too, have distinct ways of talking. One author writes that women are cautious about their language usage today because of the hold-overs from previous times (Haas, 1979). In other words, the role modeling provided by mothers and other groups or individuals influences our contemporary behavior to some extent. Differing language systems are detrimental to both men and women since they limit their behavioral options. In addition, the divergent language systems are conducive to misunderstandings between women and men.

Should women adopt a male style? Some authors have suggested that women use male structures (Lakoff, 1975). Specific research findings support this suggestion. Wright and Hosman (1983) determined that male or female witnesses in a courtroom setting were both perceived as more credible when they used a lower number of hedges. Stake and Stake (1979) posited that in women, confidence is followed by assertiveness. They imply that assertiveness is a characteristic which women should adopt.

All of the research does not encourage women to adopt male structures. While Wright and Hosman's investigation recommended the use of fewer hedges by both women and men, they also found that women were perceived to be more attractive when they used numerous intensifiers, a traditional form for women.

Another study shows that women who appear to be confident in small group interaction exert influence, but they are not viewed as positively as are confident men (Bradley, 1980). In other words, even when women adopt male strategies and behaviors, they may not succeed. Kramer (1978) notes that women find themselves in a paradoxical situation when they identify men as their oppressors but use a rhetoric which reflects a male-oriented culture that is being challenged. In other words, oppression is viewed as undesirable by women, yet they use the oppressive techniques on others to achieve their goals. Adopting a male style, then, does not appear to be the answer, since it does not necessarily assist women to attain their goals, and indeed tends to call into question the basic assumptions and values of women.

We observed in the last section that the female style has positive attributes. Kramer (1978) determined that many female language characteristics are rated as close to ideal speech. Baird and Bradley (1979) concluded that female managers were perceived as more effective than male managers. McMillan, Clifton, McGrath, & Gale (1977) questioned whether the qualities characterizing female speech are actually perceived negatively by listeners. Mulac and Lundell (1980) demonstrated that female speakers are rated as more pleasant and more attractive in aesthetic quality than males.

Bradac, Hemphill and Tardy (1981) examined the effects of "powerful" and "powerless" speech on the attribution of blame to a defendant and a plaintiff in an artificial courtroom situation. The "powerless" style was comparable to the female style as it included hedges, intensifiers, polite forms, and hesitation forms. The "powerful" style included short or one-word replies. In one instance, respondents attributed greater fault to the individual who used the "powerful" style. These results imply that the "powerless" female style may be advantageous in eliciting less attribution of blame.

Though feminine linguistic style is not without positive attributes, it is more than questionable to recommend it as the style that should be adopted by all speakers. Earlier in this chapter, we determined that the feminine style may result in being devalued, may be less effective, and that it encourages dominance by others. The female style of communication has both positive *and* negative characteristics, so that it cannot be indiscriminatingly recommended. Men in positions of authority and power who acquired and maintained their status through "man talk" would tend to resist change. Other men may be discouraged from adopting a female style because of ridicule and denigration by others in the culture. Finally, persons who have strong instrumental inclinations, including women, would find that this style of communication was not suitable to their personality and individual style.

Women and men who wish to communicate with each other with minimal misunderstanding and with maximal effectiveness should consider a wide language repertoire, one which incorporates elements of the masculine and the feminine styles that have been outlined in this chapter. We should freely select from a variety of behaviors the appropriate cues for the situation. A woman who is dealing with a man who is attempting to control a conversation by interruptions, overlaps, and delayed responses, might adopt a similar aggressive stance rather than submit to domination. A man conversing with a woman who is unusually silent, might consider listening more than talking. Adopting a flexible stance and moving in and out of traditionally masculine and feminine behaviors is not a solution that will meet with immediate success. Men who behave in ways which are associated with stereotypical females and women who behave in a manner that is correlated with stereotypical males are still questionable characters in our culture. Nonetheless, this approach appears to hold the most promise for alteration of our language styles. To the extent that we can adapt new behaviors as necessary, we can eradicate the sexism which is harmful to all of us. Our language, as a symbol system, can move us from a social order in which discrimination is codified to a higher level of social organization in which distinctions between males and females are minimized.

Conclusions

In this chapter, we considered the differences in the language usage of women and men. We found that a number of stereotypes exist which influence our thinking about the language of women and men and that many of these attitudes are simply not borne out of the actual practices which research studies have uncovered. The literature on conversational differences is not broad, but it indicates that women and men exhibit both substantive and structural differences in their communication. There are a number of explanations for these differences; these include the culture with its underlying power structure which places men in a dominant role, the sex role differences between women and men that encourage different behaviors, and a variety of other less developed theories. Women and men who wish to communicate effectively with each other and to attain other goals as well are encouraged to be sensitive to the communication situations in which they are involved and to respond appropriately, without regard to the traditional "maleness" or "femaleness" of the linguistic act.

7 Interpersonal attraction and physical attractiveness

Introduction

In the last chapter, we began to discuss the codes individuals use in order to communicate. Verbal codes or language were the topic of that chapter. In this chapter we begin a discussion of nonverbal codes which are used in the communication between women and men. Physical appearance is frequently the first information that we have about another person, and this appears to be highly important in the communication process. Closely related to physical appearance is interpersonal attractiveness. In this chapter we will focus our attention on these concepts and attempt to determine the implications for communication among women and men.

In the past few years, a number of psychologists, communication researchers, and other social scientists have become interested in the role of interpersonal attraction, a phenomenon which, in its simplest form, may be viewed as liking or loving another person. In its more accurate depiction, interpersonal attraction is far more complicated than simply stating whom we like or love. Individual preferences vary; thus, one researcher found that the attractive person generally is someone who is kinder, more genuine, more sincere, warmer, more sexually responsive, more poised, more modest, more sociable, more sensitive, more interesting, stronger, more exciting, more nurturing, and of better character than the less attractive individual (Berscheid & Walster, 1969).

Physical appearance constitutes a significant component of interpersonal attraction and is sometimes used synonymously. Evidently physical appearance is important in our interactions with others and is a notable determinant in interpersonal attraction, since it provides the earliest information that we generally have about another person. When we initially meet others, we know very little about them and experience what Berger and Calabrese (1975) label "uncertainty." We rid ourselves of this uncertainty by drawing inferences from the physical data which we perceive; in other words, we tend to fill in unknown information on the basis of the image which the other person presents. This tendency is the perceptual process known as *closure*, which was discussed in chapter 5. You will recall that closure means that we fill in unknown areas or blanks with reasonable guesses about information that seems to complete the picture. Examples of visual closure are provided in the following figures in which we fill in the first two figures by completing the lines, and we create a cat out of the sketch by filling in the areas between the darkened areas.

An example of closure in the perception of a person occurs when we observe a women wearing a t-shirt that states "59¢," and we recognize that this symbol stands for the idea that women make 59¢ for every dollar that men earn. We assume that this woman supported the Equal Rights Amendment and is concerned about women's issues. In other words, based upon her clothing, we fill in her attitude toward a particular group. In chapter 8 we will

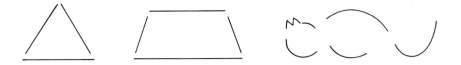

consider more extensively the role of clothing in communication, but we should recognize in this chapter that clothing provides initial information in interactions and that we recognize the cues which clothing provides in order to fill in other information about the person.

Interpersonal attraction is affected by a number of factors, some of which we shall discuss in this chapter. Further, as we shall see, physical and interpersonal attraction elicit a number of different reactions in individuals. Interpersonal attraction interacts with gender differences, and some of these findings are essential to our understanding of communication between persons of the same and opposite sex. Finally, interpersonal attraction is especially prominent in the area of romantic involvement and in understanding both short-term and long-term relationships. We will consider these topics in this chapter.

Causes of interpersonal attraction

One topic which interests many people is the consideration of those factors which contribute to interpersonal attraction. We may be interested in this area because we wish to use the information prescriptively; that is, we want the information in order to make ourselves more attractive to others. As we shall see in this section, we can alter our appearance, our personality, and certain other factors so as to appear more attractive to others. At the same time, some of the causes of interpersonal attraction remain out of our control.

Gender variables and interpersonal attraction

Biological sex

Gender variables appear to interact with interpersonal attraction. In chapter 1, we distinguished between gender, sex type, and sexism as three gender variables. Each of these has been examined as elements of interpersonal attraction. Gender, biological sex differences, do not appear to account for differences in judgment about interpersonal attraction, since women and men have similar tastes with respect to physical attractiveness (Cavior & Dokeck, 1973). As we try to draw conclusions about whether a member of the opposite sex would find someone attractive, we may look to our own assessment as a clue. Also, persons of the opposite sex may be drawing similar conclusions about the attractiveness of others.

What's Attractive to You?

You may agree with others about those characteristics which are attractive in others, or you may disagree about specific features of other people which you find attractive. Before you read the next section of the text and examine the findings of the research in this area, complete this exercise. First, mark those items which are highly essential to your decision to describe another person as attractive. Then, arrange these items from *1*, most important, to *20*, least important. After you have completed this checklist alone, discuss your responses with your friends or fellow students. How do you agree? On which items do you disagree? Why? Do you perceive any female/male differences in determining which items are important? How do you account for these?

Category	Place an "X" in blank for those items that are important to you.	Rank Order for those items that are important.
1. Attractive hair		
2. Nice legs		
3. Attractive face		
4. Intelligent		
5. Sense of humor		
6. Nice buttocks		
7. Appropriate height		
8. Appropriate weight		
9. Kind		
10. Nice chest/ breasts		
11. Complex		
12. Good to children		
13. Concerned about others		
14. Ambitious		
15. Attractive hands		
16. Independent		
17. Wealthy		
18. Attractive feet		
19. Spontaneous		
20. Conservative		

Psychological sex type

An individual's sex type appears to interact with interpersonal attraction. One study investigated an individual's sex type as feminine, masculine, androgynous, or undifferentiated and then determined her or his preference of others who were identified as feminine, masculine, androgynous, or undifferentiated. That study tabulated the following results. Women overwhelmingly preferred androgynous males in terms of platonic and romantic attraction. Men preferred androgynous women at the platonic level, but were more attracted to feminine or sex-typed women at the romantic level. Men appear to be more traditional in their attitudes toward women, distinguishing between their preferences for a friend or a lover. Individuals who were identified as undifferentiated were the least likely to be selected as attractive at either the platonic or romantic level (Kulik & Harackiewicz, 1979). Undifferentiated persons, you will recall, are those who have low levels of both femininity and masculinity. Apparently, certain levels of feminine and masculine traits are necessary for attraction, and androgyny may be the most desirable category for predicting attraction.

Sexism

Sexism appears to show some relation to interpersonal attraction. The Macho Scale, a 28-item measurement of personal differences related to sexist attitudes, behaviors, and stereotypes, was administered to a number of women and men. These people were categorized into high machos (sexist) and low machos (nonsexist) groups. High scorers on the Macho Scale reported the greatest liking for attractive people and the least liking for unattractive people. Low scorers were less affected by physical attractiveness as a determinant for liking. In addition, those who scored low on the Macho Scale were found to recall more biographical information about the person they rated, used the biographical information in making assessments of liking, and differed significantly from the high scorers in their notions of physically attractive traits (Touhey, 1979). We will observe that this study provides results which are consistent with a study reported in chapter 10 concerning the influence of sexism in public speaking criticism.

Another gender variable which interacts with interpersonal attraction is people's attitudes toward the women's liberation movement or feminism. In a somewhat provocative investigation, Goldberg, Gottesdiener, and Abramson (1975) reported that individuals who were asked to identify, from photographs, women who supported the women's liberation movement chose the photographs of less attractive women.

Another study furnished more specific findings. College-age students and persons who were older than college students participated in this second study. This time the ratings of the physical attraction of the photographed women were not related to the attitude scores of the individuals who were making judgments about them; however, the males perceived supporters negatively (unattractive) and females perceived supporters positively (attractive) (Johnson, Doiron, Brooks, & Dickinson, 1978).

Women who violate conventional sex role expectations are often evaluated more negatively than are women who behave according to conventional sex role patterns. Banziger and Hooker (1979) predicted that feminists would be rated as less attractive than people who were perceived to be nonfeminists. They further predicted that profeminist males would rate profeminist women as more attractive than nonfeminist women while nonfeminist men would rate nonfeminist women as more attractive than profeminist women. Their study confirmed the second notion, since profeminist men rated profeminist women as more attractive, and nonfeminist men rated nonfeminist women as more attractive. The first hypothesis, that feminists would be rated as less attractive than nonfeminists, supported in earlier studies, did not receive support in this study.

In some ways Banziger and Hooker's research clarifies the earlier studies and in other respects it contradicts them. These authors suggest that a "negative halo" effect, the tendency to devalue all of the characteristics of a person when you devalue one of her or his characteristics, rather than a belief in the unattractiveness of feminists, provided the rationale for their findings. They imply that association with the feminist movement produces a negative stigma, but this negative stigmatization seems to occur only with males who originally are negatively disposed toward feminism.

Banziger and Hooker's study points to another area of research in interpersonal attraction. The men in this study felt that women who supported a perspective which was significantly different from their own attitudes were less attractive. Interpersonal attraction appears to be closely associated with similarity of attitudes, beliefs, values, and other characteristics, as we shall observe in the next section.

Similarity and interpersonal attraction

A large number of studies demonstrate a correlation between attractiveness and the perception of attitude similarity (cf. Mashman, 1978; McGinley, Nicholas, & McGinley, 1978; Siegel, 1977). When a person is attracted to another on the basis of physical or interpersonal attractiveness and that individual perceives that the other person has similar values and attitudes, then the observer concludes that she or he holds consistent beliefs.

Attractiveness and similarity appear to complement each other. When we perceive a person whom we believe to be attractive, we also perceive that individual to be similar to ourselves (Mashman, 1978). Moreover, when we perceive someone to be similar to ourselves, we believe that person is attractive (McGinley, Nicholas, & McGinley, 1978; Siegel, 1977; Krivonis, 1980). Similarity lowers the uncertainty level of a situation, and a lowered uncertainty level leads to an increase in interpersonal attraction. It does not appear to matter whether these similarities are merely perceived or are real, but perceived similarities seem to have a greater impact on liking than do actual similarities.

Relationship development

Specific perceptions of similarity have been examined in a variety of contexts, including the romantic setting and between dating partners. Let us examine some of these studies. Similarity has been studied in a number of investigations in intimate communication, and appears to be a significant factor in the selection of a mate (Centers, 1972). Both similarity of attitudes and physical attractiveness affect the desirability of dating and of friendship (Black, 1974; Byrne, Ervin, & Lamberth, 1970; Curran, 1972, 1973; Byrne, London, & Reeves, 1968; Touhey, 1972).

Physical attractiveness

Similarity in level of physical attractiveness has received special attention. Early research in this area indicated that individuals would select the most attractive person they could in identifying the preferred date, but more recent research implies that an individual's own attractiveness plays a role in the selection of someone to date (Berscheid & Walster, 1974). This *matching hypothesis,* which appears to be validated, indicates that individuals select romantic partners who are similar in physical attractiveness rather than selecting the most attractive person possible.

In the area of general similarity among females and males who are potentially dating partners, two theories have competed as explanations of romantic selection. Freud developed the notion of a *completion principle* which postulates that we tend to fall in love with someone who possesses the traits we are seeking to acquire. He hypothesized that the romantic partner is viewed as a goal for which one strives.

A competing hypothesis, known as the *instrumental theory* postulates that partners choose each other because of similar qualities and characteristics. Research on romantic attraction, courtship, and mate selection reports that the instrumental theory may have more explanatory value. However, one study indicates that factors like physical appeal have an effect on initial attraction while complementary characteristics, the extent to which another person can satisfy our needs, have some additive value in understanding romantic attraction (Siegel, 1977).

In a variety of settings, similarity appears to have greater effect for females than for males with respect to *liking.* (Stroebe, Insko, Thompson, & Layton, 1971). Whether men and women are interacting at work, in dating relationships, or are considering marriage, similarity is more significant to women than to men.

Remote matters

Similarity is important in even remote matters. An investigation which considered the attitudes of women and men toward religion and toward traditional sexual standards provides some interesting findings. Individuals were presented with descriptions of opposite-sex persons who had either similar or dissimilar attitudes on one of these two subjects. Men were most affected by the similarity or dissimilarity of the women's attitudes about sexual values. They tended to like the women who had the same attitudes which they had about sexuality, more than they liked women who had the same attitudes about religion. Women's responses were different. Women were more affected by the men's attitudes about religion, and they tended to like those men who had similar attitudes about religion more than they liked those men who had similar attitudes about sexual values (Touhey, 1972). Sexuality appears to be more salient to men, while religious values appear to be more important to women.

Smoking or nonsmoking can also result in different evaluations. In general, smokers are perceived as less attractive than nonsmokers, but nonsmokers find other nonsmokers more attractive, while smokers find smokers more attractive (Polivy, Hackett, & Bycio, 1979). In other words, similarity or dissimilarity of smoking is more influential than refraining from smoking. These findings are particularly notable in view of the campaigns against smoking which have been waged in the past few years. The significance of this investigation and of the previous study on sexual and religious values does not lie in the specific attitudes or behaviors they consider, but rather in their demonstration that attractiveness indicated by similarity may include a myriad of factors.

Physical characteristics and interpersonal attraction

We have considered the role which physical attractiveness plays in dating and courtship. Specific physical factors which appear to contribute to the composite quality of attractiveness have been identified. Cash (1980) has noted a number of these characteristics, including bright eyes, symmetrical features, and thin or medium build. Facial attractiveness has been identified as a significant factor in the perception of physical attractiveness, both in social and professional felicity and in social desirability (Milford, 1978; Nielsen & Kernalegun, 1976).

Height is a physical feature which appears to affect perceptions of attractiveness. Regardless of the height of the woman, women perceive tall men to be more attractive, dateable, and likeable than short men. However, men of medium heights are considered to be the most attractive, dateable, and likeable (Graziano, Brothen, & Bercheid, 1978). The extremes of physical characteristics may not be as desirable as the normative standard. This perspective is supported by another study on height which demonstrated that

David Chan, A *Playboy* photographer, was interviewed and he discussed his selection of models for features in the magazine. He explained that he had very specific ideas about what was required in order to be a good model.

"You won't believe what I look for first," Chan stated. "I look for smiling eyes. The smiling eyes mean a lot. That's what attracts me first, then the lips and the hair, and from there I go down."

Chan said that in spite of his ideas about the importance of physical beauty, he stated that he preferred an "inner beauty."

> It's there forever, once they've got it. Physical beauty—it's here today and gone tomorrow. (O'Donnell, 1982, IC).

Do men prefer physical beauty or an inner beauty? Do women look for men with specific physical characteristics or do they show a preference for inner qualities? Examine your own experiences and try to formulate a reasoned argument for what you believe women look for in men and what men look for in women. Use evidence to support your argument in a class exchange of views or in a small group discussion. This exercise works best if both women and men participate and if each person listens to the others, as well as expressing his or her position. Try to reach some agreement in the group and explain why differences in perception occur among the group members.

friends were frequently very similar in height rather than disparate on this seemingly irrelevant characteristic (Berkowitz, 1968).

Before we leave the question of the influence of physical characteristics on attractiveness, we should consider two alternative perspectives on the importance of physical traits. Some research has implied that appearance alone accounts for the rewards received by attractive people, while behavioral characteristics such as charm, sociability, and sincerity are largely irrelevant. A study which pointed to this conclusion found that attractive men and women obtain greater rewards in heterosexual relationships but not in same-sex social exchanges (Mathes & Edwards, 1978). Another study indicates that factors other than physical attractiveness result in overall positive evaluations of persons with respect to interpersonal attraction (Smits & Cherhoniak, 1976). The extent to which other factors contribute to interpersonal attraction may be irrelevant to our discussion here; however, it is evident that physical features actually affect interpersonal attraction.

Nonverbal behaviors and interpersonal attraction

One factor which appears to influence attraction is *propinquity,* which simply refers to physical or geographical closeness. A number of studies have demonstrated that persons who are closer to each other develop more liking and are more attracted to each other than are persons who are somewhat farther away from one another (cf. Festinger, Schachter, & Back, 1950; Byrne & Buehler, 1955; Zander & Havelin, 1960). Similarly, research on *proxemics,* the use of space by people, shows that individuals are more attracted to those who sit close to them than toward those who sit farther away. (Krivonos, 1980).

However, some limitations in closeness appear evident. Norms exist concerning physical distance in social interactions, and people become constrained or ill at ease when the distance is too close just as they are disturbed when the distance is too great. Violating the norms by standing too close has a more adverse effect than standing too far away; a moderate distance is preferred by most individuals. Similarly, an investigation of interviews demonstrated that interviewers and the persons interviewed preferred a moderate degree of proximity; this suggests that very close, personal distances were uncomfortable, particularly between or among strangers (Patterson & Sechrest, 1970). Interpersonal attraction occurs when individuals choose a moderate distance at which to interact (Geldman, 1980).

In general, high immediacy nonverbal behaviors result in more liking by others (Slane & Leak, 1978). *High immediacy* behaviors include closer positions, more direct posture, and increased eye contact. When we like someone we tend to engage in high immediacy behavior with them. Moreover, when we engage in high immediacy behaviors with others, an observer typically infers that liking is present. We appear to be drawn to others whom we like and we avoid people whom we dislike.

Eye contact is evident when people are attracted to each other. We tend to look more at people we like and less at people we dislike (cf. Rubin, 1970; Goldberg, Kiesler, & Collins, 1969; Murray & McGinley, 1972; Thayer & Schiff, 1974). Our eyes tend to dilate when we are attracted to another person, and we find people with dilated eyes as more attractive than persons who do not have dilated eyes (Burgoon & Saine, 1978). In addition, eye contact relates to attraction, in that interpersonal attraction occurs when people use eye contact to reinforce the verbal message (Goldman, 1980). We will observe in the next chapter that women and men use eye contact differently; at this point, we need only recognize that eye contact, like other nonverbal behaviors, is related to interpersonal attraction.

Other nonverbal factors are related to increased attraction. People who are drawn toward each other engage in more nodding and smiling (LaCrosse, 1975). They tend to lean toward each other, maintain erect posture, and turn their bodies toward each other (Burgoon & Saine, 1978). They also tend to demonstrate similarity in clothing style (Pinaire-Reed, 1979).

Other variables affecting interpersonal attraction

In addition to gender variables, similarity, physical features, and nonverbal cues, a few other factors have been identified which appear to make some difference in the attraction equation. Among these are status, self-disclosure, positive descriptions, and interpersonal variables such as warmth. Occupational status affects interpersonal attraction. Persons who are identified as holding high status occupations are viewed as more physically attractive, more likeable, and as having more vocational competence (Hickling, Noel, & Yutzler, 1979).

Self-disclosure, which was discussed in chapter 3, also appears to affect interpersonal attraction. Persons who self-disclose too much too early arouse discomfort in others and are rated lower in interpersonal attraction (Horenstein & Gilbert, 1978).

Interpersonal attraction can be manipulated (Oliver, 1977). We can alter the amount of attraction which one person feels for another. One method of altering the attraction that someone holds for another person is through suggestion (Oliver, 1977). Another method is to offer a positive description of a person. Two researchers gave individuals a short description of an hypothetical stimulus person, then showed them photographs of the individual, and finally asked them to rate the person. People who were positively described were rated as having more social desirability and making a more favorable impression. In addition, women responded to the character information about the stimulus person by giving them higher attractiveness ratings, but men did not (Owens & Ford, 1978). Suggestion and positive evaluation of a person before meeting the individual can result in increased attraction.

Interpersonal variables are also useful in increasing attraction. Though physical attractiveness is an important predictor of interpersonal attraction, one study demonstrated that a consideration of physical features alone might not be a salient factor in all social situations. This research identified warmth as an influential factor in interpersonal encounters and indicated that additional interaction variables may add to physical attractiveness as a predictor of interpersonal attraction, or may be even more important in some situations (LaVoie & Adams, 1978). We should note that the argument about which is more important, physical features or interpersonal variables, is not salient; our conclusion from this review of literature should be that both physical attraction and variables like warmth appear to contribute to a person's attraction in an interpersonal encounter, and that these elements may have varying levels of importance in different situations.

In this section we have observed that a variety of factors contribute to our judgments about interpersonal attraction. Gender variables including biological sex, sex type, sexism, and attitudes about women and men affect interpersonal attraction assessments. Similarity of physical characteristics,

attitudes, beliefs, and values manifest a difference. Specific physical features of other persons and nonverbal behavior appear to alter our perceptions of attractiveness. Finally, factors like status, self-disclosure timing, positive evaluations, and interpersonal variables have an effect. In the next section we will examine what results when we find someone who is interpersonally attractive. As we shall observe, the research in this area is as abundant as in the area of the causes of interpersonal attraction.

The importance of physical appearance

Earlier in this chapter we stated that physical appearance is often the first information available to us about another person. Physical appearance thus strongly influences our perception of the interpersonal attractiveness of others. As we shall determine in this section of the chapter, physical appearance can not be over estimated.

Treatment of children based on physical attractiveness

Emphasis on physical appearance in our culture extends even to children, particularly to little girls, as this cartoon implies. While we may find it extremely distasteful, attention to physical attractiveness and other features of interpersonal appeal begin earlier than we realize.

Teacher preference
By the age of four, children are affected by beauty attraction (Cash, 1980). Teachers discriminate against unattractive children in favor of their more attractive students. When children are attractive, they are assumed to be more intelligent, to have parents who are interested in their child's education, and to possess a wide range of other favorable attributes (Bennetts, 1978). It appears that teachers prefer attractive children to unattractive students (Langlois & Downs, 1979).

Peer preference

Children also distinguish between each other on the basis of their physical appeal. The popular children reported in one study of nursery-school children were those who were good looking. The researchers stated that "Attractive children of either sex were perceived to be more independent, not afraid of anything and not needing help from anyone." In contrast, unattractive children were given negative evaluations; and when the nursery-schoolers were asked to name someone who scared them, they selected the unattractive classmates (Bennetts, 1978).

Another study examined Black, Mexican-American, and Anglo-American children, and found that they have similar stereotypic behavioral expectations for attractive and unattractive peers. Physical attractiveness was more influential than ethnicity in determining children's attributions and peer preferences in this investigation. Boys tended to like those who were physically attractive, while girls tended to like or dislike other children on the basis of ethnicity. In general, physical attractiveness is more important than race, and a child's perception of the physical attractiveness of other children has wide-ranging implications for friendship choices, peer interaction, and ethnic relations (Langlois & Stephan, 1977).

Behavior and attractiveness

When children misbehave, they are regarded differently if they are attractive or unattractive. When unattractive children behave inappropriately, their behavior is viewed as evidence of a chronic tendency to be bad, whereas the misbehavior of attractive children is viewed as an isolated, momentary aberration rather than a basic character flaw (Bennetts, 1978). Children who are determined to be unattractive are believed to act anti-socially and to act aggressively. According to two researchers, labeling children as attractive or unattractive and treating them differently may have some effect on how they behave. (Langlois & Downs, 1979).

The question of whether children behave differently because they are treated different or whether they are treated differently because they behave differently is difficult to answer. However, some differences in behavior between attractive and unattractive children occur. Unattractive children frequently behave in ways that are associated with masculinity, regardless of their sex, and they tend to prefer to play with masculine toys. Attractive children, on the other hand, tend to play in feminine ways and play with feminine toys. Boys who are viewed as attractive may be discriminated against by others because of their lower levels of activity (Langlois & Downs, 1979).

Finally, in a study of children who were institutionalized in a mental hospital, differences in treatment were found, based on attractiveness. The small number of attractive children received the overwhelming share of attention offered by attendants and workers. In addition, the attractive children were viewed as more mentally competent than were the unattractive children, even though no real differences in the children's mental competence could be determined (Bennetts, 1978).

Summary

Interpersonal attraction and physical attractiveness affect the way others view us from the time we are very young, and as we shall determine, this continues throughout our lives. The notion that what is beautiful is good has been examined in countless studies. Our cultural values encourage us to believe that persons have equal opportunities to succeed, that we are innocent until proven guilty, and that superficial characteristics like appearance are less important than other factors. Nonetheless, as we shall see, attractive people appear to have more opportunities and advantages than do less attractive individuals.

Evaluation based on physical attractiveness

In general, attractive people are viewed more positively than unattractive people. However, two studies do not lend complete support to this notion. In the first study, males' achievements were correlated positively with attractiveness, while female's achievements showed no relationship to attractiveness. In other words, attractive males had higher achievement than did unattractive males, but achievement showed no correlation with attractiveness for women.

In the second study, attractiveness was not associated with achievement for boys, but was negatively associated for girls. In this study, the boys' attractiveness showed no relationship to achievement, but less attractive girls had higher achievement while more attractive girls had lower achievement (Sparacino & Hansell, 1979). These conflicting findings were noted at the high school level, and thus may be better understood in a context in which peer pressure operates and popularity for girls particularly may be based on physical attractiveness rather than on high achievement.

One investigation sought to determine whether the relationship between physical attractiveness and a piece of writing that was the product of either an attractive or unattractive person. In one study, men judged an essay that was purportedly written by a female author who was either attractive or unattractive. The men rated the attractive author as significantly more talented. Women who made the same judgment rated the attractive author as less talented. When essays were reported to have been written by attractive or unattractive male authors, no difference in evaluation occurred on the basis of attractiveness (Kaplan, 1978). The positive "halo" effect which is often reported in the literature did not appear to work for men. Men appear to be judged on the basis of their work rather than on the basis of their appearance.

At the same time, when judged by females, the work of women appears to be evaluated more negatively if it is attributed to an attractive female author, but evaluated more positively when it is evaluated by males. A positive "halo" effect occurs for male judges, while women appear to believe that "beauty and brains don't mix!" Alternatively, the females may have been jealous of the attractive female author.

Another study which considered the evaluation of an essay provided different results. In this investigation, opposite- and same-sex evaluations were examined and were shown to be different. Highly attractive authors received the highest evaluations from members of the same sex (Anderson & Nida, 1978). Similarly, Lapitsky and Smith (1981) examined the influence of attractive clothing and unattractive clothing on judgments of the essays of female authors. On most dimensions, women judged the essays of the attractively dressed females as superior to those of the unattractively dressed females. These findings are surprising, in view of the research reported above, but they are consistent with the notion "what is beautiful is good." Consistently, the more people like each other and feel interpersonal attraction for each other, the more they approve of each other's lifestyle (Cohen, 1979).

Influence based on physical attractiveness

Attractiveness appears to account for differences in behavior in influencing or persuading others. When physically attractive and physically unattractive communicators delivered persuasive messages to audiences, there are different reactions. Attractive communicators achieved a greater level of persuasion than unattractive communicators. The research implies that physical attractiveness alone might not account for these results, since physically attractive and physically unattractive persons may have different communication skills and other pertinent traits which affect communication effectiveness (Chaiken, 1979).

Additional information on the correlation of attractiveness and influence has been determined: Stacks and Burgoon (1981) found that both physical attractiveness and violations of the use of physical space were sources of distraction for individuals. They indicated that attractive individuals who sit closer to, or further from, others may serve as positive sources of distraction which will lead to greater susceptibility to persuasion or influence.

Credibility

Attractive people receive higher initial credibility ratings than those who are unattractive (Widgery, 1974). Similarly, they are perceived to be more credible. Aronson and Mills (1965) found that a stated desire to influence audience opinion was more effective if the speaker was physically attractive than if she or he was physically unattractive. Gender differences may be operating, however, because physically attractive men were perceived to be more successful influencers than attractive females. Moreover, physically attractive females were perceived to be less successful persuaders than were unattractive females (Hoffman, 1977).

Gaining compliance

Related to one's ability to persuade or influence others is the amount of assistance one can encourage others to give. Nonverbal cues affect compliance behavior, as we shall note in chapter 8. Physical attractiveness also affects how others will respond to our request for assistance. Studies which deal with emergency and nonemergency situations are conclusive in demonstrating that attractive people are provided with more assistance than are nonattractive persons. (cf. Mims, Hartnett & Nay, 1975; Genson, Karabenick & Lerner, 1976; West & Brown, 1975).

Let us consider some of the specific studies. In one experiment, both an attractive and an unattractive woman asked in a neutral way for directions to a specific building on the campus of a large university. The attractive woman received far more help than the unattractive woman (Wilson, 1978). In another study, again in a neutral situation, an attractive and an unattractive woman each asked a number of different men to mail a letter for her. Ninety-five percent of the males mailed the letter for the attractive female, while only 45% of the males mailed the letter for the unattractive female (Wilson, 1978).

One investigation combined requests for help with self-disclosure. Attractive and unattractive females asked for directions to a health services building, and sometimes self-disclosed, sometimes did not. The results indicated that more time was spent giving directions when the women were attractive rather than when they were unattractive. Self-disclosure appeared to influence helping only when it is combined with attractiveness. The least amount of help was given to the self-disclosing but unattractive woman. Indeed, the self-disclosure of the unattractive woman may have discouraged further interaction from the passersby; actually, the self-disclosure may have had the appearance of initiating a relationship. The passerby may have viewed this as undesirable because of the unattractiveness of the woman (Harrell, 1978).

Avoiding punishment

People who are convicted of crimes may be viewed as a group of people who have unsuccessfully influenced others. In cases of burglary, more harsh judgments are rendered toward people who are believed to have committed a crime if they are attractive than if they are unattractive; but no significant differences occurred in a conviction for swindle if the person was attractive or unattractive (Hed & Smith, 1979). If an offender is attractive the culprit may be treated more leniently than this person would if he or she was unattractive, unless the offender is viewed as having used his or her appearance in committing a crime or in "conning" someone (Bennetts, 1978).

Changes in physical appearance affect the likelihood of an unattractive person continuing in a life of crime. A three year study of adult criminals conducted in New York demonstrated that unless the criminal was a heroin addict, plastic surgery could influence his or her future. Convicts with visible deformities had a 36% lower recidivism rate after they underwent plastic surgery than those who did not have any correction of their deformities (Bennetts, 1978).

Relationship development based on physical attractiveness

Attractiveness affects the quantity of interaction we have with others, our sociability, our friendships, our initial interactions, our dating behavior, and our selection of marital partners. We choose friends and mates of similar attractiveness (Cash, 1980). Physical attractiveness of same-sexed close friends, whether male or female, is significantly less discrepant than would be expected on the basis of chance. Persons whose appearances are alike rather than disparate tend to affiliate (Cash & Derlega, 1978).

People who are physically unattractive are actually more asocial, more socially isolated, and less heterosocially skillful (Cash & Derlega, 1978). The impact of physical attractiveness on social interaction has been examined. Over an 8-month period, first year college students were the subjects in one study.

The rationale for this study was based on the idea that many research projects had demonstrated that beautiful people are highly regarded, but few investigations have considered the effects of attractiveness on the course of everyday social life. Students kept a journal-style record of their socializing, and the researchers related their entries to the individual's physical attractiveness. They found that this trait was significantly related to the quantity of social interaction for males: attractive males had more social interaction with members of the opposite sex and less with members of the same sex. No significant difference occurred in quantity of social interaction of attractive and unattractive females. For both sexes, especially with opposite-sex interactions, satisfaction with a relationship had a positive correlation with attractiveness.

Initiating interactions

The initiation of interactions also appears to vary on the basis of attractiveness. Physically attractive males tended to have more mutually initiated, and fewer self- or other-initiated, interactions with the opposite sex. The kind of interaction in which people participate also varies as a function of attractiveness. Attractive males spend more of their interactions conversing and less in activities; attractive females also report a lesser proportion of task interactions and more dates and parties (Reis, Nezlak & Wheeler, 1980).

This study demonstrates that physical attractiveness plays a noticeable role in a variety of social interactions with others. Similarly, attractive men and women appear to obtain greater rewards in heterosexual relationships, although they do not necessarily find greater rewards in friendships (Mathes & Edwards, 1978).

Initial contacts with others, or initiating interactions, are affected by the attractiveness of the individuals involved. As we noted above, physically attractive men tend to have more mutually initiated and fewer self- or other-initiated interactions with women (Reis, Nezlek, & Wheeler, 1980). For both men and women, physical attractiveness exercises a positive influence on initial social contact among members of the opposite-sex. (Krebs & Adinolfi, 1975). Even before people interact, physical attractiveness appears to play a role, since interpersonal attraction appears to be the greatest toward physically attractive strangers (Byrne, London, & Reeves, 1968).

Relationship development

Physical attractiveness not only affects initial impressions and early interaction, it continues to play a part in relationship development. Dating behavior has been examined with regard to physical attractiveness, and this trait is found to be positively correlated with the *likelihood* of being asked for a date (Stroebe, Insko, Thompson, & Layton, 1971) as well as the *desirability* of being asked for a date (Brislin & Lewis, 1968; Walster, Aronson, Abrahams, & Rottman, 1966).

Does the gender of the dating partner alter the importance of physical attractiveness? Some research seems to indicate that physical attractiveness is an equally important characteristic which individuals look for in both men and women (cf. Walster, Aronson, & Abrahams, 1978). Other investigations have indicated that physical attractiveness is more important for potential female dating partners (cf. Krebs & Adinolfi, 1975).

Self-rating of attractiveness was determined to be related to date selection. Unattractive persons are more likely to consider other persons who are unattractive, and less likely to consider attractive individuals as a date when these interactions are compared with the choices of attractive persons (Stroebe, Insko, Thompson, & Layton, 1971). Physical attractiveness exerts an influence on whether or not a person is asked for a date and who is likely to ask that person.

Can a person be too attractive for the dating game? This might be the case. Two researchers hypothesized that both attractiveness and probability of accepting a date played a role in identifying persons who would be likely to be asked to date. They contended that a person's appearance as well as this individual's probability of being accepted were taken into account when decisions about asking another for a date were made. A date who ranks very low in attractiveness or very low on probability of acceptance would be less likely to be asked out than someone who ranks higher on these dimensions. However, very attractive persons might be less likely to accept a date because of their high attractiveness. Thus, the most likely person to be asked on a date might be someone of moderate attractiveness who was quite likely to accept. The results of this study support their hypothesis that persons appear to prefer dates of intermediate attractiveness; the findings indicate the probability of being asked on a date seemed related to these intermediate choices (Shanteau & Nagy, 1979).

We conclude this subsection on dating by agreeing with a recent researcher who examined the role of physical attraction in romantic relationships and concluded that physical attraction plays a more significant role than has long been contended (Mathes, 1975). The role of physical attractiveness in dating may be a rather superficial and crude measure, but it appears greatly to influence peoples' frequency of dating.

Marital partner choice

Although physical attraction is initially the most important factor in romantic attraction, other elements or traits become more important over a period of time. Physical attractiveness appears to play a role in whom we choose to marry (Stroebe, Insko, Thompson, & Layton, 1971), but differences in how potential partners view physical attractiveness begin to emerge. Typically, people select marital partners of the same level of attractiveness (Cash, 1980; Centers, 1972; Murstein, 1972, Murstein & Christy, 1976), but some evidence also indicates that people attempt to marry others who are, at least, better endowed, or more attractive than themselves (Centers, 1972).

A number of theorists attempt to explain whom we identify as a romantic partner. The *instrumental theory* which postulates that partners choose each other for similar qualities appears to be the most often reported when examining the physical attractiveness of couples. Individuals seem to favor attractive marital partners over unattractive ones when given the choice. In addition, within the context of marriage, feminine traits appear to be more highly valued than masculine traits (Nida & Williams, 1977). Expressive traits like understanding, empathy, cooperation, and yielding appear to be more highly valued than instrumental skills, including competitiveness, analytical ability, and self-sufficiency.

Although persons select others of equivalent physical attractiveness or who are slightly more attractive, we should not assume that these marriages are the happiest or last the longest. *Complementarity,* selecting a mate by how much she or he can satisfy our needs, is most significant in predicting success of a marriage (Siegel, 1977). Satisfaction in romantic relationships appears to be associated with an equality of power rather than desirability. Though people usually form couples with others of similar attractiveness (Murstein, 1972), similar physical attractiveness of a couple does not correlate with marriage adjustment (Murstein & Christy, 1976).

Marital adjustment can be predicted on the basis of whether the husband feels his wife is more attractive than he is (Murstein & Christy, 1976). Attractiveness is of more importance to males than to females in selecting a marital partner. Perhaps men feel more pressure to marry attractive women than women feel pressure to marry attractive men. Men are evaluated more favorably when their mates are attractive than when they are intelligent (Meiners & Sheposh, 1977). Unattractive men married to attractive women were believed to possess all positive qualities, including a good job, status, income, and intellect (Bar-Tal & Saxe, 1976).

Couples who had been married a long time were asked whether marriage partners must match each other in physical attractiveness for a successful marriage. In general, they did not feel that physical attractiveness had to be equal in order for a marriage to endure; but in this study attractiveness was reported as more important to the female respondents, who claimed that their physical attractiveness was more important to their husbands than their husbands' physical attractiveness was to them (Bailey & Price, 1978).

Perhaps ironically, unattractive females and males appear to have the happiest marriages (when compared to attractive females and males, or compared to one partner being attractive and the other being unattractive) (Bar-Tal & Saxe, 1976). Marital satisfaction appears to be one area in which attractiveness does not presage automatic success.

Liking or loving

Persons who are the recipients of our liking or loving are determined on the basis of their attractiveness. Regardless of a person's own attractiveness, the greatest determinant of how much his or her partner is liked is the attractiveness of the partner (Walster, Aronson & Abrahams, 1978). A positive relationship exists between liking and physical attractiveness (cf. Stroebe, Insko, Thompson, & Layton, 1971).

In the next decade perhaps other variables will be discovered which will help us better to understand the relationship between physical attractiveness and liking. Currently, we know that physical attractiveness appears to be as important for men as it is for women, and that it contributes to our affective feelings of liking of others (Walster, Aronson & Abrahams, 1978).

Importance over a period of time

If you are discouraged by the preeminance of physical attraction in relationship development, you may be encouraged by the findings of couples who have been dating for some time, who have been married, or who state that they are involved in a loving relationship. Contrary to expectations, no relationship between overall physical attractiveness and romantic love has been demonstrated. In other words, physically attractive persons are neither loved more by their partners nor do they love their partners more than do unattractive persons. At the same time, people who believe that their partners are the more attractive member of the two also love their partners more and indicate greater submission in their relationships than do those who believe that they are the more attractive members (Critelli & Waid, 1980). These results indicate that as romantic relationships progress, the relative difference in attractiveness between the partners may become a more important determinant of attraction than the overall level of attractiveness. Similarity in attractiveness may be more critical than physical attractiveness in marital settings.

Physical attractiveness and nonverbal behaviors

People do not treat each other in identical ways. We tend to treat attractive people differently than we treat unattractive people. Through a variety of nonverbal behaviors we appear to show dislike of unattractive people, and we show liking through a different set of behaviors. In an earlier section of this chapter, we considered the nonverbal behaviors in which we engage when we are interpersonally attracted to another person. In this section, we will consider the effect of physical attractiveness on our nonverbal behaviors; that is, we will consider how we nonverbally respond to attractive and unattractive persons.

Physical space

An intriguing characteristic was found in people's choice of space in interactions with attractive objects and attractive persons. A number of people were shown posters of both attractive and unattractive people, and the distance they stood from these posters was measured. Following this experience, the individuals were interviewed by a passer-by, and the distance they stood from these strangers was measured. In the poster situation, persons stood closer if they felt it was of an attractive person, but attractiveness made no difference in the live confrontations with the interviewer (Powell & Dabbs, 1976). Beauty, in and of itself, appears to confer a kind of status which may discourage persons from standing very close when actual people are involved. When pictures of beautiful people are involved, the status dimension seems to disappear. In chapter 8 we will further investigate the influence of status differences on the space we choose to put between ourselves and others when we are interacting with them.

Speed of pace

Related to the use of space and the choices that persons make in interacting with others is a study on the speed of one's pace. In this investigation, people who were alternatively attractive and unattractive crossed a road. It was found that when the people were physically attractive, others who were similarly crossing the street did so at a much slower pace than they did when the person was physically unattractive (Kmiecik, Mausar & Banziger, 1979). Perhaps people use a slower pace in their encounters with others in order to allow opportunity for an interaction, while they may wish to discourage interactions with unattractive people.

The use of gestures

The relationship between nonverbal behavior and attractiveness has been investigated in a study of nonverbal emblems. Nonverbal emblems are head nods, head shakes, shoulder shrugs, and indicating or signaling numbers with the fingers. Emblems are directly related to verbal communication to the extent that they convey specific ideas or messages known within a specific cultural group and elicit visual attention from those to whom the messages are directed. Thus, they serve to transmit messages in a visual medium. In this investigation, females appear to be more inclined to use emblems than are males. Further, females scoring high in physical attractiveness displayed far more emblems than did less attractive females or males who were either high or low in attractiveness (Poling, 1978). In nonverbal fashion, attractive females may be attempting to draw more attention to themselves as they provide more visual information to others.

The effects of physical attractiveness on other communication behaviors

A number of variables appear to be related to physical attractiveness, but we will only summarize a few of the findings which are most relevant to our understanding of female/male communication. Persons who are attractive also rate high in social attractiveness (Smits & Cherhoniak, 1976).

Comparison/contrast

Persons who are attractive elicit more positive affective reactions from others, but they appear to be overruled by other factors. In one study, male dormitory residents watched a popular TV show, whose main characters were three strikingly attractive females and were asked to rate a photo of an average female. These men rated the photo of the woman as significantly less attractive than did a comparable group who had not been watching television (Kenrick & Gutierres, 1980). Context and comparison affect judgments of affective response.

Judgments about attitudes

Judgments about a person's attitude and personality are also drawn on the basis of attractiveness. As the attractiveness of a photograph increased, individuals' perceptions of attitude similarity also increased (Mashman, 1978). Attractive people are perceived to have certain personality characteristics even when they do not actually possess these traits (Shea, Crossman & Adams, 1978).

The dyad

Physical attractiveness has also been examined in specific communication settings. In a dyad, or two-person group, more self-disclosure appears to be offered to an attractive person and more self-disclosure occurs from an unattractive person (Pellegrini, Hicks, Meyers-Winton, & Antal, 1978). It may be that attractive people allow their looks to speak for them and appear to have a kind of status which does not require them to share personal information with others. You will recall that we discussed the notion of status in terms of self-disclosure in chapter 4. Attractive people may have a greater degree of choice in determining with whom they will establish personal relationships and thus discriminate more among those to whom they self-disclose.

The counseling setting

In the counseling setting, attractive counselors appear to have different interactions with their clients. Specific findings in one study concluded that unattractive, nondisclosing counselors were viewed less favorably with respect to expertise, interpersonal attraction, and trustworthiness than were attractive, disclosing counselors. They were also perceived as having less empathy,

With a friend of the opposite sex (a person with whom you are intimately involved, a platonic friend, or a member of your class), complete the following exercise. First, respond individually to the items that are requested. Then, exchange papers and have the other person complete the requested items. Finally, discuss your agreements and disagreements. How do you feel about your partner now that you know his or her perceptions about the attractive characteristics of women and men?

1. I feel attractive when I wear (describe the clothing, jewelry, and other items with which you adorn yourself) _____
   _____
   _____ .

2. I feel a person of the opposite sex is attractive when he or she wears
   _____
   _____
   _____ .

3. I feel attractive when I am exhibiting the personality characteristic best described as _____
   _____ .

4. I feel a person of the opposite sex is attractive when he or she exhibits the personality characteristic best described as _____
   _____ .

having less regard for another person, and being less genuine. Persons assigned to such counselors showed signs of weaker motivation to return to the counselor and had less confidence in expecting the successful outcome of visits with them. In this study, personal self-disclosure was shown to mediate in the effects of attractiveness of the counselors. The physically unattractive counselor who carefully reveals appropriately personal feelings can improve the initial appeal to his or her client (Cash & Salzbach, 1978).

The small group

The small group has also been examined to determine the effects of physical attractiveness on the outcomes of such communication. In a study which used task-oriented small groups, with emphasis on performance/nonperformance as well as personal satisfaction, some significant conclusions were reached. No consistent relationships were found between attraction and performance, but attraction was found to promote significantly greater satisfaction in the small

5. I feel unattractive when I am wearing _____

_____ .

6. I feel a person of the opposite sex is unattractive when he or she is wearing _____

_____ .

7. I feel unattractive when I exhibit the personality characteristic described as _____

_____ .

8. I feel that a person of the opposite sex is unattractive when he or she exhibits the personality characteristic described as _____

_____ .

9. In general, I feel that the most important characteristics which people of my sex can possess, those which make them appear to be attractive to others, are (list three to five) _____

_____

_____ .

10. In general, I feel that the most important characteristics of people of the opposite sex, which make them appear to be attractive to others, are (list three to five) _____

_____

_____ .

group setting (Rosenthal, 1978). These studies of specific communication settings indicate that context may be an influential factor when we consider the effects of attractivenss on communication between the sexes.

Negative assessments

Before we leave this section on the effects of interpersonal attraction on other variables, we will offer a caveat. Thus far we have identified a variety of positive outcomes which are related to physical attractiveness, as well as a number of negative results for persons who are less physically attractive. Nonetheless, physical attractiveness can have negative effects. Persons who are particularly attractive are often perceived as self-centered, materialistic, and intimidating (Stroebe, Insko, Thompson, & Layton, 1971). However, these negative perceptions are greatly outweighed by the positive effects we have already discussed in this section; when all factors are considered, the effect of physical attractiveness is generally positive.

Gender differences in interpersonal attraction

We have considered the causes of interpersonal attraction and have identified some of its effects. During our discussion, we have specified, or alluded to, some of the gender differences that appear evident in interpersonal attraction. Let us consider some of these gender differences in a more systematic way.

Among the observations that we have already made are that men perceive supporters of the women's liberation movement as unattractive while women perceive them as attractive (Johnson, Doiron, Books & Dickinson, 1978). Women appear to be more vulnerable to changing their opinions about others based on character information than are men (Owens & Ford, 1978). Finally, attractive men self-disclose more than unattractive men, but attractive women self-disclose less than unattractive women (Cash & Soloway, 1975).

We have observed that age interacts with gender in the influence of physical attractiveness. Young boys appear to be more concerned with physical attraction in friendship choices than are young girls (Langlois & Stephan, 1977). Attractive little boys may be discriminated against by others while attractive little girls are not (Langlois & Downs, 1979). Some positive correlation occurs between attractiveness for high school age boys and their academic achievement, and some negative correlation has been found between attractiveness for high school age girls and their academic achievement (Sparacino & Hansell, 1979).

Judgments of competence and ability to influence others are affected by attractiveness. Men who judge essays purportedly written by an attractive or an unattractive female author view the essay written by the attractive author as better, while women who judge the same essays view the essay written by the unattractive author as better (Kaplan, 1978). Similarly, physically attractive men are more influential than are unattractive men, while attractive women are less influential than are unattractive women (Hoffman, 1977).

The area of interpersonal relationships, especially, exhibits gender differences vis-a-vis physical attractiveness. Women believe that their own attractiveness is more important than the attractiveness of their partners (Bailey & Price, 1978). These perceptions are probably accurate. Men more frequently reject unattractive women than they reject attractive women as marital partners. At the same time, women do not discriminate very much between attractive and unattractive men in marital partner choice (Byrne, London & Reeves, 1968). Further, marriage adjustment appears to depend upon whether the husband believes his wife to be more attractive than he is (Murstein & Christy, 1976). Finally, men who marry attractive women are evaluated more favorably than are men who do not have attractive wives (Meiners & Sheposh, 1977).

Women are more positively valued as wives if they are attractive than if they are unattractive, but they appear to be devalued in terms of judgments of writing ability, academic achievement, and general intelligence. The attractiveness of women appears to have a positive effect in traditional relational contexts, but a negative influence on less traditional behaviors. Men are viewed more highly when they "possess" a beautiful wife. Beautiful women are viewed as one-dimensional, that is, without other positive attributes. Attractive women are perceived as excelling in traditional, personal roles; unattractive women are viewed as excelling in professional roles. Only men appear to be viewed as persons who are complex enough to combine success in personal and professional spheres, whether they are attractive or not.

Before we leave this section on gender differences in interpersonal attraction, we should note that although physical attractiveness appears to be an important consideration of both women and men in their judgments about others, their concern with physical attractiveness varies in the selection of a partner of the opposite sex. As we have observed, men appear to be more concerned with the physical attractiveness of an opposite-sexed partner than are women (cf. Stroebe, Insko, Thompson & Layton, 1971; Combs & Kenkel, 1966). At the same time, the characteristics of men have been examined for attractiveness to women.

What do women find attractive in men? A cross-cultural study revealed that English, Chinese, and Indian women tended to agree upon the characteristics of men that were valued most and least. Among the most influential characteristics were height, confidence, and warmth; among the least important characteristics were age, outgoing personality, and an interesting conversational style (Thakerar & Iwawaki, 1979). In terms of personality characteristics, women describe their ideal as a man who is assertive and dominant while men prefer women who are dependent (Curran, 1972). In their stated preferences, women and men can be differentiated on the basis of what they find attractive in the opposite sex. In actual behavior, we may determine that they are really not so far apart in this dimension as we have noted throughout this chapter.

Conclusions

In this chapter, we have considered the variable of interpersonal attraction including its causes, effects, and the gender differences which appear to occur. We have examined gender variables, including biological sex, sex type, sexism, and attitudes toward the women's movement, in terms of interpersonal attraction. Similarity appears to be an important factor which influences interpersonal attraction. Physical characteristics contribute to interpersonal attractiveness; we identified some of these which seem to have a particular effect on perceptions of attractiveness. Nonverbal factors like physical closeness, positive facial expression, and similarity in clothing style affect our perceptions of interpersonal attraction. In addition, status, self-disclosure, positive descriptions, and interaction variables also induce us to conclude that another person is attractive.

We determined that physical attraction and interpersonal attractiveness result in differences in the behavior of other people. Children, as well as adults, respond differently to persons who are attractive, as contrasted with those who are unattractive. Attractive people are generally viewed more positively than unattractive people, are able to influence others more easily, and can more readily achieve compliance from others. Relationships develop differently for attractive and unattractive people, and physical attractiveness appears to be especially important in the initiation of relationships. Nonverbally, we tend to nod, smile, and establish eye contact with people we like. In addition, we sit closer, use more erect posture, and walk more slowly past those persons we find attractive. We examined other specific effects of physical attractiveness, as well, including social attractiveness, perception of attitude similarity, perception of personality characteristics, self-disclosure, and satisfaction with small group interaction.

We concluded this chapter with a consideration of gender differences in interpersonal attraction. We summarized a number of differences in the perception of interpersonal attraction by women and men. In addition, we noted that interpersonal attraction has different significance for attractive or unattractive women than it has for both types of men in relationship development, but attractiveness may be a problem for women who are attempting to establish themselves as credible and competent.

8. Nonverbal communication

Introduction

In the last two chapters, we have been considering the verbal and nonverbal codes which women and men use. In chapter 7, we considered the role of interpersonal attraction and physical attractiveness. We also discussed the importance of a variety of nonverbal cues. In this chapter, we continue our investigation by systematically considering the major nonverbal codes that women and men use: proxemics, kinesics, tactile communication, paralinguistics, and artifactual communication. These codes do not include all the possible nonverbal cues. Knapp (1980) mentions the environment, Burgoon and Saine (1978) include chronemics, or time considerations, and Malandro and Barker (1983) include both of these and add taste and smell, or olfaction. We will limit our consideration to those cues that we can see (proxemics, kinesics and tactile and artifactual communication), hear (paralinguistics), or feel (tactile communication), recognizing that we may be myopic in excluding cues which we taste or smell. We will observe that women and men use nonverbal codes differently and that they are also different in their ability to decode the meaning expressed in the nonverbal medium. Our observations will necessarily be brief, since they constitute only one part of this text; a more thorough discussion can be found in Mayo and Henley's (1981) comprehensive treatment of gender differences in nonverbal behavior or in one of the nonverbal texts referenced above.

Nonverbal communication is clearly as important, if not more important, than verbal communication. The contribution of nonverbal cues to the impact of the message varies from situation to situation. In any case, the results of research in this area demonstrate the significance of those cues (cf. Hegstrom, 1979). *How* we say something is as important as, or more important than, the verbal component of the message, or *what* we say.

Specific differences in various codes

Proxemic differences

Proxemics, the human use of space, was recognized as important as early as 1966 by Edward T. Hall in his book, *The Hidden Dimension;* it was further examined in 1969 by Robert Sommer in *Personal Space: The Behavioral Basis of Design.* These and other writers analyzed the relevance of space considerations to communication. Burgoon and Jones (1976) clarified the complex set of factors that govern proxemic usage. In the past decade, researchers have paid particular attention to the different ways in which women and men use space. In this section we will examine some of those differences.

Personal space

Two subtopics are basic to our examination of proxemics. *Personal space* is the area surrounding a person which moves with her or him. It is the amount of physical distance a person maintains between herself or himself and others. Although you may rarely consider your own personal space needs, you are likely to be very conscious of them when someone invades your space. Clear norms exist concerning physical distance in social interactions, and individuals frequently experience discomfort when others violate those norms. In general, individuals become more disturbed when others stand too close rather than when they stand too far away (Goldman, 1980). A variety of responses may occur when one individual violates the expected spatial needs of another; these may include flight, withdrawal, avoidance, and conflict (Baron & Needel, 1980). Both liking and persuasiveness appear to be positively related to culturally appropriate interpersonal spacings (Baron & Needel, 1980); however, we tend to stand and sit close to people for whom we feel interpersonal attraction (cf. Graves & Robinson, 1976; Burgoon, 1978).

Territoriality

A great deal of research has been conducted which considers gender differences and personal space. Very little research has considered a second subtopic of proxemics, and gender differences. *Territoriality* is defined as our need to establish and maintain certain spaces of our own. This subject has been investigated more with animals than with people, but actually it represents a common need for animals and people. While personal space is the area that surrounds us and moves with us as we move, territoriality refers to an un-moving area or set of areas. We establish our territoriality in a variety of ways: by fencing our yards, by moving furniture so that certain spaces are not easily accessible to others, and by leaving personal items on desks, chairs, or tables to indicate that the territory is occupied. The invasion of one's personal space may result in withdrawal or in conflict. It is more likely to involve conflict. Threats and aggression are typical responses to an invasion of territory. These threats are sometimes expressed in the form of signs that warn, "Beware of dog," "Private Property," and "No trespassing."

Territory, like personal space, is often associated with dominance and status. Women, in general, are allowed to have less territory than men. For instance, few women have a particular and unviolated room in their homes while many men have dens, studies, or work areas which are off-limits to others (Frieze, 1974). Similarly, it appears that more men than women have particular chairs reserved for their use. Women's rooms, like the kitchen or sewing room, and their chairs, are typically not reserved as exclusively for their use.

Territoriality serves at least two functions. We communicate or transfer our personal identity including our personalities, values, and beliefs to the physical environment, and we regulate social interaction by establishing barriers or bridges to communication through the communication setting. The establishment of individual territories may lead to greater feelings of personal control. To the extent that we control our environment, we feel in control of the world. Women appear to have fewer opportunities to communicate their personal identity and therefore they may feel less in control of their environment and the interactions that they have with others.

You may find that you can enhance your persuasiveness with others, and you may increase their positive regard for you by your sensitivity to appropriate proxemic behavior. However, the norms governing proxemics appear to be different for women and men, as we discover in Table 8.1.

Kinesics

While proxemics refers to our use of space, *kinesics* is the term that is used to refer to bodily movements. When we study kinesic behavior, we examine such nonverbal communication as eye contact, facial expression, posture, bodily movement, and gestures. The importance of kinesics was underlined by two researchers who have demonstrated that our faces give other people information about how we feel, and our bodies communicate the *intensity* of the particular emotion (Ekman & Friesen, 1967). As we shall determine, normative behavior in this area of communication is different for women and men in our culture.

Table 8.1 Proxemic differences of women and men

Female Behavior	Male Behavior
Women are approached more closely (cf. Leventhal & Matturio, 1980; Barios, Corbitt, Estes & Topping, 1976; Juhnke, Golman & Buchanan, 1976).	Men are approached less closely.
Women approach others more closely (cf. Fisher, 1973; Sommer, 1959; DeJulio, 1977; Giesen & McClaren, 1976; Snyder & Endelman, 1979; Argyle & Dean, 1965).	Men approach others less closely.
Women discriminate more about whom they approach (Dosey, 1969).	Men discriminate less about whom they approach.
Women's approach creates less anxiety.	Men's approach creates more anxiety (Bleda & Bleda, 1978).
Women prefer to interact side-by-side (Leventhal, Lipshultz, & Chiodo, 1978).	Men prefer to interact face-to-face.
Women are least comfortable with side-by-side invasions (Patterson, 1971; Ahmed, Krail & Leventhal, 1976).	Men are least comfortable with frontal invasions (Fisher & Byrne, 1975).
Women are more likely to be placed on the side of a rectangular table (Roger & Reid, 1978).	Men are more likely to be placed at the head of a rectangular table (Lott & Sommer, 1967).
High self-concept women approach others more closely than do low self-concept women, and than men of high or low self-concepts (Stralton, Tekippe & Flick, 1973).	High self-concept men approach others more closely than low self-concept men, but not as closely as high self-concept women.
Sociability and status of females has no effect on the amount of space they are given (Wittig & Skolnick, 1978).	Unsociable, low status males are given more room than sociable, high status males and than all women.
Women stand farther away from people who are speaking loudly (Ford, Cramer & Owens, 1977).	Men maintain the same distance away from people who are speaking loudly or softly.
Women respond as easily in close quarters as in larger spaces.	Men respond less in crowded conditions than in larger spaces (Prerost, 1980).
Women flee more quickly when invasion is accompanied by talk (Sundstrom & Sundstrom, 1977; Polit & LaFrance, 1977).	Men flee more quickly when invasion is not accompanied by talk.
Women have less territory (Frieze, 1974).	Men have more territory.

Eye contact

Eye contact serves a variety of functions. It may consist of a mutual communion-signifying glance, it may mean watchful attention, it may include brief periods of watchfulness followed by an averted gaze, or it may be an extended stare. Eye contact can signal positive affect or liking, status, or dominance; or it may serve as a regulator of communication between communicators. Let us consider each of these functions further.

Liking   Early studies demonstrated that increased eye contact often indicated liking for the other person (Mehrabian, 1971). Eye contact may express friendship or a desire for affiliation with another person (Argyle & Dean, 1965). Extended eye contact signals that you are interested in the other person and may wish to become further involved, that you will demonstrate polite attention when he or she is speaking (Muirhead & Morton, 1979), and that you wish to be attentive to the available nonverbal cues being offered (Nelson, 1981). At the other end of the continuum, extended eye contact may indicate that you wish to become more intimately involved with the other person since eye contact has been shown to be similar to physical proximity (Argyle & Dean, 1975; Thayer & Schiff, 1975). Sexual attraction is generally communicated through extended eye contact. Most men direct a three seconds-plus look at attractive women; and attractive women are usually not surprised by the duration of the look. If a look is held longer than three seconds, however, the signal that is conveyed is that of sexual interest. The look suggests further involvement (Fast, 1978).

Status   Eye contact may also be used to indicate status or to achieve dominance over another person (cf. Mehrabian, 1971; Argyle & Dean, 1965). One of the most common threat displays among primates is the extended stare (Iawick-Goodall, 1971). People also use hard stares to signal danger to others. When my older children were young, the oldest chlid was overheard to tell his younger sister, "Mom's really mad—look at her eyes!" He was referring to the long stare that he and his sister had just received and was sharing information about dominance behavior and anger which are expressed through the extended look.

  In one person staring may serve to assert dominance; when both persons in an interaction stare at one another they may be engaging in a struggle for dominance in which the last person to look away achieves dominance over the other. Children frequently engage in this form of aggression, as do their adult counterparts. Status may also be communicated to the other person by not looking at them. The apparent indifference shown by the superior to her subordinate when the superior looks out the window, glances at papers, and appears visually distracted is a clear status indicator. As we examine a variety of superior-subordinate relationships in our culture such as lawyers and clients, teachers and students, parents and children, or business managers and their

Table 8.2 Kinesic (eye contact) differences of women and men

Female Behavior	Male Behavior
Women establish more eye contact than do men (cf. Thayer & Schiff, 1975; Rubin, 1970; Russ, 1975; Ellsworth, 1972; Muirhead & Morton, 1979; Ellsworth & Ludwig, 1972).	Men establish less eye contact than women.
Women engage in a higher percentage of mutual looking than do men. (Exline, Gray & Scuette, 1965).	Males engage in more mutual eye gazing as they age (Muirhead & Goldman, 1979).
Women avert their gaze more than do men (Dierks-Stewart, 1979).	Men engage in staring behavior rather than in gaze aversion.
Women appear to value eye contact more than do men. (Kleinke, Busto, Meeker, & Staneski, 1973; Argyle, Lalljee & Cook, 1968).	Men do not appear to be disturbed by people who do not watch them.

employees, we observe the typical pattern of the subordinate engaged in watchful attention to the superior and the superior failing to reciprocate the same careful watchfulness.

Communication regulation   Eye contact also serves to regulate the conversations in which we engage (Ellsworth & Ludwig, 1972). Observing another person provides significant feedback in the communication process. Increased eye contact encourages the other person to engage in interaction, while decreased eye contact discourages him or her from communicating. Eye contact signals that the communication channel is open (Weinstein, 1973).

In addition, eye contact is used to transfer the floor from one speaker to another. Typically, when a speaker is nearing the end of an utterance, she or he looks away from the other person briefly and then, on concluding her or his comments, returns her or his gaze to the other person; this has the effect of transferring the floor to her or him (Ellsworth & Ludwig, 1972; Henley, 1977). Finally, staring can be used as a regulator of interaction. If the recipient of a stare recognizes a clear and appropriate response, she or he will increase involvement with the person who is staring. In one particular investigation, a woman supposedly lost her contact lenses and used staring behavior in order to elicit help from male passers-by. When used in unambiguous ways, the stare can arouse, elicit attention, or encourage a sense of interpersonal involvement. (Ellsworth & Langer, 1976).

Eye contact serves a variety of purposes and women and men use eye contact in differing ways. Table 8.2 summarizes those differences.

Facial expression

Facial expressions serve a number of different purposes. They provide corrective feedback to speakers, they express emotions, and they demonstrate responsiveness or involvement (Mehrabian, 1971). Smiling is one type of facial expression that may be used for a variety of different purposes. Smiling may indicate liking or a positive affect (Mehrabian, 1971; Jorgenson, 1978; Laird, 1974). People attribute many positive characteristics to others who smile; these include intelligence, a good personality, and being a pleasant person. Men who smile receive higher evaluations on such characteristics than do women (Lau, 1982).

Smiling may have a social motivation. For example, bowlers in a bowling alley smiled frequently when they were socially engaged, but did not necessarily smile after they scored a spare or a strike (Kraut & Johnson, 1979). Mothers in lower-class families were shown to smile considerably less than their middle-class counterparts. The larger number of smiles by the middle class mothers may have been motivated by the societal expectations of being a "good mother" (Bugental, Love, & Gianetto, 1971).

Finally, smiling may be a demonstration of submissiveness. In the animal kingdom, chimpanzees have been observed to smile when they wish to avoid confrontation with higher-status chimpanzees (Lawick-Goodall, 1971). Similarly, first year college students exhibit the nonverbal characteristics of low-status individuals; including an increase in smiling, while upper class students smile less frequently (McKenna & Parlee, 1979). Submission may also be shown by a raised brow while a lowered brow suggests dominance (Keating, Mazur, & Segall, 1977). Smiling may suggest that no harm is intended by the person who is smiling.

An interesting sidenote to the discussion of smiling is the wearing of beards by men. In the same way that smiles and facial expression tend to reveal one's emotions to another person, the beard serves to hide and conceal one's facial expressions and his emotions from other people. How do people perceive bearded men as opposed to nonbearded men? A bearded face is more forbidding than a nonbearded face, and an unbearded face is equated with youthfulness. Men who sport beards are viewed as independent, extroverted, masculine, sophisticated, and mature. A beard heightens sexual magnetism. One suggestion for the increase in sexual arousal is that a number of animals cannot mate unless the female is at least somewhat frightened, and the beard may serve the same function with people (Freedman, 1969).

Facial expressions are a fairly fine-tuned means of communicating nonverbally, and people may observe facial expressions more than they do other nonverbal cues. Women and men do not use the same facial expressions, nor do they use facial expressions in the same way. The article which is reprinted below discusses one difference in the way that women and men use facial expression.

Who Can Resist Smiling at a Baby?

By Dick Pothier

HAVERFORD, PA.—Who could resist smiling at cute babies and puppies?

Most men, apparently, if there is another man around.

A majority of male subjects in a Haverford College research project apparently thought that smiling at a baby or a puppy somehow made them less masculine.

The research, carried out by two Haverford College students under the guidance of psychology professor Sidney Perloe, found that male students smiled much less often and less noticeably at babies and puppies presented in a videotape if there was another man—an experimenter—present in the viewing room.

But if there were no other men present, most male subjects smiled "to beat the band," Perloe said.

Women Smile Regardless

Women tested under the same conditions and with the same videotape of cute babies or puppies smiled a lot regardless of whether a male experimenter was around during the test, Perloe said.

"We think there are certain cultural rules among men that inhibit some emotional responses in men," Perloe said, "especially a response of tenderness or affection. This may all sound theoretical and academic, but I think there is some practical significance to this finding.

"For one thing, it seems to indicate that you can change the behavior of males in all-male groups—which is often boorish, crude and insensitive—by adding the presence of a woman."

In addition, Perloe said, the human smile is the evolutionary result of facial actions among non-human primates, such as apes and monkeys, "and as such, study of smiles is an important part of studying evolutionary behavior."

"Besides, I just think it's good for people to know about this kind of thing," he said. "If, for cultural and social reasons, many males are showing an inability to express tenderness toward a baby in the presence of another male, it's just useful to know about."

The finding does not include male parents, who probably are as affectionate as they can be toward their children, he said.

Senior Research Project

Perloe, who presented the smile-research project at a meeting of the International Primatological Association in Atlanta a few weeks ago, said that two Haverford students who have since graduated—Gregg Solomon and Samuel Blumberg—designed the experiment as their senior research project.

Men smiled more often before female experimenter

The concept of "toughness" or "masculinity" or "macho" behavior is almost entirely something that concerns men only in relation to other men, not in relation to women, Perloe said, which is why the presence of a female experimenter did not lead to the suppression of smiles. Indeed, nearly all the male subjects—all students at Haverford—smiled more broadly and more often when there was a female experimenter in the room.

During the experiments, while the test subjects—20 males and 20 females—watched a 12-minute videotape of babies and puppies, an unseen camera recorded their facial expressions, Perloe said.

Then a second group of 50 volunteers was shown films of the first group and was asked to guess what kind of response the test subjects were showing. The second group, which did not know the purpose of the test, found that some men smiled a lot and other men not much at all.

Later the experimenters compared the findings and found that men who were in the presence of another man suppressed their smiles far more often than men who knew they were alone.

Judging Degree of Smiling

The experimenters also measured the smiles of both groups using a research method called the "facial action scoring system," a method of judging and scoring the degree of smiling and its frequency.

"Smiles are really a very basic kind of signal," Perloe said. "In fact, most parents report that the first time their baby smiled at them was an ecstatic moment, and we believe smiles are the most communicative facial expression there is."

Table 8.3 Kinesic (facial expression) differences of women and men

Female Behavior	Male Behavior
Women use more facial expression and are more expressive than are men (cf. Mehrabian, 1972; Caul, 1974; Buck & Miller, 1974).	Men use less facial expression and are less expressive than women.
Women are better at conveying emotions than are men (Schiffenbauer & Babineau, 1976).	Men do not convey their emotions through their faces.
Women demonstrate superior recognition memory of their own facial expressions (Yarmey, 1979).	Men do not recall their own facial expressions.
Women smile more than men (cf. Argyle, 1975; Dierks-Stewart, 1976; Frances, 1979; Parlee, 1979).	Men smile less than women.
Women are more apt to return smiles when someone smiles at them (Henley, 1977).	Men are less likely to return a smile than are women.
Women are more attracted to others who smile (Lau, 1982).	Men are not more attracted to others who smile.

Let us examine some of the major differences in the facial expression used by women and men. Table 8.3 summarizes these differences.

Gender differences in facial expressiveness　　Young children are aware of the differences in the frequency of smiling behavior in women and men. When children were asked to determine whether their parents were expressing positive or negative sentiment, the children used the facial cue of the smile to decide that their fathers were offering positive comments, but they were unable to determine whether their mothers were making a positive or negative comment, even when they were smiling. The authors explained that mothers smile so frequently that their mood cannot be determined by their smile alone (Bugental, Love & Gianetto, 1971). In another study, children used females' verbal messages rather than their smiles to determine the favorability or unfavorability of messages (Bugental, Kaswan, Love, & Fox, 1970). Just as the child calling "wolf" lost effectiveness by overusing the warning, women appear to lose their effectiveness as communicators of positive affect when they rely so heavily on the smile.

　　Women also lose power and effectiveness when they smile and use a great deal of facial expression. Not only do they appear to be less than genuine if they smile when they are only responding to societal expectations rather than genuine happiness, they become increasingly vulnerable when they mirror their

Women tend to smile more than do men, and, as a consequence, their smiles are more difficult to interpret. A smiling woman may be attempting to convey that she is genuinely happy, that she is behaving in a socially approved way, or that she is nervous and is smiling to cover her feelings. Because men smile less frequently, their smiles are easier to interpret; they generally communicate positive feelings. Women's smiles suggest more affiliation and friendliness, while men's inexpressive faces tend to make them seem less approachable.

During the next few days, experiment with facial expression. If you are a woman, purposely try to smile less and show less facial expressiveness; if you are a man, try to smile more frequently than normal and to indicate your feelings through your face. Try to note sensitively the responses of others. Do you perceive any differences in how other people respond to you? For instance, did anyone ask if you were feeling differently than normal? Did people approach you less or more? Did people tend to try to communicate with you more or less frequently? How do you explain these differences? What implications does smiling behavior have for communication? What inferences can you draw about the differences in communicative behaviors between women and men? For example, do you believe that women have more opportunities to communicate with others because of their facial expression?

feelings on their faces. As a young faculty member, I recall the difficulty that I had determining the positions that colleagues held in departmental and college meetings. My colleagues, of course, were primarily men who had learned early to conceal their feelings and emotions. I have often wondered subsequently how frequently they were able to determine my reaction to particular issues simply by looking at my face. In the same way that women have learned to be expressive and show their emotions, they can learn to be less expressive, to show their emotions only under appropriate or safe conditions. A recent study demonstrates that women who use nonverbal cues that are associated with high status, less smiling, and less facial expressiveness are perceived to indicate higher status (Parlee, 1979). In other words, though women's facial expressiveness and smiling behavior may have served them poorly in the past, they can become more behaviorally flexible and regain some of the power and status they have relinquished.

Posture and bearing
Posture and bearing comprise another area of investigation in kinesics. The research indicates that postural information can be used to determine relational messages between communicators. Head cues appear to communicate

Table 8.4 Kinesic (posture and bearing) differences of women and men

Female Behavior	Male Behavior
Women tend to hold their legs more closely together.	Men tend to have their legs apart at a 10- to 15-degree angle.
Women maintain their arms close to their body.	Men hold their arms about 5- to 10-degrees away from their bodies.
Women rely on more closed body positions.	Men rely on more open body positions (Aries, 1982).
Women tend to engage in less body lean.	Men tend to engage in more backward lean (Aries, 1982).
Women walk with their pelvis rolled slightly forward.	Men walk with their entire pelvis rolled slightly back.
Women present their entire body from their neck to their ankles as a moving entity when they walk (Birdwhistell, 1970).	Men move their arms independently and exhibit a slight twist of their rib cage.

Table 8.5 Kinesic (gestural) differences in women and men

Female Behavior	Male Behavior
Women use fewer gestures than do men. Women discriminate in their use of gestures as they use fewer gestures with other women and more with men (Peterson, 1976).	Men use more gestures than women. Men do not discriminate between male and female partners in their use of gestures.
Women tend to keep their hands down on the arms of a chair more than do men (Peterson, 1976).	Men rarely keep their hands down on the arms of a chair.
Women use fewer one-handed gestures and arm movements (Shuter, 1979).	Men use more one-handed gestures and arm movements.
Women play with their hair or clothing, place their hands in their lap, and tap their hands more frequently than do men (Peterson, 1976).	Men use sweeping hand gestures, stretching the hands, cracking the knuckles, pointing, and using arms to lift the body from a chair or table more frequently.
Women tend to cross their legs at the knees or cross their ankles with their knees slightly apart (Peterson, 1976).	Men tend to sit with their legs apart or with their legs stretched out in front of them and their ankles crossed.
Women tap their hands.	Men exhibit greater leg and foot movement including tapping their feet (Peterson, 1976).

Women and men do not move or carry themselves in the same way. You may sometimes make judgments about the biological sex of people who are ahead of you on the street, simply on the basis of their posture and bearing. Perhaps you rarely discuss proxemic differences between women and men and you seldom consciously alter your own behavior to reflect your biological sex. At the same time, definite proxemic differences exist between women and men.

In this exercise, you will have an opportunity to experiment with masculine and feminine posture and bearing. In a group of about six people, discuss feminine proxemic behavior. Consider arm and leg placement, the position of the pelvis, and the way people move when they walk. Assume these positions and experiment with walking around the room. Have the other members of the group evaluate the success you have in depicting feminine proxemics. After each of you has had the opportunity of displaying feminine postures and bearing, discuss masculine proxemic behavior. Each person should attempt to enact these movements and placement of their limbs. Again, respond to how successfully each person is able to assume the proxemic behaviors of masculine people.

When every person in the group has enacted both feminine and masculine proxemics, discuss the experience. How did you feel when you were behaving as a woman? How did this contrast with how you felt when you were behaving as a man? What attitudes or values seem to be associated with feminine proxemics? How do these perspectives differ from those which seem consistent with masculine proxemic behavior? For instance, you may find that the way that women place their legs together contrasted with the way men place theirs farther apart is suggestive of different attitudes about sexuality. People with their legs pressed tightly together may seem more restrained than do people with their legs open. How does proxemic behavior relate to differences in female and male socialization? What other reactions do you have to this exercise?

informaton that may be considered as elements on a pleasantness/unpleasantness dimension, while body cues communicate more information that may be considered on a relaxation/tension continuum (Mehrabian, 1965). Let us consider some of the specific differences in the posture and bearing of women and men in our culture.

In general, we may conclude that male posture and bearing appear to be the more relaxed of the two sexes. In addition, male posture and bearing are closely related to male proxemic behavior. Men tend to establish more trunk relaxation, greater backward lean, and open leg positioning. Women, too, reflect their proxemic behavior as they tend to sit and stand in a more closed position and demonstrate more trunk rigidity (Peterson, 1976). Women appear to show more sensitivity and flexibility in their behavior to the other person than do men. Men maintain their more relaxed postures, regardless of the sex of the other person (Mehrabian, 1972). Women maintain their more erect and more tense postures until they become quite old and have difficulty in maintaining such postures and positions. In general, communicators are more relaxed with women than with men.

Gestures

Gestures have been observed less in research than some of the other areas of kinesics. A few studies have reported that women and men use gestures differently and use different gestures. These differences are summarized in Table 8.5.

The differences between the use of gestures by women and men are so evident that masculinity and femininity can be distinguished on the basis of gestures alone. A recent study determined that "naive" judges, i.e., individuals with no training or background in nonverbal communication or in psychology, could identify masculinity and femininity on the basis of expressive cues. The author concluded, ". . . 'naive' judges are far from naive: They showed themselves to be sophisticated and accurate observers of expressive masculinity and femininity" (Lippa, 1978).

Tactile communication

Tactile communication is the use of touch in human communication. When you consider touching behavior, you may think about the warm feelings you have when a friend puts a hand on your arm, the love you feel for a baby sister or brother held in your arms, or the feelings associated with kissing another person. On the other hand, you may think about the physical abuse of that touching expressed in spanking, behavior control which touch makes possible when law officers physically seize a person who is being arrested, or the sense of pain and offense which is caused in countless business settings when superiors make unwanted sexual advances on their subordinates.

Touching may be positive or negative. On the positive side, we know that touch is essential to the growth and development of persons from birth onward. A variety of studies have demonstrated that persons who receive insufficient touching may develop such disorders as speech problems, allergies, exzema, and delayed symbolic recognition. Research conducted during major world wars, at times when care for infants was severely limited, indicates that when babies' physical needs are met but not their need to be held and touched, they become ill and die (Montague, 1971; Bowlby, 1951; Adler & Towne, 1978).

Touch is positive when it is considered in the context of intimacy. Some writers have contended that touching is generally equated with sexual interest, either consciously or unconsciously (Jourard & Rubin, 1968) and suggests social and psychological intimacy (cf. Burgoon, Buller, Hale & deTurck, 1982). As we shall determine later in this section, an attitude toward touch as an instrumental act, to encourage sexuality, is a masculine bias in our culture. Nonetheless, when touch is viewed in a context of intimacy, it may intimate higher status.

To understand the positive nature of touch, one should determine whether it is being used reciprocally or unilaterally. In general, if touch is used reciprocally, it indicates solidarity among people (Henley, 1973). In relationships among equals, touch is not perceived as an assertion of power, but rather as a reinforcer of the bonds of friendship or love (Summerhayes & Schner, 1978).

Touch may be viewed as negative when it is used unilaterally. When one person has access to another person's body, but the first person is not allowed the same privilege in return, touch becomes an indicator of status rather than of solidarity. In this light, touch may be viewed as the ultimate invasion of personal space. When we consider the variety of contexts in which unilateral touching occurs, e.g., doctors touching nurses, customers touching waitresses, teachers touching students, managers touching subordinates, police officers touching accused persons, counselors touching clients, and ministers touching parishioners, it becomes evident that touch demonstrates power or status in these contexts. In the animal world, as well, unilateral touch occurs between dominant and subordinate animals as a sign of superiority or status (Lawick-Goodall, 1971). We can determine whether touch is reciprocal or unilateral by considering whether the superior would view initiation of touch by the subordinate as appropriate. For instance, may the waitress initiate touch with the customer, may the student touch the teacher's arm, may the accused touch the police officer in the same manner as he or she has been touched, and do nurses have the same access to physicians' bodies as they sometimes appear to have to the nurses?

Although parents appear to be engaging in more touching behavior with their children, women are still touched more than men. The family members between whom the least amount of touch occurs is between fathers and sons. One researcher has discussed the gender differences in familial touching and has contended that women are socially oriented to dependence and learn to view themselves as the objects of manipulation rather than as the manipulators of their environments (Lewis, 1972). To the extent that children, based on their gender, are touched differently by their parents, and the children are touched, but not allowed to touch their parents in return, these actions provide relational messages about women and men in our culture and about the use

Table 8.6 Tactile differences between women and men

Female Behavior	Male Behavior
Women touch others less than men do.	Men touch others more than women do (Henley, 1973a; 1973b; 1977; Heslin & Boss, 1975).
Women are touched more by others (Austin, 1965; Henley, 1973a, 1973b).	Men are touched less than women.
Women value touching more than do men (Fisher, Rytting, & Heslin, 1976).	Men do not value touch as much as women.
Women distinguish between touching behavior which indicates warmth and touching behavior which suggests sexual intent.	Men do not make distinctions between various kinds of touch (Druley, Casriel, & Hollender, 1980).
Women view touch as an expressive behavior which demonstrates warmth and affiliation.	Men generally view touch as an instrumental behavior leading to sexual activity, or as behavior which is childish, indicative of dependency and a lack of manliness (Druley, Casriel & Hollender, 1980; Henley, 1973).

of touch as an indicator of status rather than solidarity in interpersonal relationships.

Touching is an important topic, enhancing our understanding of the communication of women and men. In this section we will examine how touch is used differently by women and men. Table 8.6 summarizes those differences.

The message that is conveyed by the accessibility of women to touch has been expressed by a number of authors. Two researchers captured this message when they wrote, ". . . the wholesale touching of women carries the message that women are community property" (Henley & Thorne, 1977, p. 215). Women are touched primarily by their opposite-sex friends, while men are touched least by their opposite-sex friends (Jourard & Rubin, 1968).

Paralanguage

Paralanguage literally means that which accompanies language and consists of all of the vocal cues that individuals use to communicate. Our vocal cues can be categorized into (1) *pitch*—the highness or lowness of our voices; (2) *rate*—how rapidly or slowly we speak; (3) *inflection*—the change or lack of change in pitch that we incorporate; (4) *volume*—the loudness or softness of

Table 8.7   Paralinguistic differences between women and men

Female Behavior	Male Behavior
Speak at a higher pitch than do men.	Speak at a lower pitch.
Speak more softly.	Speak louder than women (Market, Prebor, & Brandt, 1972).
Speak with more expressive intonation patterns (O'Neill, 1969).	Speak with less expression.
Intonation patterns are characterized by a sense of uncertainty, questioning, and helplessness.	When making a statement, do not use the rising intonation associated with asking a question (Rosengrant & McCroskey, 1975).
More likely to pronounce the complete "ing" ending on words.	Likely to substitute "in" for "ing" ending (cf. Shuy, Wolfram, & Riley, 1967).
Come closest to standard speech norms (Levine & Crockett, 1966).	Use a greater number of nonstandard and stigmatized words (Labov, 1972).

our voices; (5) *quality*—the pleasant or unpleasant characteristics of our voices including such characteristics as breathiness, harshness, nasality, or whininess; and (6) *enunciation*—our pronunciation and articulation. In addition to these vocal cues, paralanguage includes the silences that we include in our speech and the non-word sounds such as "mmmh," "oooh," and "uh?"

Paralanguage clearly serves to communicate a variety of different features about a person such as her or his sex, age, and emotional response. Studies have demonstrated that paralanguage conveys a great deal (Mehrabian & Ferris, 1967) and that listeners can identify both the race and sex of a speaker even under temporally altered conditions (Lass, Mertz, & Kimmel, 1978). As we shall see in this section, paralanguage appears to be considerably different for women and for men.

One interesting sidenote to the discussion of paralinguistic differences between women and men is the impact of gender differences on the interpretation of voice qualities. Two vocal characteristics yielded the same impression when each was associated with women and with men. Both men and women who exhibited the vocal quality of *flatness* were perceived to be sluggish, cold, withdrawn, and masculine. Similarly, both women and men who had *nasal* voices were viewed as having a number of undesirable characteristics. Other vocal characteristics, however, had different implications when they were heard as part of a female's voice rather than a male's voice. A female speaker who had a *breathy* voice was viewed as pretty, petite, feminine, highstrung, and shallow; a male speaker with a breathy voice was seen as young and artistic.

A *thin* female voice resulted in perceptions of immaturity of the woman, a good sense of humor, and more sensitivity; a thin male voice did not affect the perception that others had of him. *Tenseness* in vocal quality causes women to be seen as younger, more feminine, more emotional, more highstrung, and less intelligent; whereas tenseness in vocal quality for men results in perceptions of being older, less yielding, and more difficult. *Throatiness* caused women to be viewed as more masculine, lazier, less intelligent, less emotional, less attractive, more careless, less artistic, more naive, more neurotic, less interesting, more apathetic, and quieter. On the other hand, throatiness in men resulted in their being viewed as older, more mature, more sophisticated, and better adjusted. Finally, *orotundity,* or a fullness, pompousness, or bombastic vocal quality, is associated with liveliness, gregariousness, pride, and humorlessness in women, and with energy, health, artistry, sophistication, pride, interest, enthusiasm, hardiness, and artistic inclination in men (Addington, 1968). Interaction between the gender of the speaker and the vocal qualities appear to account for these differences.

Artifactual communication

Artifactual communication, or exchange of messages by means of objectics, or object language, refers to our display of material things, including our hair styles, clothing, jewelry, cosmetics and other adornments. Artifactual communication provides a variety of functions and is an extension of the image we have of ourselves. It allows others to determine our age, status, role, values, lifestyle, occupation, nationality, socioeconomic class, group memberships, and personality, as well as our sex. Clothing and other artifacts have valuable communicative functions (Rosenfeld & Plax, 1977). Lurie (1981) presented a socioeconomic interpretation of fashion, considering such variables as age, time, place, status, opinion, gender and sexuality.

Our clothing serves to clarify for each of us the sort of person we believe we are (Fisher, 1975); it allows us individualistic and personal expression (Proctor, 1978); clothes satisfy our need for creative self-expression (Horn, 1975); thus interest in clothing indicates a high level of self-actualization (Perry Schutz, & Ruck, 1983). Clothes allow us to identify ourselves with a particular social culture or subculture (Procter, 1978; Hillestad, 1974), as well as to express group affiliation and agreement with the values and standards of the group (Hillestad, 1974).

While we may dress for warmth and comfort, we also use clothing to express particular levels of modesty or immodesty, inasmuch as clothing can accentuate erogenous zones (Proctor, 1978). We may attempt to attract members of the opposite sex through our clothing choices. Clothing satisfies sensual needs as it touches the surface of our bodies; our overall sensitivity allows clothing to become a source of sensual pleasure (Rosencranz, 1972). Clothing may display physical and economic resources (Rosencranz, 1972), personal power and/or individual status.

A number of studies and books have considered the evolution of clothing fashions for women and men (cf. Pollhemus & Proctor, 1978; Brain, 1979). Such features as restrictiveness, restraints, comfort, and utility have been examined in connection with specific clothing styles. Modesty appears to be a more frequent characteristic of women's clothing than of men throughout history (Flugel, 1930; Lurie, 1981). Such modesty may be associated with the various taboos which affect women, including childbirth, menstruation, and other physical features. Differences in disrobing similarly indicate that women are required to be more modest. An author writing over 50 years ago stated,

> A woman is required by convention to retain her hat and outer garments until asked to remove them. A man may immediately do so. Here again the removal of garments is a sign of *male respect*. Men's garments are treated as though they were used for purposes of *display,* women's garments as though they were used for purposes of modesty (Flugel, 1930).

The differences which appear in womens' and mens' clothing may be due to physiological differences, as this writer suggests; however, we should not dismiss the influence of socialization or social pressures. The dominance/submission theme so prevalent in nonverbal communication may have some explanatory value in artifactual differences as well. One researcher postulates that differentiation in clothing arose from the male's desire to assert superiority over the female and to hold her to his service. He contends that men were able to accomplish this goal by providing women with clothing that hampered or impeded their movements and activities (Langer, 1959). The consideration of specific eras provides revealing information. For example, a recent study examined the effect of clothing worn by the Victorian woman on her activity and perceived personality. The lack of comfort and the restraining nature of the clothing created an image of submissiveness, fragility, and deficient seriousness. Mens' clothing, during the same period, provided them with an image of seriousness, strength and activity (Roberts, 1977).

Other historians have demonstrated a correlation between womens' clothing styles and the sexual mores of the time. Before the 1920's, women wore long skirts, high heels, and had well defined waist lines. During the liberating era of the 1920's, women adopted the loose flapper dress which was considerably shorter and which fitted loosely around a woman's waist. Consistently, following the Second World War when women turned from industrial positions to the traditional nurturing role in the home, their clothes became more restrictive (O'Neill, 1969).

Women's roles and their clothing needs have dictated changes in styles. Changes were required in moving from the home to industry and back to the home. A book published in 1929 adds more insight.

> Until recent years, changes in women's fashions have not been necessitated by changes in life conditions in the same manner as has been true of men. Their duties for the most part have been restricted to the home. But with the entrance of women into the world of business this has been changed. Short skirts and the discarding of corsets came about as the result of the modern girls' interest in athletics. High heeled shoes and heavy skirts went out when the business world opened its doors to women. The busy life of the woman of today leaves little time for the afternoon affairs that our grandmothers so much enjoyed, and with their disappearance has come the disappearance from the wardrobe of the modern woman of dressy afternoon clothing (Hurlock, 1929, pg. 81–82).

The author might have been amazed by the current "changes in life" which have encouraged women to discard additional pieces of their underwear, to replace skirts with pants, and to have special clothing for "afternoon affairs," unlike any their grandmothers might have enjoyed.

The trend toward "unisex" clothing which originated in the 1960's provided an interesting diversion for the fashion industry. Women and men enjoyed similar, if not identical, oufits of a variety of colors, textures, and designs. Nonetheless, most of these styles were more masculine than feminine. Women simply adopted the more comfortable, practical, and durable clothing which men had worn for some time. In addition to practicality and comfort, women may have been making the statement that they wanted equal rights or the same privileges which had been afforded men in our culture. At any rate, the unisex styles had a tendency to reduce the differences between women and men, rather than accenting them. As one author wrote, in response to the similar styles for women and men, "Whatever reduces the false separations between men and women is bound to reduce their suspicions and hostilities, and thus permit them a fuller expression of their human potentiality" (Hurlock, 1971). Havelock Ellis suggested as early as 1929 that "The extreme importance of clothes would disappear at once if the two sexes were to dress alike" (Langer, 1929). We have not observed disinterest in clothing in the past twenty years as women and men have begun to dress more similarly; instead, fashion designers have taken the most basic pieces of clothing, jeans, for example, and given them new interest and appeal.

Table 8.8 Artifactual differences between women and men

Female Behavior	Male Behavior
More sensitive to artifactual cues of others (Robertson, 1978).	Less sensitive to artifactual cues (Haley & Hendrickson, 1974).
More concerned about wearing normative clothing (Kelley, Daigle, LaFleur, & Wilson, 1974).	Less concerned about normative clothing.
More likely to be observed or watched (Argyle & Williams, 1969).	Less likely to be observed or watched.
Dress to win approval (Fisher, 1975).	Dress to avoid disapproval.

As a sidenote, unisex clothing styles have not appeared to affect children's perceptions of appropriate mode of dress, their parents' classification of the same clothing, their parents' attitudes toward gender roles, or other family attitudes. Instead, the results of the study indicated that differentiation rather than similarity of sex-appropriate clothing is still accepted by many adults and transmitted to children. To the 5-year-old child, clothing appears to be for women *or* men, but not for both sexes. The ambiguity expressed by adult fashions and parental mode of dress evidently has little influence on preschool children's perception of clothing. (Wenige, 1977).

Furthermore, the past decade has encouraged fashion consciousness and has rewarded the discriminating buyer. The multiplicity of roles played by women and men require fine distinctions in appropriate clothing. Morganosky & Creikmone (1981) determined that clothing attractiveness and clothing awareness were related to leadership traits for females and males. Women who wore form-fitting oufits rather than loose-fitting outfits, the layered look rather than an unlayered look, and high necklines rather than low or moderate necklines made a more positive first impression in applying for a job (Rucker, Taber, & Harrison, 1981). Finally, Gordon, Tengler and Infante (1982) found that women who were more clothing conscious dressed more conservatively on the job and had higher levels of job satisfaction.

In this section we will identify a variety of gender differences that appear to occur in the clothing choices and the artifactual communication of women and men. These differences are summarized in Table 8.8.

Men and women dress in different costumes for different events. Both men and women alter their clothing as they move from classroom settings to dating situations to job interviews. However, the changes may be less pronounced for one sex than for the other. Moreover, the costumes which a woman might wear in one of these situations may be very different from that of her male counterpart. Select three situations in which you would wear quite different clothing. Draw pictures, or explain in careful detail, exactly what you would wear. Then, draw, or explain, exactly what you would wear if you were of the opposite sex.

Situation	Male Outfit	Female Outfit

Compare your responses with others. How do males and females differ in each of the situations you have selected? What generalizations can you draw? Do you believe that women and men are changing their clothing styles to become more similar to each other than they have historically? How? What changes would you predict in clothing styles of the future for men and women? How do you believe men and women should dress?

You will recall that we discussed how women and men feel about themselves in chapter 2. Women and men have different body images. For instance, at least as many adult men as women are overweight. Nonetheless, most diets and exercise programs are geared toward women. Weight problems appear to be more salient to women than to men. Consider the physical configurations of men and women and discuss how clothing is used to conceal, emphasize, or alter particular physical characteristics. For example, why do men wear tight pants? Why do women wear low cut tops? As you envision an ideal mode of dress for women and men, which bodily parts would you emphasize or deemphasize? How would women's and men's bodily parts be covered or exposed differently? Why? Discuss your reactions with your classmates.

Table 8.9   Nonverbal sensitivity differences between women and men

Female Behavior	Male Behavior
Better judges of nonverbal behavior (Hall, 1978). More accurate decoders of nonverbal communication (Zuckerman, DeFrank, Hall, & Rosenthal, 1976; Kestenbau, 1977; Henley, 1977).	Men who have occupations such as acting, art, and mental health are equal to, or superior to, females in decoding nonverbal cues (Rosenthal, Archer, DiMatteo, Koivumaki & Rogers, 1974).
More sensitive to verbal-nonverbal cue conflicts in the perception of sincerity (Friedman, 1979). Not superior to men in decoding brief, unintended, uncontrolled or "leaked" nonverbal cues (Rosenthal & DePaulo, 1979).	More accurate in judging deception (Siegal, 1980).
Use gestures in making assessments of the relationships between people (*Time,* 1980).	Use actions in making assessments of the relationships between people.

Nonverbal sensitivity

Women and men are different in their sensitivity to nonverbal communication. These decoding differences are summarized in Table 8.9.

Nonverbal sensitivity varies between women and men. We will explore some possible explanations for this gender difference as well as for the other gender differences in nonverbal communication that we uncovered in this chapter. We should note, however, that nonverbal sensitivity is positively related to trust (Sabatelli, Buck, & Dreyer, 1983), that we do not become better decoders of others in the duration of a relationship (Sabatelli, Buck, & Dreyer, 1982), but that marital partners are better at decoding each other's messages than are unbiased judges (Sabatelli, Buck, & Dreyer, 1982).

Explaining gender differences in nonverbal communication

Let us consider some reasons or explanations for the gender differences in the usages of nonverbal communication. The tables presented in this chapter summarize the differences. As you examine the tables, do any explanations occur to you? A number of explanations have been offered in the literature. We will consider some of those that occur most frequently.

Physiological differences

The traditional response to nonverbal gender differences contends that primary and secondary sex characteristics are responsible. In other words, men stand with their legs farther apart because of their genitalia, female students carry their books in front of themselves rather than on their hip as do their male counterparts because of the distinctive bone structure of their arms, and men have a longer stride than women because they are physically larger.

Closely related to these explanations for differences between female and male nonverbal behavior is the notion that women and men are innately or "naturally" different. Consistent with this position is the woman who explains that she is "more comfortable" when she crosses her legs rather than sits with both feet on the floor, the man who states that it is not "natural" for men to kiss each other, or the individual who discusses the propriety of nonverbal behavior on the basis of "the way I have always behaved." In adopting this perspective, we are not necessarily implying that primary and secondary sex characteristics account for our nonverbal behavior. But we are clearly asserting that men and women behave differently, and that these differences are best explained on innate grounds rather than on the basis of learning, culture, personality, or other psychological factors.

Although widely accepted, theories of nonverbal sex differences in communication which rely upon physiological or innate factors are without sufficient scientific support. Interestingly, research in this area seems to indicate that the absence of physiological differences may account for nonverbal differences. In brief, researchers suggest that when examined on the basis of secondary sex characteristics, humans, like a large number of other animals, are more alike than different. Thus, women and men are said to be more *unimorphic* than *dimorphic*. If we were rated on a spectrum on the basis of our secondary sex characteristics, we would tend to cluster together rather than to be clearly differentiated into two distinct groups (Birdwhistell, 1970). Because we are "naturally" more alike than different, we establish elaborate codes that allow others to determine our gender. The parent who feels compelled to dress a new baby in appropriate sex-typed colored clothing exhibits this behavior. It is very difficult to distinguish between male and female children on any basis other than objective language (the length of their hair, their clothing, and their jewelry); it is not much simpler to distinguish between adults, except on the basis of nonverbal cues.

If we are more alike than different, why have we established such extensive nonverbal codes for distinguishing between women and men? Originally, such distinctions might have been useful to protect the species. In order for men and women to procreate, they may have more immediate need for gender identification. The population explosion, a variety of "baby booms," the emphasis on birth control and family planning, and the scarcity of goods and services for the world's peoples, conditions which are characteristic of our contemporary culture, suggest that such justification is outdated. We do not appear to be even remotely among the endangered species.

Female socialization

Socialization differences may be more useful in explaining the manner in which women and men are distinguished nonverbally. In general, we can conclude that women appear to *react* while men tend to *act* in their nonverbal communication (La France & Mayo, 1976). This distinction is in line with differences in socialization between the sexes. First, we will consider female socialization as an explanation and then examine male socialization. Proxemic differences between women and men may be due to the distinct nature of female socialization. Women are higher in affiliation and in sensitivity. Women may be allowed to approach others more closely because they are less threatening. The socialization of women, which encourages affiliation and discourages confrontation, suggests that it may be more appropriate for women to approach others more closely than it is for men. Women may use interpersonal proximity as an instrumental affiliative act, that is, as a means of inducing approval in other persons (Rosenfeld, 1965). Men do not avail themselves of this behavior for the same purpose since interpersonal closeness may be viewed as threatening or confrontational. Women view closeness as a positive state, while men view closeness as negative (Leventhal & Matturro, 1980).

Affiliation or relationship development affects the human use of space. Strangers interact at greater distances than do acquaintances (Willis, 1966), and persons who dislike each other interact at greater distances than do persons who like each other (Leventhal, Matturro, & Schanuman, 1978). Women appear to be more sensitive to such distinctions than are men. Women tend to stand closer to intimate friends than they do to persons they simply identify as friends, while men do not appear to make this distinction (Rosegrant & McCroskey, 1975).

Women's sensitivity to other people and to cues in the environment were considered in chapter 5. Women may alter their use of physical space in interactions with others because they are more aware of alternative cues. In other words, women alter the distance from others, i.e., where they stand and sit, because of a variety of factors of which they are aware. Men, on the other hand, may not perceive the nuances of behavioral cues which are available. Differences in perception and in sensitivity to particular kinds of cues may account for differences in proxemic behavior.

A variety of explanations have been offered for the distinction between the use and importance of eye contact for women and men. Included among these explanations are the facts that women are more inclined toward social and interpersonal relationships than are men and that women need more social approval than do men. Regardless of sex, people with a high need for affiliation engage in more eye contact (Ellsworth & Ludwig, 1972). It follows that affiliation needs may account for the greater amount of eye contact demonstrated by women. Women may be socialized to have a higher affiliative nature than do their male counterparts (Russo, 1975), and are more expressive and externally oriented (Chandler, 1977; Stern, 1977; Deaux, 1977).

Gaze appears to be an avenue of emotional expression for women in a way that is not characteristic for men (Rubin, 1970). As we discussed above, women appear to value nonverbal information more than males do (Exline & Winter, 1965). The brevity of facial expression and other nonverbal cues may necessitate closer observation if we wish to receive accurate messages from others (Ekman & Friesen, 1975). Women's needs for affiliation and communion, then, may serve as one explanation for observed differences in eye contact.

Women need more social approval than do men; this explanation is closely related to women's needs for affiliation. In general, all people tend to have more eye contact with those from whom they desire approval (Efran & Broughton, 1966). Women are expected to respond in interactions. In a sense, they are simply attempting to fulfill those expectations as they observe others and respond to them (Russo, 1975). In this manner, women seek to receive approval from others. A greater display of eye contact results in social approval from others (Efran & Broughton, 1966; Henley, 1977).

Differences in patterns of smiling have been explained on the basis of female socialization, too. For instance, women tend to smile to cover up nervousness or to meet social expectations, while men only smile when they feel comfortable or wish to express solidarity or union (Beekman, 1973). Both women and men feel threatened by a woman who does not smile very frequently and yet is apparently not unhappy (Chesler, 1972).

Pronunciation differences between women and men have been explained on the basis of female socialization. This implies that "proper" speech, like concern over manners and etiquette, are within the female domain and provide little interest for men. Incorrect usage, like the barroom brawl, is symbolic of masculinity. Proper and improper pronunciation are thus associated with the traditional feminine stereotype.

Male socialization

Men's socialization has also been used to explain gender differences in nonverbal communication. In nonverbal communication, just as in verbal communication, men act, while women react (La France & Mayo, 1979). In the area of proxemics, male socialization has been offered as an explanation: men are socialized to be more competitive and aggressive which includes face-to-face confrontation. They may perceive unusual proximity as menacing. We observed that men are more familiar with face-to-face interactions than with side-by-side affiliative positions. Males may feel more threatened when they are approached from the front than by the side, since the frontal invasion suggests the danger of confrontation, while the side by side approach suggests affiliation, which is not typically part of their behavioral repertoire. Females feel more threatened by lateral or flank approach, since custom imposes this form of affiliation. Men's willingness or unwillingness to yield or not yield the way to an oncoming person may be the result of the males' desire to avoid confrontation or to be confrontational.

Male socialization has been postulated as an explanation of differences between women and men in their use of facial expression and smiling. One hypothesis states that men are internalizers and are taught not to express their feelings or to allow their emotions to show, while women are externalizers who are encouraged to express their feelings (Caul, 1974). Men avoid facial expression and smiling, while women rely on them.

Salience of sexuality

Another explanation for gender differences proposes that sexuality is a salient factor. Opposite-sex dyads interact in closer proximity than do female-female dyads (Baxter, 1970; Hartnett, Bailey, & Gibson, 1970; Liebman, 1970). Communicators may assume a certain level of sexual interest in the dyadic setting. In one study in which the personal space of sunbathers was invaded, women allowed others to come closer to them more frequently than did men; but the opposite-sexed pairs maintained the longest period of proximity. The explanation offered by the individuals whose personal space was invaded was that they assumed a level of sexual interest by the invader (Skolnick, Frasier, & Hadar, 1977).

The same pattern of opposite-sex dyads operating most closely was determined for friends and acquaintances. When the friend or acquaintance invaded the other person's personal space, the behavior was explained by sexual intent. As a consequence, persons in same-sex dyads were confused and bewildered when closely approached by a friend or acquaintance. Not surprisingly, this confusion and embarassment was particularly acute among male-male dyads (Patterson, 1968).

A final set of studies confirms the explanation that sexuality is salient in interactions. The known bisexuality of an interviewer causes those who are interviewed to sit farther away from the interviewer in the interviewing process (Barrios, Corbitt, Estes, & Topping, 1976). Conversely, individuals for whom interest in heterosexual behavior is salient, tend to sit closer to opposite-sexed interviewers than do persons who have low interest in such activities (Hartnett, Bailey & Gibson, 1970).

Communication regulation

Differences in the nonverbal behavior of women and men may occur as a result of other variations in the communication interaction. Variations in the use of eye contact between women and men provide a typical instance. Thus, listeners observe speakers more than speakers observe listeners. As we noted in chapter 6, men tend to talk more than women (cf. Argyle, Lalljee & Cook, 1968). Women may engage more in looking at the other person since, as was just stated, listeners observe the speaker to a greater extent than speakers observe listeners (Exline, 1963; Duncan, 1969). In addition, looking at another person signals that the communication channel is open (Weinstein, 1973). For example, men were observed initiating conversations with women after they glanced at them a second time (Horn, 1974).

Dominance-submission

A final explanation relies on a dominance and submission model. This procedure is more complicated than those discussed thus far. When nonverbal cues are used in a reciprocal manner, they indicate interpersonal solidarity. When they are used unilaterally, they indicate status. In other words, if one person touches another person on the arm and the other person responds by touching the first in a similar way, we infer correctly that the two have achieved a similar level of interpersonal solidarity. However, if the touch of one person results in the second person yielding to the touch, but not responding with reciprocal touching behavior, we may surmise that this is a display of status awareness. As early as 1956, the status component of asymmetrical behavior was discussed. An early researcher wrote, "Between superordinate and subordinate, we may expect to find asymmetrical relations, the superordinate [superior] having the right to exercise certain familiarities which the subordinate is not allowed to reciprocate" (Goffman, 1956).

Proxemic differences have been accounted for by using the dominance-submission explanation. Anthropologists and others have observed that the dominant animal or person is generally not approached as closely as is the weaker or more submissive member of the species. Dominant persons and animals maintain a larger personal space, while individuals and animals who are weaker appear to be wary of approaching more dominant members (Sommer, 1959; Sommer, 1969; Henley, 1977). Women, then, may be approached more closely than are men because women appear to have subordinate status when compared to their male counterparts.

The dominance explanation of who approaches whom more closely can be extended. In general, if one animal intrudes upon another's personal space, the first animal will withdraw or will engage in conflict. The subordinate has the choice of withdrawing, in which case the space that she or he was occupying is forfeited; or, by engaging in conflict. If she or he is the subordinate and weaker than the invader, she or he similarly loses the physical space.

Women appear to forfeit their space when it is invaded. When an interviewer deliberately invaded the space of women, the women tended to look away and to smile less (Couts & Ledden, 1977). Women attempt to compensate for the discomfort of personal space invasion by creating psychological barriers or distractions. Withdrawal, rather than confrontation, appears to be the norm.

Differences in eye contact have also been explained as expressions of dominance and submission. Women's traditionally subordinate position in our culture may necessitate more eye contact and an averted gaze. Because women are not part of the dominant group, they are required to observe the members of the dominant group more in order to learn about the appropriateness of their behavior (Rubin, 1970). Strangers, for instance, gaze more at others than do friends in order to learn about each other and to formulate appropriate response patterns (Cohen, 1979).

The averted gaze serves to demonstrate submissiveness and to restrain or check aggression. An averted gaze in autistic children has been shown to be a gesture of submissiveness (Hutt & Ounsted, 1966). When women maintain a prolonged gaze, they frequently do so with a slight tilt of their heads which appears to lessen the act as a threat display (Henley, 1977). The dominance of men and the submissiveness of women appear to help explain the increased watchfulness of women as well as their averted gaze.

Differences in kinesic behavior may also indicate differences in dominance and submissiveness. When persons of different status communicate, those who are superiors frequently indulge in relaxed positions and postures. A hospital study demonstrated that nurses and attendants showed far more circumspection in their kinesic behavior than did the physicians with whom they worked (Goffman, 1956).

Male postures appear to communicate a more dominant attitude (Mehrabian, 1968; 1972). They also seem to be more active and potent (McGinley, LeFevre, & McGinley, 1975). The more open body position which is demonstrated by men is also associated with diversity or alteration of opinion (McGinley, LeFevre, & McGinley, 1975). When communicators have similar attitudes, one person will judge another who demonstrates an open body position as more positive than she or he will judge an individual with a closed body (McGinley, Nicholas, & McGinley, 1978). Men appear to have an advantage in the bodily posture and bearing they maintain, in that they communicate dominance, activity, and potency. They appear to be more likely to affect opinion change; when others have similar attitudes, they are more likely to be judged positively than are their female counterparts who typically have closed body positions.

Women show submission as they maintain less space and appear to be more "proper" in their posture and bearing. At the same time, they appear to show more flexibility with persons of varying status, while men tend to assume the same postures, regardless of the status of the other person. If they assume a less relaxed posture, women may be communicating that they do not like the other person.

Finally, we should note that women who try to assume male postures may be frustrated in their efforts, since people expect women to sit with their knees together, not cross-legged or bending over (Henley & Freeman, 1975). Women who violate these norms may be judged harshly or may be objects of humor or ridicule. It is not feasible to encourage women to sit with their feet up, to sit with their legs apart, to take long strides when they walk, or to use their bodies in forceful ways. Nonetheless, women's bodily postures appear to encourage others to treat them in submissive and negative ways and are, at the very least, awkward and difficult to maintain.

In explaining gender differences in the use of gestures, it has been postulated that women and men may use differing gestures because of societal expectations of dominance and submission (Key, 1975; Henley, 1977; Frieze & Ramsey, 1976). In general, dominant people use more gestures in cross-sexed dyads (Poling, 1978). Men appear to use a variety of gestures of dominance with women, including aggressive gestures such as moving them by pushing or pulling on their arms or other parts of their body, and playful gestures such as picking them up, spanking them, punching them, and threatening to drop them into water or onto a bed. All these gestures of dominance, whether playful or serious, serve to allow men to control women's bodies.

A number of other gestures used primarily by men, such as pointing and sweeping gestures, likewise serve to dominate. The larger amount of space that men use by stretching their arms and legs out when they sit, as compared to the small space that women use as they cross their legs or ankles, and place their hands in their laps, also imply a power differential, as was described in our consideration of proxemics.

If women are viewed as more submissive in their use of gestures, how do we account for the increased number of gestures that they use with men rather than with women? One writer theorizes that since men are known to dominate conversations, interrupt in conversations, initiate conversations, speak more than women, and control the topic of conversations, women are forced to express themselves in more covert ways; hence, they rely on gestures (Scheinfeld, 1944). Women may also be viewed as using more gestures when they are talking to men than when they are talking to women, because they find themselves in an approval-seeking situation. When women are placed in such situations, they rely on more gestures than do males (Rosenfeld, 1966). Women may seek more approval from men than they do from other women.

Differences in pronunciation have been explained as manifestations of dominance and submissiveness. It has been asserted that as the dominated group, women are required to be more concerned about their speech than are the members of the dominant group, as in the case of other minority groups.

In a variety of ways, persons with minority status are required to be more concerned about proper and appropriate behavior. It is conjectured that persons with low status must be more concerned about the appropriateness of their behavior in order to achieve upward mobility and not to lose their present status. High status persons, on the other hand, are allowed the luxury of informality and lack of concern for the proprieties, since they have already achieved success.

At the same time, some theorists have contended that women have fewer signs of status than do men. While men can rely on their positions and income to establish their credibility and status in society, women have fewer opportunities to establish their status. As a consequence, women may rely on proper speech as a method of signalling their societal role to others (Eakins & Eakins, 1978).

Do men and women behave differently in the nonverbal realm as a result of status differences, or do status differences between men and women result in differing nonverbal behaviors? This question is similar to the chicken-or-egg controversy. What is evident is that men and women behave differently in their nonverbal communication and that the cues assigned to each sex are asymmetrical, with male cues indicating superior status and the female providing subordinate nonverbal responses. These cues may have originated in order to maintain the social order of men in a dominant position; it is evident that they function to maintain status differences between men and women in our contemporary culture. To the extent that we determine whether the current social order of men as superordinate and women as subordinate is appropriate, we may wish to perpetuate such nonverbal differences; to the extent that we believe that asymmetrical power relationships between men and women are inappropriate, we may wish to consider alterations in our nonverbal behavior.

We need to recognize that nonverbal changes are difficult and hazardous. The difficulty of altering any habit is well established and is compounded by the additional problem of behaving in a manner that is discrepant, or different, from the expectations of others. Rosenthal and DePaulo (1979) note these obstacles and further observe that, in general, women have been determined to be "more polite in the nonverbal aspects of their social interactions" (p. 95). They state that when women are less accomodating in their nonverbal behaviors, they experience less successful interpersonal outcomes. Alteration in nonverbal behaviors holds the possibility of social change, but not without attendant personal risk.

Conclusions

Let us review some of the findings in this chapter. We began by discussing the importance of nonverbal communication in our understanding of interactions among people. We discussed proxemics and determined that women are approached more closely than men and that women approach others more closely than do men. In our consideration of kinesics, we noted that eye contact may serve to indicate liking or status, as well as to regulate communication. We found that women use more eye contact than do men, but they also are more likely to avert their gaze. Facial expression also varies between men and women; women tend to use far more facial expressions than do men and tend to smile more. Men and women use distinctive bearing, posture, and gestures. Indeed, the gender of the person may be predicted by his or her bodily movements. Men touch others more than women do, and women are the recipients of more touching than are men. Paralinguistics varies between women and men. Women and men wear different clothing, and their clothing appears to hold differing importance for them. Women are more sensitive to nonverbal cues than are men.

A variety of explanations have been offered for the differences in male-female nonverbal behaviors. Physiological differences have been largely discredited as an explanation. Female and male socialization offers explanatory value. The salience of sexuality and communication regulation also enhance our understanding of gender differences. Status differences, or dominance-submissiveness, may account for nonverbal sex differences. To the extent that women and men are confined to differing and limiting roles as a result of their nonverbal behaviors, those behaviors become questionable prescriptions to offer to flexible and fully functioning human persons.

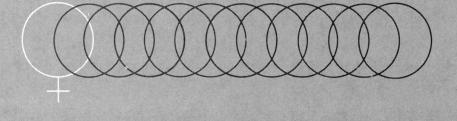

Section 4

This final section of the text integrates the material you have read and applies the research to specific communication contexts. We do not communicate in a vacuum, and the effects of the situation critically alter our communication behaviors. Chapter 9 considers the personal context of intimacy. Sexuality is explored for women and for men. This includes couple communication, with some emphasis on initial attraction and dating; traditional and nontraditional couples; dual career marriages; conflict and stress; power and dominance; and marital satisfaction and improvement. Family communication is examined within the increasingly diverse types of family we find in our contemporary culture.

Contexts

Chapter 10 focuses on the public contexts of communication. We will consider specific communication behaviors, such as small group interaction, leadership behaviors, and public speaking. Communication in the business world may be more important for women and men than ever before. Business communication is discussed in chapter 10, with an emphasis on occupational choices, employment interviews, discrimination in securing new positions, and women as managers. This section of the text completes the exploration of gender and communication.

9 Contexts of intimacy

Introduction

In this chapter some of the more intimate phases in which men and women communicate will be discussed. We will consider the role of human sexuality as one area of communication between the sexes. Non-marital sex, the double standards which exist for women and men, differences between women and men in their sexual behavior, the influence of sex roles and beliefs about women and men on sexuality, contemporary practices, and perceptions of sexuality, will be discussed. Couple communication occurs between people who are dating, engaged, or married. In the first section of the chapter, we will consider initial attraction and dating behavior, traditional and nontraditional couples, dual-career marriages, conflict and stress in marriage, power and dominance, and marital satisfaction. The chapter will conclude with a section on family communication, including infant-parent verbal and nonverbal exchanges of messages, communication with children who are normal or abnormal, and the increasing alternative family structure—the single-parent family. This consideration will clarify research findings and offer some assistance to persons who wish to develop nonsexist, useful approaches to communication within intimate contexts.

Sexuality

A great deal has been written about the sexual revolution which purportedly took place in our culture in the 1960s. This revolution was said to have been related to other, similar liberalizing influences, such as the women's movement. We read in the popular literature that the sexual revolution had a tendency to liberate both men and women from prior restraints, allowing people to feel less guilt about their feelings of sexuality. But what has actually occurred? In order to gain a better understanding of the cultural mores surrounding our contemporary sexual practices and attitudes, we find that an historical overview is helpful.

Importance and universality

The importance and universality of sexuality can be found in statements as early as 1929:

> To the average normal person, in whatever type of society we find him [her], attraction by the other sex and the passionate and sentimental episodes which follow are the most significant events of his [her] existence (Malinowski, 1929).

Sexuality has been regarded as universally important, but only in recent times has it been approved outside the sanctions of marriage.

Within marriage

The Bible, the church, and the laws of the land have contributed to a history in which sexuality was viewed as inappropriate behavior when practiced outside marriage. The Old Testament prescribes punishment that should be inflicted upon persons who engage in adultery. The proof of virginity by brides was required by the exhibition of a bloody sheet on the morning after the wedding. Within the Catholic Church, non-marital intercourse was viewed as a deadly sin, and persons who were not absolved were condemned to eternal hell. State legislatures adopted the values which originated in the Bible and the church, and in nearly every state, in the nineteenth century, coitus between non-married persons was subject to corrective action (Hunt, 1974).

The terminology which has been used traditionally to describe non-marital sex has also contributed to our disapproval of it. For instance, we seldom use the term "non-marital" sex, using, instead, such words as "pre-marital," "extra-marital," "unfaithfulness," and "adultery." The pejorative nature of these commonly used words clearly delineates a right-wrong perspective about sexuality outside of marriage. Furthermore, these words are frequently inaccurate. "Pre-marital," for instance, suggests that the intercourse is occurring before a marriage, when, in fact, it may not be preceding any wedding plans. "Extra-marital" suggests that something is occurring which is in addition to something else, although it may be the only sexuality that a person experiences. "Non-marital" sex may be more accurate and less pejorative than some of these other terms. Similarly, we may distinguish between "relational" and "non-relational" sex, a distinction which would allow us to discriminate between sex that occurs within the confines of an established relationship and sex that occurs spontaneously or between persons with no prior relationship commitment. Traditional terminology encourages sex within marriage while some newly coined words, like those listed above encourage sexuality within a variety of contexts.

Perceptions of women and men

In addition to our historical belief in the sanctity of sexual activity within marriage, there are varying beliefs about how women and men differ in their perceptions of sexuality. Sexuality has been viewed traditionally as a biological need which is frequently included among other physical needs such as food, water, and air. The psychologist Freud maintained this view in his psychoanalytic theory, and the well-known sex researcher at Indiana University, Kinsey, based a great deal of his work on Freud's perspective. Both these men asserted that male and female sexuality are different.

Kinsey noted that sexual variety was reasonable and normal for human males, but that females did not appear to engage in the same range of sexual activity. He concluded that females were less interested in sex because of physiological differences. In fact, Kinsey attributed male/female differences in sexuality to the nervous system (Kinsey, 1953).

Today, most of us would agree that socialization processes and cultural influences better explain the differences between sexual practices and attitudes of women and men, as well as the historical preference for sex within marriage. Birth control improvements, progress in controlling venereal diseases, greater mobility, and more opportunity have allowed women and men more freedom to engage in sex within and without marriage. Nonetheless, as we shall see, some of the vestiges of an earlier time still remain and tend to influence the behavior of people.

The "double standard" versus an "individual ethic"

A controversial issue regarding sex between women and men is the *double standard* which implies that behavior that is deemed appropriate for men is not appropriate for women. The emphasis on a double standard is probably a contribution of some of the studies which Kinsey conducted; it was reinforced by later work by Chesser (1956). Twice as many men as women approve of the double standard, but a majority of persons prefer a single standard (cf. Christensen, 1973; Hunt, 1974). The double standard, which is held by a minority of adolescents, appears to be in the process of being replaced by the *individual ethic,* which assumes that individuals behave in a manner with which they feel comfortable (Haas, 1979).

A certain amount of confusion occurs for women and men. Perhaps we are in the midst of a paradigm shift or change in perspective concerning acceptable sexual practices. Women are frequently confused by the sexual transition and feel caught between two sets of sexual values, while some men are threatened by the pressure to perform and to be good lovers (Bardon, 1978). Although people are no longer satisfied with the beliefs and practices of another time, they also appear to be dissatisfied with current practices, and are not completely satisfied sexually (Dychtwald, 1979). The manner in which we communicate the changes is unclear, and the messages which we wish to share are uncertain.

Reactionary materials such as Donald Symons' book, *The Evolution of Human Sexuality,* published in 1980, create confusion. Symons and others suggest that male and female sexuality is different and that these differences are based on differing neurological systems in women and men. His book, similar to Darwin's theory of survival of the fittest, traces the evolution of sexuality and contends that human sexuality is dominated by men. Materials such as this cause confusion. People become uncertain as to whether differences in sexuality are due to differences in socialization and cultural influences, or are a result of neurological and biological differences between the sexes.

Homophobia, the fear of homosexuality, is more common than we may realize. Aggression toward homosexual people, in such expressions as sexual humor, frequently occurs because of deep-seated fears. In order to understand your own feelings about homosexuality, complete the following exercise.

On a blank sheet of paper, individually answer the following question anonymously, "I am not homosexual because _____ " or "I am homosexual because _____." Complete the sentence that you have selected (that you are or are not homosexual) ten times. After you have provided at least ten reasons why you are or are not homosexual, place your paper with those of your classmates in a single pile. Each person should randomly select one of the pieces of paper and share what another person wrote. After each person has read the rationale provided by another class member, the class may wish to discuss the responses. It is essential that the person who authored the reasons not identify himself or herself, unless he or she wishes to provide this disclosure.

After all of the papers have been read, you may wish to discuss homosexuality and bisexuality in general terms. The fear of homosexual relationships frequently interferes in the expression of sexual loving in same-sex sexual relationships. The strong cultural taboos against homosexuality have been called into question within the last decade. As homosexuality is demythologized and people share their feelings as well as new information on same-sex sexual relationships, lower levels of homophobia may occur. Homosexuality or bisexuality may not be your preference; at the same time, it is important for each of us to be informed and free from fear about this important topic.

Actual male-female differences

A variety of male/female differences in sexuality have been demonstrated. A study conducted slightly over ten years ago suggests that coital activity among college women drastically increased, but that men still appeared to engage in more nonmarital coital activity than did women (Kaats & Davis, 1970). More recent studies report that men remain the initiators in sexual activity, even though the attitude of the woman in the couple determines whether or not the two will engage in intercourse (Peplau, Rubin, & Hill, 1977). Men tended to overestimate their partner's desire for sex and thus to advocate a higher desirability of sex for men and women than did women (Peplau, Rubin, & Hill, 1977). Males were inclined to be more sexually permissive about their own behavior than were females. Males will often accept nonmarital sexual intercourse for themselves or other males, but not for females (Gray, White &

Libby, 1978). Female sexual behavior is primarily related to being in love and going steady, while male sexuality is more indirectly and less exclusively associated with romanticism and intimacy in relationships. Women prefer permanent relationships, while men prefer diversity and more casual sexual partners (Kirkendall & Sibley, 1966). Men show a slightly higher frequency of coitus and a slightly higher number of coital partners than do women. Men report a significantly higher sexual urge than do women; and women are more tolerant of marrying a non-virgin than are men (Mercer & Kohn, 1979).

Perceptual male-female differences

These differences in self-report data must be interpreted cautiously, however, since they may be an artifact or symbol of social acceptability. For instance, one study demonstrated that men reported their first coital experience to others sooner and that they told more people (almost exclusively male peers) than did women. Women told fewer persons, waited longer to self-disclose this information, and shared the information with greater frequency with the opposite sex. Males tended to receive approval from those whom they informed, while women were more likely to receive mixed or disapproving reactions (Carns, 1973). Since men are more likely to receive approval when they disclose information about their sexual activity, they may be more willing (and even eager) to discuss it with interviewers or experimenters than are women.

When women and men were asked about the strategies that would be used in "come-ons" and "put-offs," they found that both sexes perceived a double standard. The majority of students felt that strategies of "come-ons" would be used by men and that the strategies of "put-offs" would be used by women. In other words, they felt that men would attempt to engage in sex while women would try to avoid it. However, when men and women were asked about their own strategies, they were found to be remarkably similar. Both men and women used indirect strategies for engaging in sex with a partner, such as seduction and body language, and both used similar strategies, including coercion, and moralizing in avoiding sex. The techniques for engaging in sex tended to be more indirect, while the techniques for avoiding sex tended to be more direct (McCormick, 1979).

Sex guilt
One difference in the perceptions of men and women which has been studied is *sex guilt,* or remorse for engaging in sexual intercourse. Women suffer from sex guilt more than do men (Mendelsohn & Mosher, 1979). Sex guilt inhibits sexual behavior in women. College women are more prone to moral condemnation of a roommate who has her first coital experience with an attractive acquaintance than when the first coital experience was with a loved fiance (Mendelsohn & Mosher, 1979). Females with high sex guilt regarded virginity as important, and males with high sex guilt portray sex as dangerous. Sex guilt

is negatively correlated with the level of sexual experience of the person and is positively correlated with a belief in sex myths (Mosher, 1979). Sexually inactive people report significantly higher sex guilt than sexually active students (Gerrard, 1980). More conservative people who are sexually inactive report higher sex guilt than less conservative people; the conservative people report that they would not consider having premarital intercourse or would even consider intercourse after they were engaged (Gerrard, 1980).

Sexual satisfaction

Shere Hite (1976), author of a number of books on male and female sexuality, reports that 24% of the women she studied had no orgasms during intercourse and that 33% seldom or rarely experienced orgasm. Women appear to have fewer orgasms than do men, but how do they view their sexuality? Satisfaction with sexual relationships correlates highly with fidelity in women. Happily married women do not have strong desires for extramarital relationships (Swieczkowski & Walker, 1978). Apparently women are able to achieve what they desire, and they tend to be able to find satisfaction in their sexual relationships.

Sex roles have been examined as a predictor of sexual satisfaction for women. Sexual satisfaction in women is not related to their femininity, however, but rather is related to their feminism and their partner's feminism. In other words, highly feminine females, described as nurturing, empathic, submissive, and tender, are not more likely than other women to report high satisfaction with their sex lives. Women who endorse equality for men and women, who perceive women to be fundamentally more like men than different from them, are more likely to report high sexual satisfaction, particularly when they have a partner who similarly endorses equality for the sexes (Kirkpatrick, 1980). This report implies that the more egalitarian the couple, the more satisfying their sex life will be.

Similarly, egalitarian beliefs appear to affect such practices as birth control. Men who hold more positive attitudes toward the use of male contraceptives tend to subscribe less strongly to stereotypic beliefs that contraception is a woman's responsibility. In other words, men who maintain stereotypic views of women tend to pursue sexual gratification regardless of the consequences, while men who reject such stereotypes are more likely to accept the responsibility of birth control (Weinstein & Goebel, 1979). The less stereotypic couples share responsibility for their sexual activity.

Women who behave in nontraditional ways were studied in another investigation. Women who ask directly for sex were found to be less traditional and more apt to be involved in a relationship with a man who also asked directly for intercourse. These females used direct verbal initiatives, were less conventional, and generally more assertive. They also tended to be involved with men who were more accepting of women, held more egalitarian beliefs, and respected the rights of women (Jesser, 1978). Again, it appears that equality within couples results in more role flexibility and acceptance of a wider repertoire of behavior.

The changes we discussed at the beginning of this section have resulted in an increased sexual permissiveness for both men and women. Some correlations occur between attitudes of permissiveness and other features. People who enjoy sex, are attractive, reject traditional religious beliefs, are more liberal in their social and political attitudes, prefer small families, or favor women entering careers, tend to be more sexually permissive (Kelly, 1978).

The way a person perceives himself or herself also correlates with his or her attitudes about sexual permissiveness. A positive relationship occurs between self-actualizing tendencies and reported sexual permissiveness and sexual satisfaction, while a negative relationship exists between self-actualization and sexual prudishness (Paxton & Turner, 1978). Self-actualizing people are more free than others in speaking about sex and in admitting their sexual attraction to other people. In order for a person to relate intimately to another person, he or she must think highly of himself or herself. People who express sexual dissatisfaction within their marriages do not similarly report general dissatisfaction with their marriages; instead sexual dissatisfaction is correlated with how people view themselves (Frank, Anderson & Robenstein, 1979). Just as couples who express equality and have positive attitudes about women and men have more satisfying sexual relationships, individuals who are self-actualizing and have positive feelings about themselves are more sexually satisfied. The picture which emerges is that sexual satisfaction is part of a larger satisfaction with self and with positive attitudes about other people.

Summary

Sexual activity occurs between women and men within and outside of marriage or established relationships. People do not randomly engage in sexual acts with others, but increased sexual permissiveness occurs today, due to advancements in medicine, greater knowledge about biological and psychological processes, and alterations in our perspectives about women and men. Persons who have positive feelings about themselves are likely to have positive feelings about intercourse and are likely to engage in intercourse with others for whom they have some affection. We must be wary of double standards and discriminatory statements about intercourse which imply that it is appropriate behavior for men, but less appropriate for women. Initiation of sexual activity, dominance behavior during intercourse, and clear statements about preferences during sex should also be practiced by both women and men. Role flexibility appears to be a predictor of sexual satisfaction.

Women and men use different verbal and nonverbal behaviors in sexual acts. For instance, women report that they frequently enjoy longer periods of foreplay than do the men with whom they have a sexual relationship. Women may engage in more touching and stroking behavior and be more relationally-oriented. Men may be more task-directed and view orgasm as the goal of a sexual interaction. Traditionally, men have assumed a more powerful physical position in lovemaking, including "being on top." Men have generally been in control of the sexual experience by initiating the encounter, making the first moves at critical points, and in terminating the sexual relationship. However, changes are occurring in our contemporary culture.

If you have been involved in sexual relationships, you may find that your own experience is similar to traditional practices, highly discrepant from traditional practices, or combines both traditional and contemporary practices. For example, as a woman, you may recall instances in which you initiated a sexual relationship with a man or in which you were highly motivated to have an immediate orgasm. As a man, you might recall experiences in which you preferred touching, stroking, and massaging and were not concerned if you reached orgasm at all.

This exercise is designed to help you consider your sexual needs, without regard to traditional expectations, and to determine how you may become more liberated in achieving those goals. The exercise works particularly well if you complete it with a sexual partner, but it can also be useful if you do it alone. Provide as many responses as you wish for each of the following categories.

Nonverbal Behaviors Typically Associated with Men
(Include body positioning, breathing, sounds associated with lovemaking, the amount of space used, clothing (or lack of clothing) that may be worn, movement, etc.)

1. _____
2. _____
3. _____
4. _____
5. _____

Verbal Behaviors Typically Associated with Men
(Include statements that might be made to initiate sexual interactions, endearing terms that are used to refer to partners, language that is likely to be used when they are aroused, etc.)

1. _____
2. _____
3. _____
4. _____
5. _____

Nonverbal Behaviors Typically Associated with Women
(You may wish to recall some of the categories you used in describing male behavior to prompt you to consider some of the female behaviors.)

1. _____
2. _____
3. _____
4. _____
5. _____

Verbal Behaviors Typically Associated with Women
(You may want to examine your list of verbal behaviors that are associated with men in order to recall some typical female behaviors.)

1. _____
2. _____
3. _____
4. _____
5. _____

Nonverbal Behaviors in Which You Would Like to Engage in Sexual Interactions

1. _____
2. _____
3. _____
4. _____
5. _____

Verbal Behaviors in Which You Would Like to Engage in Sexual Interactions

1. _____
2. _____
3. _____
4. _____
5. _____

Nonverbal Behaviors in Which You Would Like Your Partner to Engage in Sexual Interactions

1. _____
2. _____

3. _____
4. _____
5. _____

Verbal Behaviors in Which You Would Like Your Partner to Engage in Sexual Interactions

1. _____
2. _____
3. _____
4. _____
5. _____

If you complete this exercise with a sexual partner, you may wish to exchange lists and discuss some experimentation in your relationship. You may want to consider how you can each engage in behavior which is desirable for you and also meet the other person's desires. You may also want to consider if you have mutually exclusive goals. For instance, if you want your partner to offer more words of endearment during sexuality and she or he wishes to verbalize less, you might find that you cannot both be satisfied simultaneously. Instead, you may have to engage in some sexuality in which she or he verbalizes less and sometimes you may find that she or he is willing to offer more verbal endearments.

If you complete this exercise in a classroom setting, you may wish to share your lists with others. Anonymity may be essential in this exercise, so that you may wish to place your paper with those of your classmates on a pile and read another student's paper to the entire group. After the lists have been shared, you may wish to consider the similarities and differences expressed. Does it appear that we do have a different set of expectations about women and men in sexual interactions? How do these differences relate to other socialization? How do they relate to our conceptions of stereotypical male and female behavior? To what extent have you been controlled by the other person's expectations of you? To what extent have people of the opposite-sex been constrained? What can, or will, you do to be more satisfied in your sexual relationships?

Couple communication

Initial attraction and dating

Communication between people who are dating, who are engaged, or who are married is being studied. Researchers are interested in recommending methods for increased satisfaction with intimate relationships and for explaining dysfunctional relationships. To whom are you most likely to intimately relate? As you learned in chapter 7, people tend to date those who are similar to themselves in physical attractiveness. Couples at less developed stages are unlikely to commit themselves further to each other if they are dissimilar in attractiveness. A less attractive person who is involved with a more attractive person is likely to worry about the differences in attractiveness and a potential break-up of the relationship. Differences in attractiveness according to gender also appear. Women who are more attractive are likely to have a greater number of opposite-sexed friends than are less attractive women, but are more likely to maintain a relationship with one man. Men who are attractive are more likely than women to discontinue the relationship with a woman (White, 1980).

Do men and women have similar or different ideals of the sex type of potential partners? Sex role expectations are more frequently different than similar. In general men prefer feminine females most often. Men who were androgynous, feminine or masculine preferred feminine sex typed females while undifferentiated men preferred undifferentiated females. Androgynous men are attractive to feminine and androgynous females; masculine men are attractive to all females; undifferentiated men are attractive to undifferentiated women; and feminine men are attractive to no set of women. In order to be attractive to men, women appear to have a narrower latitude of sex role definition than do men (Kimlicka, Wakefield, & Goad, 1982).

The sex roles of married persons have been similarly examined. Androgynous people prefer less sex typed marital roles than do others. A mother's role may have a bearing on a daughter's preference for a traditional or egalitarian role. When the mother is not satisfied with her role, regardless of whether she works outside the home or stays at home, the daughter prefers an egalitarian role. When she is satisfied with her out-of-home work, the daughter similarly prefers an egalitarian role. Only when the mother stays at home and shows satisfaction with her role does the daughter prefer a traditional role (Pursell, Banikotes, & Sebastian, 1981).

Both verbal and nonverbal cues can be used to predict an existing relationship between two people. The acquaintance process is characterized by increasing intimacy and decreasing reciprocity of intimate communication. Persons who are intimately involved communicate with more descriptive intimacy (personal facts about themselves), but not more evaluative intimacy (their personal feelings or opinions). Intimates are less likely to reciprocate when the other person tells them something of an intimate nature than are strangers. Women tend to offer more evaluative intimacy than men in all stages of relationship development. Intimates are likely to personalize non-intimate topics while strangers are likely to minimize intimate ones. Increased acquaintance appears to be related to an increase in the intimacy of information exchanged and with a transition in the processes used to regulate interactions. Intimates are more likely to engage in simultaneous talking, interruptions, and rapid turnover of dialogue than are strangers (Morton, 1978).

Nonverbal cues also indicate relationship development. Couples who are in love spend more time gazing into each other's eyes than do couples who are not as strongly involved. Men and women who are strongly involved spend about an equal amount of time gazing into each other's eyes even though women are found to spend more time looking at men than men spend looking at women (Rubin, 1970). People who care about each other similarly tend to sit closer, stand closer, and use increased touching. It is generally quite simple to predict increased attraction and relationship development from nonverbal cues.

Just as nonverbal and verbal cues can be used to gauge the development of a relationship, the amount of influence one partner has on the other may indicate relationship development. The person with whom you are intimately involved is likely to influence the decisions you make. One study examined the influence that young women have on young men's career aspirations and achievements. The female dating partner is highly influential during the years when her male friend is coordinating his educational, occupational, and marital plans. Her interests tend to be associated with his plans and her encouragement is likely to affect his career decisions (Otto, 1977).

Traditional/nontraditional couples

In the past, couples met, dated, became engaged and then married. At the present time, a variety of alternatives are possible. Some people decide to remain or to become single (cf. Cargan & Melko, 1982), while others choose alternative coupled states. Cohabitation has become a frequently recurring step intervening in the dating—becoming engaged—marrying cycle, and for many couples cohabitation has also replaced marriage. This lifestyle has sharply increased during the past decade. Researchers infer that this represents a new dimension in the courtship process and does not threaten the institution of marriage.

Cohabitation
What kind of people are likely to cohabit? Cohabitants are similar in their background to non-cohabitants, with the exception of religion; cohabitants have weaker religious beliefs than non-cohabitants. People who have experienced multiple marriages are more likely to cohabit than are persons who have not

been married previously. Cohabitation does not alter sex roles, however, co-habiting couples describe themselves in less sex role stereotypic terms than non-cohabitating couples. No differences in behavioral commitment are evident in cohabiting and noncohabiting couples (Risman, Hill, Rubin, & Peplau, 1981). The most significant gratifications that occur by cohabiting are companionship, sexual activity, and economic gain. The negative consequences include conflict over property rights and increased risks for females due to differing expectations concerning sexual fidelity and the permanence of the relationship. Children who are born to persons who are cohabiting face negative consequences, too, since they lack legal protection in custody cases and in the procurement of support (Newcomb, 1978).

Marriage

Is the marital state desirable? Marriage seems to be good for one's health, especially for men. Both single women and men are more likely to report stress, to use drugs, and to contemplate suicide than do married people of both sexes. Divorced men demonstrate the most stress and drink the heaviest of any group (Cargan & Melko, 1981).

Moreover, married people are perceived more highly than single people. Married people are rated as happier, more secure, and more reliable than others. However, married people are seen as less successful in their jobs than the unmarried. Finally, marital status has more effect than gender on person perception (Etaugh & Malstrom, 1981).

At one time, people may have entered into marriage for survival, sex, and other physiological needs. Today, people indicate that they marry to fulfill emotional and psychological needs. When these needs are not fulfilled or when individuals have different expectations, disappointment and conflict frequently result. One cause appears to be lack of communication about one's needs, because this deficiency can contribute to misunderstanding. In addition, stereotypical expectations and differing degrees of sex drive create marital problems for many couples (Sager & Hunt, 1979).

For instance, the gender variable, sexism, causes problems in marriage. One investigation found that sexist attitudes affect the communication patterns in marital couples and that sexist individuals tend to engage in power struggles. Women offer more information than do men in both nonsexist and sexist relationships. However, women tend to view themselves as less positive and they disclose less when they are engaged in sexist relationships. Similarly, women have negative self-concepts and low levels of self-disclosure when they are engaged in conflict with their husbands. The power struggles that ensue in sexist relationships decrease the amount of information exchanged and polarize the individuals. In this way the patterns become circular. Couples who become aware of their sexist biases and learn how they affect their interactions are able to solve this vicious cycle of conflict and dysfunction (Alsbrook, 1976).

Marital partners are frequently highly similar. Some of these similarities may be conducive to marital satisfaction, while others seem largely irrelevant to a couples' satisfaction. Married couples typically have a similar ethnic origin, are usually from similar social backgrounds, and generally have the same, or approximately the same, educational level (Chronkite, 1977). Couples are frequently alike in vocabulary, somewhat alike in reasoning abilities, and to a smaller degree, similar in perceptual speed. Couples are typically similar in age, with husbands being about two or three years older than their wives, and similar in size, with husbands being slightly larger in height and weight than their wives *(Detroit Free Press,* 1981).

One area in which women and men have been distinctive in the past, but are now similar is the area of work. Most couples, in the past, had single-career marriages. Today, many couples are involved in dual-career marriages. Let us consider the influence of the dual-career nature of marriages on other factors.

Dual-career marriages

Dual-career marriages, marriages in which both the husband and wife have careers, represent a life style which is distinct from traditional marriages (cf. Aldous, 1982). From an economic standpoint, many couples find it necessary for both partners to work outside the home in order to reach or approximate their desired standard of living. In general, dual-career marriages are relatively prosperous. These couples use family planning to insure that they have only one or two children. Researchers found that women who have a high level of commitment to their jobs use birth control more effectively and have fewer children than other women (Safilios-Roschild, 1970).

Men whose wives work make fewer long-distance moves than do other men when the opportunities arise for a job transfer. The loss of job mobility is compensated for, in part, by higher living standards in the same geographical area. Although economic necessity encourages dual-career couples, small children in the home consistently exert a strong negative effect on the likelihood of the wife working (Ewer, Crimmins, & Oliver, 1979). At the same time, there is some evidence that a large number of older children is often correlated with the wife working (Ewer, Crimmins, & Oliver, 1979).

Contrasting traditional and dual-career marriages
Dual-career marriages have been contrasted with traditional marriages. In some instances, there is little to distinguish the two styles. One couple writing about two-career couples noted that women in two-career relationships still bear the major responsibility for household management and child care, which means that when women enter the job market, their workday simply grows longer (Shaevitz & Shaevitz, 1980).

One investigation compared traditional couples (the wife did not work and did not plan to work), neo-traditional couples (the wife did not work, but planned on working), and pioneer couples (the wife worked). The study found that husbands with wives who had great need for personal achievement, perceive this need and want wives to participate in career-related decisions and socio-economic decisions, more than do husbands with wives needing average achievement. Husbands with wives who have a high need for achievement also think that they should perform more household tasks than husbands of wives with average need for achievement. Pioneer husbands perceive their wives participating more in financial decisions and socio-economic decisions. These husbands perform more child-care related activities than the traditional husbands, but the wives think they should do more. Traditional wives are satisfied with the amount of domestic work performed by their husbands (Russell, 1975).

The wives

What are the wives of dual-career couples like? They are more physically active than are traditional housewives (Burke & Weir, 1976). A high proportion of them are the only child or the oldest child in their families, had no other adult relative living within their family setting, had work-oriented mothers, experienced tension of some kind with their fathers, had a prolonged separation from parents during childhood or some other disturbing experience, and were members of a relatively high social class (Beddington, 1973). Working women tend to have uniformly high non-traditional philosophical beliefs, as contrasted with traditional women who tend to be feminine females or engage in sex-linked role behavior (Deutsch, 1978). High status professional women demonstrate a will to succeed that is far beyond that demonstrated by the average American woman.

The husbands

The husbands in the dual-career couple have also been considered in research. Dual-career professional men are the least traditional in philosophical orientation and actual role behavior, while men who are the sole wage-earners are the most traditional on both counts (Deutsch, 1978). The husband's attitude in favor of feminism is largely unrelated to his, or his wife's, reported marital adjustment (Hardesty & Betz, 1980). On the other hand, Goldstein (1978) found that the marital satisfaction of wives could be predicted best on the basis of the husbands' attitudes toward women and the husbands' level of femininity. She also found that the marital satisfaction of husbands in androgynous dyads was greater than for husbands in non-androgynous dyads.

Husbands of housewives are more physically active than are husbands of working women (Burke & Weir, 1976). For men, there is a positive correlation between their job satisfaction and their marital adjustment, which is not shared by women: women tend to demonstrate no correlation between their job satisfaction and their marital adjustment (Ridley, 1973). Both members of the two-career couple have lower needs for social interchange in the areas of affection, inclusion, and control. In other words, these people tend to be more self-reliant and self-sufficient than are persons in traditional relationships (Burke & Weir, 1976).

Marital satisfaction

What effects do two careers have on marital satisfaction? Will dual-career marriages last longer or not as long as traditional marriages? It is not clear whether dual career marriages are happier or less happy than traditional marriages. The level of satisfaction is influenced by the attitudes and behavior of each spouse. Thus, it appears that marital adjustment is high when both spouses are evaluated as high or low in job involvement, or when the husband is medium and the wife has low ratings in job involvement. When either spouse becomes highly involved in a job, marital adjustment seems to suffer (Ridley, 1973). Women with high work commitment demonstrate higher marital satisfaction than do women who are not working outside the home (Safilios-Rothschild, 1970). Both partners are less happy when the wife works because of economic necessity rather than by choice, and more strain exists in marriages when there are preschool children in the family (Hopkins & White, 1978).

Recent evidence indicates that dual-career couples may have increased satisfaction, particularly when the wife's employment is by choice rather than necessity, when the wife is not more successful in her career than her husband, and when the couple shares common values about working women (Yoger, 1982).

In a second study, levels of *career salience*, or the importance or conspicuousness of the career, and profeminist attitudes were shown to relate to marital happiness in dual-career marriages. Husbands and wives report high levels of marital adjustment when they have relatively high profeminist attitudes and moderate levels of career salience, or view their careers as holding importance or being relevant to their lives. Better marital adjustment is reported when greater family income is contributed by the husband (Hardesty & Betz, 1980).

Difficulties

What are the special problems of the dual-career marriage? Perhaps the most outstanding problem in such marriages is the high level of stress which couples report. Leslie (1977) states that couples maintain that they frequently lack the energy or the time to complete all of their many tasks. Couples point out that two full-time careers, management of a home and family, and other responsibilities place enormous demands on both partners. Relationship stress also occurs as a result of differential personal growth and role changes, generally on the part of the woman, with an inability of the marital relationship to adapt to the changes (Rice, 1979).

The women in dual-career marriages probably face the most stress. Frequently they are called upon to accept a large portion of the responsibilities at home, while also maintaining a full-time position. Women are more likely to face stress due to work overload, identity problems, lack of social networks, as well as the discrepancies between personal and social norms of women in our culture (cf. St. John-Parsons, 1978; Johnson & Johnson, 1977). Child-rearing is frequently viewed as the primary province of the woman rather than the man in the dual-career family as well as in single-career families (Johnson & Johnson, 1977).

Not only do women face problems within their family units, but managers and executives may not respond flexibly to the women's role redefinition. Women may perceive themselves primarily in terms of their careers, while their superiors may limit their options by viewing them as wives and mothers. Conversely, women may request leaves, flexitime—working an eight hour day, but beginning and ending earlier or later than the typical 9-to-5 job—or seek other benefits which will help them in their roles as wives and mothers, and these concessions may be denied to them because they are perceived by their superiors as persons who should put their jobs first.

Solving the difficulties

Couples who share the household duties seem to face fewer problems than couples who do not. Maples (1981) found that flexibility tends to provide a feeling of deep satisfaction for couples. Among the flexible methods of solving household problems are sharing the work of childcare from early ages, hiring household help, planning carefully to make the best of limited leisure time, and foregoing many of the routine social activities engaged in by more traditional couples. Couples who are experimenting with new modes of communication and are willing to go beyond stereotyped ways of relating provide stability for each other. Dual-career couples have to work particularly hard at remaining close to each other. Schedules, deadlines, children, and other obligations may contribute to a sense of distance, alienation, or isolation. Open communication, touching, and sexual contact can alleviate the distance that is sometimes experienced (Shaevitz & Shaevitz, 1980).

What kind of people engage in role sharing? Several factors seem to contribute. People who had mothers who worked outside the home, people with postgraduate liberal arts educations, and people maturing in the late 1960s and early 1970s are favorable to role sharing. Women who view work outside the home as leading to greater self-actualization and men who did not view work as a major source of self-esteem engage in role sharing. Factors such as job flexibility, sufficient child care, the earning potential of the wife, and a nontraditional child-rearing philosophy are also important (Haas, 1982).

Husbands and wives can each contribute to the success of the dual-career marriage. Husbands who identify with their wives' career goals, who derive satisfaction from their accomplishments, and who do not feel threatened by their wives, contribute to more successful marriages (Leslie, 1977). Wives can contribute to more successful marriages by defining their own notions of "the full life" rather than accepting societal expectations and norms (Pogrebin, 1978). Women may also find some assistance in separating their professional lives from their home lives in the way that men have traditionally done. They might isolate their more expressive-emotional selves at home and demonstrate their instrumental-rational selves at work. Women may also find it useful to establish priorities for domestic roles; spend time with children focusing on them, rather than on other matters; and consider domestic problems that arise on an immediate basis rather than putting them off (Johnson & Johnson, 1977).

Solving the special problems which are encountered in dual-career couples may be aggravated by the personalities of the people involved. For persons who are involved in dual-careers, achievement and recognition are important. They are willing to invest a great deal of their time and energy in achieving career goals. As a result, they are somewhat rigid and rather single-minded at times. These qualities do not always lend themselves to solving marital or domestic difficulties (Rice, 1979).

Are dual-career marriages worth the difficulties that are faced? Apparently they are for many individuals, since people appear to be entering into dual-career marriages at an increasing rate. The intellectual and psychological benefits which appear to accrue from such marriages seem to outweigh the difficulties. Furthermore, no evidence exists to indicate that there are any disadvantages for the children in dual-career families (St. John-Parsons, 1978). No significant differences have been demonstrated in the values and norms of the partners in single-career or dual-career marriages. (Beddington, 1973), and people seem to be able to respond in a variety of ways in both types of marriage. As we shall determine in the next section, conflict and stress exists to some extent in all marriages.

Conflict and stress in marriage

The discussion of the special problems which occur in dual-career marriages introduces a topic that is relevant to all marital interactions. Husbands and wives all face conflict and stress in varying proportions in their marriages, and conflict appears to recur in a fairly predictable cyclical way in most relationships (cf. Feldman, 1979). On the negative side, it appears that distressed and nondistressed couples can be differentiated on the basis of two behaviors. Distressed couples tend to criticize each other more than do nondistressed couples; nondistressed couples tend to be more responsive than do distressed couples (Koren, Carlton & Shaw, 1980). It appears that criticism may be a negative factor in relational development, while responsiveness is positive.

At the same time conflict is not necessarily a negative factor in marital satisfaction, since it may present an opportunity for couples to develop increased access to each others' interpersonal perceptions. As a consequence of this greater access, the individuals are better able to adapt to stress and change within the relationship. Couples who avoided discussion of the problem as their primary means of conflict management were found to achieve greater perceived agreement, while actually moving farther apart (Knudson, Summers, & Golding, 1980). Superficially, the marriage appeared to be calm and placid, but beneath the surface, there was little understanding. Conflict, then, appears to hold some positive value in interaction.

Marital partners who indicate greater stress in different aspects of their lives also report being less satisfied with their marriages and with their lives in general. It appears that high levels of stress and dissatisfaction are related. Marriage partners can receive help from their spouses, however, in dealing with their individual stresses and difficulties. In marriages in which the partners were satisfied with the help that they received from their spouses, the partners were also more likely to report experiencing less stress. Marital helping can act as a barrier between the partners and the world, lowering the level of stress, and increasing the amount of satisfaction that the partners perceive in their marriages and their lives (Burke & Wier, 1977).

Power and dominance

One area in which conflict may occur in marriages is disagreement concerning which of the two partners has control or is able to dominate. Traditionally, men dominated in most marriages and exhibited the most power. Kidd (1975) reviewed some of the recommendations offered in popular magazines, noting, for instance, an article in the *Ladies Home Journal,* in 1956, which recommended that women and men behave according to traditional patterns. The article implied that when women and men did not behave in traditional ways, it was their sexuality which was at fault (Kidd, 1975). Similarly, an article published in a 1957 issue of *Reader's Digest* recommended that women deceive their husbands deliberately during sexual intercourse. Marion Hillard, the author, wrote,

> A man can feel kinship with the gods if his wife can make him believe he can cause the flowering within her. If she doesn't feel it, she must make every effort to pretend (Kidd, 1975).

Beginning slowly in the early 1960s and increasing steadily thereafter, a new notion of appropriate interpersonal relations evolved, challenging the dominant positions of husbands. As the "self" increased in importance, social institutions were suubordinated and their power to define relationships diminished. (Kidd, 1975). In 1967, for instance, 48% of all spouses expected their husbands to have the greater share of influence, 10% expected wives to have most or somewhat more influence, and 42% responded that they thought each of the mates would have about the same amount of influence. In actual interaction, husbands were more likely to have a high degree of influence on their wives. Role differentiation was also stressed in the reports of this study, too, as 80% of the wives contributed most or more of the social-emotional support (Smith, 1967).

Competence

Does dominance of one partner occur as a result of his or her competence? The control of husbands is greatest when the husband is more competent and when the cultural norms are patriarchal; that is, the expectations are that men are in charge. Patriarchal norms become unimportant when the husband is not perceived as competent. Egalitarian, or shared, marital control occurs when the norms are egalitarian and when the husbands' levels of competence are perceived to be the same as wives' (Nye, 1982). Competence, then, appears to mediate in decision-making.

Education and salary levels

Education and salary levels also affect power in the family. The more educated both spouses are, the more egalitarian is the authority between them. The husband's authority increases with his salary. Only in the area of family budgeting does the traditional wife have a disadvantage in relation to the working wife. The working wife makes 25% of the financial decisions by herself, 53% with her husband; and she does not participate at all in 22% of the decisions. Non-working wives make about 14% of the financial decisions by themselves, 44% with their husbands; and they do not participate at all in 43% of the decisions (Gottman, Markman, & Notarius, 1970). Working mothers participate in household tasks less than non-working mothers, and their husbands participate more. Working mothers make fewer decisions about routine household matters than non-working mothers, while their husbands participate more. At the same time no differences occur between husbands and wives in comparisons involving working and non-working wife situations. Regardless of whether women work or do not work, husbands tend to make more decisions for the family (Hoffman, 1970).

Marital satisfaction

Are husbands and wives satisfied in their marriages, regardless of who has the power? The persons most dissatisfied with their marriages are wives who are very dominant. The women who are most satisfied are those who are not particularly dominant but who do show some authority, and those who have no authority and have notably dominant husbands (Gottman, Markman & Natarius, 1970). Only in cultures in which egalitarian ideals exist do women and men appear to have the same opportunities of gaining and maintaining power and being perceived positively when they hold power (Bah & Rollins, 1976).

Communication behaviors

Subtle differences occur in the communication behavior of persons who have control in a relationship. Partners who perceive themselves to have power in a marital dyad tend to use more bilateral strategies as well as more direct strategies. *Bilateral strategies* are those in which persuasion is used as opposed to the person simply doing what she or he desires. *Direct strategies* are those in which persons state what they want outright rather than trying to manipulate the other person through hinting, making subtle suggestions, or using other forms of manipulation. In heterosexual relationships men are more likely to use direct and bilateral strategies than are women, possibly because they expect compliance. Women perceive themselves as influencing their partners from a subordinate position, while men perceive themselves in a position of relative power (Falbo & Peplau, 1980).

Millar and Rogers-Millar have completed a great deal of research on marital interactions. They first noted that a difference exists between dominance and domineeringness. *Domineeringness* was defined as the extent of one-up statements a person made. A one-up statement is defined as that which attempts to assert definitional rights. For instance, a woman might assert, "I really enjoy my night class this quarter; I think I'll plan on enrolling in night classes every quarter."

Dominance was viewed as a measure which derives from the interactions between two people. A measure of dominance is determined by comparing the interactions between two people in which a one-up statement is followed by a one-down statement by the other person, as contrasted with a one-up statement by the other person. In the example of the wife asserting her feelings about night classes and her plans to enroll in more night courses, dominance would be exhibited if her husband responded, "Oh no, you're not. I'm tired of being at home with the kids when you're out every night of the week." Dominance would not be exhibited if the husband offered a one-up statement such as, "I know what you mean—some of my best courses were at night, too. I think I might enroll in a graduate course at night next quarter myself."

Millar and Rogers-Millar posit that domineeringness is part of dominance as measured; but it is not a predictor of dominance nor should it be conceptually or operationally equated with dominance. They found that while domineeringness does not allow statements about one's own dominance, it decreases the likelihood of the other person's dominance. In order to avoid being dominated, a person could increase his or her own domineeringness.

They also found that a relationship exists between wives' and husbands' scores on these attitudes and marital satisfaction. The larger the wife's domineeringness score, the less communication satisfaction both the husband and wife report, and the less marital satisfaction the wife reports. Although the husband's domineeringness score is also inversely related to marital and communication satisfaction, the relationship is not as well-established as is the wife's domineeringness score. In addition, husband dominance explains some of the reported levels of marital satisfaction in couples. In other words, when husbands make one-up statements followed by the wife's one-down statements rather than combative one-up statements, then the husbands and wives report more marital satisfaction (Rogers & Millar, 1979; Courtright, Millar, & Rogers, 1979). These findings support traditional relationships in which husbands serve as the dominant person. At the same time they call into question the efficacy or usefulness of domineeringness in marital interaction. Domineeringness appears to be a negative factor which militates against the member of the couple who relies upon it. Most of us desire marital satisfaction and are willing to alter behaviors in order to achieve improved levels of marital happiness. In the next section we will consider this topic.

Improving marital satisfaction

Marital satisfaction is difficult to achieve. Changing conceptions of women and men as well as new and different relational styles contribute to the problem. Men have difficulty dealing with women who are ambitious and independent, and women have trouble when men are unemotional or overly emotional. Cohabitation by friends, homosexual relationships, and frequent dissolutions of relationships add to the confusion. People who marry desire satisfying relationships, yet few appear to maintain long and happy marriages.

The changes that are occurring in our culture make it increasingly imperative for people to rely upon communication to negotiate role expectations and definitions. While Rawlins (1983) details the dilemmas associated with achieving relational satisfaction through communication, we can point to some communication practices which encourage relational satisfaction.

Interaction

Interaction, in and of itself, appears to be a predictor of marital success. A review of the 1960s contended that mutual expressiveness between the husband and wife contributed to the woman's feeling of role satisfaction (Hicks & Platt, 1970). More recently, Birchler and Webb (1977) determined that one could discriminate between happy and unhappy couples on the basis of amount of interaction. Happy couples enjoyed more activities together, including sexual intercourse. Further, they did not withdraw from each other as did unhappy couples.

Communicator style

The communicator styles of the spouses is also relevant. Happily married couples report that they alter their communication styles within their marriage more than when they are communicating in general. These couples tended to communicate in a relaxed, friendly, open, dramatic, and attentive style within their marriages. Men who are expressive and women who are attentive report happiness in their marriages (Honeycutt, Wilson & Parker, 1982).

Self-disclosure

Self-disclosure is valuable in satisfying marriages, but we observed earlier that the amount of self-disclosure which is desirable is not clear, pointing out in chapter 4 that "more" may be "better" but that this is not universally true. Current studies indicate that reciprocity in self-disclosure may be more important than high levels of self-disclosure (cf. Davidson, Balswick, & Halverson, 1983; Hendrick, 1981). Imbalance in self-disclosure, rather than low amounts, appears to be related to lower levels of marital satisfaction.

Trust

Trust is also related to satisfying marriages. Persons who are married for long periods of time appear to score high on trust, and partners appear to reciprocate trust more than they do love or self-disclosure. Failure to reciprocate trust appears to be a predictor of failing relationships. Couples who dissolved their relationships showed the highest discrepancy in levels of trust of the other person. The highest levels of trust appear in couples who live together, are newly married, or who have been married for more than twenty years (Larzelere & Huston, 1980).

Parental identification and role expectations

At the beginning of the contemporary women's movement, in 1960, parental identification was shown to affect personal reports of marital satisfaction. Luckey (1960) found that men who identified with their fathers were more often in satisfactory marriages than in unsatisfactory ones, but that women who identified with their mothers were not necessarily more satisfied in their marriages than were women who did not identify with their mothers. The predictor for women's satisfactory marriages was related to how similar they viewed their husbands and fathers to be. The investigator in this study concluded that in satisfying marriages, the relationship is similar to that between parent and child, that satisfied women are those who interact with their husbands as fathers. This study might be of even more interest if it were conducted on couples of the 1980s. Current research leads us to the conclusion that people of either gender who hold high self-concepts generally report that they have more satisfactory marriages, as we noted earlier.

At the present time, we know that the communication of role expectations plays a significant part in satisfactory marriages. Women and men are provided with a larger range of roles than those couples participating in the 1960s research. Marital satisfaction, at least for women today, is related to their success in meeting, and exceeding, the role expectations expressed to them by their spouses (Petronio, 1982). The importance of interpersonal communication in the negotiation process cannot be overemphasized.

Satisfaction in marriages

We can have satisfying marriages. We can apply information about the variables which predict success in marriages. People who marry after their teens, people with a high school education or more, and people who had parents in happy marriages are all more likely to succeed (cf. Bahr, 1980; Locks, 1982). The avoidance of extremes within marriages—including community involvement, visits with relatives, time spent with friends, and even church attendance—has been demonstrated to enhance marital relationships (Holman, 1981).

Assistance available for troubled marriages

When marriages need assistance, communication training (Epstein & Jackson, 1978) and other skill development (Warmbrook, 1982) have been shown to be useful. A variety of agencies and groups offer support systems and training sessions for marital improvement. Many of these organizations focus on communication skills such as listening, empathy, openness, self-disclosure, assertiveness, and clarity. Both women and men can become successful marital partners and develop more effective and mutually satisfying interaction patterns. Couples probably realize greater growth by attending workshops and seminars together rather than separately. As we observed in chapter 1, communication is a negotiated process, and successful communication in the marital setting is probably dependent upon both persons interacting in useful ways rather than only one person learning new skills and behaviors.

Improving marital communication

Marital satisfaction between women and men is difficult to achieve because of the behavioral differences which are discussed in this book. Women and men have different perceptions, use different verbal and nonverbal symbols, and are distinctive in their abilities to self-disclose, be empathic, listen, and be assertive. The frustrations which occur when others do not reciprocate our behaviors mitigate against successful and satisfying marriages. Men tend to show a greater investment in a relationship during its early, premarital stages than during the post-marital period (cf. Dawkins, 1976;). Women tend to adopt a more relational stance toward their partners in the early phases than later on. Researchers recommend androgyny as the ideal standard of mental health (Kraevetz & Jones, 1981). We recommend flexibility in communication behavior and the development of larger behavioral repertoires as keys to more successful and satisfying relationships.

Contemporary authors offer specific recommendations. Virginia Satir, author of *Conjoint Family Therapy*, writes that a woman's and man's perceptions of her or his own communication and the communication of the other person is essential in understanding the development of deterioration of a relationship (1964). Montgomery (1981) finds that quality communication within marriages consists of four skills. *Openness* requires self-disclosure on both parts; *confirmation* involves the acceptance of oneself and of the spouse; *transactional management* requires the ability to control the communication situation; and *situational adaptability* is the ability to change appropriately given a particular situation.

Pearson (1983) states that four stages are especially relevant in the development of intimate relationships. She identifies these stages as (1) sharing the self, (2) affirming the other, (3) becoming "one," and (4) transcending "one." Sharing the self is similar to self-disclosure. Sharing yourself is particularly important in the establishment of a close personal relationship. Self-disclosure in this setting should be open, personal, and direct. People frequently equate intimate communication with self-disclosure since the two are almost synonymous. Consider your own intimate relationship(s): Do you self-disclose openly and honestly? Do you express your thoughts and feelings? Are you responsive to the self-disclosures of your partner and attempt to reciprocate the level of self-disclosure which she or he offers?

Affirming the other person may be considered as similar to empathy. When we affirm another person we attempt to validate who that person is. We acknowledge that this individual is unique and imply that he or she is important. While we try to put ourselves in the other person's place, we do not necessarily agree with all his/her perceptions, beliefs, attitudes, or values. Do you affirm your partner? Do you let him or her know that you really understand who he or she is and appreciate that individual's unique qualities and characteristics? Do you try to understand his or her perceptions, values, and attitudes?

When we become "one" with another person, we experience a kind of bonding. A new unit is created from two previous and distinct personalities. People who have been married for some time may appear to look the same, behave similarly, and speak in the same way. Although this does not necessarily happen, it is generally true that couples develop special ways of communicating that are unique to their relationship. Special words, pet names, and shared experiences all contribute to the "us" that is created from a "you" and a "me." Do you feel that you and your intimate partner have become one? What characteristics make your relationship as a couple different from the qualities which each of you contribute? How are you, as a couple, different from other couples you know?

Transcending "oneness" in intimate relationships resembles self-actualization in personal development. When we feel truly secure in our intimate relationships, we are able to gain and to offer independence and equality. Each partner has the security of a loving, understanding relationship and the freedom to develop as an independent person, too. She or he is able to put "we" and "me" together in an harmonious way rather than allowing them to be mutually exclusive conditions. Do you feel that you can be yourself in the intimate relationship in which you are involved? Do you allow your partner the freedom to grow independently as well as within your relationship?

Summary

Couple communication is an emerging area of interest. While the literature is fairly new and sometimes insufficient for sweeping generalizations, we can draw some conclusions. Individuals who are initially attracted to each other and begin dating are frequently similar in a number of respects including in attractiveness. People who are dating self-disclose personal information to each other and exhibit reciprocity in communication. Intimates frequently talk simultaneously, interrupt each other, and exchange talk turns rapidly. Nonverbally, dating couples tend to gaze into each others eyes, sit closer, stand closer, and use increased touching.

Cohabitation has become increasingly popular in the past decade. Individuals who cohabit are not very different from their peers who marry. Legal problems can arise in the cohabiting situation that are different from the legal problems that occur when a marriage dissolves. Married people are perceived more positively and appear to be more healthy than are unmarried people. Similarity between the members of the couple is a relevant predictor of marital satisfaction.

Dual-career marriages have become increasingly prevalant in the past decade. Dual-career marriages include wives who have a pronounced "will to succeed" and other characteristics that are different from traditional housewives. Although the men in dual-career marriages are not highly discrepant from the men in single-career marriages, they also have some unique qualities. Even though a high level of stress is often present in dual-career marriages, many people feel that the gains are worth the added difficulties. Marital success in the dual-career couple is dependent upon the flexibility and support of the two members. Role sharing at home and at work is important as are new communicative strategies.

Conflict and stress exist to some extent in every marriage, appear to be cyclical in occurrence, and may have positive impact on the success of the marriage. Conflict may encourage openness and it provides valuable information to the other spouse. Power and dominance in marriages has changed in the past two decades. Power has shifted from a male domain to a shared function. The person who is more competent, more educated, and has a higher salary level often has more control than the other spouse. It is not surprising that our male-oriented society encourages people to perceive marriages in which the man is dominant, but where the woman has no authority or where she has some authority, as the most satisfying. Different communicative strategies are pursued by those individuals who perceive that they have power in the marital dyad than by those who perceive that they do not. A distinction between dominance and domineeringness in communicative behaviors are useful in our consideration of this topic.

Marriages can be highly satisfying and they can be improved in satisfaction. Communication behaviors are highly related to marital satisfaction.

First, interaction is related to marital satisfaction. Second, specific characteristics of Norton's Communicator Style are related to marital satisfaction. Self-disclosure and trust are related to marital satisfaction. Parental identification and role expectations affect marital satisfaction. A variety of resources are available for people who wish to remedy problems in troubled marriages or improve good ones. Marital communication can be improved by sharing our self, affirming our spouse, becoming "one" with him or her, and transcending that "oneness."

These four stages are important in the successful marriage. Other factors may intervene, however, as we shall determine in the next section. In order to bridge the information on marital satisfaction that we have been discussing to the information on family communication that we will discuss, we might consider the impact having a child may have on marital satisfaction. In a single statement, the arrival of children alters the marital relationship and the level of marital satisfaction. Couples with children report the most satisfaction when the children are young, before their teenage years, and then again after the children leave home (Lampe, 1980). With this transition, let us turn to interaction patterns in the family.

Family communication

Parent-child interaction

Family communication is a newly emerging area of investigation. Researchers have become increasingly interested in interaction patterns between parents and their children (cf. Nye, 1982), with studies of infant-parent communication largely focusing on mother-infant interaction. These studies demonstrate that mothers adjust their speech when they are interacting with children in order to gain the child's attention, to probe the child's language ability, to provide the child experience with conversational turn-taking, and to teach grammatical structure (cf. Sachs, 1977; Snow, 1977). These maternal speech adjustments have been labeled motherese (Newport, 1976). *Motherese* includes reduced sentence length and complexity (cf. Phillips, 1973; Snow, 1972), higher pitch, and exaggerated intonation patterns (Garnica, 1977; Nelson, 1978; Ryan, 1978; Snow, 1977, 1979). It frequently includes many questions and imperatives, few subordinate clauses, few past tenses, and longer pauses between utterances (Snow, 1977).

Mothers and infants have been studied to determine how they mutually regulate each others' speech. Mothers and infants appear to be mutually responsive to each others' vocalizations (Anderson, Vietze, & Dokecki, 1977). From early infancy to preschool years, mothers, by means of their speech adaptations, are able to engage and assist their children in conversations (Snow, 1978). As they grow older, children are given a more active role in the conversations which they have with their mothers.

Fathers and mothers do not speak the same way to their children (cf. Malone, 1982; Bellinger & Gleason, 1982), nor do parents speak the same way to their daughters and their sons (Snow, Jacklin, & Maccoby, 1983). The communication between fathers and infants, as well as between mothers and infants, was examined in the case of 19-month old infants and their parents in a laboratory playroom. Researchers found that fathers spoke less and took fewer conversational turns, but their speech to their children was similar to the mothers in the average length of the conversational turns, average length of the utterances, average number of verbs, and relative proportion of questions, declaratives, and imperatives. Depending on the child's sex, fathers and mothers responded differently to the children. Both mothers and fathers took more conversational turns with sons than with daughters and had longer conversations with daughters (Golinkoff & Ames, 1979).

Another study examined the speech of five French-speaking couples with their male children who were aged from 18 to 36 months. Paternal speech displayed the same simplification that has been regularly found in mothers. As the child becomes older, parents increase their vocabulary, utterance length, and complexity of their sentences, while decreasing repetitions, expansions, and commands. Differences between paternal and maternal speech style emerged in this study. In the language development of their children, mothers and fathers may play roles which complement each other. Mothers used longer average lengths of utterances compared to fathers. They also corrected the incorrect speech of their children to a greater extent than did fathers. The longest utterances to children, however, were by fathers, and these were related to a larger number of requests for clarification (Rondal, 1980).

A final study on infant-parent interaction demonstrates that mothers and fathers provide different language contexts for their year-old infants. Mothers are more likely to have longer dialogues with infants of either gender, and fathers are more likely to have shorter dialogues with sons. Mothers and fathers tend to respond similarly to daughters. Fathers and daughters talk more and longer than do fathers and sons. Fathers may play an important role in the language development of their infants. Fathers may be more responsible than mothers in encouraging language ability differences between boys and girls at early ages, since they discriminate between boys and girls in the amount of interaction. Mothers do not discriminate between boys and girls.

Earlier work in this area appeared to indicate that from the early ages of the sons, fathers and sons demonstrate a preference to interact. (Lamb, 1977; Parke & O'Leary, 1976; Parke & Sawin, 1975; Rendina & Dickerscheid, 1976). While the finding that fathers and daughters talk more appears to contradict these findings, another conclusion in this study supports the special relationship that appears to exist between fathers and sons. Sons responded more contingently, or conditionally, to their fathers' verbal initiations than to their mothers'. For example, sons might offer indirect responses, one-syllable responses such as "yeah," "huh?" or "hmm;" may respond with a comment about a different topic, or may offer no verbal response at all. Sons responded more contingently than did daughters to their fathers' verbal initiations, too. Fathers tend to terminate conversations with sons if their sons are not responding, thus providing a context in which conversations, when they do occur, are mutual. With daughters, both fathers and mothers are more likely to continue to talk even if no response is forthcoming.

Differing conversational patterns occur more often when parents are individually talking with their infants than if both parents are present and conversing with the child. The lengths of the dialogues increase in the dyadic setting and non-reciprocal dialogue are proportionately less likely to occur. This conclusion suggests that the dyad consisting of parent and child is the ideal context for parent-child interaction rather than the triadic context including both parents and the child (Killarney & McCluskey, 1981).

Parents engage in more touching with their infants and small children than they do with their older children, but our culture does not encourage touching among family members to the same extent as do some other cultures. Some researchers have pointed out that a lack of body contact with the mother and prolonged social isolation results in abnormal adult social and sexual behaviors (Harlow, 1963). Countries like Japan have cultures with intense early attachments and extensive physical contact in mother-child interactions until the child is at least ten years of age (Caudill & Weinstein, 1969). Cultural norms of the United States encourage early separation of the infant from the mother, with the social reinforcement of independent behaviors on the part of the child occurring at the same time. Some writers have postulated that children in the United States may not be receiving as much stimulation as they need from their caretakers, and that we may be headed for a national crisis as these children become adults (Bronfenbrenner, 1970; Fraiber, 1977). The alienation that is felt by school-age children in the United States has been viewed to be due to a possible lack of early parent-child nonverbal interaction (Bronfenbrenner, 1970).

In addition to examining infant-parent interactions, research studies have focused on adolescent-parent interrelations. Many of these studies have concerned issues such as dependence-independence and harmony-conflict (cf. Douvan & Adelson, 1966; Offer, 1969). More recently some of these studies have examined the extent to which interaction between adolescents and parents is egalitarian rather than authoritarian. A recent investigation indicates that while egalitarian ideals tend to be increasing in American families, egalitarian interaction is not keeping pace. The researchers find that complete egalitarianism is difficult in families in which the resources are not evenly divided. They found that egalitarianism is possible at the level of the *content* of family interaction, but it is probably not possible at the level of the *structure* of family interaction (Papini & Datan, 1981).

As we know, children are not all the same. Not only do we find a great deal of difference among normal children; some children are born with special problems. When children have such problems, communication patterns with them are different than they are with normal children. For example, researchers examined the different interaction patterns that occurred between schizophrenic and normal children. Families with a schizophrenic child were characterized by fathers who communicated much less with their children and sons who communicated less with their fathers. A role reversal occurred for the mothers, thus creating a situation of maternal dominance in families with a schizophrenic child. In addition, mothers of schizophrenic children tended to be withdrawn and cold (Ferreira & Winter, 1970). The difficulties of dealing with children with special problems is evident in the communication patterns in the family.

Single parenting

Single parenting is a topic which should be considered in this section of the text. Our contemporary social reality forecasts that one adult in every four will become a single parent. Half of the women in our society are likely to be single mothers. *Single parent families,* those families which include one parent and at least one dependent child living in the same household, may occur as a result of divorce, separation, widowhood, non-marriage, or adoption. The childbearing decision, once left to chance, has become an area of increasing interest. Both couples and single individuals face a large number of choices about how, when, why, and whether to have children (Fox, 1982).

These new choices alter the complexion of the family unit and result in larger numbers of single parent families. A current estimate suggests that of the 30 million families in the United States, 19% are headed by a single parent (Weiss, 1979). One out of every six children, or eleven million children, were living in single parent families in 1979 (Mandes, 1979; Weiss, 1979). Estimates suggest that by the time children reach the age of 18, 50% of them will have spent some part of their lives in a single parent family unit (Schorr & Moen, 1979; Weiss, 1979).

Although single parent families are prevalent in our society, single parenting is not yet a routinized form of family functioning. The role expectations of the single parent are ambiguous and the behaviors which she or he should exhibit are unclear. Incompatibility between the number of single parent families and the lack of acceptance of this type of family result in stress for individuals in single parent families.

The problem most commonly reported by persons who become single parents is that of loneliness. Single parent status is socially stigmatized because it tends to threaten our ideals and our myths about marriages and families. Single parents have less time for social participation and they are more isolated from their neighbors (Smith, 1980). Single parents are more likely to express a need to have someone to talk to than are individuals in *nuclear families,* those families which have a wage-earning father, a home-making mother, and children (Koch-Nielsen, 1980). Fathers are particularly vulnerable to not having friends with whom to interact (Weiss, 1979). Single women feel more restricted in their relationships with others and may face problems such as sexual propositions and loss of status and respect (Kitson, Lopata, Holmes, & Meyering, 1980).

Solutions to the problem of loneliness which are faced by single parents include gearing activities in our culture to single parents as well as coupled parents, increasingly accepting alternative family styles, and coming to grips with the notion that the nuclear family is a myth rather than reality in twentieth-century America. Unrelated substitute parents, who might include housekeepers or lovers, can assist the single parent in overcoming loneliness and in caring for the children. Relatives, too, can function as auxilary parents. In any case, we need to become more responsive to the interaction needs of a group of people who are increasing in size each day. Keep in mind that one out of every four of us will become a single parent!

Alternative family structures

Family communication is changing. The traditional nuclear families are being replaced by a variety of different kinds of families, including the single-parent family. Interaction between parents and children is also changing. Fathers may be spending more time interacting with infants and small children. More egalitarian talk may be replacing the superior-subordinate interaction among parents and their adolescents.

The changing nature of the talk which occurs within the family challenges each of us to be flexible in our interactions with our own family members and with other families. We need to consider whether we are discriminating in our communication behavior between children of different sexes and what those differences may cause. We need to examine our openness and acceptance of a wide variety of different kinds of families. As Jane Howard, author of *Families,* writes,

> They're saying that families are dying, and soon. They're saying it loud, but we'll see that they're wrong. Families aren't dying. The trouble we take to arrange ourselves in some semblance or other of families is one of the most imperishable habits of the human race. What families are doing, in flamboyant and dumfounding ways, is changing their size and their shape and their purpose. Only 16.3 percent of this country's 56 million families are conventionally "nuclear," with breadwinning fathers, homemaking mothers, and resident children. That leaves 83.7 percent to find other arrangements, which are often so noisy that the clamor resulting is easily mistaken for a death rattle (Howard, 1978).

As we ourselves readjust, we must be careful to demonstrate our respect for others and our willingness to adapt to new circumstances.

Improving family communication

Family communication patterns can encourage or discourage satisfying relationships. Pearson (1983) states that three needs should be met in our interactions with the members of our families: 1) establishment of the individual's need for autonomy, 2) maintenance of the family's need for interdependence, and 3) development of an awareness of the recurring interactional patterns and the changes within the family system.

We allow members to be autonomous, or separate, functioning people when we permit open and honest self-disclosure for all family members. People of both genders and all ages need the opportunity to share their feelings, thoughts, and ideas, even when they are discrepant from the rest of the family. Consider your own family: Do you allow others to self-disclose? Do you tell your parents or children how you feel? Do members of your family feel free to disagree? Autonomy may also be dependent upon assertiveness skills. Examine the members of your family and the extent to which each is assertive. Do any of them regularly display aggressiveness with the others? Do some members of the family typically behave nonassertively?

We learn about sex roles as we grow and mature; similarly, we learn about family roles. We learn that the role of mother may be different than the role of father or child. In order to understand better some of these roles, complete the following exercise. Provide as many descriptive terms as you wish for each of the following categories.

1. The characteristics that best describe a father are

_____
_____
_____

2. The characteristics that best describe a mother are

_____
_____
_____

3. The characteristics that best describe a son are

_____
_____
_____

4. The characteristics that best describe a daughter are

_____
_____
_____

The family is an interdependent unit which means that each member of the family has needs that are satisfied by the others in the group, and each in turn satisfies the needs of the others. Interdependence is maintained as family members engage in active listening and empathic understanding. Consider the level of listening and empathy in your family. Do people seem to listen to and care for each other? Are family members willing to put their own needs aside from time to time in order to try to understand the problems of the others from their point of view? Do family members avoid defensiveness, dominating the conversation, evaluation, disconfirming statements, and other negative behaviors?

We need to develop an awareness of the recurring interaction patterns and the changes that occur within our family systems. In the cartoon on page 312, Linus and Lucy demonstrate the sometimes negative recurring interaction patterns that occur between brothers and sisters. The changes in sex roles

5. If I become a mother/father, I would like to be described as

_____

_____

_____

6. As a son/daughter, I could best be described as

_____

_____

_____

7. I would like my daughters, if I have any, to be described as

_____

_____

_____

8. I would like my sons, if I have any, to be described as

_____

_____

_____

After you have completed the sentences individually, discuss your responses with the other members in your class. What similarities occur among your lists? What differences? How do family roles relate to sex roles? How can family roles be separated from traditional sex roles? To what extent do you envision a family which is similar to the family in which you grew up? To what extent do you envision your family to be different from the family in which you grew up?

which have been discussed in this text are only one example of the rapid alterations occurring in our culture. The modifications in the family unit discussed in this section are another example of rapid change.

In addition to these changes, individual families go through major alterations. Family members are born, others die, some move away, and others move back home. Some family members work while others lose their jobs, some begin to attend college while others graduate or drop out. As they mature, family members agree to take on new tasks within the home and are able to perform them; others relinquish particular duties because they feel the tasks are no longer appropriate for them to do. These changes strongly impact on the communication patterns in the family and on the resulting satisfaction that people feel. To the extent that we understand that all families go through changes and that we must be willing to adapt in order to cope and to grow, we will be involved in a family which is fully functioning.

Conclusions

In this chapter we explored communication which occurs in intimate contexts. Sexuality is an important and universal behavior within and outside of marriages. We learned in this chapter that women and men are perceived to be different in their sexual behavior. The "double standard" implies that men can experiment with sexuality with less fear of negative sanctions than can women. We considered the topics of sex guilt and sexual satisfaction which have interesting and differing implications for women and men.

The communication that occurs within couples has been studied and some generalizations are warranted. Patterns for initial attraction and dating behavior were considered. Traditional and non-traditional couples provide similar and differing behavioral patterns. The dual-career marriage, like cohabitation, has increased in recent times. New and complicated problems occur within dual-career marriages. We examined conflict, stress, power, and dominance in marriages. We proposed methods of improving marital satisfaction and included a discussion of interaction patterns, communicator style, self-disclosure, trust, parental identification, and role expectations.

Family communication has become the focus of research recently. Parents and children interact in somewhat predictable ways, and these interactions vary, depending upon the gender of the parent and the gender of the child. Single parent families have become more prevalent and present special problems for individuals within such families. While family structures are going through shifts and changes, family communication can be highly satisfying and can be improved.

10 Public contexts

Introduction

In the last chapter, we considered differences in the communicative behaviors of women and men in intimate settings; in this chapter, we will examine communicative behaviors which occur in public contexts. We will identify differences which exist in communication between women and men in small group interaction, differences in their leadership behaviors, and their public speaking skills. Communication in the business setting will be highlighted as we consider occupational choices, employment interviews, discrimination in obtaining new positions, and women as managers. We will observe that women and men are distinctive in their public communication behaviors and are treated differently in the workplace.

Specific communication behaviors

Earlier in this text, we noted that women and men exhibit a variety of differences in their verbal and nonverbal communication. We determined that men and women vary in their expressions of self-awareness, self-disclosure, and self-assertion. Men and women are perceived to be different in their abilities to listen and to empathize with others. Interpersonal attraction appears to be a different variable for men than for women. In this section of the text, we will determine how some of these specific differences in communication skills interact with particular communication settings. We will begin with small group communication.

Small group interaction

Baird (1976) provided a very thorough review of female/male differences in small group interaction. We will consider some of those findings as well as additional research that has been provided subsequently. In small groups, men tend to initiate more verbal activity than do women and demonstrate more task-related behavior than do women. Women tend to offer more positive responses than do men, and men tend to be more informative, objective, and goal-oriented; women tend to be more opinionated (cf. Heiss, 1962; Gouran, 1968). In unpleasant interactions, women tend to withdraw while men are inclined to talk more (Young, 1969). These conclusions are consistent with the findings in the earlier chapters which report that men are more instrumental, women are more expressive, and men tend to talk more than do women.

One of the more common purposes for small group communication is problem-solving. Early research in this area implied that women were superior at tasks which were personally interesting, while men were superior on abstract multiple-choice problems (South, 1927). Men may be superior to women in problem-solving ability, but this difference is reduced when mixed sex groups are examined, and when women are highly motivated to solve problems (cf. Hoffman & Maier, 1961).

Women are sometimes perceived to be less competent in problem-solving or decision-making in the small group (cf. Meeker & Weitzel-O'Neill, 1977). Women may be able to overcome these perceptions by increasing their demonstrated competence. Bradley (1980) found that women who demonstrated high task-related competence were treated with friendliness, reason, and relatively few displays of dominance from their male interactants. She also found, however, that these women were not particularly well liked, in the sense that they held high interpersonal attraction for the men. The quality of competence appears to carry a price tag for women in the small group setting.

Risk-taking

Risk-taking appears to be higher in small group communication than in individual behavior. Are women and men equally likely to take risks in the small group? Studies which have focused on individuals indicate that men are more prone to take risks than are women (cf. Maier & Burke, 1967; Minton & Miller, 1970; Bauer & Turner, 1974). The "risky shift" phenomenon refers to the tendency of groups to take larger risks in decision-making than individual members will take in making the same decisions. This tendency occurs in all combinations of sex-composed groups, including mixed-sex groups, all-female groups, and all-male groups, but it occurs most frequently in mixed—sex groups, followed by all-male groups, and all-female groups (Harper, 1970). Women's greater risk-taking behavior in groups is replaced by more conservative behavior when they are alone (Wallach, Kogan & Bem, 1962).

Cooperativeness/competitiveness

The differences between women and men in their cooperativeness and competitiveness also affect their small group behavior. You will recall from chapter 1, that women tend to be more cooperative than men; similarly, they seem to be more willing to share resources with their opponents than are men (Leventhal & Lane, 1970; Benton, 1973). Some theorists have conjectured that men play to win, while women play to avoid losing. Women appear to be more interested in fair outcomes than in winning (cf. Phillips & Cole, 1970; Hattes & Kahn, 1974). Female motivation may be based on "fear of success," a greater need for acceptance and affiliation, or a lesser need for dominance and achievement. At the end of this section, we will observe that these results appear to be in a state of flux.

Conflict and conflict resolution

Men and women appear to be different in their engagement in conflict and in their methods of conflict-resolution. Men appear to be far more likely to engage in aggression than are women (Sears, 1961; Gordon & Cohn, 1961; Lefkowitz, Eron, Walder & Huesmann, 1977). Men are more likely to be *Machiavellian,* attempting to gain their own way through deception and deceit, than are women (Christie, 1970; Kaplowitz, 1976). Women, on the other hand, are more likely to engage in socially acceptable behavior to resolve conflict than are men (Jourard, 1971; Roloff, 1980). Men are more likely to use anti-social modes of behavior in conflict resolution such as *regression* (resolving the conflict by internalizing feelings or by seeking help), *revenge* (getting even), *verbal aggression* (attacking the other person's self-concept), and *physical violence* (physically attacking). Women are more likely to resort to socially acceptable modes of behavior, including reasoning and understanding.

An interesting study examined the relationship of adolescent male and female choices of modes of conflict resolution in their lives and in their favorite television characters. Roloff and Greenberg (1979) found that females were more likely to use verbal aggression, socially acceptable modes, and revenge, as contrasted with males, who were more inclined to use verbal aggression, physical aggression, and revenge in their real lives. Females perceived that their favorite television characters were more likely to use regression and socially acceptable modes, while males perceived their characters as using more physical aggression and revenge. Some relationship exists between our own choices of modes of conflict resolution and those of our favorite characters.

Coalition formation

Coalitions, or sub-groups, sometimes form in the small group setting. Both women and men tend to join the majority coalition, but women are more likely to do so when they are weak, while men are more likely to do so when they are strong (Bond & Vinacke, 1961). When three men are placed together, the men tend to engage in a dominance struggle in which the two strongest males tend to form a coalition and the weakest male is excluded (Uesugi & Vicacke, 1963). When triads (three-person groups) include two men and a woman, the men compete for the woman's attention (Amidjaja & Vinacke, 1965). When women are in the majority, they tend to include any person who may be left out, regardless of his or her sex (Amidjaja & Vinacke, 1965; Vinacke, 1955).

Sex composition of the group

Do men and women prefer to work in same-sex or mixed-sex groups? Women prefer all women if the group is small; they prefer the inclusion of men only if the group is large. Men, on the other hand, prefer to have women present in both a small and a large group situation. Furthermore, cohesiveness within a small all-male group takes a longer time to materialize. (Marshall & Heslin, 1975). Women appear to perceive communication in the smaller group as more personal, or more appropriate for same-sexed persons, whereas men do not discriminate between smaller and larger groups.

As our culture changes, do women and men behave differently in the small group setting? Fisher (1983) found that the sexual composition of groups did not affect the interaction patterns they displayed, although the cooooperative-competitive orientation prescribed influenced both the content and relationship patterns of interaction. Yamada, Tjosvold, and Draguns (1983), conversely, determined that the sex composition and the sex appropriateness of situations affected the style of interaction more than did cooperation. In addition, the sex of the participant and the sex composition of the group were not found to affect cooperation. These conflicting findings may be explained in a variety of ways, not the least of which is our changing culture and concurrent role expectations.

Ellis and McCallister (1980) hypothesized that psychological sex type might be more useful than biological sex in their examination of relational control patterns in the small group. They determined that masculine individuals compete for control in predictable patterns of relational interaction, that feminine individuals use equality and submissiveness, but not according to predictable patterns, and that androgynous individuals are more moderate and use patterns of idea initiation. Ellis and McCallister thus support the notion that conflicting findings concerning the role of biological sex may be due to differences in the expression of internalized sex roles.

Summary

We may summarize the research on small group interaction by observing that men tend to dominate, are goal-oriented, are competitive, are aggressive, are Machiavellian, and are more likely to use anti-social modes of behavior. Women tend to be submissive, cooperative, pro-social, and more concerned with including all of the group members. Mixed sex-groups are more likely to engage in risk-taking, are preferred by men, are preferred by women if the group is large, and may provide outcomes which are superior to all-male or all-female groups. Finally, the changing times are reflected in conflicting research which demonstrates, or fails to demonstrate, differences in interactions in the small group setting on the basis of biological sex, but does demonstrate differences on the basis of psychological sex roles.

We explained above that in the small group setting men tend to initiate, while women tend to respond or react to the comments of others. This proactive behavior of men and reactive behavior of women is consistent with male/female differences in other spheres of life. In order to explore your own proactive or reactive style, complete the following exercise.

First, list five to eight events that you expect or hope will occur. They might include places you wish to visit, conversations in which you wish to engage, relationships which you wish to establish or terminate, tasks you wish to begin or complete, or information you wish to learn. Then, list the person, event, or circumstance you believe is responsible for your reluctance to achieve your goal. For example, you might list a parent, or friend, an employer, an instructor, or an intimate; you might list an event such as your graduation from college, your accumulation of a certain amount of money, your "meeting the right person," or a certain point in time.

I Am Waiting for   **Because**

_____   _____
_____   _____
_____   _____
_____   _____
_____   _____
_____   _____

Now list some situations or circumstances in which you have made the "first move." Consider recent events, conversations, difficult interactions, places you have visited, information you have learned, relationships you have initiated or ended, jobs you have been offered, or tasks you have accomplished. After you

Leadership behaviors

The higher level of activity in men than in women and their tendency to talk more than women help men in asserting leadership in small group settings. Men tend to initiate more verbal acts, make more suggestions, defend their ideas more strongly, yield less readily to interruptions, and, in general, to dominate (Kaess, Wittyal, and Nolan, 1961; Hall, 1972). Men emerged as leaders in small groups more often than females and were found to be ranked higher than women as group leaders in a variety of different tasks (Tindall, Boyler, Cline, Emberger, Powell, & Wions, 1978).

have made your list, identify people or circumstances which you could have used as an excuse for not accomplishing this particular goal.

Recently, I Initiated   **And I Did Not Wait for**

_____   _____

_____   _____

_____   _____

_____   _____

_____   _____

Examine your two lists and attempt to determine how they are distinct from each other. In what circumstances do you try to allow others to control your life? When do you proact? How can you account for these differences in your life? Discuss your lists with your classmates. Do you perceive any male/female differences? Why do they occur? How do these differences generalize to the small group setting? For example, if you observe that men tend to react in personal relationships while they affirmatively proact in work-related situations, you might consider some differences between women and men in responding to their personal needs versus the goal-oriented needs of the members of the small group discussion. What effects do these differences have on the outcome of a discussion in a small group? How can the situation be altered? To what extent do you believe it should be changed? As you consider alterations which can occur, do not overlook the relationship between other experiences which women and men have in the small group setting. Consider the experiences of children in play situations, the relationships of men and women engaged in an intimate setting, and the roles of women and men in other situations.

Megargee (1969) also found that dominant persons emerged as leaders over submissive persons. When dominant and submissive men and women were paired, the following results occurred: 1) dominant males and females emerged as leaders over their same-sexed submissive partners; 2) in mixed-sex groups, dominant males emerged over submissive females; 3) in mixed-sex groups, submissive males emerged over dominant females. The author noted that, in general, the dominant females conceded the leadership position to their partners. In this study, sex, rather than personality, determined leadership emergence.

Women and men as capable leaders

Women appear to be as capable as men to serve as leaders. For instance, when women are provided with a solution to a problem, they are as capable and careful in obtaining group acceptance as are men (Maier, 1970). At the same time, women are less able to gain acceptance with a group when they are not provided with a solution to a problem. It appears that they are less confident and consequently less able to secure attitudinal or behavioral change. Similarly, in high task clarity conditions, no differences between women and men as leaders could be ascertained (Ruch & Newton, 1977). Females appear to exercise significantly less control over groups of people whom they are supervising, than do males, but women do not alter their behaviors because of the sex of the subordinates. Another author points out that while traditional sex-stereotyping is pervasive, the notion that women are inferior leaders does not appear to be true in actual behavioral situations (Brown, 1979; Stitt, Schmidt, Price, & Kipnis, 1983). Finally, two researchers found that although men and women perform equally well as leaders, group members perceive men to be more successful than women in leadership roles (Jacobson & Effertz, 1974). Later in this chapter, we will give further consideration to women in management roles.

The impact of sex roles on leadership behaviors

A number of studies have examined the impact of sex roles on leadership behavior. Male leaders are expected to be independent, aggressive, analytical, competitive, self-disciplined, objective, and task-oriented, while it is anticipated that female leaders will be dependent, passive, non-aggressive, sensitive, subjective, and people-oriented. As a consequence of these expectations, it has been conjectured that leadership behavior is logically related to sex-role identification. In general, males appear to possess masculine characteristics consistent with the instrumental or task-oriented behaviors expected of a male leader, while females display expressive or relational behaviors when serving as a leader (Fowler & Rosenfeld, 1979; Baird & Bradley, 1979; Bartol & Butterfield, 1976; Haccoun, Sallay, & Haccoun, 1978; Day & Stogdill, 1972; Welsh, 1979).

Task-orientation and socio-emotional orientation

Leadership in small groups has frequently been considered in terms of task-orientation and a socio-emotional orientation. A number of writers have indicated that both leadership functions must be present. The task leader insures that the job is completed, and the socio-emotional leader insures that the group members are satisfied with the group process and the group outcome (cf. Hersey & Blanchard, 1977; Hill, 1973). Accordingly, it appears that women are more likely to serve as social leaders and men as task leaders. However, the research does not demonstrate that a person's sex predicts his or her leadership style (Barol, 1974, 1978; Bartol and Wortman, 1975, 1976). At the

322   Contexts

same time, two research studies examined those behaviors of men and women which are directly analogous to leadership style, and found that females are highly associated with expressive behaviors, such as concern and consideration, while males are linked to instrumental activities such as initiating structure and giving direction (Baird & Bradley, 1979; Bartol & Butterfield, 1976).

Sex roles and leadership orientation

The contradiction among such studies led some researchers to transfer the question of differences in leadership behavior from biological sex to psychological sex role. These studies have been consistent in their findings and have demonstrated that masculine individuals engage in more controlling behaviors than feminine or androgynous individuals. Feminine individuals engage in more submissive acts and in fewer competitive dominance behaviors than either masculine or androgynous individuals. Androgynous individuals exhibit a more equal distribution of both dominant and submissive acts than do either of the other two sex-typed groups (Patton, Jasnoski, & Skerchock, 1977; Serafini & Pearson, 1983). Similarly, Ellis and Skerchock (1979) found that masculine people made significantly more dominant control bids than either feminine or androgynous persons. In addition, Ellis and McCallister (1980) determined that sex-typed males communicated in more instrumental and assertive ways, which appeared to indicate a need for direct interaction and structure in the environment, but sex-typed females communicated relational submissiveness more than any other group. Just as individuals prefer a male leader rather than a female leader, they also demonstrate a strong preference for a masculine leader (Inderlied & Powell, 1979).

What should women do if they wish to serve as task-oriented leaders? The studies above imply that women who are cross-sexed (masculine) in their orientation may serve as effective task leaders. As women serve in leadership roles in which they are in charge of an increasing number of males, they become task-oriented (Chapman, 1975). In addition to including masculine behaviors in one's repertoire, confidence appears to be essential to women who wish to lead. An earlier study indicated that women who are provided with a solution to a problem and probably appear to others to be confident, are effective as leaders. Confidence and instrumental characteristics such as assertiveness, analytical skills, independence, self-discipline, and competitiveness, may serve women well, as they seek to function as leaders. Two authors conjecture that the leadership imbalance between women and men may be altered if low status persons (such as women) are assigned non-task related duties which will serve to enhance their competence and their confidence. Reinforcement of women as leaders and encouragement of role flexibility by group members may be useful both in altering the existing equation and preferences (Lockheed & Hall, 1976).

Men who wish to serve as socio-emotional leaders or as followers are well advised to consider role flexibility, as well. Two theorists asserted that the flexible, adaptable leader will be the most effective and that a wide range of behaviors should be exhibited (Hersey & Blanchard, 1977). A variety of leadership behaviors is required in differing situations in order to achieve effectiveness (Hill, 1973). Apparently the notion of *androgyny* and behavioral flexibility which we discussed in chapter 1 may be useful to women and to men who wish to alter traditional leadership behavior and perceptions of leadership.

Summary
The communicative behaviors of men, including the initiation of more verbal acts, a greater number of suggestions, strong defense of their ideas, the tendency not to yield to interruptions, and dominance, cause them to emerge as leaders more often than do women. In addition, prejudice mitigates against women serving as leaders, since they are perceived less favorably in positions of leadership. Nonetheless, both women and men can serve as effective leaders. As stated earlier, men tend to be more task-oriented, while women tend to be more socio-emotionally oriented; but leadership orientation appears to be more closely related to psychological sex role than to biological sex. Women can learn to become effective task-oriented leaders and men can learn to become effective socio-emotional leaders.

Public Speaking

Public speaking differences among men and women have been examined. Some of the studies have considered the sex of the speaker, or source, of the message, and others have studied the influence of the sex of the listener, or receiver, of the message. Let us begin our review by examining the findings of studies which have considered the sex of the source.

The source

In general, people with high status, including men and Anglo-Americans, have been shown to be more effective as communicators and have been favored for high status positions, while persons with low status, including women, Mexican-Americans, and blacks, have been viewed less favorably (Ramírez, 1977; Noel & Allen, 1976; Wheeler, Wilson, & Tarantola, 1976; De La Zerda & Hopper, 1979). These conclusions have been drawn even when messages are identical, a finding which have led researchers to speculate that women, among other groups, have lower credibility than have men. A frequently cited study demonstrated that audiences respond more favorably to messages attributed to a male than to a female communicator (Goldberg, 1968).

Specific components of credibility have been examined. Male sources of messages received higher competence ratings than did female sources in an investigation of persuasive discourse (Miller & McReynolds, 1973). In another study, females received higher scores on three dimensions of credibility that were examined: trustworthiness, dynamism or dynamic enthusiasm, and competence (Vigliano, 1974). A more recent study indicates that women may be viewed to be higher in trustworthiness and coorientation, or perceived similarity, whereas men may be viewed to be higher in competence and dynamism (Pearson, 1982). In addition, males were given higher dynamism ratings in a study on male and female speakers, while females were given higher aesthetic quality ratings, and no difference was determined between men and women on socio-intellectual status (Mulac & Torborg, 1980).

Studies which have focused on the communication classroom have confounded our understanding of sex differences in the source of a message (cf. Pearson, 1981b). Females appear to receive higher grades than males on their classroom speeches (Pearson & Nelson, 1981; Barker, 1966). Moreover, female students receive proportionately more positive than negative comments than do male students (Pearson, 1975; Sprague, 1971). At least one component of self-concept changes for female students, while male students do not report changes in self-concept from the beginning to the end of a communication class (Judd & Smith, 1977).

Other studies demonstrate no difference in the public speaking of men and women. One study showed that sex did not correlate significantly with public speaking ability ratings, but that women received higher grades in the basic speech communication classroom (Hayes, 1977). Another study revealed no difference in the persuasiveness of female and male speakers (Sloman, 1974).

A recent study examined the influence of sex role on grading in the classroom. Rather than focus on the biological sex of the speaker, this study examined the effect of psychological sex role on grading. The research showed that feminine individuals received higher grades than did masculine individuals (Pearson, 1981a). This study, added to the others that we reviewed, implies that women may be uniquely suited for the public speaking setting, and/or that women may be especially responsive to the classroom situation. Stereotypical characteristics associated with women such as sensitivity to the needs of others, understanding, compassion, and warmth, may assist them in the public speaking setting; while feminine personality traits including compliance, yielding, and responsiveness may help women in achieving higher grades in the classroom.

Communication apprehension which is associated with the avoidance of oral communication and a feeling of discomfort when communicating, has been examined for both biological sex and psychological sex type. Women report slightly more public speaking apprehension than do men (Infante & Fisher, 1974; McCroskey, Simpson, & Richmond, 1982). Greenblatt, Hasenauer, and

Freimuth (1980) found that feminine females report more communication apprehension than masculine males, that androgynous males and androgynous females do not report differences in communication apprehension, and that androgynous females report less communication apprehension than feminine females. This study implies that femininity, rather than biological femaleness, results in higher levels of communication apprehension.

The research on communication apprehension, a self-report variable, is intriguing in the light of the findings that women and feminine people receive higher grades in the communication classroom. It appears that women and feminine individuals may report greater levels of fear, but actually perform better. Conversely, women and feminine individuals may receive higher grades because of prejudice in their favor on the part of evaluators. Let us consider the impact of the gender of the evaluator or receiver of the message further.

The receiver

The studies on the sex of the receiver have been conducted in and out of the classroom setting. Some of the earliest work on sex differences in receivers considered persuasibility. Some studies indicated that women were more easily persuaded than were men (cf. Scheidel, 1963; Carmichael, 1970; Rosenfeld & Christie, 1974; Tuthill & Forsythe, 1982). Other studies revealed no differences between women and men in persuasibility (Miller & McReynolds, 1973). Conflicting findings and differing conceptualizations of persuasibility have questioned some of these findings.

Factors other than sex differences may account for the differences in persuasibility which have been reported. Montgomery and Burgoon (1977) assert that persuasibility is a personality trait which refers to an individual's propensity to shift his or her attitude toward *any* topic, but that the results of prior studies may be due to the specific topics that were used. Many of the investigations of persuasibility have used male-oriented topics, and women may have demonstrated more attitude change since they were less committed to a position on the issue. In addition, they might have less information on the topic since it is less salient to them. According to Saltiel and Woelfel's theory of accumulated information and attitude change, people resist changing their attitudes to the extent that they have information accumulated about it (Saltiel & Woelfel, 1975). In other words, women may not resist attitude change in studies which utilize male-oriented topics since they have little information about them.

Psychological sex role has replaced biological sex as the independent variable in more recent studies. Montgomery and Burgoon (1977) determined that feminine females changed attitudes more than did masculine males, and that this difference was greater than that obtained between androgynous males and androgynous females. In other words, psychological sex role had more predictive value than did traditional considerations of biological sex.

In the classroom, the rating, or evaluation behavior, of men and women has been examined. Some studies indicate that females are more lenient evaluators. Female student evaluators rated both male and female speakers higher than did male student evaluators (Pfister, 1955). Women rated persuasive speeches higher for persuasiveness than did men, both immediately after a speech and after ten weeks (Sikkink, 1956). Miller and McReynolds (1973) showed that women tend to rate a male speaker higher than do men. Bock, Powell, Kitchens, and Flavin (1976) demonstrated that female raters made more leniency errors.

Women do appear to be more generous than men in rating certain aspects of the speeches of their peers. Thus, female listeners tend to score speakers, regardless of sex, higher than male listeners, on trustworthiness and dynamism, but not on competence (Vigliano, 1974). Female college speech instructors made significantly more delivery comments (as opposed to content comments), positive comments (as opposed to negative comments), and personal comments (as opposed to impersonal comments) than did male college instructors (Sprague, 1971).

Personality traits as well as the attitudes and predispositions of the evaluator appear to affect evaluation. Rigid evaluators tend to rate speakers lower than do people who are not rigid (Bostrom, 1964). People who are difficult to persuade rate speakers lower than do critics who are easy to persuade (Bock, 1970). Sexist people, who see more differences than similarities between women and men, tend to rate all speakers lower than do people who are nonsexist (Pearson, 1980).

In the classroom setting, women tend to receive higher scores than do men, and they also tend to give higher scores, and criticism which is more positive and perceived to be more helpful. In addition, women may more readily adapt their responses to persuasive messages as they seem to alter their attitudes in line with those of the speaker. Stereotypic feminine qualities may account for many or all of these differences. At the same time, we must be aware of the impact of the classroom setting upon female and male behavior. In this section of the chapter, we have observed some differences as we moved from classroom to non-classroom settings. In the next section, we will focus our attention on the educational setting when we discuss classroom interaction and textbook and other written materials.

Individuals of high status are generally perceived to be more effective speakers than are those with low status. Gender differences in public speaking favor women, but most of these studies were made in communication classrooms and the context may have affected the results. Feminine individuals receive higher grades on their speeches and they also report higher levels of communication apprehension. Differences in evaluation of public speaking may be in the eyes of the beholder, and the evaluators may be responding more favorably to speakers because of their gender or because of behaviors stereotypically associated with their gender. Dogmatic, rigid, difficult to persuade, sexist individuals are all shown to evaluate speakers lower than do others. Although it has been determined that women are more easily persuaded than men, many of these studies have been questioned on methodological grounds. It appears, however, that feminine individuals may be more easily persuaded than masculine individuals and that psychological sex roles have more predictive value than biological sex.

Communication in the business world

The world of business has taken on new significance as women in large numbers have entered traditionally male fields like accounting and management. People in business have sometimes been slow to respond to these changes, so that sometimes decisions about hiring, firing, retention, benefits, and other personnel matters have not kept pace with the changing times. We will see sexism operating as we examine the research that has been completed in this area.

"In 1919, Senator Reed Smoot established a salary ceiling for the staff of the Women's Bureau. 'No woman is worth more than $2,000 a year,' he told Mary Anderson, the first director" (Bird, 1970). We will note that although the economy has changed in the sixty-five years since the Senator made the statement, the underlying attitude about employing women, particularly in managerial jobs, has not. Women make up a larger percentage of the work force today than in earlier times, rising from about 20% in 1920 to about 42% at the current time (Hayt, 1977). Nonetheless, women still make less money for the same work. During the 1970s, women wore buttons that were inscribed, "59¢" to remind people that women typically made 59¢ for every dollar made by men. During the second fiscal year of the Reagan administration, that figure slipped from 59¢ to 57¢.

Occupational choices

Women and men are not employed in the same numbers in the same professions. As we know, women tend to be placed in low-ranking, low-paying positions in business, journalism health-related fields, and teaching (cf. Vladeck, 1981; Holly, 1979). Men tend to engage in more adventurous or high-status occupations such as the military, the police force, management positions, or governmental positions. Occupations are perceived to be appropriate for men or for women, and men and women tend to agree on those distinctions (Krefting, 1979; Jackson, 1983).

Butler (1981) provides the following two job descriptions and asks which advertisement fits reality:

Wanted: Insurance Executive

Affectionate, childlike person who does not use harsh language to head our Investment Division. We want someone who is cheerful and eager to sooth hurt feelings. The position requires gullibility. This is the perfect job for the tender, yielding individual.

Wanted: Insurance Executive

Competitive, ambitious person with leadership ability needed to head our Investment Division. We want someone who is self-sufficient and dominant. The position requires strong analytical ability. This is the perfect job for an independent, self-reliant person.

Butler created these job descriptions by selecting adjectives from the Bem Sex Role Inventory which was discussed in Chapter 2. Her point is that stereotypical feminine qualities interfere with women and men perceiving jobs as equally appropriate for both sexes. In other words, if a person believes that she or he possesses stereotypic feminine qualities that individual might not feel that the second job description is appropriate. On the other hand, the first job description is one that we may never see.

Perceptions of children

Children as young as three years old recognize that jobs are sex-typed. When children between the ages of three and six were asked the traditional question, "What do you want to be when you grow up?" the boys tended to choose adventure careers, including police work, sports areas, etc.; while the girls selected quieter careers, such as nursing. Seventy percent of the boys and 73% of the girls chose stereotypical careers for themselves. In addition, 14% of the children felt that it was not proper for men to feed babies; 20% felt it was not proper for men to pour coffee for seated women; and 49% felt that it was not proper for women to be repair-people (Beuf, 1974). More recent research confirms that nursery school children continue to select stereotyped occupations for themselves and that boys personal aspirations were more stereotyped than girls (O'Keefe & Hyde, 1983).

Children in the fourth, fifth, and sixth grades were surveyed regarding career choices. The children were Black, Hispanic, and Anglo-American. The responses were analyzed by ethnic membership as well as by sex. Hispanic and Anglo-American girls chose more nontraditional, higher status occupations than did Black girls. No interactions occurred between sex and ethnic groups for boys. Both females and males in all ethnic groups preferred careers

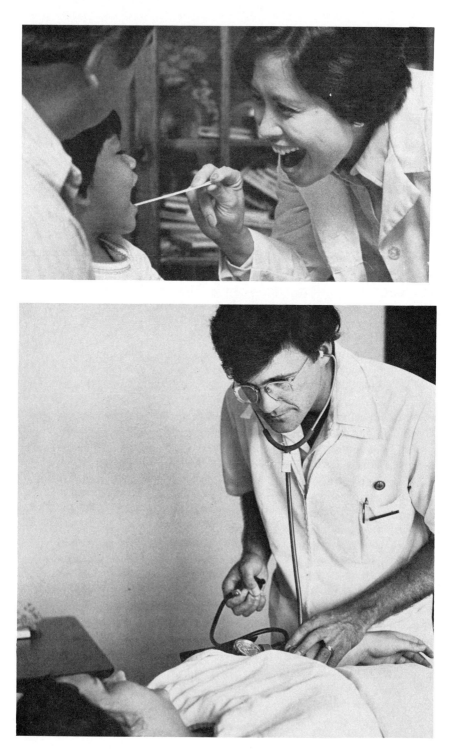

which were stereotyped for their own sex, although girls, particularly Anglo-American girls, showed a greater tendency to cross the stereotyped lines. While boys regarded themselves as being suited for the male-appropriate jobs only, girls considered the males to be appropriate for either male-typed or female-typed jobs. In general, the Black girls tended to hold the most stereotypic views of job appropriateness. Girls appear to adhere less to societal norms than do boys (Coles, 1978).

An intriguing study on children's perceptions of occupational choices were conducted. Five- and six-year-old children watched a series of four films in which the sex of the physician and the nurse were altered. In each of the two-minute films, the physician examined a small boy and wrote a prescription for him while a nurse took his temperature. Of all the subjects who were shown the female physician/male nurse film, 53% said they had observed a movie about a male physician and a female nurse. Of those shown the female physician/female nurse film, 91% identified the sexes of the actors in each occupation correctly. All of the subjects who viewed the male physician/female nurse were able to identify accurately by sex the person in each occupation. The authors of this study contend that children tend to see sex role regularities as "lawful relationships," a perception which causes them to deny the fact that a female can be a physician or a male can be a nurse (Cordua, McGraw & Drabman, 1979). This study, like the one above, demonstrates that men have a more limited occupational choice than do women, since the tendency to misidentify the female physician was not as great as the tendency to mislabel the male nurse.

Perceptions of adolescents and young adults

We have observed that psychological sex type has been used in countless studies that previously considered biological sex. In occupational choices, one study sought to determine whether androgynous individuals were more flexible in their selection of potential occupation. Fifty-seven percent of college females who have androgynous sex roles are enrolled in female-dominated majors, while 43% of them are enrolled in male-dominated majors. Males with feminine sex roles do not appear to select nontraditional majors. Men may refrain from entering female-dominated fields because of the greater restrictions on men or because the occupations tend to be low-status and low-pay (Stochton, 1980).

American adolescents were asked about educational expectations and occupational expectations. Men and women expressed similar educational expectations, but the correlation between educational and occupational expectations is lower for females than for males, a finding which implies that women do not have the same, high occupational expectations held by men. The authors theorize that achievement results in conflict for socialized females (Anashensel & Rosen, 1978). Women frequently fear high occupational success, particularly in traditionally male jobs, because their success can result in disapproval from males.

Martha Friedman, psychotherapist and author of *Overcoming the Fear of Success* (1982), summarized some of indicators of fear of success. She explains that people who fear success undermine their own efforts by doing such things as arriving late to work, not completing an assignment on time, selecting the wrong mate, sleeping through final exams, and behaving inappropriately in social situations. Though fear of failure frequently leads people to strive harder to achieve a goal, the fear of success is often an unconscious impediment. Examples of fear of success include the single man who only dates married women, the female executive who quits her job to have a baby, the man who has 20 years of experience but tells others that he will lose his job because he has no college degree, the married woman who is involved in infidelity on a routine basis, the graduate student who drops courses and insults his or her professors, and the woman who desires a permanent relationship but discourages relational development.

If you answer any of the following questions with a "yes," you may be afraid of doing too well, according to Friedman:
(Place an "X" next to any item which is true for you.)

_____ 1. Do you think if people really knew you, they wouldn't like you?
_____ 2. Do you feel like you are a fraud and that sooner or later you will be discovered?
_____ 3. Do you fear making a mistake?
_____ 4. Are you a perfectionist?
_____ 5. Do you procrastinate?
_____ 6. Are you overly critical of your own, or of others, work?
_____ 7. Do Sundays depress you?
_____ 8. Are you a workaholic?
_____ 9. Do you feel guilty when you are having a good time?
_____ 10. Do you fear exposure of something about yourself?

If you responded **yes** to any of these, Friedman contends that you may be afraid of doing too well. Many of us are in some degree afraid of success. When the fear of success is pushed to an extreme, it may lead to tragedy. Among famous people, Richard Nixon, John Belushi, and Judy Garland are still cited as classic examples. Fear of success is an avoidance mechanism.

Since we believe that success will have negative outcomes such as disappointment, abandonment, rejection, and discouragement, we avoid it. We reason that when things are going well, they cannot continue; we believe that our luck cannot hold.

The fear of success may come from the mixed messages we receive. We are told to live up to our potential, to be all that we can be. On the other hand, we are informed with equal emphasis that the meek shall inherit the Earth, that money is not everything, and that it is lonely at the top. The fear of success is a special problem for women. They are susceptible because of socialization processes which suggest that successful women have jealous mothers, poor relationships with men, and are viewed as "castrating" inhuman beings. Friedman explains that people who combine low self-esteem with high guilt feelings are prime candidates for fear of success.

All psychologists do not agree that the phenomenon of "fear of success" exists. Betsy Brown, psychologist and director of the Center for Family Consultation in Mountainside, New Jersey, thinks fear of success is "nonsense." Brown concludes that both men and women have "achievement-related conflicts," and that some people may not wish to pay the price of success. Nonetheless, she argues that good reasons are frequently offered for refusing to strive for success, and that it is not at all an unconscious process. Harvey Ruben, psychiatrist and assistant clinical professor of psychiatry at Yale, believes that most people have a fear of failure. He states that success is a rare outcome and the phenomenon called "fear of success" is actually fear of failure.

Do you believe that a phenomenon such as "fear of success" exists? Do you believe that you, or others that you know, have experienced this fear? Describe the condition as you understand it. Could "fear of success" be "fear of failure" with a different label? For instance, do people become so concerned with succeeding that they fail because of the pressure they place on themselves? Discuss differences between women and men in relation to the fear of success. Compare your responses on the ten questions listed above with those of your classmates. How can you account for differences? What can you, and others, do to avoid negative behavior which results in failure? What particular changes should occur that will help women? What changes would assist men in avoiding behaviors associated with "fear of success"?

Fear of success in adults

Fear of success appears to be a dominant theme for women; a number of researchers have investigated the importance of this concept. In one study, career salience was examined in light of fear of success. The author defined *career salience* as the degree to which people are career-motivated, the degree to which occupations are important as a source of satisfaction, and the degree of priority that is ascribed to occupations, among other sources of satisfaction. The investigation demonstrated that career salience is highest when fear of success is lowest and when women are non-traditional in their sex role attitudes. Career salience is lowest when fear of success is highest and when women are traditional in their sex role attitudes. Neither fear of success nor sex role attitudes alone predict career salience; they appear to interact to encourage or discourage career salience (Illfelder, 1980). In other words, women who experience a fear of success, but are non-traditional in their sex role attitudes, will still have career salience. Similarly, women without fear of success, who are traditional in their sex role attitudes, will have career salience.

Another study demonstrates that female fear of success is not reflective of female motive, but reflects a perception that is common to both men and women concerning the negative social consequences attending female success in competitive situations (Bremer, 1980). In other words, women do not experience fear of success without validation from men. Both men and women recognize that successful women may gain disapproval from others in the culture. In addition, fear of success is not related to a personality trait. This suggests that the fear is not a characteristic of a person, but rather an accurate perception of the state of affairs (Illfelder, 1980).

Furthermore, the fear of success syndrome appears to be in a state of change. Garland, Hale and Burnson (1982) reported that men may predetermine that women will fail while women predetermine that they will succeed. They found that when men had positive attitudes toward women in management, they believed that success was based upon ability and efforts. When women responded to the failure of particular women in management, they explained that it was due to the job itself rather than the females' abilities or deficiencies. Further, women who are already in management positions do not attribute the failure to succeed of other female managers to bad luck. Similarly, Jabes (1980) found that women managers were biased toward other women managers in positive ways. She concludes, too, that women no longer appear to have a motive to avoid success.

Summary

Children from the age of 3 perceive occupations as sex-typed. Adolescents and young adults similarly concur that some jobs are for women and some are for men. It is not surprising that adults make choices about occupations based on stereotypical conceptions that have been internalized for a lifetime. The "fear of success" may be a legitimate response to women's (and men's) recognition of barriers to particular occupational paths for persons of one gender or the other. Both the "fear of success" and the limited sex-appropriateness of particular jobs appear to be gradually diminishing.

Employment interviews

Prior notions about appropriate jobs, occupational goals which are different from men, and social attitudes which imply that women should not compete with men, all contribute to women's perceptions of their employability. What occurs in the employment interview? When women are interviewed for positions, they should not be surprised if they are asked illegal and sexist questions (Garrison, 1980). Women may be asked questions about their marital status, plans to have children, and other personal questions; they may be sexually propositioned or treated differently than men.

Employers who have been surveyed about women in the employment interview have identified some factors which may impair women's chances of being hired. They asserted that women tend to look at a position in terms of the "short-run" rather than as a long-term career goal, that marital status tends to hinder women in managerial roles (i.e., married women are less willing to spend extra hours on the job, are less willing to travel, and are less willing to engage in other unusual requirements of the job), and that women appear to be more nervous and less self-confident during interviews than are men.

Women who want to improve their opportunities of being hired can use the findings in these studies to assist them. They should consider, before they occur, how they will handle sexist questions and sexual suggestions. Women should familiarize themselves with the guidelines established by the EEOC (Equal Employment Opportunity Commission) regarding legal and illegal questions. If you are asked an illegal question, it is probably better for you to explain your concern about the question than to stall, offer a circumvented answer, or not answer at all. Consider methods of answering such questions which will not offend the interviewer, but will clarify your position.

Consider ways of demonstrating your confidence during the employment interview. Before you go to an employment interview, attempt to "second guess" the interviewer and write down some of the questions you will probably be asked. Then, prepare answers which are complete, honest, accurate, and specific. Avoid extra verbiage, euphemisms, platitudes, or ambiguous language. Answer the question completely, but stick to the point of the question. Consider, too, your nonverbal communication in the employment interview. Do you appear nervous as you straighten your clothing, constantly move your glasses, or play with a piece of jewelry or a strand of hair? Attempt to be poised as you practice answering the questions that you have drawn up. Show confidence through your nonverbal communication by using meaningful, clear,

Women and men both participate in a variety of interviews. One of the most important interviews may be that in which we engage to secure a job. One method of preparing for the employment interview is to write probable questions and to prepare responses which you believe are appropriate. Try to write down the comments and questions that an employer might state or ask in a legal employment interview. Then write the same interview again, this time including sexist comments and asking personal questions which are not relevant to the job. After you have written the two interview plans, compare them. What kind of questions do you believe are illegal? What comments should an employer avoid? What should you do if an employment interviewer asks you an inappropriate question? After you have considered some of these issues, practice the interviews. Interview at least one man and one woman with each of your two interviews. Exchange roles so you are interviewed in an appropriate and an inappropriate way. Discuss your findings in each of these situations. How did you feel when you were *asking* inappropriate questions? How did you feel when you were *asked* inappropriate questions? How much information was acquired in each situation? Discuss such issues as: working for someone who regularly conducts inappropriate interviews; conflict in the interview setting; differences in perception about what constitutes an appropriate and an inappropriate set of questions; motivation for asking illegal questions; the differences in power between the interviewer and interviewee; and nonverbal behaviors which might accompany illegal and legal questions.

and confident gestures; sitting with both feet on the floor, establishing direct eye contact, and using responsive facial gestures rather than simply smiling throughout the interview. Verbal and nonverbal communication cues may make the difference between being hired and continuing to look for work!

Discrimination in hiring practices

A special problem which appears to occur more frequently at this time than in the past is the situation in which a dual-career couple attempt to find new employment. At the present time, it appears that more women than men find it necessary to seek positions in or near the cities where their spouses are employed. Nearly always a dual career couple finds that the job of one person affects the job of the other. Typically, the man's job is given precedence because the man is able to earn more money than the woman. Women are more likely to be primarily responsible for child care, and both find it difficult to deviate from societal expectations (Foster, 1980). Even in supposedly egalitarian dual-career marriages, women do not have the same opportunities as men.

Attempts to equalize the hiring situation for women have been met in certain quarters by charges of "reverse discrimination." Some writers have held that reverse discrimination is just as detrimental as is direct discrimination, and that women have not been denied opportunities as have other groups such as Blacks (Sher, 1977). Other authors have maintained that reverse discrimination may be justified so as to shift present practices and to achieve equal opportunities for women (Jones, 1977). The problem of discrimination and reverse discrimination is very complex; it involves considerations such as persons losing self-respect because of special treatment, identifying individuals and groups who could and should benefit, and the extent to which such practices should extend.

Both primary and secondary sexism occur in contemporary hiring practices. *Primary sexism* is unfair discrimination on the basis of sex; *secondary sexism* is found in differential hiring practices on the basis of sex-correlated factors. For instance, if a person is not hired because of pregnancy, she is a victim of secondary sexism. Similarly, anti-nepotism laws, last hired-first fired policies, promotion of full-time employees over part-time employees, previous salary establishing present rank, and preference for persons who have an uninterrupted work record, are examples of secondary sexism. A consideration of secondary sexism, as well as primary sexism is essential as we attempt to offer women equal opportunities in employment (Warren, 1977). Secondary sexism is more elusive and more complex than primary sexism; frequently people will point to a lack of primary sexism to prove that sexist practices do not occur.

Let us consider one of the examples of secondary sexism cited above to illustrate the complexity of this issue. Anti-nepotism laws are designed to prevent members of the same family having administrative or managerial control over each other. For instance, if a man is a manager in a company, his wife cannot be a member of his unit. If a woman is a college president, her husband cannot be one of the deans. Who is more likely to hold the advanced position in a husband and wife team? To date, the husband is. It is more probable that the husband earns more money, has a more advanced position, and has proceeded through the ranks more quickly than his wife. This is due to a number of factors, including the likelihood that women are younger than their husbands, that they put aside career obligations for relational or personal concerns, are less goal-oriented in their careers, and assume positions of support rather than leadership. Regardless of the cause, the result is the same: Anti-nepotism laws keep women from working in units in which they are prepared and for which they are appropriate candidates simply because their spouses are in charge of those units.

Sexism in hiring practices and discrimination against women must be considered from an ethical standpoint. For centuries, women have had more difficulty in gaining and maintaining employment outside the home than have men. All decisions regarding personnel are ambiguous; that is, we rarely, if ever, are asked to choose between two equally qualified persons. Choices about hiring persons are based on unstated, ambiguous factors, as well as on the basis of specific job descriptions. In a sense, employers always run the risk of making errors in their judgments. If, for example, they decide that they will hire one candidate because of his or her superior educational background, they may be forced to lose the candidate who has years of reputable experience. Similarly, in the past, employers have been determined to hire men rather than women because of some of the factors of secondary sexism mentioned above. The employer's mistake, in these cases, has been to lose women with unique capabilities and special experience.

Perhaps it is time for employers to begin selecting personnel who tend to be more sensitive, empathic, and understanding, rather than persons who are highly competitive, objective, and analytical. We are liable to err when we hire men rather than women, and we may err when we hire women rather than men. It is surprising that years of discrimination against women have not aroused the same outrage as has concern about far fewer cases in which reverse discrimination has occurred. Is reverse discrimination wrong? Yes, but thus far it has been far less of a problem than is discrimination. Our goal should be to reject errors in judgment which favor either women or men. It is evident that large institutions and businesses can do a great deal to reduce the adverse effects of sexual stereotyping in hiring practices (cf. Heilman, 1980).

Women as managers

One of the most widely studied issues in business settings concerning women and men is the role of women as managers. Bormann, Pratt and Putnam (1978), for instance, conducted research which demonstrated the importance of considering female dominance and male response to that dominance in organizations. In their study, they found that fantasies accompany perceptions of male and female leadership. One of the most common fantasies linked leadership with male potency. Men perceived female leadership associated with their own loss of sexual potency. Their study indicates that women may have powerful mythology to overcome if they are to succeed in management.

A number of myths have been dispelled concerning women's abilities to manage. Some of the stereotypes about women that appear to be unsupported are that women are too emotional to make rational decisions (Biles & Pryatel, 1978; Dipboye, 1975); women have a low commitment to work, compared to men (Biles & Pryatel, 1978); women lack motivation to achieve (Biles & Pryatel, 1978); men are inherently more assertive than women (Dipboye, 1975); and men are intellectually superior to women (Dipboye, 1975). While such myths are being dispelled in the literature, women appear to remain at a disadvantage because of such stereotypes (Larwood, Wood, & Inderlied, 1978; Collins, Waters, & Waters, 1979) and because individuals prefer managers who possess masculine characteristics (Brenner & Bromer, 1981).

Self-perception of women and men managers

Both women and men may perceive themselves differently as managers. Women view themselves as having additional health problems because they "experience unique problems—stresses and strains which are not undergone by their male counterparts" (Davidson, 1981). Women may perceive additional problems in their jobs than do men. In self-evaluations, women and men provide significantly different responses. Male managers view themselves as performing better than women in comparable jobs, and as having more abilities and higher intelligence. Also, men rate their jobs as more difficult than the jobs that women hold, an impression which is corroborated by their subordinates (Deaux, 1979). Indeed, it appears that at this time, men have more demanding jobs, than do women. It is also true that men are more likely than women to view themselves as successful and to attribute their success to their own abilities.

Are women and men different as managers? The jury is still not in. A number of studies have determined that women and men are not significantly different (Marcum, 1976; Wexley & Hunt, 1974; Bartol, 1974, 1978; Bartol & Wortman, 1975, 1976; Inderlied & Powell, 1979). Men and women do not appear to differ in motivation to manage (Miner, 1974); subordinates do not distinguish between male and female leaders in their use of positive and punitive rewards (Szilagyi, 1980); male and female supervisors have been perceived to exhibit similar patterns of leadership behavior and to be similar in terms of effectiveness (Day & Stodgill, 1972); and male and female leaders who exhibit similar behaviors are not judged differently by their subordinates (Alvares & Lee, 1979).

However, other studies have reported differences between female and male managers. One study indicates that while there may be no significant difference in male and female leadership styles, there is a difference in leadership behaviors (Chapman & Luthans, 1975). Males exhibit stereotypic masculine characteristics, whereas females exhibit stereotypic feminine characteristics in their management roles (Baird & Bradley, 1979; Bartol & Butterfield, 1976; Haccoun, Sallay & Haccoun, 1978; Day & Stodgill, 1972; Welsh, 1979).

In terms of specific communication behaviors, women managers who are considerate of subordinates are viewed more positively, while male managers who engage in goal-oriented behavior are viewed more positively (Petty & Miles, 1976; Petty & Lee, 1975). Men may be more assertive or aggressive in their interactions with others and thus emerge more frequently as the leader, while women reveal more information about their feelings, beliefs, and concerns than men and are more person-oriented (Hyman, 1980). Men generally dominate in their conversations and interviews with subordinates, while female managers supply more information to subordinates than males (Hyman, 1980).

Explaining the findings concerning women and men as managers

How do we account for the inconsistent findings concerning men and women? Do male leaders behave in stereotypic feminine ways? Some of the differences in the findings may be due to the procedures the researchers used. For instance, when students are asked to role-play managers, they may behave differently than do persons who actually serve as managers. Women who are actually in the management field may behave similarly to men who are in the management field. Female managers may be self-selected. In other words, female managers may possess traditionally masculine characteristics. Male and female Master of Business Administration (M.B.A.) students differ, inasmuch as female M.B.A. students possess stronger self-report attributes on several levels. These women seem to be consistently more creative, more willing to initiate change in their own lives, and more self-assured. It appears that the female M.B.A. has little or no fear of sex role inappropriateness (Foster, 1979). Similarly, male and female graduate students enrolled in introductory business courses at three American universities both had higher stereotypical masculine traits than did individuals in the normal population (Powell & Butterfield, 1981). These findings suggest that women and men in management and business may be self-selected and hold masculine traits.

Two studies on female managers strengthened the contention that women in management may hold those characteristics, attitudes, and temperaments more commonly ascribed to men. Schein (1973, 1975) found that female middle managers are perceived to possess traditionally masculine characteristics. In addition, women corporate presidents are more task-oriented in their leadership style than are men in the same positions, a finding which implies that women in management may exhibit even more extreme traditionally masculine characteristics than do their male counterparts (Helmich, 1974).

Another explanation of differences that have been perceived between men and women as managers may be contextual, that is, the specific occupation or organization being investigated may account for differences. Some positions may be viewed as more appropriate for men or for women. For example, one study indicated that women have not actively pursued careers as school administrators because a strong norm exists that this is a man's job (Schmuck, 1975). Another study contends that significant patterns of male-female differences in work attitudes are not evident when occupation and organization level are held constant (Brief, 1976). It is clear that the structure and socialization of the organization are the most important factors regarding the presence of women (Valden & Lynn, 1979). The willingness to accept women as managers may greatly reduce the perceived differences between them and their male counterparts. The situation in which a male or female manager finds himself or herself must be taken into consideration.

Effective managers

To the extent that a woman or a man can accurately perceive the organizational climate and adapt to it, she or he will probably be successful and will be perceived as successful (Bedeian, Armenakis, & Kemp, 1976). Indeed, Hersey and Blanchard (1977) assert that the flexible, adaptable leader will be the most effective. Hill (1973) notes that different leadership behaviors are required in different situations in order to achieve effectiveness.

Women and men are both capable of management roles. At the present time, fewer women than men perform in such roles. A survey of high-school students indicates that female occupational aspirations are not lower than those of males, but they are different. Females tend to aspire to professional and technical occupations more, while males tend to aspire to management (Fottler, 1980). We must continue to eradicate inaccurate stereotypes about management and provide appropriate training for women and men. Desexing training materials, for instance, would be useful in demonstrating that women, as well as men are functionally appropriate for the job (Alpander & Gutnam, 1976).

Women managers may provide some unique qualities and some special experience that men do not possess or have not developed. In a recent survey, women managers were described as proving their competence and winning increased acceptance (Wood, 1976). Women may bring a balance to organizations that has been missing because of domination by men. It is informative that among the most notable reasons that top level executives are fired are their lack of sensitivity and caring for employees, their bullying style, and their cold and arrogant behavior which are stereotypical masculine traits (McCall, 1983). Traditional roles of women including consumers, interior decorators, cooks, and seamstresses may be conducive to their developing particular sensitivity for serving in management roles in organizations which have such functions. For instance, women may be especially adept at restaurant management, retail management, and management roles in the fashion industry.

However, women may not be given the same opportunities that men have traditionally enjoyed. Difficult economic times cause positions of management, with their higher status and salaries, to be more competitive. In addition, people are not equally accepting of men and women in management roles. Women may find that their subordinates do not accept their authority (Forgionne, 1977; Yerby 1975). Also, women may have to learn styles of leadership which are distinct from those of their male counterparts. One recent study demonstrated that female supervisors who behaved in a directive, authoritarian style were viewed as less effective than were female supervisors who adopted a rational or friendly style (Haccoun, Sallay & Haccoun, 1978).

Another study discussed four potential power outcomes. A person could have a high need or desire to exert influence over others and a high degree of control in his or her interactions with others (high/high), a high need to exert influence, but a low degree of control (high/low), a low need and a low degree of control (low/low), or a low need and a high degree of control (low/high). Men have typically fallen into the high/high category and have been very successful. When women adopt this posture, they are viewed negatively (Swanson & Wagner, 1979). It is suggested that the high/high state may have only been successful because men have used it, not because it is inherently better. Similarly, women who have adopted stereotypical masculine interaction styles have not found that they have been the recipients of less bias against them (Wiley & Eskilson, 1982). Women should consider that simply adopting male behaviors in all situations may result in less than success.

Success is a topic that is familiar to women and men who have perused the best selling women's self-help books. Bate and Self (1983) recently stated that women's self-help books can be categorized into three different orientations: 1) Those that define success in terms of external indications such as money, power, and advancement to high-status positions (i.e., *Games Mother Never Taught You: Corporate Gamesmanship for Women; Beating Men at Their Own Game; The Woman's Selling Game;* and *Is Networking for You?*); 2) Those that define success ambiguously, which means they present a mixed view of that which constitutes success (i.e., *Women at Work; Networking;* and *Skills for Success*); and 3) Those that define success in terms of internal markers or the way that a woman integrates her numerous roles according to her own priorities (i.e., *Having It All, Paths to Power,* and *Targeting the Top*). Bate and Self observe that the diversity of advice available to women implies that we are in a period of cultural transformation and that women's choices will have far-reaching significance.

Koester (1982) similarly examined women's self-help books, but she used a fantasy theme analysis. She writes that, according to the books, "Successful women managers operate as Machiavellian princesses controlling the impact of their gender in an organizational setting filled with intrigue and inuendo" (p. 165). Successful women, according to Koester's analysis are those who balance the negative stereotypes of women, but retain essential femininity. Koester, like Bate and Self, notes that the books present contradictory advice. She adds that their advice may be incomplete and debilitating as well.

We will conclude this section of the chapter with the extended excerpt from an article which appeared in the *Wall Street Journal*. The article is informative, since it provides a descriptive picture of women as executives in the contemporary culture. The views expressed may be more realistic than those espoused by the authors of the popular self-help books.

Female Bosses Say Biggest Barriers Are Insecurity and 'Being a Woman'

By Jennifer Bingham Hull
Staff Reporter of THE WALL STREET JOURNAL

They are senior executives at large U.S. companies with average salaries of about $92,000. Their titles range from corporate secretary to president and chief executive officer, and while most are single, those who are married say they are both the main breadwinner and the main homemaker.

They attribute their successes to ambition, drive and a willingness to take risks, and they blame their failures on a male world and their lack of confidence in it. They were more often the first-born or only child in their families and favored their fathers.

This is part of a picture that emerges from a study of executive women recently completed by Korn/Ferry International, an executive search firm, and the University of California, Los Angeles, Graduate School of Management. The study is based on 300 responses to 600 questionnaires mailed to women at the level of vice president and above at Fortune magazine's lists of the top 1,000 industrial concerns and 300 of the largest companies in specialized areas. Most of the respondents are vice presidents. Their average age is 46.

While the study makes it clear that women are on the way up, it also shows that it has been a bit lonely being among the few women at the top.

Work-Place Problems

Asked whether "barriers to women have fallen at the senior management level," 63% of the women say no. And 70% say women don't receive equal pay for comparable jobs. Female executives most frequently mention "being a woman" as their major career obstacle, citing "the old-boy network," "insecure men," and the attitude that they're "too good looking to take seriously . . . will run off and get married" as work-place problems.

In comments on her questionnaire, a vice president of corporate finance says her biggest career obstacle has been her appearance. I "didn't look or sound the part—5'3½", female, with a Southern accent," she says. A vice president and director of manpower development complains of "lack of acceptance based on competence . . . the unwillingness of people to give me the toughest assignments." And a regional vice president says her biggest barrier to success has been her "tendency to unconsciously intimidate male superiors."

After "being a woman," lack of confidence was most frequently cited as the main obstacle to success. A senior vice president of marketing says she was forced to overcome "my own fears of not being as good or strong as the men I worked with because of lack of education and being the first woman." Asked to name her greatest career challenge, another woman simply responded, "myself."

These comments sound familiar to Barbara Franklin, a senior fellow of public management of the University of Pennsylvania's Wharton School. She serves on the boards of Dow Chemical Co., Westinghouse Electric Corp. and Aetna

Life & Casualty Co. Miss Franklin cites isolation and upbringing as reasons for insecurity. "Women aren't brought up with male egos. And . . . in the corporate scene nobody tells you when you've done a good job. There's just this deafening silence."

Lack of confidence, Miss Franklin says, comes from corporate women's inability to break into men's informal networks. "I see it now. Everybody I know plays golf. I don't play golf."

The study by Korn/Ferry and UCLA follows a similar survey done in 1979. Then, the researchers set out to analyze the characteristics of senior executives, surveying about 1,700 people in senior positions below the level of chief executive officer at Fortune's top 500 companies and the 300 more specialized concerns. When 99% of the respondents turned out to be men, the researchers decided to survey executive women and compare the two groups. Presidents, chief executive officers and chief operating officers were included in the female study in order to get a sufficient sample. The average age of the men surveyed was 53.

"I know men who say, 'I support your career. It's wonderful.' But that's not what they mean," says a woman who is a director of several companies.

Comparison shows the biggest difference between executive men and women to be marital and family status. Fifty-two percent of the women surveyed are single, compared with only 4% of the men. In addition, 61% of the women are childless, while 97% of the men were parents.

Executive women are far more likely to be divorced than their male counterparts. Of the women studied, 17% are divorced, compared with only 2.4% of the men. More than half of the executive women who are divorced say their career played a part in the separation.

A study recently completed by James Baron, assistant professor of organizational behavior at Stanford University and William Bielby, associate professor of sociology at the University of California, Santa Barbara, yields similar results.

Using data from the 1960s, the two men studied about 1,000 men and women in a cross-section of occupations. Some 86% of their male respondents were married, compared with only 61% of the women.

"As you move up the ladder, these pressures become even greater," Mr. Baron says. "Not only is being married a disadvantage to a woman in that position, but it's an asset for a man."

Paychecks and Housekeeping

In 1971, Miss Franklin was appointed to the Nixon White House to recruit women for high-level jobs in the federal government. "Many of them were either single or divorced," she recalls. "It's hard to find men in this age group willing to be supportive and understanding of the demands on a successful woman. I know men who say, 'I support your career. It's wonderful.' But that's not what they mean. They mean I support it as long as it doesn't interfere with someplace I want you to be."

Executive women who are married are generally running the home and bringing home more of the money. On the average these women provide 56% of their household income. Sixty-eight percent of the women say their careers have been more financially rewarding than their husbands', and 78% say their careers have progressed better. About half of the women say they're responsible for the housekeeping, and 29% say they share the work with their spouse. A majority of the women with children say they have the primary responsibility for their care.

"I'm out there writing notes to the housekeeper and arranging meals," says an executive search manager queried about the study. The woman is married to an executive at a large corporation and makes more money than her husband. She says she prefers to do the housework. "I find it easier in life to manage and administer that which I've been trained to do," she says, describing how they divide the work at home.

Refusing Transfers

Another difference between executive men and women is mobility. While 33% of the female respondents have been asked to relocate, only 21% have done so, compared with 81% of the men. Of the women who refused a transfer, the majority say their refusal hasn't hurt their careers.

While the survey portrays an executive woman who is still bumping into obstacles along the path to success, it also shows her making progress. Nearly half of the women over 52 years of age started in clerical positions, compared with only 23% of the younger female executives, who more often started in management. The younger women also have more earning power than their elders. Some 60% of the women earning more than $106,000 are between 38 and 52, compared with only 20% of those over 52.

Although executive women have more limited educational backgrounds than their male counterparts, more than in the past are graduating from college. Some 20% of the respondents don't have a college degree, compared with 8% of the men surveyed. But 34% of the younger women surveyed have advanced degrees, compared with only 14% of the older women.

Comparison of the two studies shows that female executives are also less conservative and less religious than male executives. Some 60% of the women say religion plays little or no role in their lives, while about the same percentage of men said religion was a significant or moderate influence on them. On economic issues, 49% of the respondents say they are conservative, compared with 74% of the men. On social issues, 21% of the women say they are conservative, compared with 42% of the men. Some 80% of the women favor passage of the Equal Rights Amendment and 90% favor a woman's right to abortion.

The studies also show a difference in family background between men and women in senior management. Sixty percent of the women surveyed say they were either the oldest or only child, compared with 49% of the men. In addition, 48% of the women say they were closer to their fathers while growing up, compared with 40% who were closer to their mothers. Fifty-four percent of these female executives say their mothers didn't work outside the home.

Conclusions

In this chapter, we have considered gender differences in communication as these occur in public contexts. In earlier chapters we noted that women tend to be less assertive than men; that men tend to be less empathic than women; that women demonstrate more sensitivity to nonverbal cues; and that men are better able to focus on a single message in a multiple-message situation. In this chapter, we viewed some of the results of those differences in communication behaviors in public contexts.

We observed that women and men have different styles in the small group setting, and concluded that mixed-sex groups might be superior to either all-male or all-female groups. We noted that people might prefer men in leadership positions, but that both men and women can be successful leaders. In public speaking, women and men exhibit different skills, and in the speech communication classroom, women appear to excell. The occupational choices of women and men are different, although we might question whether they should be. The employment interview is sometimes different when it is conducted with a woman than with a man; however, federal guidelines define discrimination in hiring as illegal. In the past, women have rarely served as managers; today they are moving rapidly into managerial positions. Their success in these positions is not simply a matter of adopting and enacting male behaviors; instead, successful female managers may have to develop unique styles which are responsive to the specific needs of their positions.

References

Adamsky, Cathryn. "Changes in Pronominal Usage in a Classroom Situation." *Psychology of Women Quarterly* 5 (1981): 773–779.

Addington, David W. "The Relationship of Selected Vocal Characteristics to Personality Perception." *Speech Monographs* 35 (1968): 492–503.

Adler, Ronald B. *Confidence in Communication: A Guide to Assertive and Social Skills.* New York: Holt, Rinehart and Winston, 1977.

Adler, Ronald and Towne, Neil. *Looking Out/Looking In.* New York: Holt, Rinehart, and Winston, 1978.

Ahmen, S. M. S. "Invasion of Personal Space: A Study of Departure Time as Affected by Sex of the Intruder, Sex of the Subject, and Saliency Condition." *Perceptual and Motor Skills* 49 (1979): 85–86.

Aiken, L. "The Relationships of Dress to Selected Measures of Personality in Undergraduate Women." *The Journal of Social Psychology* 59 (1963): 119–128.

Alberti, Robert E., and Emmons, Michael L. *Your Perfect Right.* San Luis Obispo, California: Impact Publishers, Inc., 1974.

Albright, D. G. and Chang, A. F. "An Examination of How One's Attitudes Toward Women Are Reflected in One's Defensiveness and Self-Esteem." *Sex Roles* 2 (1976): 195–198.

Aldous, Joan. (ed.) *Two Paychecks: Life in Dual-Earner Families.* Beverly Hills, California: Sage Publications, 1982.

Alpander, Guvenc G. and Gutmann, Jean E. "Contents and Techniques of Management Development Programs for Women." *Personnel Journal* 55 (1976): 76–79.

Alreck, Pamela L.; Settle, Robert B.; and Belch, Michael A. "Who Responds to Gendered Ads, and How?" *Journal of Advertising Research* 22 (April/May, 1982): 25–32.

Alsbrook, Larry. "Marital Communication and Sexism." *Social Casework* 57 (1976): 517–522.

Altman, Janet H. and Wittenborn, J. R. "Depression-Prone Personality in Women." *Journal of Abnormal Psychology* 89 (1980): 303–308.

Alvares, Kenneth M. and Lee, Dennis M. "Effects of Sex on Descriptions and Evaluations of Supervisory Behavior in a Simulated Industrial Setting." *Journal of Applied Psychology* 64 (1977): 405–410.

Amerikaner, Martin. "Self-Disclosure: A Study of Verbal and Coverbal Intimacy." *The Journal of Psychology* 104 (1980): 221–229.

Amidjaja, I. Mat and Vinacke, W. Edgar. "Achievement, Nurturance, and Competition in Male and Female Triads." *Journal of Personality and Social Psychology* 2 (1965): 447–451.

Anchor, K. N.; Sandler, H. M.; and Cherones, J. H. "Maladaptive Antisocial Aggressive Behavior and Outlets for Intimacy." *Journal of Clinical Psychology* 33 (1977): 947–949.

Anderson, Barbara J.; Vietze, Peter; and Dokechi, Paul R. "Reciprocity in Vocal Interactions of Mothers and Infants." *Child Development* 48 (1977): 1676–1681.

Anderson, Rosemarie and Nida, Steve A. "Effect of Physical Attractiveness on Opposite and Same Sex Evaluations." *Journal of Personality* 46 (1978): 401–413.

Aneshensel, Carol S. and Rosen, Bernard C. "Sex Differences in the Educational-Occupational Expectation Process." *Journal of Social Forces* 57 (1978): 164–186.

Archer, Richard L. and Berg, John H. "Disclosure Reciprocity and Its Limits: A Reactance Analysis." *Journal of Experimental Social Psychology* 14 (1978): 527–540.

Archer, R. L. and Burleson, J. A. "The Effects of Timing of Self-Disclosure on Attraction and Reciprocity." *Journal of Personality and Social Psychology* 38 (1980): 120–130.

Argyle, Michael. *Bodily Communication.* New York: International Universities Press, 1975.

Argyle, Michael and Dean, Janet. "Eye Contact, Distance and Affiliation." *Sociometry* 28 (1965): 289–304.

Argyle, Michael; Lalljee, Jansur; and Cook, Mark. "The Effects of Visibility on Interaction in a Dyad." *Human Relations* 21 (1968): 3–17.

Argyle, M. and Williams, M. "Observer or Observed? A Reversible Perspective in Person Perception." *Sociometry* 32 (1969): 396–412.

Aries, Elizabeth. "Verbal and Nonverbal Behavior in Single-Sex and Mixed-Sex Groups." *Psychological Reports* 51 (1982): 127–134.

Aronson, Elliot and Mills, Judson. "Opinion Change as a Function of the Communicator's Attractiveness and Desire to Influence." *Journal of Personality and Social Psychology* 1 (1965): 173–177.

Ashby, Marylee Stull and Wittmaier, Bruce C. "Attitude Changes in Children after Exposure to Stories about Women in Traditional or Nontraditional Occupations." *Journal of Educational Psychology* 70 (1978): 945–949.

Ashworth, Clark; Furman, Gail; Chaikan, Alan; and Derlega, Valerian. "Physiological Responses to Self-Disclosure." *Journal of Humanistic Psychology* 16 (1976): 71–80.

Austin, David W. "Nonverbal Cues Influencing Client and Nonclient Perception of Counselors." Unpublished doctoral dissertation, University of Wyoming, 1973.

Ayres, Joe. "Relationship Stages and Sex as Factors in Topic Dwell Time." *Western Journal of Speech Communication* 44 (1980): 253–260.

Bahr, S. J. "Premarital Antecedents of Marital Stability." *Family Perspective* 14 (1980): 103–109.

Bahr, Stephen and Rollins, Boyd. "A Theory of Power Relationships in Marriage." *Journal of Marriage and the Family* 38 (1976): 619–627.

Bailey, Roger C. and Price, James P. "Perceived Physical Attractiveness in Married Partners of Long and Short Duration." *The Journal of Psychology* 99 (1978): 155–161.

Baird, John E. "Sex Differences in Group Communication: A Review of Relevant Research." *The Quarterly Journal of Speech* 62 (1976): 179–192.

Baird, John E. and Bradley, Patricia Hayes. "Styles of Management and Communication: A Comparative Study of Men and Women." *Communication Monographs* 46 (1979): 101–111.

Baker, Michael J. "The Impact of Physically Attractive Models on Advertising Evaluations." *Journal of Marketing Research* 14 (1977): 538–555.

Bales, R. F. *Interaction Process Analysis: A Method for the Study of Small Groups.* Reading, Mass.: Addison-Wesley, 1950.

Ball, Joe M. "The Relationship between the Ability to Speak Effectively and the Primary Mental Abilities, Verbal Comprehension and General Reasoning." *Speech Monographs* 25 (1958): 285–290.

Balswick, Jack and Avertt, Christine Parker. "Differences in Expressiveness: Gender, Interpersonal Orientation, and Perceived Parental Expressiveness as Contributing Factors." *Journal of Marriage and the Family* 39 (1977): 121–127.

Balswick, Jack O. and Balkwell, James W. "Self-Disclosure to Same- and Opposite-Sex Parents: An Empirical Test of Insights from Role Theory." *Sociometry* 40 (1977): 282–286.

Bannatyne, A. *Language, Reading, and Learning Disabilities.* Springfield, Illinois: Charles C. Thomas, 1971.

Banziger, George and Hooker, Lynn. "The Effects of Attitudes Toward Feminism and Perceived Feminism on Physical Attractiveness Ratings." *Sex Roles* 5 (1979): 437–442.

Barbara, D. A. "On Listening—the Role of the Ear in Psychic Life." *Today's Speech* 5 (1957): 12–15.

Bardon, Edward J. *The Sexual Arena and Women's Liberation.* Chicago: Nelson-Hall, 1978.

Barker, Larry L. "Irrelevant Factors and Speech Evaluation." *Southern Speech Journal* 32 (1966): 10–18.

Barker, Larry L. *Listening Behavior.* Englewood Cliffs, N.J.: Prentice-Hall, 1971.

Barnlund, Dean C. "A Transactional Model of Communication." In *Foundations of Communication Theory,* ed. Kenneth K. Sereno and C. David Mortensen. New York: Harper & Row, 1970.

Baron, Robert A. and Bell, Paul A. "Physical Distance and Helping: Some Unexpected Benefits of 'Crowding In' on Others." *Journal of Applied Social Psychology* 6 (1976): 95–104.

Baron, Rueben M. and Needel, Stephen P. "Toward an Understanding of the Differences in the Responses of Humans and Other Animals to Density." *Psychological Review* 87 (1980): 320–326.

Barratt, Robin. "If the 'Miss' Fits, Use It—Sexist Language Is Appropriate to Describe Sexist People." *The Chronicle of Higher Education* (March 31, 1982) p. 21.

Barrios, Billy A.; Corbitt, L. Claire; Estes, J. Philip; and Topping, Jeff S. "Effect of a Social Stigma on Interpersonal Distance." *The Psychological Record* 26 (1976): 343–348.

Bar-Tal, Daniel and Saxe, Leonard. "Perceptions of Similarly and Dissimilarly Attractive Couples and Individuals." *Journal of Personality and Social Psychology* 33 (1976): 772–781.

Barthel, J. "The World Has Turned More than 3200 Times, and 8 Million People Keep Watching." *New York Times Magazine,* March 23, 1968.

Bartol, Kathryn M. "Male Versus Female Leaders: The Effects of Leader Need for Dominance on Follower Satisfaction." *Academy of Management Journal* 17 (1974): 225–232.

Bartol, Kathryn M. "The Sex Structuring of Organizations: A Search of Possible Courses." *Academy of Management Review* 3 (1978): 805–813.

Bartol, Kathryn M. and Butterfield, D. Anthony. "Sex Effects in Evaluating Leaders." *Journal of Applied Psychology* 61 (1976): 446–454.

Bartol, Kathryn M. and Wortman, Jr., Max S. "Male Versus Female Leaders: Effects on Perceived Leader Behavior and Satisfaction in a Hospital." *Personnel Psychology* 28 (1975): 533–547.

Bartol, Kathryn M. and Wortman, Jr., Max S. "Sex Effects in Leader Behavior Self-Descriptions and Job Satisfaction." *Journal of Psychology* 94 (1976): 177–183.

Bate, Barbara. "Nonsexist Language in Transition." *Journal of Communication* 28 (Winter 1978): 139–149.

Bate, Barbara and Self, Lois S. "The Rhetoric of Career Success Books for Women." *Journal of Communication* 33 (1983): 149–165.

Bateson, G. *Steps to an Ecology of Mind.* New York: Ballantine, 1972.

Bauer, Richard and Turner, James H. "Betting Behavior in Sexually Homogeneous and Heterogeneous Groups." *Psychological Reports* 34 (1974): 251–258.

Baxter, L. A. "Self-Disclosure as a Relationship Disengagement Strategy: An Exploratory Investigation." *Human Communication Research* 6 (1979): 215–222.

Bayer, Alan E. "Students in American Colleges: A Descriptive Note." *Journal of Marriage and the Family* 37 (1975): 391–397.

Beck, Kay. "Sex Differentiated Speech Codes." *International Journal of Womens Studies* 1 (1978): 566–572.

Beddington, A. C. "The Function of Stress in the Establishment of the Dual-Career Family." *Journal of Marriage and the Family* 35 (1973): 530–537.

Bedeian, Arthur G.; Armenakis, Archilles A.; and Kemp, B. Wayne. "Relation of Sex to Perceived Legitimacy of Organizational Influence." *The Journal of Psychology* 94 (1976): 93–99.

Beekman, Susan J. "Sex Differences in Nonverbal Behavior." Paper, Michigan State University, 1973.

Bell, Nancy J. and Carver, William. "A Reevaluation of Gender Label Effects: Expectant Mothers' Responses to Infants." *Child Development* 51 (1980): 925–927.

Bellinger, D. C. and Gleason, J. B. "Sex Differences in Parental Directives to Young Children." *Sex Roles* 8 (1982): 1123–1139.

Bem, Sandra Lipsitz. "Androgyny vs. the Tight Little Lives of Fluffy Women and Chesty Men." *Psychology Today* 9 (September 1975): 58–59.

Bem, Sandra. "The Measurement of Psychological Androgyny." *Journal of Consulting and Clinical Psychology* 42 (1974): 155–162.

Bem, Sandra. "Sex-role adaptability: One consequence of Psychological Androgyny." *Journal of Personality and Social Psychology* 31 (1975): 634–643.

Bem, Sandra L. and Bem, Daryl J. "Does Sex-biased Job Advertising 'Aid and Abet' Sex Discrimination?" *Journal of Applied Social Psychology* 3 (1973): 6–18.

Bender, V. Lee; Davis, Yvonne; Glover, Oliver; and Stapp, Joy. "Patterns of Self-Disclosure in Homosexual and Heterosexual College Students." *Sex Roles* 2 (1976): 149–160.

Bennetts, Leslie. "Beauty is Only Skin Deep, But . . ." *New York Times,* 1978.

Benson, P. L.; Karabenick, S. A.; and Lerner, R. M. "Pretty Pleases: The Effects of Physical Attractiveness, Race, and Sex on Receiving Help." *Journal of Experimental Social Psychology* 12 (1976): 409–415.

Benton, Alan H. "Reactions to Demands to Win from an Opposite Sex Opponent." *Journal of Personality* 41 (1973): 430–442.

Berger, Charles R. "Sex Differences Related to Self-Esteem Factor Structure." *Journal of Consulting and Clinical Psychology* 32 (1968): 442–446.

Berger, Charles and Calabrese, R. "Some Explorations in Initial Interaction and Beyond: Toward a Developmental Theory of Interpersonal Communication." *Human Communication Research* 1 (1975): 98–112.

Berger, C. R.; Gardner, R. R.; Clatterbuck, G. W.; and Schulman, L. S. "Perceptions of Information Sequencing in Relationship Development." *Human Communication Research* 3 (1976): 29–46.

Berkowitz, William R. "Perceived Height, Personality, and Friendship Choice." *Psychological Reports* 24 (1969): 373–374.

Berlo, David K. *The Process of Communication.* New York: Holt, Rinehart and Winston, 1960.

Berryman, Cynthia L. and Wilcox, James R. "Attitudes Toward Male and Female Speech: Experiments on the Effects of Sex-Typical Language." *The Western Journal of Speech Communication* 44 (1980): 50–59.

Berscheid, Ellen. "Physical Attractiveness" in L. Berkowitz (ed.) *Advances in Experimental Social Psychology.* New York: Academic Press, 1974, pp. 157–215.

Berscheid, Ellen and Walster, Elaine Hatfield. *Interpersonal Attraction.* Reading, Mass.; Addison-Wesley, 1969.

Beuf, Ann. "Doctor, Lawyer, Household Drudge." *Journal of Communication* 24 (1974): 142–145.

Bianchi, B. D. and Bakeman, R. "Sex-typed Affiliation Preferences Observed in Pre-Schoolers: Traditional and Open School Differences." *Child Development* 49 (1978): 910–915.

Biles, George E. and Pryatel, Holly A. "Myths, Management and Women." *Personnel Journal* 57 (1978): 572–577.

Birchler, Gary R. and Webb, Linda J. "Discriminating Interaction Behaviors in Happy and Unhappy Marriages." *Journal of Consulting and Clinical Psychology* 45 (1977): 494–495.

Bird, Caroline. *Born Female: The High Cost of Keeping Women Down.* New York: David McKay Co., 1968.

Birdwhistell, Ray L. "Masculinity and Femininity as Display." In *Kinesics and Context,* by Ray L. Birdwhistell. Philadelphia: University of Pennsylvania Press, 1970.

Black, Harvey K. "Physical Attractiveness and Similarity of Attitude in Interpersonal Attraction." *Psychological Reports* 35 (1974): 403–406.

Blackwell, Lorna and Kernaleguen, Anne. "Men's Fabric Preferences Related to Age, Inherent Color Vision, and Perceptual Disembedding Ability." *Perceptual and Motor Skills* 51 (1980): 551–557.

Bleda, Paul R. and Bleda, Sharon Estee. "Effects of Sex and Smoking on Reactions to Spatial Invasion at a Shopping Mall." *The Journal of Social Psychology* 104 (1978): 311–312.

Bloom, L. Z.; Coburn K.; and Pearlman J. *The New Assertive Woman.* New York: Delacorte, 1975.

Bloomenthal, Howard. *Promoting Your Cause.* New York: Funk and Wagnalls, 1971.

Bloxham, Thine Lu Cochrane. "Adolescents' Awareness of Dress Norms." Master's Thesis, Washington State University, 1974.

Bock, Douglas G. "The Effects of Persuasibility on Leniency, Halo, and Trait Errors in the Use of Speech Rating Scales." *Speech Teacher* 19 (1970): 296–300.

Bock, Douglas G. and Bock, E. Hope. "The Effects of Sex on the Experimenter, Expectancy Inductions, and Sex of the Rater on Leniency, Halo, and Trait Errors in Speech Rating Behavior." *Communication Education* 26 (1977): 298–306.

Bock, Douglas, G.; Powell, Larry; Kitchens, James T.; and Flavin, James W. "The Influence of Sex Differences in Speech Evaluation: Situational and Media Effects." *Communication Education* 26 (1977): 143–153.

Bochner, Arthur, "On the Efficacy of Openness in Close Relationships." In *Communication Yearbook 5*, ed. Michael Burgoon. New Brunswick, New Jersey: Transaction Books, 1982, pp. 109–124.

Bochner, Arthur P. and Kelly, Clifford W. "Interpersonal Competence: Rationale, Philosophy, and Implementation of a Conceptual Framework." *Speech Teacher* 23 (1974): 279–301.

Bogen, J. E., and Bogen, G. M. "The Other Side of the Brain III: The Corpus Callosum and Creativity." *Bulletin of the Los Angeles Neurological Societies* 34 (1969): 191–200.

Bond, J. and Vinacke, W. "Coalition in Mixed Sex Triads." *Sociometry* 24 (1961): 61–75.

Borges, Marilyn A., and Laning, Beverly. "Relationships Between Assertiveness, Achievement Motivation, Feminist Attitudes, and Locus of Control in the College Population." *Psychological Reports* 44 (1979): 545–546.

Bormann, Ernest G.; Pratt, Jerie; and Putnam, Linda. "Power, Authority, and Sex: Male Response to Female Leadership." *Communication Monographs* 45 (1978): 119–155.

Bostrom, Robert N. "Dogmatism, Rigidity, and Rating Behavior." *Speech Teacher* 13 (1964): 283–287.

Bostrom, Robert N. and Bryant, Carol L. "Factors in the Retention of Information Presented Orally: The Role of Short-term Listening." *Western Journal of Speech Communication* 44 (1980): 137–145.

Bostrom, Robert N.; Humphreys, Rebecca J.; and Roloff, Michael E. "Communication and Helping Behavior: The Effects of Information, Reinforcement, and Sex on Helping Responses." *Communication Quarterly* 29 (1981): 147–155.

Bostrom, R. N. and Kemp, A. P. "Type of Speech, Sex of Speaker, and Sex of Subject as Factors Influencing Persuasion." *Central States Speech Journal* 30 (1968): 245–252.

Bostrom, Robert N. and Waldhart, Enid S. "Components in Listening Behavior: The Role of Short-Term Memory." *Human Communication Research* 6 (1980): 221–227.

Bouska, Marvin L. and Beatty, Patricia A. "Clothing as a Symbol of Status: Its Effect on Control of Interaction Territory." *Bulletin of the Psychonomic Society* 11 (1978): 235–238.

Bowlby, John. *Maternal Care and Mental Health.* Geneva: World Health Organization, 1952.

Bradac, James J.; Hemphill, Michael R.; and Tardy, Charles H. "Language Style on Trial: Effects of 'Powerful' and 'Powerless' Speech on Judgments of Victims and Villains." *Western Journal of Speech Communication* 45 (1981): 327–341.

Bradac, J. J.; Tardy, C. H.; and Hosman, L. A. "Disclosure Styles and a Hint at Their Genesis." *Human Communication Research* 6 (1980): 228–238.

Bradley, Patricia Hayes. "The Folk-Linguistics of Women's Speech: An Empirical Examination." *Communication Monographs* 48 (1981): 73–90.

Bradley, Patricia Hayes. "Sex, Competence and Opinion Deviation: An Expectation States Approach." *Communication Monographs* 47 (1980): 105–110.

Brain, Robert. *The Decorated Body.* New York: Harper & Row, 1979.

Bralowe, Mary. "Advertising World's Portrayal of Women is Starting to Shift." *The Wall Street Journal* (October 28, 1982): 33.

Brandt, D. R. "A Systematic Approach to the Measurement of Dominance in Human Face-to-Face Interaction." *Communication Quarterly* 28 (1980): 31–43.

Breisinger, Gary D. "Sex and Empathy, Reexamined." *Journal of Counseling Psychology* 23 (1976): 289–290.

Bremer, Teresa Hargrave and Wittig, Michelle Andrisin. "Fear of Success: A Personality Trait or a Response to Occupational Deviance and Role Overload?" *Sex Roles* 6 (1980): 27–46.

Brenner, O. C. and Bromer, John A. "Sex Stereotypes and Leader's Behavior as Measured by the Agreement Scale for Leadership Behavior." *Psychological Reports* 48 (1981): 960–962.

Brenner, Otto C. and Vinacke, W. Edgar. "Accommodative and Exploitative Behavior of Males vs. Females and Managers versus Nonmanagers as Measured by the Test of Strategy." *Social Psychology Quarterly* 42 (1979): 289–293.

Bridgwater, Carol Austin, "When a Man Talks, You Listen." *Psychology Today* 14 (December 1980): 25–26.

Brief, Arthur P. and Oliver, Richard L. "Male-Female Differences in Work Attitudes Among Retail Sales Managers." *Journal of Applied Psychology* 61 (1976): 526–528.

Brislin, Richard and Lewis, Stephen. "Dating and Physical Attractiveness: Replication." *Psychological Reports* 22 (1968): 976.

Britton, G. E. and Lumpkin, M. C. "For Sale: Subliminal Bias in Textbooks." *Reading Teacher* 31 (October, 1977): 40–45.

Brofenbrenner, U. *Two Worlds of Childhood.* N. G.: Russell-Sage, 1970.

Brooks, Linda. "Interactive Effects of Sex and Status on Self-Disclosure." *Journal of Counseling Psychology* 21 (1974): 469–474.

Brooks, R. "The Relationship Between Piagetian Cognitive Development and Cerebral Cognitive Asymmetry." Greeley, Colorado: University of Northern Colorado, 1979. (ERIC Document Reproduction Service No. ED 160 224).

Brophy, Jere E. and Good, Thomas L. "Teachers' Communication of Differential Expectations for Children's Classroom Performance: Some Behavioral Data." *Journal of Educational Psychology* 61 (1970): 365–374.

Brouwer, Dede; Gerritsen, Marinel; and DeHaan, Dorian. "Speech Differences Between Women and Men: On the Wrong Track?" *Language in Society* 8 (1979): 33–49.

Broverman, Donald M.; Broverman, Inge K.; Clarkson, Frank E.; Rosenkrantz, Paul S.; and Vogel, Susan R. "Sex-role Stereotypes: A Current Appraisal." *Journal of Social Issues* 28 (1972): 59–78.

Broverman, Inge K.; Broverman, Donald M.; Clarkson, Frank E.; Rosenkrantz, Paul S.; and Vogel, Susan R. "Sex-Role Stereotypes and Clinical Judgments of Mental Health." *Journal of Consulting and Clinical Psychology* 34 (1970): 1–7.

Broverman, Inge K.; Vogel, Susan R.; Broverman, Donald M.; Clarkson, Frank E.; and Rosenkrantz, Paul S. "Sex Role Stereotypes: A Current Appraisal." *Journal of Social Issues* 28 (1972): 59–78.

Brown, Stephen M. "Male versus Female Leaders: A Comparison of Empirical Studies." *Sex Roles* 5 (1979): 595–611.

Brundage, Toni E.; Derlega, Valerian J.; and Cash, Thomas F. "The Effects of Physical Attractiveness and Need for Approval on Self-Disclosure." *Personality and Social Psychology Bulletin* 3 (1977): 63–66.

Brunner, Claire C. and Phelps, Lynn A. "Interpersonal Communication Competence and Androgyny." Paper presented to the International Communication Association Convention, Acapulco, 1980.

Bryan, A. I. and Wilke, W. H. "Audience Tendencies in Rating Public Speakers." *Journal of Applied Psychology* 26 (1942): 371–381.

Bryant, J.; Crane, J. S.; Comisky, P. W.; and Zillman, D. "Relationship Between College Teachers' Use of Humor in the Classroom and Students' Evaluations of Their Teachers." *Journal of Educational Psychology* 72 (1980): 511–519.

Buchanan, Douglas R.; Juhnke, Ralph; and Goldman, Morton. "Violation of Personal Space as a Function of Sex." *The Journal of Social Psychology* 99 (1976): 187–192.

Buchli, Virginia and Pearce, W. Barnett. "Listening Behavior in Cooriential States." *Journal of Communication* 24 (1974): 62–70.

Buck, Ross; Miller, Robert E.; and Caul, William F. "Sex, Personality, and Physiological Variables in the Communication of Affect Via Facial Expression." *Journal of Personality and Social Psychology* 30 (1974): 587–596.

Bugental, Daphne E.; Love, Leonore R.; and Gianetto, Robert M. "Perfidious Feminine Faces." *Journal of Personality and Social Psychology* 17 (1971): 314–318.

Bugental, Daphne E.; Kaswan, Jacques W.; Love, Leonore R.; and Fox, Michael N. "Child Versus Adult Perception of Evaluative Messages in Verbal, Vocal, and Visual Channels." *Developmental Psychology* 2 (1970): 367–375.

Burge, Penny Lee. "Parental Sex-Role Attitudes Related to Self-Concept and Sex Role-Identity of Pre-School Children." Unpublished doctoral dissertation The Pennsylvania State University, 1979.

Burgoon, Judee K. "A Communication Model of Personal Space Violations: Explication and an Initial Test." *Human Communication Research* 4 (1978): 129–142.

Burgoon, J. K.; Buller, D. B.; Hale, J. L.; and de Turck, M. A. "Relational Messages associated with Immediacy Behaviors." Paper presented at the International Communication Association Convention, Boston, April 1982.

Burgoon, J. K. and Jones, S. B. "Toward A Theory of Personal Space Expectations and their Violations." *Human Communication Research* 2 (1976): 131–146.

Burgoon, Judee K. and Saine, Thomas. *The Unspoken Dialogue: An Introduction to Nonverbal Communication.* Boston, Mass.: Houghton Mifflin Company, 1978.

Burke, Ronald J. and Weir, Tamara. "Marital Helping Relationships. The Moderators Between Stress and Well-being." *The Journal of Psychology* 95 (1977): 121–130.

Burke, Ronald J. and Weir, Tamara. "Some Personality Differences Between Members of One-Career and Two-Career Families." *Journal of Marriage and the Family* 38 (1976): 453–459.

Burke, Ronald J.; Weir, Tamara; and Harrison, Denise. "Disclosure of Problems and Tensions Experienced by Marital Partners." *Psychological Reports* 38 (1976): 531–542.

Burr, Elizabeth; Dunn, Susan; and Farquhar, Norma. "Women and the Language of Inequality." *Social Education* 36 (1972): 841–845.

Busby, Linda J. "Sex Role Research on the Mass Media." *Journal of Communication* 25 (1975): 107–131.

Butler, Pamela E. *Self-Assertion for Women.* San Francisco: Harper & Row, 1981.

Byrne, D. and Buehler, J. A. "A Note on the Influence of Propinquity upon Acquaintanceships." *Journal of Abnormal and Social Psychology* 51 (1955): 147–148.

Byrne, Donn; Ervin, Charles R.; and Lamberth, John. "The Continuity Between the Experimental Study of Attraction and Real-Life Computer Dating." *Journal of Personality and Social Psychology* 16 (1970): 157–165.

Byrne, Donn; London, Oliver; and Reeves, Keigh. "The Effects of Physical Attractiveness, Sex, and Attitude Similarity on Interpersonal Attraction." *Journal of Personality* 36 (1968): 259–271.

Caffrey, J. "Auding Ability at the Secondary Level." *Education* 75 (1955): 303–310.

Camden, Carl and Kennedy, Carole. "Interruptions as an Index of Communication Dominance." Paper presented at the Western Speech Communication Association, Denver, 1982.

Cantor, J. R. "What is Funny to Whom? The Role of Gender." *Journal of Communication* 26 (1976): 164–172.

Cargan, L. and Melko, M. "Is Marriage Good for your Health?" *Family Perspective* 15 (1981): 107–114.

Cargan, L. and Melko, M. *Singles: Myths and Realities.* Beverly Hills, California: Sage Publications, 1982.

Carmichael, Carl W. "Frustration, Sex, and Persuasibility." *Western Speech* 34 (1970): 300–307.

Carns, Donald E. "Talking About Sex: Notes on First Coitus and the Double Sexual Standard." *Journal of Marriage and the Family* 35 (1973): 677–688.

Carroll, Lewis. *Through the Looking Glass.* New York: Random House, Inc., 1965.

Casciani, J. M. "Influence of Model's Race and Sex on Interviewees' Self-Disclosure." *Journal of Counseling Psychology* 25 (1978): 435–440.

Cash, Thomas. "If You Think Beautiful People Hold All the Cards, You're Right Says a Researcher." *People Weekly* 14 (July 7, 1980): 74–79.

Cash, Thomas F. and Derlega, Valerian J. "The Matching Hypothesis: Physical Attractiveness Among Same-Sexed Friends." *Personality and Social Psychology Bulletin* 4 (April 1978): 240–243.

Cash, T. F. and Salzbach, R. F. "The Beauty of Counseling: Effects of Counselor Physical Attractiveness and Self-Disclosure on Perceptions of Counselor Behavior." *Journal of Counseling Psychology* 25 (1978): 288–291.

Cash, Thomas F. and Soloway, Deborah. "Self-Disclosure Correlates of Physical Attractiveness: An Exploratory Study." *Psychological Reports* 36 (1975): 579–586.

Cassata, Mary B.; Skill, Thomas D.; and Boadu, Samuel Osei. "In Sickness and In Health." *Journal of Communication* 29 (Autumn 1979): 73–81.

Caudill, William and Weinstein, Helen. "Maternal Care and Infant Behavior in Japan and America." *Psychiatry* 32 (1969): 12–43.

Cavior, N. and Dokeck, P. R. "Physical Attractiveness, Perceived Attitude Similarity, and Academic Achievement as Contributors to Interpersonal Attraction Among Adolescents." *Child Development* 44 (July 1973): 44–54.

Cegala, Donald J. "Interaction Involvement: A Cognitive Dimension of Communicative Competence." *Communication Education* 30 (1981): 109–121.

Centers, Richard. "The Completion Hypothesis and the Compensatory Dynamic in Intersexual Attraction and Love." *The Journal of Psychology* 82 (1972): 111–126.

Chaikin, Alan L. and Derlega, Valerian J. "Variables Affecting the Appropriateness of Self-Disclosure." *Journal of Consulting and Clinical Psychology* 42 (1974): 588–593.

Chaiken, Alan; Derlega, Valerian; Yoder, John; and Phillips, David. "The Effects of Appearance on Compliance." *The Journal of Social Psychology* 92 (1974): 199–200.

Chaiken, Shelly. "Communicator Physical Attractiveness and Persuasion." *Journal of Personality and Social Psychology* 37 (1979): 1387–1397.

Chandler, Theodore A.; Cook, Bettyanne; and Dugovics, David A. "Sex Differences in Self-Reported Assertiveness." *Psychological Reports* 4 (1978): 395–402.

Chandler, T. and Dugovics, D. "Sex Differences in Research on Locus of Control." *Psychological Reports* 41 (1977): 47–53.

Chang, M. and Gruner, C. R. "Audience Reaction to Self-Disparaging Humor." *The Southern Speech Communication Journal* 46 (1981): 419–426.

Chapman, A. J. and Gadfield, N. J. "Is Sexual Humor Sexist?" *Journal of Communication* 26 (1976): 141–153.

Chapman, J. Brad "Comparison of Male and Female Leadership Styles." *Academy of Management Journal* 18 (1975): 645–650.

Chapman, J. Brad and Luthans, Fred. "The Female Leadership Dilemma." *Public Personnel Management* 4 (May–June, 1975): 173–178.

Chasser, El. *The Sexual, Marital and Family Relationships of the English Woman.* Watford: Hutchenson Medical Publications Ltd., 1956.

Cherlin, Andrew. "Hereditary Hyphens." *Psychology Today* 12 (1978): 150.

Chelune, Gordon J. "Reactions to Male and Female Disclosure at Two Levels." *Journal of Personality and Social Psychology* 34 (1976): 1000–1003.

Chelune, Gordon J. "Summary, Implications, and Future Perspectives." In Gordon J. Chelune (Ed.) *Self-Disclosure.* San Francisco, California: Jassey-Bass Publishers, 1979.

Chelune, Gordon G. J.; Sultan, Faye E.; and Williams, Carolyn L. "Loneliness, Self-Disclosure, and Interpersonal Effectiveness." *Journal of Counseling Psychology* 27 (1980): 462–480.

Chesler, Phyllis. *Women and Madness.* Garden City, N.Y.: Doubleday, 1972.

Christensen, Harold. "Attitudes Toward Marital Infidelity: A Nine-Culture Sampling of University Student Opinion." *Journal of Comparative Family Studies* 4 (1973): 197–215.

Christiansen, John B. "Television Role Models and Adolescent Occupational Goals." *Human Communication Research* 5 (1979): 335–337.

Christie, Richard. "Social Correlates of Machiavellianism." In Richard Christie and Florence L. Geis, *Studies in Machiavellianism.* New York: Academic Press, 1970, 314–338.

Chronkite, Ruth. "The Determinants of Spouses Normative Preferences for Family Roles." *Journal of Marriage and the Family* 39 (1977): 575–585.

Clay, Vidal S. "The Effect of Culture on Mother-Child Tactile Communication." *Family Coordinator* 17 (1968): 204–210.

Clifton, A. K. and Lee, D. E. "Self-Destructive Consequences of Sex-Role Socialization." *Suicide and Life-Threatening Behavior* 6(1) (1976): 11–22.

Cline, Rebecca J. "Revealing and Relating: A Review of Self-Disclosure Theory and Research." Paper presented to the International Communication Association Convention, Boston, Massachusetts, May 1982.

Cohen, David. "The Avid Gazes of Strangers." *Psychology Today* 13 (October 1979): 40–115.

Coles, Ruth J. "Occupations in Regard to Ethnic Groups." *Journal of Vocational Behavior* 14 (1978): 43–45.

Colins, Michael; Waters, L. K.; and Waters, Carrie Wherry. "Relationships between Sex-Role Orientation and Attitudes toward Women as Managers." *Psychological Reports* 45 (1979): 828–830.

Combs, Robert H. and Kenkel, William F. "Sex Differences in Dating Aspirations and Satisfaction with Computer Selected Partners." *Journal of Marriage and the Family* 28 (1966): 62–66.

Compton, Norma H. "Personal Attributes of Color and Design Preferences in Clothing Fabrics." *The Journal of Psychology* 54 (1962): 191–195.

Condry, J. and Condry, S. "Sex Differences: A Study of the Eye of the Beholder." *Child Development* 47 (1976): 812–819.

Conner, Barbara Hunt; Peters, K.; and Nagasawa, R. H. "Person and Costume: "The Influence of Clothing on the Formation of First Impressions." Effect on the Formation of First Impressions." *Home Economics Research Journal* 4 (1975): 32–41.

Connor, Jane M., and Serbin, Lisa A. "Children's Responses to Stories with Male and Female Characters." *Sex Roles* 4 (1978): 637–645.

Corbett, Michael et al. "Sexism Among College Students—Do Males and Females Differ?" *Youth and Society* 9 (1977): 171–190.

Cordua, Glenn D.; McGraw, Kenneth O.; and Drabman, Ronald S. "Doctor or Nurse: Children's Perception of Sex Typed Occupations." *Child Development* 50 (1979): 590–593.

Coser, R. L. "Laughter Among Colleagues." *Psychiatry* 23 (1960): 81–95.

Courtney, Alice. "Women in T.V. Commercials." *Journal of Communication* 24 (Spring 1974): 110–117.

Courtney, Alice E. and Lockeretz, Sarah Wernick. "A Woman's Place: An Analysis of the Roles Portrayed by Women in Magazine Advertisements." *Journal of Marketing Research* 8 (1971): 92.

Courtney, Alice E. and Whipple, Thomas W. "How to Portray Women in TV Commercials." *Journal of Advertising Research* 20 (1980): 53.

Courtright, John A.; Millar, Frank E.; and Rogers-Millar, L. Edna. "Domineeringness and Dominance: Replication and Expansion." *Communication Monographs* 3 (1979): 180.

Coutts, Larry M. and Ledden, Maribeth. "Nonverbal Compensatory Reactions to Changes in Interpersonal Proximity." *The Journal of Social Psychology* 102 (1977): 283–290.

Coyne, J. C.; Sherman, R. C.; and O'Brien, K. "Expletives and Woman's Place." *Sex Roles* 4 (1978): 827–835.

Cozby, P. "Self-Disclosure: A Literature Review." *Psychological Bulletin* 79 (1973): 73–91.

Cozby, P. "Self-Disclosure, Reciprocity, and Liking." *Sociometry* 35 (1972): 151–160.

Critelli, Joseph W. and Dupre, Kathleen M. "Self-Disclosure and Romantic Attraction." *The Journal of Social Psychology* 106 (1978): 127–128.

Critelli, Joseph W. and Neumann, Karl F. "An Interpersonal Analysis of Self-Disclosure and Feedback." *Social Behavior and Personality* 6 (1978): 173–177.

Critelli, Joseph W. and Waid, Lewis R. "Physical Attractiveness, Romantic Love, and Equity Restoration in Dating Relationships." *Journal of Personality Assessment* 44 (1980): 624–629.

Crosby, Faye and Nyquist, Linda. "The Female Register: An Empirical Study of Lakoff's Hypotheses." *Language in Society* 6 (1977): 313–322.

Culbert, S. A. "Trainer Self-Disclosure and Member Growth in Two T-Groups." *Journal of Applied Behavioral Science* 4 (1968): 47–73.

Culley, James D. and Bennett, Rex. "Selling Women, Selling Blacks." *Journal of Communication* 26 (1976): 160–174.

Currant, Elaine F.; Dickson, Andrew L.; Anderson, Howard N.; and Faulkender, Patricia S. "Sex Role Stereotyping and Assertive Behavior." *Journal of Psychology* 101 (1979): 223–228.

Curran, James P. "Differential Effects of Stated Preferences and Questionnaire Role Performance on Interpersonal Attraction in the Dating Situation." *The Journal of Psychology* 82 (1972): 313–327.

Curran, James P. "Correlates of Physical Attractiveness and Interpersonal Attraction in the Dating Situation." *Social Behavior and Personality* 1 (1973): 153–157.

Dalto, C. A.; Ajzen, I.; and Kaplan, K. J. "Self-Disclosure and Attraction: Effects of Intimacy and Desirability on Beliefs and Attitudes." *Journal of Research in Personality* 13 (1979): 127–138.

Davidson, B.; Balswick, J.; and Halverson, C. "Affective Self-Disclosure and Marital Adjustment: A Test of Equity Theory." *Journal of Marriage and the Family* 45 (1983): 93–102.

Davidson, Marilyn. "What Women Managers Face." *Management Today* 62 (1981): 80–83.

Davis, John D. "Effects of Communication About Interpersonal Process on the Evolution of Self-Disclosure in Dyads." *Journal of Personality and Social Psychology* 35 (1977): 31–37.

Davis, John D. "When Boy Meets Girl: Sex Roles and the Negotiation of Intimacy in an Acquaintance Exercise." *Journal of Personality and Social Psychology* 36 (1978): 684–692.

Davis, Junetta. "Sexist Bias in Eight Newspapers." *Journalism Quarterly* 59 (1982): 456–460.

Dawkins, Richard. *The Selfish Gene*. Oxford: Oxford University Press, 1976.

Day, David R. and Stogdill, Ralph M. "Leader Behavior of Male and Female Supervisors: A Comparative Study." *Personnel Psychology* 25 (1972): 353–360.

Dayhoff, Signe A. "Sexist Language and Person Perception: Evaluation of Candidates from Newspaper Articles." *Sex Roles* 9 (1983): 527–539.

Deaux, Kay. "Self-Evaluations of Male and Female Managers." *Sex Roles* 5 (1979): 571–580.

Deaux, K. and Farris, E. "Attributing Causes for One's Own Performance: The Effects of Sex, Norms, and Outcome." *Journal of Research in Personality* 11 (1977): 59–72.

De Forest, C. and Stone, C. L. "Effects of Sex and Intimacy Level on Self-Disclosure." *Journal of Counseling Psychology* 27 (1980): 93–96.

De La Zerga, Nancy and Hopper, Robert. "Employment Interviewers' Reactions to Mexican American Speech." *Communication Monographs* 46 (1979): 126–134.

Densmore, Dana. *Speech is a Form of Thought.* Pittsburgh, PA: KNOW, Inc., 1970.

Derlega, Valerian J. and Chaikin, Alan L. "Norms Affecting Self-Disclosure in Men and Women." *Journal of Consulting and Clinical Psychology* 44 (1976): 376–380.

Derlega, Valerian J. and Chaikin, Alan L. "Privacy and Self-Disclosure in Social Relationships." *Journal of Social Issues* 33 (1977): 102–115.

Detroit Free Press. "We Tend to be Attracted to Mates Most Like Us." April 20, 1981, sec. D, 1.

Deutsch, Morton and Krauss, Robert M. "Studies of Interpersonal Bargaining." *Journal of Conflict Resolution* 6 (1962): 52–76.

Deutsch, Robin Ann. "Sex-Linked Role Behavior. Philosophical Orientation, and Coping Styles in Three Marital Groups." Unpublished doctoral dissertation, California School of Professional Psychology, Berkeley, 1978.

Dibble, Harold L. "More on Gender Differences and the Origin of Language." *Current Anthropology* 17 (1976): 744–49.

Dierks-Stewart, K. "The Effects of Protracted Invasion on an Individual's Action Territory." Unpublished Master's Thesis, Bowling Green State University, 1976.

Dierks-Stewart, K. "Sex Differences in Nonverbal Communication: An Alternative Perspective." In *Communication, Language and Sex: Proceedings of the First Conference,* ed. Cynthia L. Berryman and Virginia A. Eman. Rowley, Massachusetts: Newbury House Publishers, Inc., 1979, pp. 112–121.

Dimond, R. E. and Hellkamp, D. T. "Race, Sex, Ordinal Positions of Birth and Self-Disclosure in High School Students." *Psychological Reports* 25 (1969): 235–238.

Dimond, R. E. and Mintz, D. C. "Ordinal Position of Birth and Self-Disclosure in High-School Students." *Psychological Reports* 21 (1967): 829–833.

Dimond, S. J. *Introducing Neuropsychology.* Springfield, Illinois: Charles C. Thomas, 1978.

Dipboye, Robert L. "Women as Managers—Stereotypes and Realities." *Survey of Business,* May/June 1975, pp. 22–26.

Dipboyle, Robert L. and Wiley, Jack W. "Reactions of Male Raters to Interviewee Self-Presentation Style and Sex: Extensions of Previous Research." *Journal of Vocational Behavior* 13 (1978): 192–203.

Dohrmand, Rita. "A Gender Profile of Children's Educational T.V." *Journal of Communication* 25 (Autumn 1975): 56–65.

Donohew, Lewis; Parker, Joanne M.; and McDermott, Virginia. "Psychophysiological Measurement of Information Selection: Two Studies." *Journal of Communication* 22 (1972): 54–63.

Dooley, D.; Whalen, C. K.; and Flowers, J. V. "Verbal Response Styles of Children and Adolescents in a Counseling Setting: Effects of Age, Sex, and Labeling." *Journal of Counseling Psychology* 25 (1978): 85–95.

Dorris, James M. "Androgyny and Pedagogy: An Analysis of Interpersonal Communication Textbooks, 1975–1979." *Communication Education* 30 (1981): 33–43.

Dosey, Michael A. and Meisels, Murray. "Personal Space and Self-Protection." *Journal of Personality and Social Psychology* 11 (1969): 93–97.

Doster, Joseph A. "Sex Role Learning and Interview Communication." *Journal of Counseling Psychology* 23 (1976): 482–485.

"Double Standard Still There in Advertising." *The Messenger,* Athens, Ohio, February 16, 1982, p. 6.

Douglas, Susan P. "Do Working Wives Read Different Magazines From Non-Working Wives?" *Journal of Advertising* 6 (Winter 1977): 40–43.

Douvan, Elizabeth and Adelson, Joseph. *The Adolescent Experiences.* New York: Wiley, 1966.

Downing, M. "Heroine of the Daytime Serial." *Journal of Communication* 24 (1974): 130–137.

Downs, Chris A. and Gowan, Darryl C. "Sex Differences in Reinforcement and Punishment on Prime Time Television." *Sex Roles* 6 (1980): 683–694.

Druley, Dawn; Cassriel, Dan; and Hollendar, March H. "A Cuddler's Guide to Love." *Self Magazine* (May 1980): 96–100.

Drummond, R. J.; McIntire, W. G.; and Ryan, C. W. "Stability and Sex Differences on the Coppersmith Self-Esteem Inventory for Students in Grades Two to Twelve." *Psychological Reports* 40 (1977): 943–946.

Dubois, Betty Lou and Crouch, Isabel. "The Question of Tag Questions in Women's Speech: They Don't Really Use More of Them, Do They?" *Language in Society* 4 (1975): 289–294.

Duker, Jacob M. and Tucker, Lewis, R. "Women Libers' Versus Independent Women: A Study of Preferences for Womens' Roles in Advertisements." *Journal of Marketing Research* 14 (1977): 469–475.

Duncan, Hugh Dalziel. *Symbols in Society.* New York: Oxford University Press, 1968.

Duncan, Starkey, Jr. "Nonverbal Communication." *Psychological Bulletin* 72 (1969): 118–137.

Duran, Robert and Wheeless, Virginia Eman. "Social Management: Toward a Theory Based Operationalization of Communication Competence." Paper presented at the Speech Communication Association Convention, 1980.

Dychtwald, Ken. "Sexuality and the Whole Person." *Journal of Humanistic Psychology* 19 (Spring, 1979): 47–60.

Eakins, Barbara Westbrook, and Eakins, R. Gene. *Sex Differences in Human Communication.* Boston, Mass.: Houghton Mifflin Co., 1978.

Eakins, Barbara and Eakins, Gene. "Verbal Turn-Taking and Exchanges in Faculty Dialogue." *Papers in Southwest English IV: Proceedings of the Conference on the Sociology of the Languages of American Women,* ed. Betty Lou Dubois and Isabel Crouch, San Antonio, TX: Trinity University, 1976, pp. 53–62.

Edelsky, Carole. "Acquisition of Communicative Competence: Recognition of Linguistic Correlates of Sex Roles." *Merril-Palmer Quarterly* 22 (1976): 47–59.

Efran, J. S. and Broughton, A. "Effect of Expectancies for Social Approval on Visual Behavior." *Journal of Personality and Social Psychology* 4 (1966): 103–107.

Ehrman, Sandra J. "Clothing Attitudes and Peer Acceptance." Master's thesis, Colorado State University, 1971, from *A Schematic Approach to Theoretical Analysis of Dress as Nonverbal Communication,* by Robert Christian Hillestad. Doctoral dissertation, The Ohio State University, 1974.

Eicher, Joanne B. and Kelly, Eleanor A. "High School as a Mating Place," from *Dimensions of Dress and Adornment: A Book of Readings,* Lois M. Gurel and Marianne S. Beeson, (eds.), Dubuque, Iowa: Kendall/Hunt Publishing Co., 1975.

Eichorn, D. H. and Bayley, N. "Growth in Head Circumference from Birth Through Young Adulthood." *Child Development* 33 (1962): 257–271.

Ekman, Paul and Friesen, Wallace V. "Head and Body Cues in the Judgment of Emotion: A Reformulation." *Perceptual and Motor Skills* 24 (1967): 711–724.

Elias, J. W.; Wright, L. L.; and Winn, F. J. "Age and Sex Differences in Cerebral Asymmetry as a Function of Competition for 'Time' and 'Space' in a Successive Auditory Matching Task." *Experimental Aging Research* 3 (1977): 33–48.

Ellis, Donald G. and McCallister, Linda. "Relational Control in Sex-typed and Androgynous Groups." *Western Journal of Speech Communication* 44 (1980): 35–49.

Ellis, Donald G. and Skerchock, Linda. "Relational Control Sequences in Sex-Typed and Androgynous Groups." Paper presented at the International Communication Association Convention, Philadelphia, 1979.

Ellison, Craig W. and Firestone, Ira J. "Development of Interpersonal Trust as a Function of Self-Esteem, Target Status and Target Style." *Journal of Personality and Social Psychology* 29 (1974): 655–663.

Ellsworth, Phoebe C.; Carlsmith, J. Merrill; and Henson, Alexander. "The Stare as a Stimulus to Flight in Human Subjects: A Series of Field Experiments." *Journal of Personality and Social Psychology* 21 (1972): 302–311.

Ellsworth, Phoebe C. and Langer, Ellen J. "Staring and Approach: An Interpretation of the Stare as a Nonspecific Activator." *Journal of Personality and Social Psychology* 33 (1976): 117–122.

Ellsworth, Pheobe C. and Ludwig, Linda M. "Visual Behavior in Social Interaction." *Journal of Communication* 22 (1972): 375–403.

Ellsworth, P. and Ross, L. "Intimacy in Response to Direct Gaze." *Journal of Experimental Social Psychology* 11 (1975): 592–613.

Engelbach, Margaret L. "Fashionability of Clothing: Its Effect on Perceptions of an Educator." Unpublished doctoral dissertation, The Ohio State University, 1978.

Epstein, H. "Growth Spurts During Brain Development: Implications for Educational Policy and Practice." In *Education and the Brain,* ed. J. S. Chall and A. F. Mirsky. Chicago, Illinois: University of Chicago Press, 1978.

Epstein, Norman and Jackson, Elizabeth. "An Outcome Study of Short Term Communication Training with Married Couples." *Journal of Consulting and Clinical Psychology* 46 (1978): 207–212.

Ernst, S. "An Investigation of Students' Interpretation of Inclusionary and Exclusionary Gender Generic Language." Unpublished doctoral dissertation, Washington State University, 1977.

Esp, Barbarann. "Campus Prisoners of Stereotypes." *Psychology Today* 12 (November 1978): 34, 36.

Etaugh, C. and Malstrom, J. "The Effect of Marital Status on Person Perception." *Journal of Marriage and the Family* 43 (1981): 801–805.

Ewer, Phyllis A.; Crimmins, Eileen; and Oliver, Richard. "An Analysis of the Relationship Between Husband's Income, Family Size and Wife's Employment in the Early Stages of Marriage." *Journal of Marriage and the Family* 41 (1979): 727–738.

Exline, Ralph; Gray, David; and Shuette, Dorothy. "Visual Behavior in a Dyad as Affected by Interview Content and Sex of Respondent." *Journal of Personality and Social Psychology* 1 (1965): 201–209.

Exline, Ralph and Winters, L. C. "Affective Relations and Mutual Glances in Dyads," from *Affect, Cognition, and Personality,* ed. S. S. Tomkins and C. E. Izard. New York: Springer Press, 1965.

Falbo, Toni and Peplau, Letitia Anne. "Power Strategies in Intimate Relationships." *Journal of Personality and Social Psychology* 38 (1980): 618–628.

Farber, Gerald Mark. "Marital Satisfaction and the Topics of Self-Disclosure for Jewish Men and Women: A Correlational Study." Unpublished doctoral dissertation, Boston University, 1979.

Farley, Jennie. "Women's Magazines and the ERA: Friend or Foe?" *Journal of Communication* 28 (1978): 187–193.

Farwell, M. "Women and Language." In Jean R. Leppaluoto (Ed.), *Women on the Move.* Pittsburgh, PA: KNOW, Inc., 1973, pp. 165–171.

Fast, Julius. "Your Eyes are Talking." *Family Health* 10 (1978): 22–25.

Feigenbaum, W. Morton. "Reciprocity in Self-Disclosure Within the Psychological Interview." *Psychological Reports* 40 (1977): 15–26.

Feldman, Larry B. "Marital Conflict and Marital Intimacy: An Integrative Psychodynamic-Behavioral Systemic Model." *Family Process* 18 (1979): 69–78.

"Female Bosses Say Biggest Barriers are Insecurity and 'Being A Woman.'" *Wall Street Journal,* (November 2, 1982): 29, 36.

Ferreira, Antonio and Winter, William. "Interaction Process Analysis of Family Decision-Making." *Family Process* 6 (1967): 155–172.

Ferrell, William Lyman. "A Comparison of Assertive Training and Programmed Human Relations Training in a Treatment Program for Problem Drinkers." Unpublished doctoral dissertation, The University of North Carolina at Chapel Hill, 1977.

Festinger, Leon; Schachter, Stanley; and Back, Kurt. *Social Pressures in Informal Groups.* New York: Harper, 1950.

Fillmer, H. Thompson and Haswell, Leslie. "Sex-Role Stereotyping in English Usage." *Sex Roles* 3 (1977): 257–263.

Fine, Marlene G. "Soap Opera Conversations: The Talk That Binds." *Journal of Communication* 31 (Spring 1981): 97–107.

Fiore, Anthony and Swenson, Clifford H. "Analysis of Love Relationships in Functional and Dysfunctional Marriages." *Psychological Reports* 40 (1977): 707–714.

Firestone, Shulamith. *The Dialectic of Sex: The Case for Feminist Revolution.* New York: William Morrow, 1970.

Fischer, R. and Rhead, J. "The Logical and the Intuitive." *Main Currents in Modern Thought* 31 (1974): 50–54.

Fisher, B. Aubrey. "Differential Effects of Sexual Composition and Interactional Context on Interaction Patterns in Dyads." *Human Communication Research* 9 (1983): 225–238.

Fisher, Jeffrey David and Bryne, Donn. "Too Close for Comfort: Sex Differences in Response to Invasions of Personal Space." *Journal of Personality and Social Psychology* 31 (1975): 15–21.

Fisher, J. D.; Rytting, M.; and Heslin, R. "Hands Touching Hands: Affective and Evaluative Affects of Interpersonal Touch." *Sociometry* 39 (1976): 416–421.

Fisher, Seymour. "Body Decoration and Camouflage," from *Dimensions of Dress and Adornment: A Book of Readings,* Lois M. Gurel and Marianne S. Beeson (eds.). Dubuque, Iowa: Kendall/Hunt Publishing Co., 1975.

Fishman, Pamela M. "Interaction: The Work Women Do." *Social Problems* 25 (1978): 397–406.

Fishman, Pamela M. "Interactional Shitwork." *Heresies: A Feminist Publication on Art & Politics* 2 (May 1977): 99–101.

Fitzgerald, Maureen P. "Self-Disclosure and Expressed Self-Esteem, Social Distance and Areas of the Self Revealed." *The Journal of Psychology* 56 (1963): 405–412.

Fitzpatrick, Mary Ann and Bochner, Arthur. "Perspectives on Self and Others: Male-Female Differences in Perceptions of Communication Behavior." *Sex Roles* 7 (1981): 523–534.

Flaherty, J. A. "Self-Disclosure in Therapy: Marriage of the Therapist." *American Journal of Psychotherapy* 33 (1979): 442–452.

Flanagan, Anna M. and Todd-Mancillas, William R. "Teaching Inclusive Generic Pronounce Usage: The Effectiveness of an Authority Innovation-Decision Approach Versus an Optional Innovation-Decision Approach." *Communication Education* 31 (1982): 275–284.

Flugel, J. C. *The Psychology of Clothes.* New York: International Universities Press, Inc., 1930.

Ford, J. Guthrie; Cramer, Robert E.; and Owens, Gayle. "A Paralinguistic Consideration of Proxemic Behavior." *Perceptual and Motor Skills* 45 (1977): 487–493.

Foreit, Karen G.; Agor, Terna; Byers, Johnny; Larue, John; Lokey, Helen; Palazzini, Michael; Patterson, Michael; and Smith, Lillian. "Sex Bias in Newspaper Treatment of Male-Centered and Female-Centered News Stories." *Sex Roles* 6 (1980): 475–480.

Forgionne, Guisseppi A. and Nwacukwu, Celestine C. "Acceptance of Authority in Female-Managed Organizational Positions." *University of Michigan Business Review* 29 (May 1977): 23–28.

Forster, Charles and Ross, Robert J. "Preferences for Sexual Symbols in the Genital Stage: A Replication." *Psychological Reports* 37 (1975): 1048–1050.

Fortenberry, James H.; MacLean, Joyce; Morris, Priscilla; and O'Connell, Michael. "Mode of Dress as a Perceptual Cue to Deference." *The Journal of Social Psychology* 104 (1978): 139–140.

Foster, Lawrence W. and Kolinko, Tom. "Choosing to be a Managerial Woman: An Examination of Individual Variables and Career Choice." *Sex Roles* 5 (1979): 627–634.

Foster, Martha A.; Wallston, Barbara Strudlor; and Berger, Michael. "Feminist Orientation and Job Seeking Behavior Among Dual-Career Couples." *Sex Roles* 6 (1980): 59–65.

Fottler, Myron D. "Managerial Aspirations of High School Seniors: A Comparison of Males and Females." *Journal of Vocational Behavior* 16 (1980): 83–95.

Fowler, Gene D. and Rosenfeld, Lawrence B. "Sex Differences and Democratic Leadership Behavior." *Southern Speech Communication Journal* 45 (1979): 69–78.

Fox, Greer Litton. *The Childbearing Decision: Fertility Attitudes and Behavior.* Beverly Hills, California: Sage Publications, 1982.

Fraiberg, Selma. *Every Child's Birthright: In Defense of Mothering.* New York: Basic Books, 1977.

Frances, Susan J. "Sex Differences in Nonverbal Behavior." *Sex Roles* 5 (1979): 519–535.

Freedman, Daniel G. "The Survival Value of the Beard." *Psychology Today* 3 (1969): 36–39.

Freedman, J. L. "The Crowd: Maybe Not So Maddening After All." *Psychology Today* 4 (1971): 58–61.

Freeman, Harvey R. "Sex-Role Stereotypes, Self-Concepts, and Measured Personality Characteristics in College Women and Men." *Sex Roles* 5 (1979): 99–103.

Friedman, H. S. "The Interactive Effects of Facial Expressions of Emotion and Verbal Messages on Perceptions of Affective Meaning." *Journal of Experimental Social Psychology* 15 (1979): 453–469.

Friedman, Martha. *Fear of Success.* New York: Warner Books, 1982.

Frieze, Irene Hanson. "Nonverbal Aspects of Femininity and Masculinity Which Perpetuate Sex-Role Stereotypes." Paper presented at the Eastern Psychological Association, 1974.

Frieze, I. H. and Ramsey, S. J. "Nonverbal Maintenance of Traditional Sex Roles." *Journal of Social Issues* 32 (1976): 133–141.

Frost, Joyce Hocker and Wilmot, William W. *Interpersonal Conflict.* Dubuque, Iowa: Wm. C. Brown Co., 1978.

Fu, Victoria R.; Korslund, Mary K.; and Hinkle, Dennis E. "Ethic Self-Concept during Middle Childhood." *Journal of Psychology* 105 (1980): 99–105.

Funabiki, D.; Bologna, N. C.; Pepping, M.; and FitGerald, K. C. "Revisiting Sex Differences in the Expression of Depression." *Journal of Abnormal Psychology* 89 (1980): 194–202.

Galejs, Irma. "Social Interaction of Preschool Children." *Home Economics Research Journal* 2 (1974): 153–159.

Galin, D. "Implications for Psychiatry of Left and Right Cerebral Specialization." *Archives of General Psychiatry* 31 (1974): 572–583.

Gardener, H. *The Shattered Mind: The Person After Brain Damage.* New York: Knopf, 1975.

Gardner, J. A. "The Effects of Body Motion, Sex of Counselor and Sex of Subject on Counselor Attractiveness and Subject's Self-Disclosure." Unpublished doctoral dissertation, University of Wyoming, 1973.

Garland, H.; Hale, K. F.; and Burnson, M. "Attributions for the Success and Failure of Female Managers: A Replication and Extension." *Psychology of Women Quarterly* 7 (1982): 155–162.

Garnica, O. "Some Prosodic and Paralinguistic Features." In C. Snow and C. Ferguson (Eds.), *Talking to Children.* Cambridge: Cambridge University Press, 1977, pp. 63–88.

Garrison, Laura. "Recognizing and Combatting Sexist Job Interviews." *Journal of Employment Counseling* 17 (1980): 270–276.

Gauthier, Joyce and Kjervik, Diane. "Sex-Role Identity and Self-Esteem in Female Graduate Nursing Students." *Sex Roles* 8 (1982): 45–55.

Gelman, Richard and McGinley, Hugh. "Interpersonal Liking and Self-Disclosure." *Journal of Consulting and Clinical Psychology* 46 (1978): 1549–1551.

Gentry, J. W.; Doering, M.; and O'Brian, T. V. "Masculinity and Femininity Factors in Product Perception and Self-Image." In *Advances in Consumer Research,* ed. H. K. Hunt. Proceedings of the Association for Consumer Research, 1978.

Gerrard, Meg. "Sex Guilt and Attitudes Toward Sex in Sexually Active and Inactive Female College Students." *Journal of Personality Assessment* 44 (1980): 258–261.

Giesen, Martin and McClaren, Harry A. "Discussion, Distance and Sex: Changes in Impressions and Attraction During Small Group Interaction." *Sociometry* 39 (1976): 60–70.

Gigy, Lynn L. "Self-Concept of Single Women." *Psychology of Women Quarterly* 5 (1980): 321–340.

Gilbert, Shirley J. "Effects of Unanticipated Self-Disclosure on Recipients of Varying Levels of Self-Esteem: A Research Note." *Human Communication Research* 3 (1977): 368–371.

Gilbert, Shirley J. and Horenstein, David. "The Communication of Self-Disclosure: Level Versus Valence." *Human Communication Research* 1 (1975): 316–322.

Gilbert, Shirley J. and Whiteneck, Gale G. "Toward a Multi-Dimensional Approach to the Study of Self-Disclosure." *Human Communication Research* 2 (1976): 347–355.

Gilley, Hoyt M. and Summers, Collier. "Sex Differences in the Use of Hostile Verbs." *Journal of Psychology* 76 (1970): 33–37.

Gitter, A. G. and Black, H. "Is Self-Disclosure Self-Revealing?" *Journal of Counseling Psychology* 23 (1976): 327–332.

Goffman, E. "The Nature of Deference and Demeanor." *American Anthropologist* 58 (1956): 473–502.

Gold, Alice Ross; Brush, Lorelei R.; and Sprotzer, Eve R. "Developmental Changes in Self-Perceptions of Intelligence and Self-Confidence." *Psychology of Women Quarterly* 5 (1980): 231–239.

Gold, Delores and Berger, Charlene. "Problem-Solving Performance of Young Boys and Girls as a Function of Task Appropriateness and Sex Identity." *Sex Roles* 4 (1978): 183–192.

Goldberg, C. N.; Kiesler, C. A.; and Collins, B. E. "Visual Behavior and Face-to-Face Distance During Interaction." *Sociometry* 32 (1969): 43–53.

Goldberg, P. "Are Women Prejudiced Against Women?" *Transaction* 6 (1968): 28.

Goldberg, P. A. "Prejudice toward Women: Some Personality Correlates." *International Journal of Group Tensions* 4 (1974): 53–63.

Goldberg, Phillip A.; Gottesdiener, Marc; and Abramson, Paul R. "Another Putdown of Women? Perceived Attractiveness as a Function of Support for the Feminist Movement." *Journal of Personality and Social Psychology* 32 (1975): 113–115.

Goldberg, S. and Lewis, M. "Play Behavior in the Year-Old Infant: Early Sex Differences." *Child Development* 40 (1969): 21–31.

Goldhaber, Gerald M. and Weaver, Carl H. "Listener Comprehension of Compressed Speech When the Difficulty, Rate of Presentation, and Sex of the Listener are Varied." *Speech Monographs* 35 (1968): 20–25.

Goldman, Morton. "Effect of Eye Contact and Distance on the Verbal Reinforcement of Attitude." *The Journal of Social Psychology* 111 (1980): 73–78.

Goldstein, Ellen Sue. "The Relationship of Sex-Role Self-Concept, Attitudes Toward Women, Job Involvement and Marital Satisfaction in Wives of Dual-Career Couples with Children." Unpublished doctoral dissertation, New York University, 1978.

Golinkoff, Roberta Michnick, and Ames, Gail Johnson. "A Comparison of Father's Speech to Mother's Speech with their Young Children." *Child Development* 50 (1979): 28–32.

Goodall, Jr., H. Lloyd. "The Nature of Analogic Discourse." *The Quarterly Journal of Speech* 69 (1983): 171–179.

Gorcyca, Diane Atkinson and Petersen, Corlice Jeanne. "Recall and Preference of Traditional and Reversed Sex-Typed Stories by Kindergarten Children." Paper presented at the International Communication Association Convention, Acapulco, 1980.

Gordon, J. and Cohn, F. "The Effects of Affiliation Drive Arousal on Aggression in Doll Interviews." Manuscript, 1961.

Gordon, William I.; Fengler, Craig D; and Infante, Dominic A. "Women's Clothing Predispositions as Predictors of Dress at Work, Job Satisfaction, and Career Advancement." *The Southern Speech Communication Journal* 47 (1982): 422–434.

Gottfredson, Gary D. "A Note on Sexist Wording in Interest Measurement." *Measurement and Evaluation of Guidance* 8 (1976): 221–223.

Gottman, John; Markman, Howard; and Notarius, Cliff. "The Typography of Marital Conflict." *Journal of Marriage and the Family* 6 (1970): 192–203.

Gouran, Dennis S. "Variables Related to Consensus in Group Discussions of Questions of Policy." *Speech Monographs* 36 (1968): 387–391.

Graham, Alma "The Making of a Nonsexist Dictionary." *Ms.* 2 (December 1973): 12–16.

Graves, James R. and Robinson, John D. II. "Proxemic Behavior as a Function of Inconsistent Verbal and Nonverbal Messages." *Journal of Counseling Psychology* 23 (1976): 333–338.

Graves, Richard L. and Price, Gayle B. "Sex Differences in Syntax and Usage in Oral and Written Language." *Research in the Teaching of English* 145 (May 1980): 147–153.

Graziano, William; Brothen, Thomas; and Berscheid, Ellen. "Height and Attraction: Do Men and Women See Eye to Eye?" *Journal of Personality* 46 (1978): 128–145.

Gray, Louis; White, Mervin; and Libby, Roger W. "A Test and Reformulation of Reference Group and Role Correlates of Premarital Sexual Permissiveness Theory." *Journal of Marriage and Family* 40 (1978): 79–91.

Green, S. B.; Burkhart, B. R.; and Harrison, W. H. "Personality Correlates of Self-Report, Role-Playing and In Vivo Measures of Assertiveness." *Journal of Consulting and Clinical Psychology* 47 (1979): 16–24.

Green, W. Paul and Giles, Howard. "Reactions to a Stranger as a Function of Dress Style: The Tie." *Perceptual and Motor Skills* 37 (1973): 676.

Greenberg, Bradley S.; Abelman, Robert; and Neuendorf, Kimberly. "Sex on the Soap Operas: Afternoon Delight." *Journal of Communication* 31 (Spring 1981): 83–89.

Greenberg, Bradley; Graef, David; and Atkins, Charles. "Sexual Intimacy on Commercials and TV During Prime Time." *Journalism Quarterly Review* (1980): 410.

Greenberg, J. "Off the Wall at U Mass." *Science News* 116 (1979): 268.

Greenblatt, Lynda; Hasenauer, James E.; and Freimuth, Vicki S. "Psychological Sex Type and Androgyny in the Study of Communication Variables: Self-Disclosure and Communication Apprehension." *Human Communication Research* 6 (1980): 117–129.

Grotjahn, M. *Beyond Laughter.* New York: McGraw-Hill Book Company, 1957.

Grush, Joseph E. and Yehl, Janet G. "Marital Roles, Sex Differences, and Interpersonal Attraction." *Journal of Personality and Social Psychology* 37 (1979): 116–123.

Haccoun, Dorothy M.; Sallay, George; and Haccoun, Robert R. "Sex Differences in the Appropriateness of Supervisory Styles: A Nonmanagement View." *Journal of Applied Psychology* 63 (1978): 124–127.

Hass, A. *Teenage Sexuality.* New York: Macmillan Co., 1979.

Haas, Adelaide. "Male and Female Spoken Language Differences: Stereotypes and Evidence." *Psychological Bulletin* 86 (1979): 616–626.

Haas, Adelaide. "Partner Influence on Sex-Associated Spoken Language of Children." *Sex Roles* 7 (1981): 225–234.

Haas, L. "Determinants of Role-Sharing Behavior: A Study of Egalitarian Couples." *Sex Roles* 8 (1982): 747–760.

Hackney, Harold. "Facial Gestures and Subject Expression of Feelings." *Journal of Counseling Psychology* 21 (1974): 173–178.

Haley, Elizabeth G. and Hendrickson, Norejane J. "Children's Preferences for Clothing and Hair Styles." *Home Economics Research Journal* 2 (1974): 179–193.

Haley, Jay. *Problem-Solving Therapy.* New York: Harper & Row, 1976.

Haley, Jay. "Research on Family Patterns." *Family Process* 64 (1965): 41–50.

Hall, James R. and Black, J. Diane. "Assertiveness, Aggressiveness, and Attitudes Toward Feminism." *The Journal of Social Psychology* 107 (1979): 57–62.

Hall, Judith A. "Gender Effects in Decoding Nonverbal Cues." *Psychological Bulletin* 85 (1978): 845–857.

Hall, K. "Sex Differences in Initiation and Influence in Decision-Making Among Prospective Teachers." Unpublished doctoral dissertation, Stanford University, 1972.

Halley, Richard D. "Distractibility of Males and Females in Competing Aural Message Situations: A Research Note." *Human Communication Research* 2 (1975): 79–82.

Hammen, C. L. and Padesky, C. A. "Sex Differences in the Expression of Depressive Responses on the Beck Depression Inventory." *Journal of Abnormal Psychology* 86 (1977): 609–614.

Hampleman, R. S. "Comparison of Listening and Reading Comprehension Ability of Fourth and Sixth Grade Pupils." *Elementary English* 35 (1958): 49–53.

Hansson, Robert O.; O'Connor, Mary Ellen; Jones, Warren H.; and Mihelich, Mary Hill. "Role Relevant Sex Typing and Opportunity in Agentic and Communal Domains." *Journal of Personality* 48 (1980): 419–434.

Hardesty, Sarah A. and Betz, Nancy E. "The Relationships of Career Salience, Attitudes Toward Women, and Demographic and Family Characteristics to Marital Adjustment in Dual-Career Couples." *Journal of Vocational Behavior* 17 (1980): 242–250.

Harlow, H. F.; Harlow, M. K.; and Haesen, E. W. "The Maternal Affectional System of Rhesus Monkey." In H. I. Rheirgold (ed.), *Maternal Behavior in Mammals.* New York: Wiley and Son, Inc., 1963, pp. 254–281.

Harper, R. "The Effects of Sex and Levels of Acquaintance on Risk-Taking in Groups." Unpublished doctoral dissertation. University of North Dakota, 1970.

Harrel, W. Andrew. "Physical Attractiveness, Self-Disclosure, and Helping Behavior." *Journal of Social Psychology* 104 (1978): 15–17.

Harris, Mary B. "Mediators Between Frustration and Aggression in a Field Experiment." *Journal of Experimental Social Psychology* 10 (1974): 561–571.

Hart, R. P. and Burks, D. M. "Rhetorical Sensitivity and Social Interaction." *Speech Monographs* 39 (1972): 75–91.

Hart, R. P.; Carlson, R. E.; and Eadie, W. F. "Attitudes toward Communication and the Assessment of Rhetorical Sensitivity." *Communication Monographs* 47 (1980): 1–22.

Hartlage, L. C. "Identifying and Programming for Differences." Paper presented at Parent and Professional Conference on Young Children with Special Needs, Cleveland, Ohio, March 1980.

Hartnett, John J.; Bailey, Kent G.; and Gibson, Frank W. Jr. "Personal Space as Influenced by Sex and Type of Movement." *The Journal of Psychology* 76 (1970): 139–144.

Haslett, Betty. "Communicative Functions and Strategies in Children's Conversations." *Human Communication Research* 9 (1983): 114–129.

Hassett, J. and Houlihan, J. "Different Jokes for Different Folks." *Psychology Today* 12 (January 1979): 64–71.

Hattes, Joseph H. and Kahn, Arnold. "Sex Differences in a Mixed-Motive Conflict Situation." *Journal of Personality* 42 (1974): 260–275.

Haugh, Susan Sterkel; Hoffman, Charles D.; and Cowan, Gloria. "The Eye of the Very Young Beholder: Sex Typing of Infants by Young Children." *Child Development* 51 (1980): 598–600.

Hayes, Daniel Truman. "Nonintellective Predictors of Public Speaking Ability and Academic Success in a Basic College-Level Speech Communication Course." Unpublished doctoral dissertation, University of Missouri, 1977.

Hayt, Grimlin (ed.). *The Women's Movement: Editorial Research Reports*. Washington, D.C.: Congressional Quarterly, 1977, p. 33.

Hecht, M.; Shephard, T.; and Hall, M. J. "Multivariate Indices of the Effects of Self-Disclosure." *Western Journal of Speech Communication* 43 (1979): 235–245.

"Heeding Those Subtle Signs." *Time* 116 (September 8, 1980): 56.

"He Gives the Orders, But I'm the Boss." *Advertising Age* 52 (Oct. 13, 1980): 7.

Hegstrom, Timothy G. "Message Impact: What Percentage is Nonverbal?" *Western Journal of Speech Communication* 43 (1979): 134–142.

Heilbrun, A. B. "Measurement of Masculine and Feminine Sex Role Identities as Independent Dimensions." *Journal of Consulting and Clinical Psychology* 44 (1976): 183–190.

Heilbrun, A. B. "Sex Role, Instrumental-Expressive Behavior, and Psycho-Pathology in Females." *Journal of Abnormal Psychology* 73 (1968): 131–136.

Heilman, Madeline E. "The Impact of Situational Factors on Personnel Decisions Concerning Women: Varying the Sex Composition of the Applicant Pool." *Organizational Behavior and Human Performance* 26 (1980): 386–395.

Heiss, J. "Degree of Intimacy and Male-Female Interaction." *Sociometry* 25 (1962): 197–208.

Helgeson, Candace. "The Prisoners of Texts: Male Chauvinism in College Handbooks and Rhetorics." *College English* 38 (1976): 396–406.

Helmich, Donald L. "Male and Female Presidents: Some Implications of Leadership Style." *Human Resource Management* (Winter 1974): 25–26.

Hendrick, S. "Self-Disclosure and Marital Satisfaction." *Journal of Personality and Social Psychology* 40 (1981): 1150–1160.

Henkin, Nancy Zimmerman. "An Exploratory Study of Self-Disclosure Patterns of Older Adults." Unpublished doctoral dissertation, Temple University, 1980.

Henley, Nancy M. *Body Politics: Power, Sex, and Nonverbal Communication.* Englewood Cliffs, N.J.: Prentice Hall, 1977.

Henley, Nancy M. "The Politics of Touch," from *Radical Psychology*, Phillip Brown, (ed.). New York: Harper and Row, 1973: 421–433.

Henley, Nancy M. "Status and Sex: Some Touching Observations." *Bulletin of the Psychonomic Society* 2 (1973): 91–93.

Henley, Nancy and Freeman, Jo. "The Sexual Politics of Interpersonal Behavior," from *Women: A Feminist Perspective*, ed. Jo Freeman. Palo Alto, California: Mayfield Publishing Company, 1975.

Henley, Nancy and Thorne, Barrie. "Womanspeak and Manspeak: Sex Differences and Sexism in Communication, Verbal and Nonverbal," from *Beyond Sex Roles*, ed. Alice Sargent. St. Paul, Minn.: West Publishing Company, 1977.

Hersey, Paul and Blanchard, Kenneth H. *Management of Organizational Behavior: Utilizing Human Resources*. 3rd Edition. Englewood Cliffs, New Jersey: Prentice-Hall, 1977.

Hess, Elizabeth P.; Bridgewater, Carol A.; Bornstein, Philip H.; and Sweeney, Teresa M. "Situational Determinants in the Perception of Assertiveness: Gender-Related Influences." *Behavior Therapy* 11 (1980): 49–57.

Hewitt, John P. and Stokes, Randall. "Disclaimers." *American Sociological Review* 40 (1975): 1–11.

Hicks, Mary W. and Platt, Marilyn. "Marital Happiness and Stability: A Review of Research in the Sixties." *Journal of Marriage and the Family* 32 (1970): 553–574.

Hickling Edward J.; Noel, Richard C.; and Yutzler, Donald F. "Attractiveness and Occupational Status." *The Journal of Psychology* 102 (1979): 71–76.

Highlen, Pamela S. "Effects of Situational Factors, Sex, and Attitude on Affective Self-Disclosure." *Journal of Counseling Psychology* 25 (1978): 270–276.

Highlen, Pamela S. and Gillis, Sheila F. "Effects of Situational Factors, Sex, and Attitude on Affective Self-Disclosure and Anxiety." *Journal of Counseling Psychology* 25 (1978): 270–276.

Hilgard, Ernest R. and Atkinson, Richard C. *Introduction to Psychology,* 4th ed. New York: Harcourt, 1967.

Hill Charles T.; Peplau, Letitia Ann; and Dunkel-Schetter, Christine. "Self-Disclosure in Dating Couples: Sex Roles and the Ethic of Openness." *Journal of Marriage and the Family* 42 (1980): 305–317.

Hill, W. A. "Leadership Style: Rigid or Flexible." *Organizational Behavior and Human Performance* 9 (1973): 35–47.

Hillestad, Robert Christian. "A Schematic Approach to a Theoretical Analysis of Dress as Nonverbal Communication." Unpublished doctoral dissertation, The Ohio State University, 1974.

Hillman, Judith Stevinson. "An Analysis of Male and Female Roles in Two Periods of Children's Literature." *Journal of Educational Research* 68 (1974): 84–88.

Hilpert, Fred; Kramer, Cheris; and Clark, Ruth Ann. "Participants' Perceptions of Self and Partner in Mixed-Sex Dyads." *Central States Speech Journal* 26 (1975): 52–56.

Hirschman, Lynette. "Female-Male Differences in Conversational Interaction." Abstracted in Barrie Thorne and Nancy Henley, *Language and Sex: Difference and Dominance,* Rowley, Mass.: Newbury House, 1975, p. 249.

Hirst, Graeme. "An Evaluation of Evidence for Innate Sex Differences in Linguistic Ability." *Journal of Psycholinguistic Research* 11 (1982): 95–111.

Hite, Shere. *The Hite Report.* New York: Macmillan Co. 1976.

Hoffman, Lois Wladis. "Effects of the Employment of Mothers on Parental Power Relations." *Journal of Marriage and the Family* 41 (1970): 27–35.

Hoffman, Martin L. "Sex Differences in Empathy and Related Behaviors." *Psychological Bulletin* 84 (1977): 712–722.

Hoffman, Richard L. and Maier, Norman, K. V. "Quality and Acceptance of Problem Solutions by Members of Homogeneous and Heterogeneous Groups." *Journal of Abnormal and Social Psychology* 62 (1961): 401–407.

Holly, Susan. "Women in Management of Weeklies. *Journalism Quarterly* 56 (1979): 810–815.

Hollandsworth, J. G., Jr. "Self-Report Assessment of Social Fear, Discomfort, and Assertive Behavior." *Psychological Reports* 44 (1979): 1230.

Hollow, M. K. "Listening Comprehension at the Intermediate Grade Level." *Elementary School Journal* 56 (1956): 158–161.

Holman, T. B. "The Influence of Community Involvement on Marital Quality." *Journal of Marriage and the Family* 43 (1981): 143–149.

Homans, George C. *Social Behavior: Its Elementary Form.* New York: Harcourt, Brace, 1961.

Honeycutt, J. M.; Wilson, C.; and Parker, C. "Effects of Sex and Degrees of Happiness on Perceived Styles of Communicating In and Out of the Marital Relationship." *Journal of Marriage and Family Counseling* 44 (1982): 395–406.

Hopkins, Jane and White, Priscilla. "The Dual-Career Couple: Constraints and Supports." *Family Coordinator* 27 (1978): 253–259.

Hoppe, Christiane M. "Interpersonal Aggression as a Function of Subject's Sex, Subject's Sex Role Identification, Opponent's Sex, and Degree of Provocation." *Journal of Personality* 47 (1979): 315–329.

Horenstein, David and Gilbert, Shirley J. "Anxiety, Likeability and Avoidance." *Small Group Behavior* 7 (1978): 423–432.

Horn, Marilyn J. "Carrying it Off in Style," from *Dimensions of Dress and Adornment: A Book of Readings,* by Lois M. Gurel and Marianne S. Beeson (eds.). Dubuque, Iowa: Kendall/Hunt Publishing Co., 1975.

Horowitz, M. J.; Duff, D. F.; and Stratton, L. O. "Body-Buffer Zone." *Archives of General Psychiatry* 11 (1964): 651–656.

Hosman, Lawrence A. and Tardy, Charles H. "Self-Disclosure and Reciprocity in Short and Long-Term Relationships: An Experimental Study of Evaluational and Attributional Consequences." *Communication Quarterly* 28 (1980): 20–29.

Hoult, T. F. "Experimental Measurement of Clothing as a Factor in Some Social Ratings of Selected American Men." *American Sociological Review* 19 (1954): 324–328.

Howe, Florence. "Sexual Stereotypes Start Early." *Saturday Review* 54 (1971): 76–94.

Howell, William S. *The Empathic Communicator.* Belmont, California: Wadsworth Publishing Company, 1982.

Hoyenga, Katherine Blick and Wallace, Benjamin. "Sex Differences in the Perception of Autokinetic Movement of an Afterimage." *The Journal of General Psychology* 100 (1979): 93–101.

Hubble, Mark A. and Gelso, Charles J. "Effect of Counselor Attire in an Initial Interview." *Journal of Counseling Psychology* 25 (1978): 581–584.

Hunt, M. *Sexual Behavior in the 1970's.* Chicago: Playboy Press, 1974.

Hurlock, Elizabeth. *The Psychology of Dress: An Analysis of Fashion and Its Motive.* New York: Hastings House, 1971.

Hutt, C. and Ounsted. C. "The Biological Significance of Gaze Aversion with Particular Reference to the Syndrome of Infantile Autism." *Behavioral Science* 11 (1966): 346–356.

Hyman, Beverly. "Responsive Leadership: The Woman Manager's Asset or Liability?" *Supervisory Management* 25 (August 1980): 40–43.

Ickes, William; Schermer, Brian; and Steeno, Jeff. "Sex and Sex Role Influences in the Same-Sex Dyads." *Social Psychology Quarterly* 42 (1979): 373–385.

Illfelder, Joyce K. "Fear of Success, Career Salience and Anxiety Levels in College Women." *Journal of Vocational Behavior* 16 (1980): 7–17.

Inderlied, Sheila Davis and Powell, Gary. "Sex-Role Identity and Leadership Style: Different Labels for the Same Concept?" *Sex Roles* 5 (1979): 613–625.

Infante, Dominic A. and Fisher, Jeanne Y. "The Influence of Receivers' Attitudes, Audience Size, and Speakers' Sex on Speakers' Pre-message Perceptions." *Central States Speech Journal* 25 (1974): 43–49.

Irvin, C. E. "Evaluating a Training Program in Listening for College Freshmen." *School Review* 61 (1953): 25–29.

Jabes, Jak. "Causal Attributions and Sex-Role Stereotypes in the Perceptions of Women Managers." *Canadian Journal of Behavioral Science* 12 (1980): 52–63.

Jacklin, C. and Maccoby, E. "Myth, Reality, and Shades of Gray: What we Know and Don't Know about Sex Differences." *Psychology Today* 8 (1974): 109–112.

Jackson, Linda A. "The Influence of Sex, Physical Attractiveness, Sex Role, and Occupational Sex-Linkage on Perceptions of Occupational Suitability." *Journal of Social Psychology* 13 (1983): 31–44.

Jackson, Philip W.; Silberman, Melvin L.; and Wolfson, Bernice J. "Signs of Personal Involvement in Teachers' Descriptions of Their Students." *Journal of Educational Psychology* 60 (1969): 22–27.

Jacobson, Marsha B. and Effertz, Joan. "Sex Roles and Leadership: Perceptions of the Leaders and the Led." *Organizational Behavior and Performance* 12 (1974): 383–396.

Janofsky, A. Irene. "Affective Self-Disclosure in Telephone Versus Face-to-Face Interviews." *Journal of Humanistic Psychology* 11 (1971): 93–103.

Jay, Winifred T. and Schminke, Clarence W. "Sex Bias in Elementary School Mathematics Texts." *The Arithmetic Teacher* 22 (1975): 242–246.

Jespersen, Otto. *Language: Its Nature, Development and Origin.* London: Allen and Unwin, 1922.

Jesser, Clinton J. "Male Responses to Direct Verbal Sexual Initiatives of Females." *The Journal of Sex Research* 14 (1978): 118–128.

Johannesen, Richard L. "The Emerging Concept of Communication as a Dialogue." *Quarterly Journal of Speech* 57 (1971): 373–382.

Johnson, Carole Shulte and Kelly, Inga Kromann "'He' and 'She': Changing Language to Fit a Changing World." *Educational Leadership* 32 (1975): 527–530.

Johnson, Colleen L. and Johnson, Frank A. "Attitudes Toward Parenting in Dual-Career Families." *American Journal of Psychiatry* 134 (1977): 391–395.

Johnson, P. J. "Personal Space as Reaction to Threat." Unpublished doctoral dissertation, Catholic University of America, 1973.

Johnson, Ronald W.; Doiron, Denyse; Brooks, Garland P.; and Dickinson, John. "Perceived Attractiveness as a Function of Support for the Feminist Movement: Not Necessarily a Put-Down of Women." *Canadian Journal of Behavioral Science* 10 (1978): 214–221.

Jolly, Eric J., and O'Kelly, Charlotte G. "Sex-Role Stereotyping in the Language of the Deaf." *Sex Roles: A Journal of Research* 6 (1980): 285–292.

Jonas, Doris F. and Jonas, A. David. "Gender Differences in Mental Function: A Clue to the Origin of Language." *Current Anthropology* 16 (1975): 626–30.

Jones, Hardy. "Fairness, Meritocracy, and Reverse Discrimination." *Social Theory and Practice* 4 (1977): 211–226.

Jones, Linda. "Sex-Role Stereotyping in Children as a Function of Maternal Employment." *Journal of Social Psychology* 11 (1980): 219–222.

Jorgenson, Dale O. "Nonverbal Assessment of Attitudinal Affect With the Smile-Return Technique." *The Journal of Social Psychology* 106 (1978): 173–179.

Jorgensen, Stephen R. and Gaudy, Janis C. "Self-Disclosure and Satisfaction in Marriage: The Relation Examined." *Family Relations* 29 (1980): 281–287.

Jourard, Sidney M. "An Exploratory Study of Two Moods of Interpersonal Encounter and Their Interrelation." *Journal of Humanistic Psychology* 5 (1966): 221–231.

Jourard, Sidney M. *Personal Adjustment: An Approach Through the Study of Healthy Personality.* (2nd Edition). New York: Macmillan, 1963.

Jourard, Sidney M. *Self-Disclosure: An Experimental Analysis of the Transparent Self.* New York: John Wiley, 1971.

Jourard, S. M. and Lasakow, P. "Some Factors in Self-Disclosure." *Journal of Abnormal and Social Psychology* 56 (1958): 91–98.

Jourard, S. M. and Rubin, J. E. "Self-Disclosure and Touching: A Study of Two Modes of Interpersonal Encounter and Their Inter-relation." *Journal of Humanistic Psychology* 8 (1968): 39–48.

Judd, Larry R. and Smith, Carolyn B. "The Relationship of Age, Educational Classification, Sex, and Grade to Self-Concept and Ideal Self-Concept in A Basic Speech Course." *Communication Education* 26 (1977): 289–297.

Judd, Larry R. and Smith, Carolyn B. "A Study of Variables Influencing Self-Concept and Ideal Self-Concept among Students in the Basic Speech Course." *Speech Teacher* 23 (1974): 215–221.

Kaats, Gilbert R. and Davis, Keith E. "The Dynamics of Sexual Behavior of College Students." *Journal of Marriage and Family* 32 (1970): 390–399.

Kaess, Walter A; Witryol, Sam L.; and Nolan, Richard E. "Reliability, Sex Differences and Validity in the Leaderless Group Discussion Technique." *Journal of Applied Psychology* 45 (1961): 345–350.

Kanna, Bernice. "Shop's Theory: It Takes a Woman to Sell One." *Advertising Age* 52 (July 21, 1980): 67.

Kanungo, Rabindra N. and Jotindar, S. Johar. "Effects of Slogans and Human Model Characteristics in Product Advertisements." *Canadian Journal of Behavioral Science* 7 (1975): 127–138.

Kaplan, Robert M. "Is Beauty Talent? Sex Interaction in the Attractiveness Halo Effect." *Sex Roles* 4 (1978): 195–204.

Kaplowitz, H. L. "Machiavellianism and Forming Impressions of Others." In Thomas Blass, (ed.), *Contemporary Social Psychology: Representative Readings.* Itasca, Illinois: F. E. Peacock, 1976, 378–384.

Karpoe, Kelly P. and Olney, Rachel L. "The Effect of Boys' or Girls' Toys on Sex-Typed Play in Preadolescents." *Sex Roles* 9 (1983): 507–518.

Karre, I. "Stereotyped Sex Roles and Self-Concept: Strategies for Liberating the Sexes." *Communication Education* 25 (1976): 43–52.

Keating, Caroline F., Mazur, Allan and Segall, Marshall H. "Facial Gestures Which Influence the Perception of Status." *Sociometry* 40 (December 1977): 374–378.

Kelley, Jonathon. "Sexual Permissiveness: Evidence for a Theory." *Journal of Marriage and the Family* 40 (1978): 455–468.

Kelly, Charles M. "An Investigation of the Construct Validity of Two Commercially Published Listening Tests." *Speech Monographs* 32 (1965): 139–143.

Kelly, Charles M. "Listening: Complex of Activities—and a Unitary Skill?" *Speech Monographs* 34 (1967): 455–466.

Kelly, Eleanor; Daigle, Caroline; La Fleur, Rosetta; and Wilson, Linda. "Adolescent Dress and Social Participation." *Home Economics Research Journal* 2 (1974): 167–175.

Kelly, J. "Dress as Nonverbal Communication." Paper presented to the Annual Conference of the American Association for Public Opinion Research, May 1969.

Kelly, Jeffrey A.; Wildman, Hal E.; and Ureg, Jon K. "A Behavioral Analysis of Gender and Sex Role Differences in Group Decision Making and Social Interactions." *Journal of Applied Social Psychology* 12 (1982): 112–127.

Kenny, Charles T. and Fletcher, Dixie. "Effects of Beardedness on Person Perception." *Perceptual and Motor Skills* 37 (1973): 413–414.

Kenrick, Douglas T. and Gutierres, Sara E. "Contrast Effects and Judgments of Physical Attractiveness When Beauty Becomes a Social Problem." *Journal of Personality and Social Psychology* 38 (1980): 131–140.

Kerin, R. A.; Lundstrom, W. G.; and Sciglimpaglia, D. "Women in Advertisements: Retrospect and Prospect." *Journal of Advertising* 8 (Summer 1979): 37–41.

Kestenbaum, Linda V. "Decoding Inconsistent Communications: Importance of Body Versus Voice Cues and an Analysis of Individual Differences." Unpublished doctoral dissertation, City University of New York, 1977.

Key, Mary Ritchie. *Male/Female Language.* Mutuchen, N.J.: The Scarecrow Press, Inc., 1975.

Kidd, Virginia. "Happily Ever After and Other Relationship Styles: Advice on Interpersonal Relations in Popular Magazines, 1951–1973." *Quarterly Journal of Speech* 61 (1975): 31–40.

Kidd, Virginia. "A Study of the Images Produced Through the Use of the Male Pronoun as the Generic." *Moments in Contemporary Rhetoric and Communication* 1 (1971): 25–30.

Kiesler, C. A.; Kiesler, S. B.; and Pallack, M. S. "The Effect of Commitment to Future Interaction on Reactions to Norm Violations." *Journal of Personality* 35 (1967): 585–599.

Killarney, Jim and McCluskey, Kathleen A. "Parent-Infant Conversations: Characteristics of and Differences Between Mothers' and Fathers' Speech to One-Year-Old Sons and Daughters." Paper presented at the Fourth Annual Communication, Language, and Gender Conference Morgantown, West Virginia, 1981.

Kimlicka, Thomas; Wakefield James; and Goad, Nancy. "Sex Role of Ideal Opposite Sexed Persons for College Males and Females." *Journal of Personality Assessment* 46 (1982): 519–521.

King, W. H. "An Experimental Investigation into the Relative Merits of Listening and Reading Comprehension for Boys and Girls of Primary School Age." *British Journal of Educational Psychology* 29 (1959): 42.

Kingston, A. and Lovelace, T. "Sexism and Reading: A Critical Review of the Literature." *Reading Research Quarterly* 13 (Winter, 1977–1978): 133–161.

Kinsey, Alfred C.; Pomeroy, Wardell B.; and Martin, Clyde E. *Sexual Behavior in the Human Female.* Philadelphia: W. B. Saunders Co., 1953.

Kinzer, N. S. "Soapy Sin in the Afternoon." *Psychology Today* (August 1973): 46, 48.

Kirkendall, A. Lester and Libby, W. Roger. "Interpersonal Relationships—Crux of the Sexual Renaissance." *The Journal of Social Issues* 22 (1966): 45–49.

Kirkpatrick, Robert. "Sex Roles and Sexual Satisfaction in Women." *Psychology of Women Quarterly* 4 (1980): 444–459.

Kitson, G.; Lopata, H.; Holmes, W.; and Meyering, S. "Divorcees and Widows: Similarities and Differences." *American Journal of Orthopsychiatry* 50 (1980): 291–301.

Klapper, J. T. *The Effects of Mass Communication.* Glencoe, Illinois: The Free Press, 1960.

Kleinke, Chris. "Effects of Dress on Compliance to Requests in a Field Setting." *Journal of Social Psychology* 102 (1977): 223–224.

Kleinke, Chris L. "Knowledge and Familiarity of Descriptive Sex Names for Males and Females." *Perceptual and Motor Skills* 39 (1974): 419–422.

Kleinke, Chris L.; Bustos, Armando A.; Meeker, Frederick B.; and Staneski, Richard A. "Effects of Self-Attributed and Other Attributed Gaze on Interpersonal Evaluations Between Males and Females." *Journal of Experimental Social Psychology* 9 (1973): 154–163.

Klos, Dennis S. and Loomis, Diane F. "A Rating Scale of Intimate Disclosure Between Late Adolescents and Their Friends." *Psychological Reports* 42 (1978): 815–820.

Kmiecik, Cynthia; Mausar, Paula; and Banziger, George. "Attractiveness and Interpersonal Space." *The Journal of Social Psychology* 108 (1979): 277–278.

Knapp, Mark L. *Essentials of Nonverbal Communication.* New York: Holt, Rinehart and Winston, 1980.

Knapper, Christopher K. "The Relationship Between Personality and Style of Dress." Unpublished doctoral dissertation, University of Saskatchewan Regina Campus, 1969.

Kness, Darlene and Densmore, Barbara. "Dress and Social-Political Beliefs of Young Male Students." *Adolescence* 11 (1976): 431–442.

Knudson, Roger M.; Summers, Alison A.; and Golding, Stephen L. "Interpersonal Perception and Mode of Resolution in Marital Conflict." *Journal of Personality and Social Psychology* 38 (1980): 751–763.

Koch, Nielsen, I. "One-Parent Families in Denmark." *Journal of Comparative Family Studies* 11 (1980): 17–29.

Koester, Jolene. "The Machiavellian Princess: Rhetorical Dramas for Women Managers." *Communication Quarterly* 30 (1982): 165–172.

Kohen, J. A. "The Development of Reciprocal Self-Disclosure in Opposite Sex Interaction." *Journal of Counseling Psychology* 22 (1975): 404–410.

Kohen, J. A. "Liking and Self-Disclosure in Opposite Sex Dyads." *Psychological Reports* 36 (1975): 695–698.

Koren, Paul; Carlton, Kathe; and Shaw, David. "Marital Conflict: Relations Among Behaviors, Outcomes, and Distress." *Journal of Consulting and Clinical Psychology* 48 (1980): 460–468.

Krail, Kristina A. and Leventhal, Gloria. "The Sex Variable in the Intrusion of Personal Space." *Sociometry* 39 (1976): 170–173.

Kramarae, Cheris. *Women and Men Speaking.* Rowley, Mass.: Newbury House Publishers, Inc., 1981.

Kramer, Cheris R. "Perceptions of Female and Male Speech." *Language and Speech* 20 (1977): 151–161.

Kramer, Cheris R. "Sex Differences in Communication Behavior." Paper presented at the Speech Communication Association Convention, Houston, 1975.

Kramer, Cheris R. "Sex Differences in Language." *Psychology Today* 8 (1978): 82–85.

Kramer, Cheris R. "Women's and Men's Ratings of their Own and Ideal Speech." *Communication Quarterly* 26 (1978): 2–11.

Kramer, Cheris R. "Women's Speech: Separate But Unequal?" *Quarterly Journal of Speech* 60 (1974): 14–24.

Kramer, Cheris; Thorne, Barrie; and Henley, Nancy. "Perspectives on Language and Communication." *Signs* 3 (1978): 638–651.

Kraut, Robert E. and Johnston, Robert E. "Social and Emotional Messages of Smiling: An Ethological Approach." *Journal of Personality and Social Psychology* 37 (1979): 1539–1553.

Kravetz, D. and Jones, L. "Androgyny as a Standard of Mental Health." *American Journal of Orthopsychiatry* 51 (1981): 502–509.

Krebs, Dennis and Adinolfi, Allen A. "Physical Attractiveness, Social Relations, and Personality Style." *Journal of Personality and Social Psychology* 31 (1975): 245–253.

Krefting, Linda A. "Masculinity-Femininity of Job Requirements and Their Relationship to Job-Sex Stereotypes." *Journal of Vocational Behavior* 15 (1979): 164–173.

Krivonos, Paul D. "The Effects of Attitude Similarity, Spatial Relationship, and Task Difficulty on Interpersonal Attraction." *The Southern Speech Communication Journal* 45 (1980): 240–248.

Kroll, H. W. and Moren, D. K. "Effect of Appearance on Requests for Help in Libraries." *Psychological Reports* 40 (1977): 129–130.

Kuhn, Deanna; Nash, Sharon Churnin; and Brucken, Laura. "Sex Role Concepts of Two- and Three-Year Olds." *Child Development* 49 (1978): 445–451.

Kulik, James A. and Harackiewicz, Judith. "Opposite-Sex Interpersonal Attraction as a Function of the Sex Roles of the Perceiver and the Perceived." *Sex Roles* 5 (1979): 443–452.

Kyle, D. W. "Changes in Basal Content: Has Anyone Been listening?" *Elementary School Journal* 78 (1978): 305–312.

"La-Affaire Derrire." *Time Magazine* (January 1, 1973): 29.

Labov, William. *Sociolinguistic Patterns.* Philadelphia: University of Pennsylvania Press, 1972.

LaCrosse, Michael B. "Nonverbal Behavior and Perceived Counselor Attractiveness and Persuasiveness." *Journal of Counseling Psychology* 22 (1975): 563–566.

LaFrance, Marianne and Mayo, Clara. "A Review of Nonverbal Behaviors of Women and Men." *Western Journal of Speech Communication* 43 (1979): 96–107.

Laird, James D. "Self-Attribution of Emotion: The Effects of Expressive Behavior on the Quality of Emotional Experience." *Journal of Personality and Social Psychology* 29 (1974): 475–486.

Lakoff, Robin, "Language and Woman's Place." *Language in Society* 2 (1973): 45, 47–48.

Lakoff, Robin. *Language and Women's Place.* New York: Harper and Row, 1975.

Lakoff, Robin. "Language in Context." *Language* 48 (1972): 907–927.

Lakoff, Robin. "Women's Language." In *Women's Language and Style,* (Studies in Contemporary Language #1). U.S.: E. L. Epstein, 1978.

Lamb, M. "The Development of Mother-Infant and Father-Infant Attachments in the Second Year of Life." *Developmental Psychology* 13 (1977): 637–649.

Lakoff, Robin "You Are What You Say." *Ms.* 3 (1974): 63–67.

Lambert, S. "Reactions to a Stranger as a Function of Style of Dress." *Perceptual and Motor Skills* 35 (1972): 711–712.

Lampe, P. E. "Husband and Wife Roles and Marital Satisfaction." *Family Perspective* 14 (1980): 145–148.

Lane, Shelley D. "Empathy and Assertive Communication." Paper presented at the Western Speech Communication Association Convention, San Jose, California, 1981.

Lane, Terrance Scott. "Children's Task Performance on a Sex-Consistent or Sex-Inconsistent Game Following Social Comparison with their Peers." Unpublished doctoral dissertation, University of Georgia, 1982.

Langner, Lawrence. *The Importance of Wearing Clothes.* New York: Hastings House, 1959.

Langlois, Judith H. and Downs, A. Chris. "Peer Relations as a Function of Physical Attractiveness: The Eye of the Beholder or Behavioral Reality?" *Child Development* 59 (1979): 409–418.

Langolis, Judith H. and Stephan, Cookie. "The Effects of Physical Attractiveness and Ethnicity on Children's Behavioral Attributions and Peer Preferences." *Child Development* 48 (1977): 1694–1698.

Larche, Douglas W. *Mother Goose and Father Gander: Equal Rhymes for Girls and Boys.* Indianola, Iowa: Father Gander Press, 1979.

Larwood, Laurie; Wood, Marion M.; and Inderlied, Shelia Davis. "Training Women for Management: New Problems, New Solutions." *Academy of Management Review* 3 (1978): 584–593.

Larzelere, Robert E. and Huston, Ed L. "Dyadic Trust Scale: Towards Understanding Personal Trust in Close Relationships." *Journal of Marriage and the Family* 42 (1980): 595–604.

Lass, Norman J.; Mertz, Pamela J.; Kimmel, Karen. "The Effect of Temporal Speech Alterations on Speaker Race and Sex Identifications." *Language and Speech* 21 (1978): 279–290.

Lau, Sing. "The Effect of Smiling on Person Perception." *The Journal of Social Psychology* 117 (1982): 63–67.

Laubach, Arlene R. "School-Controlled Conformity of Dress for Teenagers and its Relation to Selected Behaviors and Security-Insecurity." Unpublished doctoral dissertation. The Pennsylvania State University, 1972.

Laver, James. "What Will Fashion Uncover Next?" from *Dimensions of Dress and Adornment: A Book of Readings,* Lois M. Gurel and Marianne S. Beeson, (eds.). Dubuque, Iowa: Kendall/Hunt Publishing Co., 1975.

LaVoie, Joseph C. and Adams, Gerald R. "Physical and Interpersonal Attractiveness of the Model and Imitation in Adults." *The Journal of Social Psychology* 106 (1978): 191–202.

Lawick-Goodall, Jane, van. *In the Shadow of Man.* Boston: Houghton-Mifflin, 1971.

Lawson, E. D. "Hair Color, Personality and the Observer." *Psychological Reports* 28 (1971): 311–332.

Lazarsfeld, P. F.; Berelson, B.; and Gaudet, H. *The People's Choice,* 2nd edition. New York: Columbia University Press, 1948.

Leary, Mark R. "Interpersonal Orientation and Self-Presentational Style." *Psychological Reports* 45 (1979): 451–456.

Lefkowitz, Monroe M.; Eron, Deonard D.; Walder, Leopold O.; and Huesmann, L. Rowell. *Growing Up to Be Violent: A Longitudinal Study of the Development of Aggression.* New York: Pergamon Press, Inc., 1977.

Leibman, Miriam. "The Effects of Sex and Race Norms on Personal Space." *Environment and Behavior* 2 (1970): 208–246.

Lemon, Judith. "Women and Blacks on Prime-Time Television." *Journal of Communication* 27 (Autumn 1977): 70–79.

Lesak, M. *Neuropsychological Assessment.* New York: Oxford University Press, Inc., 1976.

Leslie, Gerald R. *Marriage in a Changing World.* New York: John Wiley and Sons, 1977.

Leventhal, Gerald S. and Lane, Douglas W. "Sex, Age, and Equity Behavior." *Journal of Personality and Social Psychology* 15 (1970): 312–316.

Leventhal, Gloria; Lipshultz, Marsha; and Chiodo, Anthony. "Sex and Setting Effects on Seating Arrangement." *The Journal of Psychology* 100 (1978): 21–26.

Leventhal, Gloria and Matturro, Michelle. "Differential Effects of Spatial Crowding and Sex on Behavior." *Perceptual Motor Skills* 51 (1980): 111–119.

Leventhal, Gloria; Matturro, Michelle; and Schanerman, Joel. "Effects of Attitude, Sex and Approach on Nonverbal, Verbal and Projective Measures of Personal Space." *Perceptual and Motor Skills* 47 (1978): 107–108.

Lever, J. "Sex Differences in the Games Children Play." *Social Problems* 23 (1976): 478–487.

Levere, Jane. "Portrayal of Women in Ads Defended by Top Ad Women." *Editor and Publisher* (June 8, 1974): 11.

LeVine, E. and Frances, J. N. "A Reassessment of Self-Disclosure Patterns Among Anglo-Americans and Hispanics." *Journal of Counseling Psychology* 28 (1981): 522–524.

Levine, J. B. "The Feminine Routine." *Journal of Communication* 26 (1976): 173–175.

Levine, Lewis and Crockett, Harry J., Jr. "Speech Variation in a Piedmont Community: Postvocalic," from *Explorations in Sociolinguistics,* ed. Stanley Lieberson. The Hague: Mouton, 1966.

Levinger, G. and Senn, D. "Disclosure of Feelings in Marriage." *Merrill-Palmer Quarterly of Behavior and Development* 13 (1967): 237–249.

Levy, J. and Levy, J. M. "Human Lateralization from Head to Foot: Sex-Related Factors." *Science* 200 (1978): 1291–1292.

Lewis, M. "Parents and Children: Sex Role Development." *Social Review* 80 (1972): 229–240.

Lewis, R. J. "Emotional Intimacy among Men." *Journal of Social Issues* 34 (1978): 108–121.

Liebert, R. M.; McCall, R. B.; and Hanratty, M. A. "Effects of Sex-Typed Information on Children's Toy Preferences." *Journal of Genetic Psychology* 119 (1971): 133–136.

Lindbeck, Joy S. "You've Come a Long Way Baby—So Tell It Like It Is: A Report on Sex Bias in Textbooks." *Educational Horizons* 54 (Winter 1975–1976): 94–98.

Lippa, Richard. "The Naive Perception of Masculinity-Femininity on the Basis of Expressive Cues." *Journal of Research in Personality* 12 (1978): 1–14.

Littlefield, Robert P. "Self-Disclosure Among Some Negro, White, and Mexican-American Adolescents." *Journal of Counseling Psychology* 21 (1974): 133–136.

Lockheed, Marlaine E. and Hall, Katherine P. "Conceptualizing Sex as a Status Characteristic: Applications to Leadership Training Strategies." *Journal of Social Issues* 32 (1976): 111–124.

Locksley, Anne. "Social Class and Marital Attitudes and Behavior." *Journal of Marriage and the Family* 44 (1982): 427–440.

Locksley, Anne; Borgida, Eugene; Brekke, Nancy; and Hepburn, Christine. "Sex Stereotypes and Social Judgment." *Journal of Personality and Social Psychology* 39 (1980): 821–831.

Locksley, Anne and Colton, Mary. "Psychological Androgyny: A Case of Mistaken Identity." *Journal of Personality and Social Psychology* 37 (1979): 1017–1031.

Loeb, Roger C. and Horst, Leslie. "Sex Differences in Self and Teachers' Reports of Self-Esteem in Pre-Adolescents." *Sex Roles* 4 (1978): 779–788.

Lombardo, John P. "Satisfaction with Interpersonal Relations as a Function of Level of Self-Disclosure." *Journal of Psychology* 2 (1979): 21–26.

Lombardo, John P. and Berzonsky, M. D. "Sex Differences in Self-Disclosure During an Interview." *Journal of Social Psychology* 107 (1979): 281–282.

Lombardo, John P. and Fantasia, Salverio. "The Relationship of Self-Disclosure to Personality, Adjustment, and Self-Actualization." *Journal of Clinical Psychology* 32 (1976): 765–769.

Lombardo, John P. and Wood, Robert D. "Satisfaction with Interpersonal Relations as a Function of Level of Self-Disclosure." *Journal of Psychology* 102 (1979): 21–26.

Lomranz, J. and Shapira, A. "Communicative Patterns of Self-Disclosure and Touching Behavior." *The Journal of Psychology* 88 (1974): 223–227.

Long, Gary T.; Selby, James W.; and Calhoun, Lawrence G. "Effects of Situational Stress and Sex on Interpersonal Distance Preference." *The Journal of Psychology* 105 (1980): 231–237.

Long, Lynette N. and Long, Thomas J. "Influence of Religious Status and Religious Attire on Interviewees." *Psychological Reports* 39 (1976): 25–26.

Long, Thomas J. "Influence of Uniform and Religious Status in Interviewees." *Journal of Counseling Psychology* 25 (1978): 405–409.

Losco, J. and Epstein, S. "Humor Preference as a Subtle Measurement of Attitudes Toward the Same and Opposite Sex." *Journal of Personality* 43 (1975): 321–334.

Lott, Dale F. and Sommer, Robert. "Seating Arrangements and Status." *Journal of Personality and Social Psychology* 7 (1967): 90–95.

Lowry, Dennis T.; Love, Gail; and Kirby, Malcolm. "Sex on the Soap Operas: Patterns of Intimacy." *Journal of Communication* 31 (Spring 1981): 90–96.

Luckey, Eleanore Braun. "Marital Satisfaction and Parent Concepts." *Journal of Counseling Psychology* 24 (1960): 195–204.

Luft, J. *Of Human Interaction.* Palo Alto, California: National Press Books, 1969.

Lull, James. "Girls' Favorite TV Females." *Journalism Quarterly Review* 57 (1980): 146–150.

Lundsteen, Sara. "Teaching Abilities in Critical Listening in Fifth and Sixth Grades." Unpublished doctoral dissertation, University of California, Berkeley, 1963.

Lundstrom, W. J. and Sciglimpaglia, D. "Sex Role Portrayals in the Media." *Journal of Marketing* 41 (1977): 72–79.

Lurie, Alison. *The Language of Clothes.* New York: Random House, 1981.

Lutwiniak, Patricia M. "The Relationship of Selected Clothing Behavior to Self Esteem." Master's thesis, University of Tennessee, 1972, from *A Schematic Approach to Theoretical Analysis of Dress as Nonverbal Communication,* by Robert Christian Hillestad. Doctoral dissertation, The Ohio State University, 1974.

Maccoby, Eleanor Emmons, and Jacklin, Carol Nagy. "Myth, Reality, and Shades of Gray: What We Know and Don't Know about Sex Differences." *Psychology Today* 8 (December 1974): 109–112.

MacDonald, Malcolm R. "How Do Men and Women Students Rate in Empathy?" *American Journal of Nursing* 77 (1977): 998.

Mackay, David C. and Fulkerson, D. C. "On the Comprehension and Production of Pronouns." *Journal of Verbal Learning and Verbal Behavior* 18 (1979): 661–673.

MacKay, Donald G. "Psychology, Prescriptive Grammar, and the Pronoun Problem." *American Psychologist* 35 (1980): 444–449.

Macmillan Publishing Company. *Guidelines for Improving the Image of Women in Textbooks.* Glenview, Illinois: Scott, Foresman and Company, 1972.

Maier, Norman R. F. "Male versus Female Discussion Leaders." *Personnel Psychology* 23 (1970): 455–461.

Maier, Norman R. F. and Burke, Ronald J. "Response Availability as a Factor in the Problem-Solving Performance of Males and Females." *Journal of Personality and Social Psychology* 5 (1967): 304–310.

Maier, Richard A. and Ernest, Robert C. "Sex Differences in the Perception of Touching." *Perceptual and Motor Skills* 46 (1978): 577–578.

Malandro, Loretta A. and Barker, Larry. *Nonverbal Communication.* Reading: Massachusetts, 1982.

Malinowski, B. *The Sexual Life of Savages in North-Western Malenesia.* New York: Eugenia Publishing Co., 1929.

Malone, Guy. "A Comparison of Mothers' and Fathers' Speech to their 3-Year-Old Sons." *Journal of Psycholinguistic Research* 11 (1982): 599–607.

Mant, Andrea. "Media Images and Medical Images." *Social Science and Medicine* 9 (November-December 1975): 613–618.

Maples, Mary F. "Dual Career Marriages: Elements for Potential Success." *Personnel and Guidance Journal* 60 (1981): 19–23.

Marcum, Patricia J. "Men and Women on the Management Team." *University of Michigan Business Review* 28 (1976): 8–11.

Marecek, Jeanne; Piliavin, Jane Allyn; Fitzsimmons, Ellen; Krogh, Elizabeth C.; Leader, Elizabeth and Trudell, Bonnie. "Women as TV Experts: The Voice of Authority?" *Journal of Communication* 28 (Winter 1978): 159–168.

Mark, Elizabeth Wyner. "Sex Differences in Intimacy Motivation: A Projective Approach to the Study of Self-Disclosure." Unpublished doctoral dissertation, Boston College, 1976.

Mark, R. A. "Parameters of Normal Family Communication in the Dyad." Unpublised doctoral dissertation, Michigan State University, 1970.

Markel, Norman N.; Long, Joseph, F. R.; and Saine, Thomas J. "Sex Effects in Conversational Interaction: Another Look at Male Dominance." *Human Communication Research* 2 (1976): 356–364.

Markel, Norman; Prebor, Layne; and Brandt, John. "Biosocial Factors in Dyadic Communication: Sex and Speaking Intensity." *Journal of Personality and Social Psychology* 23 (1972): 11–13.

Marlatt, G. A. "Comparison of Vicarious and Direct Reinforcement Control of Verbal Behavior in an Interview Setting." *Journal of Personality and Social Psychology* 16 (1970): 695–703.

Marshall, Joan E. and Heslin, Richard. "Boys and Girls Together: Sexual Composition and the Effect of Density and Group Size on Cohesiveness." *Journal of Personality and Social Psychology* 31 (1975): 952–961.

Martin, J. N. and Craig, R. T. "Selected Linguistic Sex Differences During Initial Social Interactions of Same-Sex and Mixed-Sex Student Dyads." *Western Journal of Speech Communication* 47 (1983): 16–28.

Martyna, Wendy. "What Does 'He' Mean? Use of the Generic Masculine."*Journal of Communication* 28 (1978): 131–138.

Mashman, Robert C. "The Effects of Physical Attractiveness on the Perception of Attitude Similarity." *The Journal of Social Psychology* 106 (1978): 103–110.

Mathes, Eugene W. "The Effects of Physical Attractiveness and Anxiety on Heterosexual Attraction Over a Series of Five Encounters." *Journal of Marriage and Family* 37 (November 1975): 769–773.

Mathes, Eugene W. and Kempher, Sherry B. "Clothing as a Nonverbal Communicator of Sexual Attitudes and Behavior." *Perceptual and Motor Skills* 43 (1976): 495–498.

Mayo, Clara and Henley, Nancy. *Gender and Nonverbal Behavior*. New York: Springer Verlay Inc., 1981.

McAllister, H. A. "Self-Disclosure and Liking: Effects for Lenders and Receivers." *Journal of Personality* 48 (1980): 409–418.

McCall, Jr., Morgan W. "What Makes a Top Executive?" *Psychology Today* 26 (1983): 26–31.

McCormick, Naomi B. "Come-ons and Put-offs: Unmarried Students' Strategies for Having and Avoiding Sexual Intercourse." *Psychology of Women Quarterly* 4 (1979): 194–211.

McCroskey, James C. and Richmond, Virginia P. "Communication Apprehension as a Predictor of Self-Disclosure." *Communication Quarterly* 25 (Fall 1977): 40–43.

McCroskey, James C.; Simpson, Timothy.; and Richmond, Virginia P. "Biological Sex and Communication Apprehension." *Communication Quarterly* 30 (1982): 129–133.

McCullough, Jacquelyn Harden. "A Multivariate Profile of Fashion Conscious College Women." Unpublished doctoral dissertation, Purdue University, 1977.

McGhee, Paul E. "Sex Differences in Children's Humor." *Journal of Communication* 26 (1976): 176–189.

McGhee, Paul E. and Frueh, Terry. "Television Viewing and the Learning of Sex Role Stereotypes." *Sex Roles* 6 (1980): 179–188.

McGinley, Hugh; LeFevre, Richard; and McGinley, Patsy. "The Influence of a Communicator's Body Position on Opinion Change in Others." *Journal of Personality and Social Psychology* 31 (1975): 686–690.

McGinley, Hugh; Nicholas, Karen; and McGinley, Patsy. "Effects of Body Position and Attitude Similarity on Interpersonal Attraction and Opinion Change." *Psychological Reports* 42 (1978); 127–138.

McGovern, Jana L. and Holmes, David S. "Influence of Sex and Dress on Cooperation: An Instance of 'Person' Chauvinism." *Journal of Applied Social Psychology* 6 (1976): 206–210.

McKeachie, W. "Lipstick as a Determiner of First Impressions of Personality: An Experiment for the General Psychology Course." *Journal of Social Psychology* 36 (1962): 241–244.

McLaughlin, Margaret L.; Cody, Michael, J.; Kane, Marjorie L.; and Robey, Carl S. "Sex Differences in Story Receipt and Story Sequencing Behaviors in Dyadic Conversations." *Human Communication Research* 7 (1981): 99–116.

McLean, Francis P. "The Process of Aging Related to Cathexis and to Clothing Satisfaction." Unpublished doctoral dissertation, Utah State University, 1978.

McMillan, Julie R.; Clifton, A. Kay; McGrath, Diane; and Gale, Wanda S. "Women's Language: Uncertainty or Interpersonal Sensitivity and Emotionality?" *Sex Roles* 3 (1977): 545–559.

McVicar, Pauline, and Herman, Al. "Assertiveness, Self-Actualization, and Locus of Control in Women." *Sex Roles* 9 (1983): 555–562.

Mead, George Herbert quoted in *Sociology: Human Society* by Melvin DeFleur *et al.* Glenview, Illinois: Scott, Foresman & Company, 1977, p. 138.

Meeker, B. F. and Weitzel-O'Neill, P. A. "Sex Roles and Interpersonal Behavior in Task-Oriented Groups." *American Sociological Review* 42 (1977): 91–105.

Megargee, Edwin E. "Influence of Sex Roles on the Manifestation of Leadership." *Journal of Applied Psychology* 53 (1969): 377–382.

Mehrabian, Albert. *Nonverbal Communication*. Chicago: Aldine-Atherton, 1972.

Mehrabian, Albert. "Verbal and Nonverbal Interaction of Strangers in a Waiting Situation." *Journal of Experimental Research in Personality* 5 (1971): 127–128.

Mehrabian, Albert and Ferris, Susan R. "Influence of Attitudes from Nonverbal Communication in Two Channels." *Journal of Consulting Psychology* 31 (1967): 248–252.

Meiners, Mary L. and Sheposh, John P. "Beauty or Brains: Which Image for Your Mate?" *Personality and Social Psychology Bulletin* 3 (1977): 262–265.

Mendelsohn, Meri and Mosher, Donald. "Effects of Sex Guilt and Premarital Sexual Permissiveness on Role Played Sex Education and Moral Attitudes." *Journal of Sex Research* 15 (1979): 174–183.

Mendes, H. "Single-Parent Families: A Typology of Life-Styles." *Social Work* 24 (1979): 189–191.

Mercer, William G. and Kohn, Paul M. "Gender Differences in the Integration of Conservatism, Sex Urge, and Sexual Behaviors Among College Students." *Journal of Sex Research* 15 (1979): 129–142.

Merritt, Sharyne and Gross, Harriet. "Women's Page/ Lifestyle Editors: Does Sex Make a Difference?" *Journalism Quarterly* 55 (Autumn 1978): 508–514.

Meyers, Karen Ann. "The Effects of Inclusive/Exclusive Language on Reading Comprehension, Perceived Aesthetic Quality and Likelihood of Adoption of Inclusive Pronoun Usage." Unpublished senior honor's thesis, Rutgers University, 1979.

Milford, James T. "Aesthetic Aspects of Faces: A (Somewhat) Phenomenological Analysis Using Multidimensioinal Scaling Methods." *Journal of Personality and Social Psychology* 36 (1978): 205–216.

Miller, Casey and Swift, Kate. "Women and the Language of Religion." *Christian Century* 93 (1976): 353–358.

Miller, Casey and Swift, Kate. "De-Sexing the English Language." *Ms.,* Preview issue, Spring 1972, p. 7.

Miller, Franklin G. and Rowold, Kathleen L. "Attire, Sex Roles, and Responses to Requests for Directions." *Psychological Reports* 47 (1980): 661–662.

Miller, Gerald R. and McReynolds, Michael. "Male Chauvinism and Source Competence: A Research Note." *Speech Monographs* 40 (1973): 154–155.

Miller, Nina S. "Visual Self-Presentation: Impact of Counselor Clothing on Potential Clients' First Impressions." Unpublished doctoral dissertation, Purdue University, 1978.

Miller, Susan H. "The Content of News Photos: Women's and Men's Roles." *Journalism Quarterly* 52 (Spring 1975): 70–75.

Miller, T. W. "Male Attitudes toward Women's Rights as a Function of their Level of Self-Esteem." *International Journal of Group Tensions* 4 (1974): 35–44.

Mims, P. R.; Hartnett, J. J.; and Nay, W. R. "Interpersonal Attraction and Help Volunteering as a Function of Physical Attractiveness." *Journal of Psychology* 89 (1975): 125–131.

Miner, John B. "Motivation to Manage Among Women: Studies of Business Managers and Educational Administrators." *Journal of Vocational Behavior* 5 (1974): 197–208.

Minnigerode, F. A. "Attitudes toward Homosexuality: Feminist Attitudes and Sexual Conservatism." *Sex Roles* 2 (1976): 347–352.

Minton, Henry L. and Miller, Arthur G. "Group Risk Taking and Internal-External Control of Group Members." *Psychological Reports* 26 (1970): 431–436.

Miyamoto, Frank; Crowell, Laura; and Katcher, Allan. "Self-Concepts of Communicative Skill among beginning Speech Students." *Speech Monographs* 23 (1956): 66–74.

Molloy, John T. *Dress for Success.* New York: Peter H. Wyden, 1975.

Molloy, John T. *The Women's Dress for Success Book.* New York: Warner Books, Inc., 1977.

Montague, Ashley. (ed.) *Touching: The Significance of the Human Skin.* New York: Harper & Row, 1971.

Montgomery, Barbara M. "The Form and Function of Quality Communication in Marriage." *Family Relations* 30 (January 1981): 21–29.

Montgomery, Barbara M. and Norton, Robert W. "Sex Differences and Similarities in Communicator Style." *Communication Monographs* 48 (1981): 121–132.

Montgomery, Charles L. and Burgoon, Michael. "An Experimental Study of the Interactive Effects of Sex and Androgyny on Attitude Change." *Communication Monographs* 44 (1977): 130–135.

Morgan, Brian S. "Intimacy of Disclosure Topics and Sex Differences in Self Disclosure." *Sex Roles* 2 (1976): 161–166.

Morganosky, M. and Creekmore, A. M. "Clothing Influence in Adolescent Leadership Roles." *Home Economics Research Journal* 9 (1981): 356–362.

Morris, William (ed.). *The American Heritage Dictionary of the English Language.* Boston, Mass.: American Heritage Publishing Company and Houghton Mifflin Company, 1975.

Mortier, Jeanne and Aboux, Marie Louise, eds. *Teilhard de Chardin Album.* New York: Harper and Row, 1966.

Morton, Terie L. "Intimacy and Reciprocity of Exchange: A Comparison of Spouses and Strangers." *Journal of Personality and Social Psychology* 36 (1978): 72–81.

Moses, P. J. *The Voice of Neurosis.* New York: Grune & Stratton, 1954.

Mosher, Donald L. "Sex Guilt and Sex Myths in College Men and Women." *Journal of Sex Research* 15 (1979): 224–234.

Moss, Howard A. "Sex, Age, and State as Determinants of Mother-Infant Interaction." In Paul Henry Mussen, John Janeway Conger and Jerome Kagan (ed.) *Readings in Child Development and Personality,* 2nd ed. New York: Harper & Row, 1970.

Moulton, Janice; Robinson, George M.; and Ellias, Cherin. "Sex Bias in Language Use: Neutral Pronouns that Aren't." *American Psychologist* 33 (1978): 1032–1036.

Muirhead, Rosalind D. and Goldman, Morton. "Mutual Eye Contact as Affected by Seating Position, Sex, and Age." *The Journal of Social Psychology* 109 (1979): 201–206.

Mulac, Anthony and Sherman, A. Robert. "Relationships Among Four Parameters of Speaker Evaluation: Speech Skill, Source Credibility, Subjective Speech Anxiety, and Behavioral Speech Anxiety." *Speech Monographs* 42 (1975): 302–310.

Mulac, Anthony and Torborg, Louisa Lundell. "Differences in Perceptions Created by Syntactic-Semantic Productions of Male and Female Speakers." *Communication Monographs* 47 (1980): 111–118.

Mulcahy, G. A. "Sex Differences in Patterns of Self-Disclosure Among Adolescents: A Developmental Perspective." *Journal of Youth and Adolescence* 2 (1973): 343–356.

Murstein, Bernard I. "Physical Attractiveness and Marital Choice." *Journal of Personality and Social Psychology* 22 (1972): 8–12.

Murray, R. P. and McGinley, H. "Looking as a Measure of Attraction." *Journal of Applied Special Psychology* 2 (1972): 267–274.

Murray, J. "Male Perspective in Language." *Women: A Journal of Liberation* 3 (1973): 46–50.

Murstein, Bernard I. and Christy, Patricia. "Physical Attractiveness and Marriage Adjustment in Middle-Aged Couples." *Journal of Personality and Social Psychology* 34 (1976): 537–542.

Natale, M. "Social Desirability as Related to Convergence of Temporal Speech Patterns." *Perceptual and Motor Skills* 40 (1975): 827–830.

Neer, Michael R. and Hudson, David D. "The Interactive Role Behaviors of Females and Males: How Differently do the Sexes Really Communicate?" Paper presented at the Western Speech Communication Association Convention, Albuequerque, New Mexico, February 1983.

Nelson, Audrey A. "Women's Nonverbal Behavior: The Paradox of Skill and Acquiescence." *Women's Studies in Communication* 4 (1981): 18–31.

Nelson, K. "Early Speech in Its Communicative Context." In F. Minifie and L. Lloyd (Eds.), *Communicative and Cognitive Abilities—Early Behavioral Assessment.* Baltimore: University Park Press, 1978.

Nesbitt, E. B. "Rathus Assertiveness Schedule and College Self-Expression Scale Scores as Predictors of Assertive Behavior." *Psychological Reports* 45 (1979): 855–861.

Newcomb, Paul R. "Cohabitation in America: An Assessment of Consequences." *Journal of Marriage and the Family* 41 (1978): 597–603.

Newcombe, Nora and Arnkoff, Diane B. "Effects of Speech Style and Sex of Speaker on Person Perception." *Journal of Personality and Social Psychology* 37 (1979): 1293–1303.

Newport, E. "Motherese: The Speech of Mothers to Young Children." In N. Castellan, D. Pisoni, and G. Potts (Eds.), *Cognitive Theory,* Vol. II. Hillsdale, New Jersey: Lawrence Earlbaum Associates, 1976.

Nichols, Ralph G. "Factors in Listening Comprehension." *Speech Monographs* 15 (1948): 154–163.

Nichols, Ralph G. and Stevens, Leonard M. "Listening to People." *Harvard Business Review* 35 (1957) 85–92.

Nida, Steve A. and Williams, John E. "Sex Stereotyped Traits, Physical Attractiveness, and Interpersonal Attraction." *Psychological Reports* 41 (1977): 1311–1322.

Nielsen, J. Paull and Kernaleguen, Anne. "Influence of Clothing and Physical Attractiveness in Person Perception." *Perceptual and Motor Skills* 42 (1976): 775–780.

Nilsen, Alleen Pace. "The Correlation Between Gender and Other Semantic Features in American English." Paper presented at Linguistic Society of America, 1973.

Nilsen, Alleen Pace. "Sexism in English: A Feminist View." *Female Studies* VI ed. Nancy Hoffman, Cynthia Secor, and Adrian Tinsley. Old Westbury, New York: The Feminist Press, 1972, 102–109.

Nilsen, Alleen Pace. "Women in Children's Literature." *College English* 32 (1971): 918–926.

Nye, F. Ivan. *Family Relationships: Rewards and Costs.* Beverly Hills, California: Sage Publications, 1982.

Noel, Richard and Allen, Mary J. "Sex and Ethnic Bias in the Evalution of Student Editorials." *Journal of Psychology* 94 (1976): 53–58.

Norton, Robert W. "Foundation of a Communicator Style Construct." *Human Communication Research* 4 (1978): 99–112.

Norton, Robert and Warnick, Barbara. "Assertiveness as a Communication Construct." *Human Communication Research* 3 (1976): 62–66.

O'Donnell, Holly Smith. "Sexism in Language." *Elementary English* 50 (1973): 1067–1072.

O'Donnell, Tom. "Playboy Photographer Looks for Inner Beauty, and Rarely Finds It." *Des Moines Register,* April 22, 1902, 1C.

O'Donnell, William J. and O'Donnell, Karen J. "Update: Sex-Role Messages in TV Commercials." *Journal of Communication* 28 (Winter 1978): 156–158.

Offer, D. *The Psychological World of the Teenager.* New York: Basic Books, 1969.

O'Keefe, Eileen S. C. and Hyde, Janet Shibley. "The Development of Occupational Sex-Role Stereotypes: The Effects of Gender Stability and Age." *Sex Roles* 9 (1983): 481–492.

Olesker, W. and Balter, L. "Sex and Empathy." *Journal of Counseling Psychology* 19 (1972): 559–562.

Oliver, Edward C. "Self-Perception Processes in Attraction: The Role of False and Real Affective Responses." Unpublished doctoral dissertation, Kansas State University, 1977.

Oliver, Linda. "Women in Aprons: The Female Stereotype in Children's Readers." *Elementary School Journal* 74 (1974): 253–259.

Ommaya, A. K. "Knowing and Doing: A Hypothesis for the Mechanisms Cerebral Asymmetry and Consciousness." Speech at Phi Sigma Rho, the George Washington University, Washington, D.C., 1978.

O'Neal, Gwendolyn S. "Clothing Effects as Nonverbal Communication on Credibility of the Message Source in Advertising." Unpublished doctoral dissertation, The Ohio State University, 1977.

O'Neill, Sylvia; Fein, Deborah; Velit, Kathryn McColl; and Frank, Constance. "Sex Differences in Preadolescent Self-Disclosure." *Sex Roles* 2 (1976): 85–88.

O'Neill, W. L. *Everyone Was Brave: The Rise and Fall of Feminism.* Chicago: Quadrangle Books, 1969.

Orenstein, H.; Orenstein, E.; and Carr, J. E. "Assertiveness and Anxiety: A Correlational Study." *Journal of Behavior Therapy and Experimental Psychiatry* 6 (1975): 203–207.

Orlofsky, Jacob L. "Sex Role Orientation, Identity Formation and Self-Esteem in College Men and Women. *Sex Roles* 3 (1977): 561–575.

Ornstein, Robert E. *The Psychology of Consciousness.* New York: Penguin Books, 1972.

Otto, Luther. "Girlfriends as Significant-Others: Their Influence on Young Men's Career Aspirations and Achievements." *Journal of Sociometry* 40 (1977): 287–292.

Owens, G. and Ford, J. G. "Further Consideration of the 'What is Good is Beautiful' Finding." *Social Psychology* 41 (1978): 73–75.

Palamatier, R. A., and McNinch, G. "Source of Gains in Listening Skill: Experimental or Pre-Test Experience." *Journal of Communication* 22 (1972): 70–76.

Paletz, David L.; Koon, Judith; Whitehead, Elizabeth; and Hagens, Richard B. "Selective Exposure: The Potential Boomerang Effect." *Journal of Communication* 22 (1972): 48–53.

Paludi, M. A. and Bauer, W. D. "Goldberg Revisited: What's in an Author's Name." *Sex Roles* 9 (1983): 387–390.

Papaleo, Stephen. "A Psychological Study of the Image of Woman as a Sexual Object: Stepping Into the Moon." Unpublished doctoral dissertation, California School of Professional Psychology, 1978.

Papini, Dennis R. and Datan, Nancy. "The Best Laid Plans . . .: Egalitarian Ideals and Sex-Typed Family Interaction." Paper presented at the Fourth Annual Communication, Language, and Gender Conference, Morgantown, West Virginia, 1981.

Parlee, M. B. "Conversational Politics." *Psychology Today* (May 1979): 48–56.

Parlee, Mary B. "Women Smile Less for Success." *Psychology Today* 12 (1979): 16.

Parke, R. and O'Leary, S. "Father-Mother-Infant Interaction in the Newborn Period: Some Findings, Some Observations, and Some Unresolved Issues." In K. Reigel and J. Meacham (Eds.), *The Developing Infant in a Changing World,* Vol. II, *Social and Environmental Issues.* The Hague: Mouton, 1976.

Parke, R. and Sawin, D. "The Father's Role in Infancy: A Re-evaluation." *The Family Coordinator* 25 (1976): 365–371.

Parrish, Susan C. "Sexual Identity and Self-Disclosure Flexibility." Paper presented at the Communication, Language, and Gender Conference, Morgantown, West Virginia, 1981.

Patterson, M. and Sechrest, L. "Interpersonal Distance and Impression Formation." *Journal of Personality* 38 (1970): 161–166.

Patterson, Miles. "Spatial Factors in Social Interactions." *Human Relations* 21 (1968): 351–361.

Patterson, Miles; Mullens, Sherry; and Romano, Jeanne. "Compensatory Reactions to Spatial Intrusion." *Sociometry* 34 (1971): 114–121.

Patton, B. R.; Jasnoski, M.; and Skerchock, L. "Communication Implications of Androgyny." Presented at the Speech Communication Association Convention, Washington, D.C., 1977.

Paxton, Anne L. and Turner, Edward J. "Self-Actualization and Sexual Permissiveness, Satisfaction, Prudishness, and Drive Among Female Undergraduates." *The Journal of Sex Research* 14 (1978): 65–80.

Pearce, W. B. and Sharp, S. M. "Self-Disclosing Communication." *Journal of Communication* 23 (1973): 409–425.

Pearson, Judy C. "The Effects of Setting and Gender on Self-Disclosure." *Group and Organizational Studies: The International Journal for Group Facilitators,* 6 (1981), 334–340.

Pearson, Judy C. "The Effects of Sex and Sexism on the Criticism of Classroom Speeches." Unpublished doctoral dissertation, Indiana University, 1975.

Pearson, Judy C. "Evaluating Classroom Speeches: An Investigation of Speaker Sex, Sexism, and Sex Role Identification." International Communication Association convention, Minneapolis, Minnesota, 1981a.

Pearson, Judy C. "A Factor Analytic Study of the Items in the Rathus Assertiveness Schedule and the Personal Report of Communication Apprehension." *Psychological Reports* 45 (1979): 491–497.

Pearson, Judy C. "Gender, Similarity, and Source Credibility." Paper presented at the Western Speech Communication Association convention, Denver, Colorado, 1982.

Pearson, Judy C. *Interpersonal Communication: Clarity, Confidence, Concern.* Glenview, Illinois: Scott, Foresman and Company, 1983.

Pearson, Judy C. "An Investigation of the Effects of Sexism and Sex Role Identification on the Criticism of Classroom Speeches." Paper presented at the Speech Communication Association Convention, New York City, New York, November 1980.

Pearson, Judy C. "The Role of Psychological Sex Type in Rhetorical Sensitivity and Self-Disclosure." Paper presented at the Speech Communication Association Convention, Anaheim, California, November, 1981.

Pearson, Judy C. "Sex and Speech Criticism in the Classroom: An Annotated Bibliography." *Women's Studies in Communication* 4 (1) (1981b): 47–54.

Pearson, Judy C. "Sex Roles and Self-Disclosure." *Psychological Reports* 47 (1980): 640.

Pearson, Judy C.; Miller, Gerald R.; and Senter, Margo-Marie. "Sexual Humor and Sex-Role Preferences." Paper presented at the annual convention of the International Communication Association, Boston, 1982.

Pearson, Judy C. and Nelson, Paul E. "The Basic Speech Communication Course: An Examination of Instructor Sex, Student Sex, and Type of Course on Grading." Paper presented at the Speech Communication Association convention, Anaheim, California, November, 1981.

Pearson, Judy C. and Nelson, Paul E. *Understanding and Sharing: An Introduction to Speech Communication,* 2nd Edition. Dubuque, Iowa: William C. Brown Company, 1982.

Pedersen, Darhl M. and Heaston, Anne. "The Effects of Sex of Subject, Sex of Approaching Person, and Angle of Approach Upon Personal Space." *The Journal of Psychology* 82 (1972): 277–286.

Pedersen, Darhl M. and Higbee, Kenneth L. "Personality Correlates of Self-Disclosure." *Journal of Social Psychology* 78 (1969): 81–89.

Pedersen, Darhl M. and Higbee, Kenneth L. "Self-Disclosure and Relationship to the Target Person." *Merrill-Palmer Quarterly of Behavior and Development* 15 (1969): 213–220.

Pedhazur, Elazar and Tetanbaum, Toby. "Bem Sex Role Inventory: A Theoretical and Methodological Critique." *Journal of Personality and Social Psychology* 37 (1979): 996–1016.

Pellegrini, Anthony. "A Speech Analysis of Preschoolers." *Child Study Journal* 12 (1982): 205–215.

Pellegrini, Robert J.; Hicks, Robert A.; Meyers-Winton, Susan; and Antal, Bruce G. "Physical Attractiveness and Self-Disclosure in Mixed-Sex Dyads." *The Psychological Record* 28 (1978): 509–516.

Peplau, L. A.; Rubin, Z.; and Hill, C. T. "Sexual Intimacy in Dating Relationships." *Journal of Social Issues* 33 (1977): 86–109.

Perry, M. O.; Schutz, H. G.; and Rucker, M. H. "Clothing Interest, Self-Actualization, and Demographic Variables." *Home Economics Research Journal* 11 (1983): 280–288.

Peterson, P. "An Investigation of Sex Differences in Regard to Non-verbal Body Gestures." Proceedings of the Speech Communication Association Summer Conference, Austin, 1975.

Petro, Carole Smith and Putnam, Barbara A. "Sex-Role Stereotypes: Issues of Attitudinal Change." *Sex Roles* 5 (1979): 29–39.

Petronio, Sandra S. "The Effect of Interpersonal Communication on Women's Family Role Satisfaction." *Western Journal of Speech Communication* 46 (1982): 208–222.

Petty, M. M. and Lee, G. K., Jr. "Moderating Effects of Sex of Supervisor and Subordinate on Relationships Between Supervisory Behavior and Subordinate Satisfaction." *Journal of Applied Psychology* 60 (1975): 624–628.

Petty, M. M. and Miles, Robert H. "Leader Sex-Role Stereotyping in a Female-Dominated Work Culture." *Personnel Psychology* 29 (1976): 393–404.

Pfister, Emil R. "A Study of the Influence of Certain Selected Factors on the Ratings of Speech Performances." Unpublished Ed.D. dissertation, Michigan State University, 1955.

Phelps, S. and Austin, N. *The Assertive Woman.* San Luis Obispo, California: Impact, 1975.

Philips, Gerald and Goodall, Jr., H. Lloyd. *Loving and Living.* Englewood Cliffs, New Jersey: Prentice-Hall, Inc., 1983.

Phillips, J. and Cole, S. "Sex Differences in Triadic Coalition Formation Strategies." In J. Phillips and T. Connor (eds.), *Studies of Conflict, Conflict Reduction and Alliance Formation,* Report 70–1 of the Cooperation/Conflict Research Group, Michigan State University, 1970, pp. 154–176.

Pinaire-Reed, J. Ann. "Interpersonal Attraction: Fashionability and Perceived Similarity." *Perceptual and Motor Skills* 48 (1979): 571–576.

Pincus, A. R. H. and Pincus, R. E. "Linguistic Sexism and Career Education." *Language Arts* 57 (1980): 70–77.

Pingree, Suzanne. "The Effects of Nonsexist Television Commercials and Perceptions of Reality on Children's Attitudes about Women." *Psychology of Women Quarterly* 2 (1978): 262–277.

Pogrebin, Letty Cobin. "Can Women Really Have It All?" *Ms.*6 (1978): 47–50.

Polhemus, Ted and Proctor, Lynn. *Fashion and Anti-Fashion: An Anthropology of Clothing and Adornment.* London: Thames and Hudson, 1978.

Poling, Tommy H. "Sex Difference, Dominance, and Physical Attractiveness in the Use of Nonverbal Emblems." *Psychological Reports* 43 (1978): 1087–1092.

Polit, Denise and LeFrance, Marianne. "Sex Differences in Reaction to Spatial Invasion." *The Journal of Social Psychology* 102 (1977): 59–60.

Polivy, Janet; Hackett, Rick; and Bycio, Peter. "The Effect of Perceived Smoking Status on Attractiveness." *Personality and Social Psychology Bulletin* 5 (1979): 401–404.

Pomerantz, Susan and House, William C. "Liberated versus Traditional Women's Performance Satisfaction and Perceptions of Ability." *The Journal of Psychology* 95 (1977): 205–211.

Post, Amy L.; Wittmaier, Bruce C.; and Radin, Mitchell, E. "Self-Disclosure as a Function of State and Trait Anxiety." *Journal of Consulting and Clinical Psychology* 46 (1978): 12–19.

Powell, Gary N., and Butterfield, D. Anthony. "A Note on Sex-Role Identity Effect on Managerial Aspirations." *Journal of Occupational Psychology* 54 (1981): 299–301.

Powell, Patricia H. and Dabbs, Jr., James M. "Physical Attractiveness and Personal Space." *The Journal of Social Psychology* 100 (1976): 59–64.

Powers-Ross, Sally Jo. Doctoral dissertation prospectus. University of Minnesota, 1978.

Prerost, Frank. "The Effects of High Spatial Density on Humor Appreciation: Age and Sex Differences." *Social Behavior and Personality* 8 (1980): 239–244.

Prisbell, Marshall A. and Andersen, Janis F. "The Importance of Perceived Homophily, Level of Uncertainty, Feeling Good, Safety, and Self-Disclosure in Interpersonal Relationships." *Communication Quarterly* 28 (1980): 22–33.

Procter, Lynn. *Fashion and Anti-Fashion.* London: Cox and Wyman, 1978.

Purnell, Sandra E. "Politically Speaking, Do Women Exist?" *Journal of Communication* 28 (1978): 150–155.

Pursell, S.; Banikotes, P. G.; and Sebastian, R. J. "Androgyny and the Perception of Marital Roles." *Sex Roles* 7 (1981): 210–215.

Rachlin, Susan Kessler and Vogt, Glenda L. "Sex Roles as Presented to Children by Coloring Books." *Journal of Popular Culture* 8 (1974): 549–556.

Raither, G. and Kasper, R. "Effect of Dress on Obtaining Directions." *Psychological Reports* 34 (1974): 246–247.

Ramirez, Albert. "Social Influence and Ethnicity of the Communicator." *Journal of Social Psychology* 102 (1977): 209–213.

Rankin, Paul Tory. "The Measurement of the Ability to Understand Spoken Language." Unpublished doctoral dissertation, University of Michigan, 1926.

Rawlins, William K. "Openness as Problematic in Ongoing Friendships: Two Conventional Dilemmas." *Communication Monographs* 50 (1983): 1–13.

Reed, J. A. P. "Clothing: A Symbolic Indicator of the Self." Unpulished doctoral dissertation, Purdue University, 1973.

Reeder, Ernestine N. "Clothing Preferences of Male Athletes in Relation to Self-Concept, Athletic Ability, Race, Socioeconomic Status, and Peer Perception." Unpublished doctoral dissertation, The University of Tennessee, 1977.

Reis, Harry T.; Nexlek, John; and Wheeler, Ladd. "Physical Attractiveness in Social Interaction." *Journal of Personality and Social Psychology* 38 (1980): 604–617.

Rendina, H. and Dickerscheid, J. "Father Involvement with First-Born Infants." *Family Coordinator* 25 (1976): 373–379.

Restak, Richard M. *The Brain: The Last Frontier.* New York: Doubleday, 1979.

Rice, David G. *Dual Career Marriage: Conflict and Treatment.* New York: The Free Press, 1979.

Rich, Elaine. "Sex-Related Differences in Colour Vocabulary." *Language and Speech* 20 (1977): 404–409.

Richmond, Virginia P. and Dyba, Paula. "The Roots of Sexual Stereotyping: The Teacher as Model." *Communication Education* 31 (1982): 265–274.

Richmond, Virginia P. and Robertson, D. Lynn. "Women's Liberation in Interpersonal Relations." *Journal of Communication* 27 (1977): 42–45.

Ridley, Carl A. "Exploring the Impact of Work Satisfaction and Involvement on Marital Interaction When Both Partners are Employed." *Journal of Marriage and the Family* 35 (1973): 229–237.

Risman, Barbara J.; Hill, Charles T.; Rubin, Zick; and Peplau, Letitia S. "Living Together in College: Implications for Courtship." *Journal of Marriage and the Family* 43 (1981): 77–83.

Rivenbark, W. H., III. "Self-Disclosure Patterns Among Adolescents." *Psychological Reports* 28 (1971): 35–42.

Roberts, Helene. "The Exquisite Slave: The Role of Clothes in the Making of the Victorian Woman." *Signs* 2 (1977): 554–569.

Robertson, Clara. "The Attractiveness of Black Counselors to Black High School Counselors Based on Sex, Age, Hairstyles, and Costumes." Unpublished doctoral dissertation, University of Denver, 1977.

Robison, Joan Tucker. "The Role of Self-Disclosure, Interpersonal Attraction, and Physical Attractiveness in the Initial Stages of Relationship Development within Single-Sex Female Dyads." Unpublished doctoral dissertation, University of Georgia, 1975.

Roger, D. B. and Reid, R. L. "Small Group Ecology Revisited—Personal Space and Role Differentiation." *British Journal of Social and Clinical Psychology* 17 (1978): 43–46.

Rogers, Carl R. *Client-Centered Therapy.* Boston: Houghton Mifflin Company, 1951.

Rogers, L. E. and Millar, F. E. "Domineeringness and Dominance: A Transactional View." *Human Communication Research* 5 (1979): 238–246.

Roll, S. and Verinis, J. S. "Stereotypes of Scalp and Facial Hair as Measured by the Semantic Differential." *Psychological Reports* 28 (1971): 975–980.

Rollman, Steven A. "Nonverbal Communication in the Classroom: Some Effects of Teachers' Style of Dress Upon Students' Perceptions of Teachers' Characteristics." Unpublished doctoral dissertation, The Pennsylvania State University, 1977.

Roloff, Michael E. "The Impact of Socialization on Sex Differences in Conflict Resolution." Paper presented at the Annual Convention of the International Communication Association, Acapulco, Mexico, May, 1980.

Roloff, Michael E. and Greenberg, Bradley S. "Sex Differences in Choice of Modes of Conflict Resolution in Real-Life and Television." *Communication Quarterly* 27 (1979): 3–12.

Rondal, J. "Fathers' and Mothers' Speech in Early Language Development." *Journal of Child Language* 7 (1980): 353–369.

Rose, Brian. "Thickening the Plot." *Journal of Communication* 29 (Autumn 1979), pp. 81–84.

Rosegrant, Teresa J. and McCroskey, James C. "The Effect of Race and Sex on Proxemic Behavior in an Interview Setting." *Southern Speech Communication Journal* 40 (1975): 408–420.

Rosencranz, Mary Lou. *Clothing Concepts: A Social-Psychological Approach.* New York: MacMillan Co., 1972.

Rosencranz, Mary Lou. "Clothing Symbolism." *Journal of Home Economics,* 54 (1972): 22, from *A Schematic Approach to a Theoretical Analysis of Dress as Nonverbal Communication,* by Robert Christian Hillestad. Doctoral dissertation, The Ohio State University, 1974.

Rosenfeld, Howard. "Effect of an Approval-Seeking Induction on Interpersonal Proximity." *Psychological Reports* 17 (1965): 120–122.

Rosenfeld, Howard M. "Approval-Seeking and Approval-Inducing Functions of Verbal and Nonverbal Responses in the Dyad." *Journal of Personality and Social Psychology* 4 (1966): 597–605.

Rosenfeld, L. B. "Self Disclosure Avoidance: Why I Am Afraid to Tell You Who I Am." *Communication Monographs* 46 (1979): 63–74.

Rosenfeld, L. B.; Civikly, J. M.; and Herron, J. R. "Anatomical Sex and Self-Disclosure: Topic, Situation, and Relationship Considerations." Paper presented at the annual meeting of the International Communication Association, Philadelphia, Pennsylvania, April, 1979.

Rosenfeld, L. R. and Christie, V. R. "Sex and Persuasibility Revisited." *Western Speech* 38 (1974): 244–253.

Rosenthal, Robert; Archer, Dane; DiMatteo, M.; Koivumaki, Robin; Hall, Judith; and Rogers, Peter L. "Body Talk and Tone of Voice: The Language Without Words." *Psychology Today* 8 (1974): 64–68.

Rosenthal, Robert and DePaulo, Bella M. "Expectancies, Discrepancies, and Courtesies in Nonverbal Communication." *Western Journal of Speech Communication* 43 (1979): 76–95.

Rosenthal, Robert and DePaulo, Bella M. "Sex Differences in Eaves-dropping on Nonverbal Cues." *Journal of Personality and Social Psychology* 37 (1979): 273–285.

Rosenthal, Saul F. "The Relationship of Attraction and Sex Composition to Performance and Nonperformance Experimental Outcomes to Dyads." *Sex Roles* 4 (1978) 887–898.

Rovner, Ralph Alan. "Ethno-Cultural Identity and Self-Esteem: A Reapplication of Self-Attitude Formation Theories." *Human Relations* 34 (1981): 427–433.

Rubble, Diana N. and Higgins, E. Tory. "Effects of Group Sex Composition on Self-Presentation and Sex-Typing." *Journal of Social Issues* 32 (1976): 125–132.

Rubin, Zick. "Measurement of Romantic Love." *Journal of Personality and Social Psychology* 16 (1970): 265–273.

Rubin, Zick and Shenker, Stephen. "Friendship, Proximity, and Self-Disclosure." *Journal of Personality and Social Psychology* 46 (1978): 1–22.

Ruch, Libby O. and Newton, Rae R. "Sex Characteristics, Task Clarity, and Authority." *Sex Roles* 3 (1977): 479–494.

Rucker, M. H.; Taber, D.; and Harrison, A. "The Effect of Clothing Variation on First Impressions of Female Job Applicants: What to Wear When." *Social Behavior and Personality* 9 (1981): 53–64.

Ruechelle, Randall C. "An Experimental Study of Audience Recognition of Emotional and Intellectual Appeals in Persuasion." *Speech Monographs* 25 (1958): 49–58.

Russell, John Hamilton III. "Need for Achievement Across Three Career Patterns of College Educated Mothers Compared With Participation in Marital Decision Making and Their Husband's Performance of Domestic Activities." Unpublished doctoral dissertation, The Ohio State University, 1975.

Russo, Nancy Felipe. "Eye Contact, Interpersonal Distance, and the Equilibrium Theory." *Journal of Personality and Social Psychology* 31 (1975): 497–502.

Ryan, M. "Contour in Context." In R. Campbell and P. Smith (Eds.), *Recent Advances in the Psychology of Language: Language Development and Mother-Child Interaction.* New York: Plenum Press, 1978.

Ryckman, R. M.; Sherman, M. F.; and Burgess, G. D. "Locus of Control and Self-Disclosure of Public and Private Information by College Men and Women: A Brief Note." *Journal of Psychology* 84 (1973): 317–318.

Rytting, Marvin B. "Self Disclosure in the Development of a Heterosexual Relationship." Unpublished doctoral dissertation, Purdue University, 1975.

Sabatelli, Ronald; Buck, Ross; and Dreyer, Albert. "Locus of Control, Interpersonal Trust and Nonverbal Communication Accuracy." *Journal of Personality and Social Psychology* 44 (1983): 399–409.

Sabatelli, Ronald; Buck, Ross; and Dreyer, Albert. "Nonverbal Communication Accuracy in Married Couple's Relationships with Marital Complaints." *Journal of Personality and Social Psychology* 43 (1982): 1088–1097.

Sachs, J. "The Adaptive Significance of Linguistic Input to Prelinguistic Infants." In C. Snow and C. Ferguson (Eds.), *Talking to Children.* Cambridge: Cambridge University Press, 1977.

Sachs, J.; Lieberman, P.; and Erikson, D. "Anatomical and Cultural Determinants of Male and Female Speech," from *Language Attitudes: Current Trends and Prospects.* Washington, D.C.: Georgetown University Press, 1973.

Safilios-Rothschild, Constantina. "The Study of Family Power Structure: A Review 1960–1969." *Journal of Marriage and the Family* 28 (1970): 539–552.

Sager, Clifford J. and Hunt, Bernice. "Intimacy." *Redbook* 153 (1979): 200–204.

Salter, Andrew. *Conditioned Reflex Therapy.* New York: Creative Age Press, 1949.

Saltiel, J. and Woelfel, J. "Inertia in Cognitive Processes: The Role of Accumulated Information in Attitude Change." *Human Communication Research* 1 (1975): 333–344.

Sanders, Janet S. and Robinson, William L. "Talking and Not Talking about Sex: Male and Female Vocabularies." *Journal of Communication* 29 (1979): 22–30.

Satir, Virginia, *Conjoint Family Therapy.* Palo Alto, California: Science and Behavior Books, Inc., 1964.

Scheibe, Cyndy. "Sex Roles in Television Commercials." *Journal of Advertising Research* 19 (1979): 23–27.

Scheidel, Thomas M. "Sex and Persuasibility." *Speech Monographs* 30 (1963): 353–358.

Schein, Virginia Ellen. "The Relationship Between Sex Role Stereotypes and Requisite Management Characteristics." *Journal of Applied Psychology* 57 (1973): 95–100.

Schein, Virginia Ellen. "Relationships Between Sex Role Stereotypes and Requisite Management Characteristics Among Female Managers." *Journal of Applied Psychology* 60 (1975): 340–344.

Scheinfeld, Amram. *Women and Men.* New York: Harcourt, Brace and Company, 1944.

Schiffenbauer, Allen and Babineau, Amy. "Sex Role Stereotypes and the Spontaneous Attribution of Emotion." *Journal of Research in Personality* 10 (1976): 137–145.

Schmuck, Patricia A. "Deterrents to Women's Careers in School Management." *Sex Roles* 1 (1975): 339–353.

Schneider, David J. "Effects of Dress on Self-Presentation." *Psychological Reports* 35 (1974): 167–170.

Schneider, Joseph W. and Hacker, Sally L. "Sex Role Imagery and Use of the Generic 'Man' in Introductory Texts: A Case in the Sociology of Sociology." *The American Sociologist* 8 (1973): 12–18.

Schneider, Kenneth C. and Schneider, Sharon Barich. "Trends in Sex Roles in Television Commercial." *Journal of Marketing* 43 (1976): 79–84.

Schorr, A. and Moen, P. "The Single Parent and Public Policy." *Social Policy* (1979, March/April): 15–21.

Schulwitz, Bonnie Smith. "Coping with Sexism in Reading Materials." *The Reading Teacher* 29 (1976): 768–770.

Schumm, Walter R.; Figley, Charles R.; and Fuhs, Nancy N. "Similarity in Self-Esteem as a Function of Duration of Marriage among Student Couples." *Psychology Reports* 47 (1980): 365–66.

Schwarzwald, Joseph; Kavish, Naomi; Shoham, Monica; and Waysman, Mark. "Fear and Sex-Similarity as Determinants of Personal Space." *The Journal of Psychology* 96 (1977): 55–61.

Scott, Foresman, and Company. *Guidelines for Improving the Image of Women in Textbooks.* Glenview, Illinois: Scott, Foresman, and Company, 1972.

Scott, Kathryn P. and Summers, Shirley Feldman. "Children's Reactions to Textbook Stories in Which Females are Portrayed in Traditionally Male Roles." *Journal of Educational Psychology* 71 (1979): 396–401.

Scruggs, Barbara J. "Clothing Attitudes, Use Practices, and Appeal of Fashion Features for Women Who Work With Emphasis on Never-Married Women." Unpublished doctoral dissertation, The Pennsylvania State University, 1976.

Seaman, David W. "La Difference or L'Egalité: Thoughts on Gender in French." Paper presented at the Communication, Language and Gender Conference, Morgantown, West Virginia, 1981.

Sears, D. O. and Freedman, J. L. "Selective Exposure to Information: A Critical Review." *Public Opinion Quarterly* 31 (1967): 194–213.

Sears, Robert R. "Relation of Early Socialization Experiences to Aggression in Middle Childhood." *Journal of Abnormal and Social Psychology* 63 (1961): 466–492.

Seegmiller, Bonni R. "Sex-Typed Behavior in Pre-Schoolers: Sex, Age, and Social Class Effects." *Journal of Psychology* 104 (1980): 31–33.

Seidner, Constance J. "Interaction of Sex and Locus of Control in Predicting Self-Esteem." *Psychological Reports* (1978): 895–898.

Serafini, Denise and Pearson, Judy C. "Leadership Behavior and Sex Role Socialization: Two Sides of the Same Coin." Paper presented at the International Communication Association Convention, Dallas, Texas, 1983.

Sereno, Kenneth K. and Weathers, Janet L. "Impact of Communication Sex on Receiver Reactions to Assertive, Nonassertive and Aggressive Communication." *Women's Studies in Communication* 4 (Fall 1981): 1–17.

Sermat, V. and Smyth, M. "Content Analysis of Verbal Communication in the Development of Relationships: Conditions Influencing Self-Disclosure." *Journal of Personality and Social Psychology* 26 (1973): 332–346.

Sexton, Donald E. and Haberman, Phyllis. "Women in Magazine Advertisements." *Journal of Advertising Research* 14 (Aug. 1974): 41–46.

Shaevitz, Margorie and Shaevitz, Morton. *Making It Together as a Two-Career Couple.* Boston: Houghton Mifflin Company, 1980.

Shamo, G. Wayne and Hill, Janice B. "Self-Concept as a Communicator: A Comparison between Novice and Advanced Speech Students." *College Student Journal* 9 (February-March, 1975): 75–79.

Shanteau, James and Nagy, Geraldine F. "Probability of Acceptance in Dating Choice." *Journal of Personality and Social Psychology* 37 (1979): 522–533.

Shea, Judy; Crossman, Sharyn M.; and Adams, Gerald R. "Physical Attractiveness and Personality Development." *The Journal of Psychology* 99 (1978): 59–62.

Sher, George. "Groups and Justice." *Ethics* 87 (1977): 174–181.

Shimanoff, Susan B. *Communication Rules: Theory and Research.* Beverly Hills: Sage Publications, 1980.

Shimanoff, Susan B. "English Lexical Gender and the Perception of Sex Markedness." Paper presented at the Western Speech Communication Association Convention, Newport Beach, California, November 1975.

Shuter, Robert. "A Study of Nonverbal Communication Among Jews and Protestants." *The Journal of Social Psychology* 109 (1979): 31–41.

Shuy, R. W. "Sex as a Factor in Sociolinguistic Research." Paper presented at the Anthropological Society of Washington meeting, Washington, D.C., 1969.

Shuy, Roger; Wolfram, Walter; and Riley, William. *Linguistic Correlates of Social Stratification in Detroit Speech,* Final Report, Project 6–1347, Washington, D.C.: U.S. Office of Education, 1967.

Siegel, Harold David. "The Effect of Attitude Similarity and Need Gratification on Romantic Attraction Toward Males in Females." Unpublished doctoral dissertation, Hofstra University, 1977.

Siegel, Jeffrey C. "Effects of Objective Evidence of Expertness, Nonverbal Behavior, and Subject Sex on Client-Perceived Expertness." *Journal of Counseling Psychology* 27 (1980): 117–121.

Siegler, David and Siegler, Robert. "Stereotypes of Males' and Females' Speech." *Psychological Reports* 39 (1976): 167–170.

Silveria, J. "Thoughts on the Politics of Touch." *Women's Press,* Eugene, Oregon. Volume I, 1972, p. 3.

Simkins Rinck. "Male and Female Sexual Vocabulary in Different Interpersonal Contexts." *The Journal of Sex Research* 18 (1982): 160–172.

Simpson, Christina. "Educational Materials and Children's Sex Role Concepts." *Language Arts* 55 (1978): 161–167.

Singer, Dorothy and Zuckerman, Diane. "What Every Parent Should Know about Television." *American Film* (Jan.—Feb. 1981): 32.

Stotko, Vincent P. and Langmeyer, Daniel. "The Effects of Interaction Distance and Gender on Self-Disclosure in the Dyad." *Sociometry* 40 (1977): 178–182.

Slane, Steve and Leak, Gary. "Effects of Self-Perceived Nonverbal Immediacy Behaviors on Interpersonal Attraction." *The Journal of Psychology* 98 (1978): 241–248.

Sloman, Carol Lee. "Sex Variables and Source Credibility: A Multivariate Investigation." Unpublished doctoral dissertation, Bowling Green State University, 1974.

Smith, Audrey. "Influence Differentiation in Family Decision Making." *Sociology and Social Research* 51 (1967): 18–25.

Smith, Dwayne M. and Self, George D. "The Influence of Gender Difference on Perceptions of Self-Esteem: An Unobtrusive Measure." *Resources in Education* (February 1978): 168.

Smith, Edward and Hed, Anita. "Effects of Offenders Age and Attractiveness on Sentencing by Mock Juries." *Psychological Reports* 44 (1979): 691–694.

Smith, Lucy Freeman. "The Effects of Non-Instructional Student Preferences Upon Ratings of Instructional Competence." Unpublished doctoral dissertation, The University of Oklahoma, 1975.

Smith, M. "The Social Consequences of Single Parenthood: A Longitudinal Perspective." *Family Relations* 29 (1980): 75–81.

Smith, M. Dwayne and Matre, Marc. "Social Norms and Sex Roles in Romance and Adventure Magazines." *Journalism Quarterly* 52 (1975): 309–315.

Smith, Mickey C. "Rationality of Appeals Used in the Promotion of Psychotropic Drugs. A Comparison of Male and Female Models." *Social Science and Medicine* April 11 (1977): 409–414.

Smits, Gerard and Cherhoniak, Irene. "Physical Attractiveness and Friendliness in Interpersonal Attraction." *Psychological Reports* 39 (1976): 171–174.

Smucker, Betty and Creekmore, Anna M. "Adolescent's Clothing Conformity, Awareness and Peer Acceptance." *Home Economics Research Journal* 1 (1972): 92–97.

Snoek, Diedrick and Rothblum, Ester. "Self-Disclosure Among Adolescents in Relation to Parental Affection and Control Patterns." *Adolescence* 14 (1979): 330–340.

Snow, C. "The Conversational Context of Language Acquisition." In R. Campbell and P. Smith (Eds.), *Recent Advances in the Psychology of Language: Language Development and Mother-Child Interaction,* New York: Plenum Press, 1978.

Snow, C. "Conversations with Children." In P. Fletcher and M. Garman (Eds.), *Language Acquisition: Studies in First Language Development,* Cambridge: Cambridge University Press, 1979, pp. 363–375.

Snow, C. "Mothers' Speech Research: From Input to Interaction." In C. Snow and C. Ferguson (Eds.), *Talking to Children,* Cambridge: Cambridge University Press, 1977, pp. 31–49.

Snow, C. "Mothers' Speech to Children Learning Language." *Child Development* 43 (1972): 549–565.

Snow, Margaret; Jacklin, Carol; and Maccoby, Eleanor. "Sex of Child Difference in Father-Child Interaction at One Year of Age." *Child Development* 54 (1983): 227–232.

Soares, Manuela. *The Soap Opera Book.* New York: Harmony, 1978.

Solomon, Martha. "The Total Woman: The Rhetoric of Completion." *Central States Speech Journal* 32 (1981): 74–84.

Sommer, Robert. *Personal Space: The Behavioral Basis of Design.* Englewood Cliffs, NJ: Prentice-Hall, 1969.

Sommer, Robert. "Studies in Personal Space." *Sociometry* 22 (1959): 247–260.

Sonnier, Isadore L. "Holistic Education: How I Do It." *College Student Journal* 16 (Spring 1982): 64–69.

Sote, G. A. and Good, L. R. "Similarity of Self-Disclosure and Interpersonal Attraction." *Psychological Reports* 34 (1974): 491–494.

Soto, Debbie Halon; Forslund, Evelyn Florio; and Cole, Claudia. "Alternative to Using Masculine Pronouns When Referring to the Species." Paper presented at the Western Speech Communication Association Convention, San Francisco, CA, November 1975.

South, Earl Bennett. "Some Psychological Aspects of Committee Work." *Journal of Applied Psychology* 11 (1927): 348–368.

Sparacino, Jack and Hansell, Stephen. "Physical Attractiveness and Academic Performance: Beauty is Not Always Talent." *Journal of Personality* 47 (1979): 449–469.

Spaulding, Robert L. "Achievement, Creativity, and Self-Concept Correlates of Teacher-Pupil Transactions in Elementary Schools." Cooperative Research Project No. 1352, U.S. Dept. of Health, Education, and Welfare, Office of Education, Washington, D.C., 1963.

Spence, J. T.; Helmreich, R.; and Stapp, J. "The Personal Attributes Questionnaire: A Measure of Sex-Role Stereotypes and Masculinity-Femininity." *JSAS Catalog of Selected Documents in Psychology* 4 (1974): 127.

Spence, J. T.; Helmreich, R.; and Stapp, J. "Ratings of Self and Peers on Sex-role Attributes and Their Relation to Self-esteem and Conceptions of Masculinity and Femininity." *Journal of Personality and Social Psychology* 32 (1974): 29–39.

Sprague, Jo. "The Reduction of Sexism in Speech Communication Education." *Speech Teacher,* 24 (1975): 37–45.

Sprague, Jo A. "An Investigation of the Written Critique Behavior of College Communication Instructors." Unpublished doctoral dissertation, Purdue University, 1971.

Stacks, Don W. and Burgoon, Judee K. "The Role of Non-verbal Behaviors as Distractors in Resistance to Persuasion in Interpersonal Contexts." *The Central States Speech Journal* 32 (1981): 61–73.

Staley, Constance. "Male-Female Use of Expletives: A Heck of a Difference in Expectations." *Anthropological Linguistics* 20 (1978): 367–380.

Staley, Constance. "Sex Related Differences in the Style of Children's Language." *Journal of Psycholinguistic Research* 11 (1982): 141–152.

Stake, Jayne E. and Stake, Michael N. "Performance—Self-Esteem and Dominance in Mixed Sex Dyads." *Journal of Personality* 47 (1979): 23–26 and 71–84.

Stanley, Julia P. "Paradigmatic Women: The Prostitute." Paper presented at South Atlantic Modern Language Association, 1972.

Stericker, Anne. "Does the 'He or She' Business Really Make a Difference? The Effect of Masculine Pronouns as Generics on Job Attitudes." *Sex Roles* 7 (1981): 637–641.

Stericker, Anne B. and Johnson, James E. "Sex-role Identification and Self-Esteem in College Students; Do Men and Women Differ?" *Sex Roles* 3 (1977): 19–26.

Sterling, F. E. "Net Positive Social Approaches of Young Psychiatric Inpatients as Influenced by Nurses' Attire." *Journal of Consulting and Clinical Psychology* 48 (1980): 58–62.

Stern, Gary and Manifold, Beverly. "Internal Locus of Control as a Value." *Journal of Research in Personality* 11 (1977): 237–242.

Stewart, John. *Bridges not Walls* (2nd ed.). Reading, Massachusetts: Addison-Wesley, 1977.

Stewig, John Warren and Knipfel, Mary Lynn. "Sexism in Picture Books: What Progress?" *Elementary School Journal* 76 (1975): 151–155.

Stitt, Christopher; Schmidt, Stuart; Price, Kari; and Kipnis, David. "Sex of Leader, Leader Behavior, and Subordinate Satisfaction." *Sex Roles* 9 (1983): 31–42.

St. John-Parsons, Donald. "Career and Family: A Study of Continuous Dual-Career Families." *Psychology of Women Quarterly* 3 (1978): 30–42.

Stochton, Nancy. "Sex Role and Innovative Major Choice Among College Students." *Journal of Vocational Behavior* 16 (1980): 360–367.

Stocking, S. H.; Sapolsky, B. S.; and Zillman, D. "Sex Discrimination in Prime Time Humor." *Journal of Broadcasting* 21 (1977): 447–455.

Stoehr, C. "Females are Crashing Comedy." *Detroit Free Press,* April 3, 1981.

Stokes, Joseph; Fuehrer, Ann; and Childs, Lawrence. "Gender Differences in Self-Disclosure to Various Target Persons." *Journal of Counseling Psychology* 27 (1980): 192–198.

Stoner, Sue and Kaiser, Lynn. "Sex Differences in Self-Concepts of Adolescents." *Psychological Reports* 43 (1978): 305–306.

Strahan, R. F. "Remarks on Bem's Measurement and a Supplementary Analysis." *Journal of Consulting and Clinical Psychology* 43 (1975): 568–571.

Strainchamps, Ethel. "Our Sexist Language." In Vivian Gornick and Barbara K. Moran (Eds.), *Women in Sexist Society,* New York: Basic Books, 1971, pp. 240–250.

Stratton, Lois O.; Tekippe, Dennis J.; and Flick, Grad L. "Personal Space and Self-Concept." *Sociometry* 36 (1973): 424–429.

Streicher, Helen White. "The Girls in the Cartoons." *Journal of Communication* 24 (Spring 1974): 125–129.

Strodtbeck, Fred L. and Mann, Richard D. "Sex Role Differentiation in Jury Deliberations." *Sociometry* 19 (1956): 3–11.

Stroebe, Wolfgang; Insko, Chester A.; Thompson, Vaida D.; and Layton, Bruce D. "Effects of Physical Attractiveness, Attitude Similarity, and Sex on Various Aspects of Interpersonal Attraction." *Journal of Personality and Social Psychology* 18 (1971): 79–91.

Stuteville, John R. "Sexually Polarized Products and Advertising Strategy." *Journal of Retailing* 47 (Summer 1971): 3–13.

Summerhayes, Diana L. and Suchner, Robert W. "Power Implications of Touch in Male-Female Relationships." *Sex Roles* 4 (1978): 103–110.

Sunderstrom, Eric and Sundstrom, Mary G. "Personal Space Invasions: What Happens When the Invader Asks Permission?" *Environmental Psychology and Nonverbal Behavior* Vol. (Winter 1977): 76–82.

Sundstrom, Eric. "An Experimental Study of Crowding: Effects of Room Size, Intrusion, and Goal Blocking on Nonverbal Behavior, Self-Disclosure, and Self-Reported Stress." *Journal of Personality and Social Psychology* 32 (1975): 645–654.

Swacker, Marjorie. "The Sex of the Speaker as a Sociolinguistic Variable," ed. Barrie Thorne and Nancy Henley. *Language and Sex: Difference and Dominance.* Rowley, Mass.: Newbury House Publishers, Inc., 1975.

Swanson, Cheryl and Wagner, Karen Van. "From Machiavelli to Ms.: Differences in Male-Female Power Styles." *Business or Public Administration Review* 39 (1979): 66–72.

Swanson, L. Anna. "Male and Female Conformity: A Study in Perception and Behavior." Master's thesis, University of Nevada, 1971, from *A Schematic Approach to a Theoretical Analysis of Dress as Nonverbal Communication,* by Robert Christian Hillestad. Doctoral dissertation, The Ohio State University, 1974.

Swieczkowski, Juliet B. and Walker, Eugene C. "Sexual Behavior Correlates of Female Orgasm and Marital Happiness." *Journal of Nervous and Mental Disease* 166 (1978): 335–342.

Szilagyi, Andrew D. "Reward Behavior by Male and Female Leaders." *Journal of Vocational Behavior* 16 (1980): 59–72.

Tahir, Laura. "Women's Wallflowerings." *Psychology Today* 13 (August 1979): 12.

Talley, Mary A. and Richmond, Virginia Peck. "The Relationship between Psychological Gender Orientation and Communicative Style." *Human Communication Research* 6 (1980): 326–339.

Tan, Alexis S. "Television Use and Social Stereotypes." *Journalism Quarterly* 59 (Spring 1982), 119–122.

Tan, Alexis; Raudy, Jack; Huff, Cary; and Miles, Janet. "Children's Reactions to Male and Female Newscasters: Effectiveness and Believability." *The Quarterly Journal of Speech* 66 (1980): 201–205.

Tan-William, Conchita. "Cerebral Hemispheric Specialization of Academically Gifted and Nongifted Male and Female Adolescents." *The Journal of Creative Behavior* 15 (Winter 1981): 276–277.

Tardy, C. H.; Hosman, L. A.; and Brodiac, J. J. "Disclosing Self to Friends and Family: A Reexamination of Initial Questions." *Communication Quarterly* 29 (1981): 263–282.

Taylor, D. A. "Some Aspects of the Development of Interpersonal Relationships: Social Presentation Process." *Technical Report No. 1,* Center for Research on Social Behavior, University of Delaware, 1965.

Taylor, Ralph B.; DeSoto, Clinton B.; and Lieb, Robert. "Sharing Secrets: Disclosure and Discretion in Dyads and Triads." *Journal of Personality and Social Psychology* 37 (1979): 1196–1203.

Tenzel, James H.; Storms, Lowell; and Sweetwood, Hervey. "Symbols and Behavior: An Experiment in Altering the Police Role." *Journal of Police Science and Administration* 4 (1976): 21–27.

Terry, Roger L. and Doerge, Suzanne. "Dress, Posture, and Setting as Additive Factors in Subjective Probabilities of Rape." *Perceptual and Motor Skills* 48 (1979): 903–906.

Telzrow, Cathy Fultz. "The Impact of Brain Development on Curriculum." *The Educational Forum* 45 (May 1981): 477–483.

Thakerar, Jitendra N. and Iwawaki, Saburo. "Cross Cultural Comparisons in Interpersonal Attraction of Females Toward Males." *The Journal of Social Psychology* 108 (1979): 121–122.

Thase, M. and Page, R. A. "Modeling of Self-Disclosure in Laboratory and Non-Laboratory Interview Settings." *Journal of Counseling Psychology* 24 (1977): 35–40.

Thayer, S. and Schiff, W. "Observer Judgement of Social Interaction: Eye Contact and Relationship Inferences." *Journal of Personality and Social Exchange* 30 (1974): 110–114.

Thayer, Stephen and Schiff, William. "Eye-Contact, Facial Expression, and the Experience of Time." *The Journal of Social Psychology* 95 (1975): 117–124.

Thibaut, J. W. and Kelley, H. H. *The Social Psychology of Groups.* New York: Wiley, 1959.

Thompson, Wayne N. "An Experimental Study of the Accuracy of Typical Speech Rating Techniques." *Speech Monographs* 11 (1944): 65–79.

Thorne, Barrie. Public speech at Michigan State University, East Lansing, Michigan, 1981.

Thorne, B. and Henley, N. "Difference and Dominance: An Overview of Language, Gender and Society." *Language and Sex: Difference and Dominance.* Rowley, Mass.: Newbury House Publishers, Inc., 1975, pp. 5–31.

Thorne, B. and Henley, N. "Sex and Language Difference and Dominance." *Language in Society* 6 (1977): 110–113.

Tibbetts, S. "Sex Role Stereotyping in the Lower Grades: Part of a Solution." *Journal of Vocational Behavior* 6 (1975): 255–261.

Tibbits, S. L. "Sex-role Stereotyping in Children's Reading Material: Update." *Journal of the National Association for Women Deans, Administrators and Counselors* (Winter, 1979): 3–9.

Tibbets, Silvia-Lee. "Sexism in Children's Magazines." Unpublished doctoral dissertation. University of Pennsylvania, 1979.

Tindall, J. H.; Boyler, L.; Cline, P.; Emberger, P.; Powell, S.; and Wions, J. "Perceived Leadership Rankings of Males and Females in Small Task Groups." *Journal of Psychology* 100 (1978): 13–20.

Todd-Mancillas, William R. "Evaluating Alternatives to Exclusive 'He.' " Paper presented at the Fifth Communication, Language, and Gender Conference, Athens, Ohio, October, 1982.

Todd-Mancillas, William. "Masculine Generics-Sexist Language: A Review of Literature and Implications for Speech Communication Professionals." *Communication Quarterly* 29 (1981): 107–115.

Touhey, John C. "Comparison of Two Dimensions of Attitude Similarity on Heterosexual Attraction." *Journal of Personality and Social Psychology* 23 (1972): 8–10.

Touhey, John C. "Sex Role Stereotyping and Individual Differences in Liking for the Physically Attractive." *Social Psychology* 42 (1979): 285–289.

Trenholm, Sarah and Todd de Mancillas, William R. "Student Perceptions of Sexism." *Quarterly Journal of Speech* 64 (1978): 267–283.

Tuthill, Douglas M. and Forsyth, Donelson R. "Sex Differences in Opinion Conformity and Dissent." *The Journal of Social Psychology* 116 (1982): 205–210.

Tyler, Leona E. *The Psychology of Human Differences,* 3rd ed. New York: Appleton-Century-Crofts, 1965.

Uesugi, Thomas K. and Vinacke, W. Edgar. "Strategy in a Feminine Game." *Sociometry* 26 (1963): 75–88.

Unger, Rhoda K. *Female and Male: Psychological Perspectives.* New York: Harper and Row, 1979.

Vaden, Richard E. and Lynn, Naomi B. "The Administrative Person: Will Women Bring a Differing Morality to Management?" *University of Michigan Business Review* 31 (1979): 22–25.

Venkatesan, M. and Losco, Jean. "Women in Magazine Ads: 1959–71." *Journal of Advertising Research* 15 (October 1975): 49–54.

Verna, Mary Ellen. "The Female in Children's T.V. Commercials." *Journal of Broadcasting* 19 (Summer 1975): 301–309.

Veroff, Joseph; Depner, Charlene; Kulka, Richard; Douvan, Elizabeth. "Comparison of American Motives: 1957 Versus 1976." *Journal of Personality and Social Psychology* 39 (1980): 1249–1262.

Viera, Kenneth G. and Miller, William H. "Avoidance of Sex-Atypical Toys by Five- and Ten-Year-Old Children." *Psychological Reports* 43 (1978): 543–546.

Vigliano, Barbara Murphy. "An Investigation of the Relationship Between the Sex of the Speaker and the Sex of the Listener on Message Comprehension and Judgment of Speaker Credibility." Unpublished doctoral dissertation. New York University, 1974.

Vinacke, W. Edgar. "Sex Roles in a Three-Person Game." *Sociometry* 22 (1959): 343–360.

Vladeck, Judith P. "Sex Discrimination in Higher Education." *Women's Rights Law Reporter* 17 (1981): 27–38.

Voss, F. "The Relationships of Disclosure to Marital Satisfaction: An Exploratory Study." Unpublished master's thesis, University of Wisconsin-Milwaukee, 1969.

Wagner, Louis C. and Banos, Janis B. "A Woman's Place: A Follow-up Analysis of the Roles Portrayed by Women in Magazine Advertisements." *Journal of Marketing Research* 10 (1973): 213–214.

Wallach, Michael A.; Kogan, Nathan; and Bem, Darlyk J. "Group Influence on Individual Risk Taking." *Journal of Abnormal and Social Psychology* 65 (1962): 75–86.

Walsh, Edward. "Petition Signing in Town and on Campus." *The Journal of Social Psychology* 102 (1977): 323–324.

Walsh, K. *Neuropsychology.* Edinburg, London: Churchill Livingstone, 1978.

Walster, Elaine; Aronson, Vera; Abrahams, Darcy; and Rottman, L. "Importance of Physical Attractiveness in Dating Behavior." *Journal of Personality and Social Psychology* 5 (1966): 508–516.

Warmbrod, M. T. "Alternative Generation in Marital Problem Solving." *Family Relations* 31 (1982): 503–511.

Warren, Denise. "Commercial Liberation." *Journal of Communication* 28 (1978): 169–173.

Warren, Mary Anne. "Secondary Sexism and Quota Hiring." *Philosophy and Public Affairs* 6 (1977): 240–261.

Warren, James Frederick. "The Effects of Assertion Training on Self-Acceptance and Social Evaluative Anxiety of University Students." Unpublished doctoral dissertation, The University of Florida, 1977.

Watson, Neil. "A Theoretical and Empirical Study of Empathy and Sex Role Differentiation." Unpublished doctoral dissertation, Harvard University, 1976.

Watzlawick, Paul. *The Language of Change.* New York: Basic Books, 1978.

Watzlawick, Paul; Beavin, Janet Helmick; Jackson, Don D. *Pragmatics of Human Communication: A Study of Interactional Patterns, Pathologies, and Paradoxes.* New York: W. W. Norton and Company, 1967.

Weaver, Carl H. *Human Listening: Processes and Behavior.* New York: The Bobbs-Merrill Company, Inc., 1972.

Weber, Marilyn Daly. "Social Situation, Uncertainty, Communication and Interpersonal Attraction." Unpublished doctoral dissertation, Northwestern University, 1977.

Weinrauch, J. Donald and Swanda, Jr., John R. "Examining the Significance of Listening: An Exploratory Study of Contemporary Management." *The Journal of Business Communication* 13 (February 1975): 25–32.

Weinstein, Henry. "Body Language." *Saturday Review of Education* 1 (1973): 77–78.

Weinstein, Sanford A. and Goebel, Gloria. "The Relationship Between Contraceptive Sex Role Stereotyping and Attitudes Toward Male Contraception Among Males." *The Journal of Sex Research* 15 (1979): 235–242.

Weiss, R. *Going It Alone: The Family Life and Social Situation of the Single Parent.* Basic Books, Inc., Publishers, 1979.

Welsh, M. Cay. "Attitudinal Measures and Evaluation of Males and Females in Leadership Roles." *Psychological Reports* 45 (1979): 19–22.

Weitz, Rose. "Feminist Consciousness Raising, Self-Concept, and Depression." *Sex Roles* 8 (1982): 231–241.

Wenige, Lynn Oliver. "Preschool Children's Classification of Adult Apparel as Related to Parents' Mode of Dress and Attitudes Toward Adult Gender Roles." Unpublished doctoral dissertation, The University of Tennessee, 1976.

Werner, Elyse K. "A Study of Communication Time." Unpublished master's thesis, University of Maryland—College Park, 1975.

West, L. W. "Sex Differences in the Exercise of Circumspection in Self-Disclosure Among Adolescents." *Psychological Reports* 26 (1970): 226.

West, S. G. and Brown, T. J. "Physical Attractiveness, The Severity of the Emergency and Helping: A Field Experiment and Interpersonal Simulation." *Journal of Experimental Social Psychology* 11 (1975): 531–538.

Wexley, Kenneth N. and Hunt, Peter J. "Male and Female Leaders: Comparison of Performance and Behavior Patterns." *Psychological Reports* 35 (1974): 867–872.

Wheelan, Susan A. "The Effect of Personal Growth and Assertive Training Classes on Female Sex Role and Self-Concept." *Group and Organization Studies* 3 (1978): 239–244.

Wheeler, Christopher; Wilson, Judith; and Tarantola, Carol. "An Investigation of Children's Social Perception of Child Speakers with Reference to Verbal Style." *Central States Speech Journal* 27 (1976): 31–35.

Wheeless, Lawrence R. "A Follow-up Study of the Relationships Among Trust, Disclosure and Interpersonal Solidarity." *Human Communication Research* 4 (1978): 143–157.

Wheeless, Lawrence R. "Self-Disclosure and Interpersonal Solidarity: Measurement, Validation and Relationships." *Human Communication Research* 3 (1976): 47–61.

Wheeless, Lawrence R. and Grotz, Janis. "The Measurement of Trust and Its Relationship to Self-Disclosure." *Human Communication Research* 3 (1977): 250–257.

Wheeless, Lawrence R., and Wheeless, Virginia Eman. "Attribution, Gender Orientation, and Adaptability: Reconceptualization, Measurement, and Research Results." *Communication Quarterly* 30 (1981): 56–66.

Wheeless, Virginia Eman; Berryman-Fink, Cynthia; and Serafini, Denise. "The Use of Gender-Specific Pronouns in the 1980's." Paper presented at the Fourth Annual Communication, Language, and Gender Conference, Morgantown, West Virginia, 1981.

Wheeless, Virginia Eman and Dierks-Stewart, Kathi. "The Psychometric Properties of the Bem Sex-Role Inventory: Questions Concerning Reliability and Validity." *Communication Quarterly* 29 (1981): 173–186.

Wheeless, Virginia Eman and Duran, Robert L. "Gender Orientation as a Correlate of Communicative Competence." *Southern Speech Communication Journal* 48 (1982): 51–64.

White, Gregory L. "Physical Attractiveness and Courtship Progress." *Journal of Personality and Social Psychology* 39 (1980): 660–668.

Whitehead, III, G. I. and Tawes, S. L. "Dogmatism, Age, and Educational Level as Correlates of Feminism for Males and Females." *Sex Roles* 2 (1976): 401–405.

Whitlow, S. Scott. "Women in the Newsroom: A Role Theory View." *Journalism Quarterly* 56 (1979): 378–383.

Widgery, Robin Noel. "Sex of Receiver and Physical Attractiveness of Source as Determinants of Initial Credibility Perception." *Western Speech* 38 (1974): 13.

Wiebe, B., and Scott, T. B. "Self-Disclosure Patterns of Hermonite Adolescents to Parents and their Perceived Relationships." *Psychological Reports* 39 (1976): 355–358.

Wildman, Robert; Wildman, Robert, II; Brown, Archie; and Trice, Carol. "Notes on Males and Females' Preferences for Opposite-Sex Body Parts, Bust Sizes, and Bust Revealing Clothing." *Psychological Reports* 38 (1976): 485–486.

Williams, John E. and Best, Deborah L. *Measuring Sex Stereotypes: A Thirty Nation Study.* Beverly Hills, California: Sage Publications, 1982.

Wiley, Mary Glenn and Eskilson, Arlene. "Coping in the Corporation: Sex Role Constraints." *Journal of Applied Social Psychology* 12 (1982): 1–11.

Wilkinson, Melvin. "Romantic Love: The Great Equalizer? Sexism in Popular Music." *The Family Coordinator* 25 (1976): 161–166.

Willet, Roslyn. "Do Not Stereotype Women—An Appeal to Advertisers." *Journal of Home Economics* 63 (1971): 549–551.

Willis, Frank N.; Gier, Joseph A.; and Smith, David E. "Stepping Aside: Correlates of Displacement in Pedestrians." *Journal of Communication* 29 (1979): 34–39.

Willis, F. N. and Hoffman, G. E. "The Development of Tactile Patterns in Relation to Age, Sex and Race." *Developmental Psychology* 11 (1975): 866.

Willis, F. N. and Reeves, D. L. "Touch Interaction in Junior High School Students in Relation to Sex and Race." *Developmental Psychology* 12 (1976): 91–92.

Wilson, Allan and Krane, Richard V. "Change in Self-Esteem and its Effects on Symptoms of Depression." *Cognitive Therapy and Research* 4 (1980): 419–421.

Wilson, D. W. "Helping Behavior and Physical Attractiveness." *Journal of Social Psychology* 104 (1978): 313–314.

Winakor, Geitel; Canton, Bernetta; and Wolins, Leroy. "Perceived Fashion Risk and Self-Esteem of Males and Females." *Home Economics Research Journal* 9 (1980): 45–56.

Winter, Clotilda. "Listening and Learning." *Elementary English* 43 (1966): 569–572.

Wise, E. and Rafferty, J. "Sex Bias and Language." *Sex Roles* 8 (1982): 1189–1196.

Witelson, S. F. "Developmental Dyslexia: Two Right Hemispheres and None Left." *Science* 195 (January 21, 1977): 309–311.

Witkowski, Terrence H. "An Experimental Comparison of Women's Self and Advertising Image." In *New Marketing for Social and Economic Progress,* ed. R. C. Carham. Chicago: American Marketing Association, 1975.

Wittig, Michele Andrisia and Skolnick, Paul. "Sex Differences in Personal Space." *Sex Roles* 4 (1978): 493–503.

Wittrock, M. D. "Education and the Cognitive Processes of the Brain," in *Education and the Brain,* ed. J. S. Chall and A. F. Mirsky. Chicago: University of Chicago Press, 1978.

Wolff, Florence I.; Marsnik, Nadine C.; Tacey, William S.; and Nichols, Ralph G. *Perceptive Listening.* New York: Holt, Rinehart and Winston, 1983.

Wolpe, Joseph and Lazarus, Arnold A. *Behavior Therapy Techniques.* New York: Pergamon Press, 1966.

Wolvin, Andrew D. and Coakley, Carolyn Gwynn. *Listening.* Dubuque, Iowa: William C. Brown Company Publishers, 1982.

Wood, Marion M. "The Influence of Sex and Knowledge of Communication Effectiveness on Spontaneous Speech." *Word* 22 (1966): 117–137.

Wood, Marion W. "Women in Management: How Is It Working Out?" *S.A.M. Advanced Management Journal,* Winter 1976, pp. 22–30.

Woodyard, Howard P. and Hines, David A. "Accurate Compared to Inaccurate Self-Disclosure." *Journal of Humanistic Psychology* 13 (1973): 61–67.

Wright, J. W. and Hosman, L. A. "Language Style and Sex Bias in the Courtroom: The Effects of Male and Female Use of Hedges and Intensifiers on Impression Information." *The Southern Speech Communication Journal* 48 (1983): 137–152.

Yamada, Elaine M.; Tjosvold, Dean; and Draguns, Juris G. "Effects of Sex-Linked Situations and Sex Composition on Cooperation and Style of Interaction." *Sex Roles* 9 (1983): 541–554.

Yankelovich, Daniel. *New Rules: Searching for Self-Fulfillment in a World Turned Upside Down.* New York: Random House, 1981.

Yarmey, Daniel A. "Through the Looking Glass: Sex Differences in Memory for Self-Facial Poses." *Journal of Research in Personality* 13 (1979): 450–459.

Yerby, Janet. "Attitude, Task, and Sex Composition as Variables Affecting Female Leadership in Small Problem-Solving Groups." *Speech Monographs* 42 (1975): 160–168.

Yogev, S. "Happiness in Dual-Career Couples: Changing Research Changing Values." *Sex Roles* 8 (1982): 593–605.

Young, Jerald W. "Willingness to Disclose Symptoms to a Male Physician: Effects of the Physician's Physical Attractiveness, Body Area of Symptom and the Patient's Self-Esteem, Locus of Control and Sex." Paper presented to the International Communication Association Convention, Acapulco, Mexico, May, 1980.

Zaidel, D. and Sperry, R. W. "Memory Impairment After Commissurotomy in Man." *Brain* 97 (1974): 263–272.

Zander, A. and Havelin, A. "Social Comparison and Interpersonal Attraction." *Human Relations* 13 (1960): 21–32.

Zeldin, Sheperd; Small, Stephen; and Savin-Williams, Ritch. "Prosocial Interactions in Mixed Sex Adolescent Groups." *Child Development* 53 (1982): 1492–1498.

Zelko, Harold P. and Dance, Frank E. X. *Business and Professional Speech Communication.* New York: Holt, Rinehart, & Winston, 1965.

Zillman, D. and Stocking, F. H. "Putdown Humor." *Journal of Communication* 26 (1976): 154–163.

Zimmerman, Don H. and West, Candace. "Sex Roles, Interruptions and Silences in Conversation." Thorne, Barrie, and Henley, Nancy, eds., *Language and Sex: Difference and Dominance.* Rowley, Mass.: Newbury House Publishers, 1975.

Zuckerman, Diana M. "Self-Esteem, Self-Concept and the Life Goals and Sex-Role Attitudes of College Students." *Journal of Personality* 48 (1980): 149–162.

Zuckerman, Miron; DeFrank, Richard; Hall, Judith; and Rosenthal, Robert. "Encoding and Decoding of Spontaneous Facial Expressions." *Journal of Personality and Social Psychology* 34 (1976): 966–977.

Zuckerman, Miron and Przewuzman, Sylvia J. "Decoding and Encoding Facial Expressions in Preschool-Age Children." *Environmental Psychology and Nonverbal Behavior* 3 (1979): 147–163.

Zweigenhaft, Richard L. and Marlowe, David. "Signature Size: Studies in Expressive Movement." *Journal of Consulting and Clinical Psychology* 40 (1973): 469–473.

Text and Visual Credits

Photos

Index